The Faded Banners

The Faded Banners

A Treasury of Nineteenth-Century Civil

Edited by Eric Solomon

Exeter Books

NEW YORK

LOUISA MAY ALCOTT
JOSEPH ALTSHELER
AMBROSE BIERCE
ROBERT W. CHAMBERS
JOHN ESTEN COOKE
STEPHEN CRANE
JOHN WILLIAM DE FOREST
GEORGE CARY EGGLESTON
HAMLIN GARLAND
SARAH ORNE JEWETT
JOSEPH KIRKLAND
SIDNEY LANIER
CHARLES LEDYARD NORTON
THOMAS NELSON PAGE
MARSHALL PUTNAM THOMPSON
MARK TWAIN

Published in 1986 by
Promontory Press
166 Fifth Avenue
New York, New York 10010
By arrangement with A.S. Barnes, a division of Oak Tree Pub-
lications, Inc.

This edition distributed by Exeter Books, a division of Bookthrift Marketing, Inc. Exeter is a trademark of Bookthrift Marketing, Inc.

Library of Congress Catalog Card Number: 86-60404
ISBN 0-671-08161-6
Printed in The United States of America

Contents

Introduction

THE CIVIL WAR HAS SHARPLY CHALLENGED THE IMAGINATIONS OF NOVELISTS AND SHORT-story writers since the first gun was fired at Fort Sumter in 1861. From the very beginning this tragic conflict—perhaps the most significant experience in the development of the American culture—has stimulated a flowering of war fiction. Much of this still-expanding body of fiction was written in the generation after the war either by men like Joseph Kirkland, John Esten Cooke, and Ambrose Bierce who had actually served in combat, or by writers like Thomas Nelson Page and Stephen Crane who spent their boyhoods close to the memories and effects of the battles.

This anthology presents some of the finest pieces of nineteenth-century Civil War fiction, stories that catch the excitement and emotional impact of the intense struggle. Although this volume attempts to balance Northern and Southern views of the Civil War—or the War Between the States—I have not sought to make a chronological organization that would give a general picture of the various campaigns that led up to Appomattox. My criterion of selection has been esthetic and artistic value; the book "covers" the war in depth, not breadth.

I

Never before in European or American literary history had a war brought forth such a large quantity of fiction in the quarter-century after the cessation of hostilities. To be sure, the writings of Tolstoy, Charles Lever, Thackeray, and Stendhal were concerned with the Napoleonic wars in greater or lesser degree; William Gilmore Simms and James Fenimore Cooper wrote volumes about the American Revolution; Zola dealt with the Franco-Prussian War, Scott with a variety of historic conflicts. But the Civil War, during the nineteenth century alone, provided subject matter not only for the sixteen authors represented here, writers of the stature of Mark Twain, Louisa May Alcott, Hamlin Garland, or Sarah Orne Jewett, but also for novelists like George Washington Cable, Harold Frederic, Wilbur Hinman, Charles King (a former officer who turned out countless Civil War adventure books for boys), Silas Weir Mitchell, Henry Morford—among others. Not until the great wars of the twentieth century was a similar outpouring of war fiction to occur. Indeed, many of the novelists of World War I, Ford Madox Ford and Ernest Hemingway, for example, acknowledged debts to the techniques developed by Civil War writers, most notably Stephen Crane and Ambrose Bierce.

A desire to re-create, to relive the emotions and tensions of the time, to regain the feelings of glory and dedication to a cause has generated much of the modern interest in the Civil War. These creative writers also attempted to evoke the wartime period; unlike twentieth-century historians and scholars, the authors here knew their material from personal experience. Nevertheless, fiction does not attempt the same process as history. The important concept for fiction is re-*creation*. For accuracy of factual detail, the reader must turn to histories, diaries, journals, records. This fiction does not necessarily document the number of guns at Gettysburg, the reasons for the losses at Shiloh, the depth of the mine at Petersburg. Although some writers may choose to stress facts (Cooke even goes so far as to include footnotes in his novels!), the creative writer establishes an ordering of fact and fantasy, the product of imaginative selection in accordance with personal predilections and a vision of life. It is the aura, the feeling, the *essence* of the war that these writers can portray. The fiction of the Civil War is at once less accurate in regard to detail and more true to the essential drama and intensity of the war years. For this reason I have made no attempt to correct an author for a minor error of fact. These works of fiction show, in Hemingway's term, the way it was, according to the author's felt experience.

Combat is central to most of these stories. Obviously, combat is only one aspect of war. Training, the pressures of discipline, problems of supply, command decisions are all important and fascinating subjects. The climax of a work of fiction, however, comes when the individual or the group goes into action; and in war, combat naturally supplies the ultimate pressure, the extreme stress, the essential test, for man and an army of men. To the army, the battle is the pay-off. To the war writer, the battle scenes are the core of his work. Ineffective war fiction may frame passages in a makeshift plot or introduce them merely for the sake of excitement. But many of the Civil War stories realize the highest possibilities of the form where combat organizes the plot and provides the work with an intellectual and spiritual center.

II

Whether considering the Union or the Confederacy, the primary problem remains: What is the unique quality of this war that has continuously motivated such an impressive amount of literature, be it poetry, history, or fiction? Is there an ascertainable reason why *this* war, more than any other, should have produced a steady flow of fiction?

Two obvious points stand out. In the first place, the war that divided the two sections of the country was an emotional event of transcendent importance to Americans. As Oliver Wendell Holmes trenchantly put it, ". . . our hearts were touched with fire . . ." One eminent historian has called the struggle a great national trauma. The very nature of the contest that split a nation accounts for both the contemporary intensity of involvement and the permanent interest. It was not simple literary convenience that led author after author to fix upon the convention of families split between Blue and Gray; it really was a war between brothers.

For all the anguish, for all the slaughter and desolation, the soldiers never actually hated their enemies. There are more tales of fraternizing among pickets than of brutality towards prisoners. Enmity came with Reconstruction. As a result, the fiction dealing with the war itself usually does not emphasize issues. Arguments were left to the politicians. Yeats has said that men make out of the quarrel with others only rhetoric, but out of the quarrel with themselves, poetry. The poetry, the emotion of Civil War fiction escapes the rhetoric of debate. The Civil War was more tragic than angry. And tragedy is the permanent substance of literature. For some writers like Kirkland or Bierce, the war meant cosmic horror, the times out of joint. To men like Page or Cooke, the war was a glorious yet painful event, marking the great moments of a doomed cause, the anguished passing of a dream.

Secondly, the Civil War was the first modern war. Certainly, the conflict bore some similarities to earlier wars. There were volunteer regiments who felt free to leave the army for spring planting; many officers were political appointees with no previous military experience; an amateur air of improvisation continued up to the very end of the war; and there remained fine opportunities for individual achievements of glory. Nevertheless, the conflict was close to the modern concept of total war. It was a war that included more than 2,200 engagements, 149 of which were important enough to be classified as battles, and a half-million casualties. At one time 50,000 men a month were being lost in the Wilderness Campaign alone. Gallantry—certainly: Pickett's charge, Thomas standing like a rock at Chickamauga, Stuart's ride around the Union army . . . these scenes are part of the national memory. But the death lists of Gettysburg, Shiloh, Malvern Hill, Antietam were appalling. This was mass warfare, including the extensive use of the draft for the first time in American history. The war directly involved four million out of a population of thirty-one million people, and millions more indirectly. Armies invaded a huge area. The tactics and weapons anticipated those that became familiar in two twentieth-century world wars. Revolvers, mines, grenades, barbed-wire entrenchments, observation balloons, railroad transportation, ironclad ships, submarines, telegraph communication all helped to increase the scope of war. Warfare was an enormity, increasingly massive and mechanized, destroying and maiming mammoth numbers of combatants.

III

"All wars are boyish and are fought by boys," wrote Herman Melville in his poem, "The March into Virginia." War has traditionally offered youth a proving ground, a place in which the young soldier must develop from innocence to maturity in order to survive. The Civil War emphasized this loss of innocence. Boys in their teens or early twenties filled the ranks of both armies. The United States itself was still a young nation, not hardened to the horrors of invasions and military hospitals. The fiction that the Civil War inspired was particularly effective because from Henry Fielding to James Joyce, novelists have found an important theme in the growth to knowledge through experience of the realities of life. The writers of Civil War stories found a theme and setting that joined perfectly—both stressing growth to maturity—and reflected the national experience as well as the specific experience of individual heroes.

Both North and South entered the Civil War with an innocence and an idealism that the brutality and extent of the conflict shattered. By the middle of the nineteenth century the memories of the American Revolution had faded. Wars such as the 1812 struggle against the British or the Mexican campaign were limited and successful. The few military men who believed that a major war would start after the South seceded went largely unheard. The two sides shared expectations of a hasty end to hostilities. The possibility of years of savage destruction seemed an absurd nightmare to soldiers and civilians alike. In 1861 the United States had no comprehension of the realities of war.

Whether the uniform was blue or gray, the soldier at the war's outbreak was quite sure that he was fighting for an ideal. The North rushed volunteers to fill Mr. Lincoln's army, volunteers not interested in the economic causes of the war but excited by high moral aims—the preservation of the union, and, for some, the end of slavery. The South framed its ideals just as clearly. The fight was to preserve a way of life, to defend institutions and homes. Young men from the North marched away to the stirring strains of "John Brown's Body," those from the South to "The Bonnie Blue Flag," equally sure of returning home, triumphant heroes, within three months. Those left behind shared the youthful optimism of the gay warriors.

That the bright new uniforms would fall to tatters, that the gleaming banners would fade, that three months would stretch into three years, and more, that ideals were insufficient guarantees for victory—these realities were chastening lessons for Americans. Young Ambrose Bierce felt the shock to his romantic sensibilities when he saw the gorgeous Virginia landscape polluted by decaying corpses. He had to learn, like all soldiers, that gallant charges against heavy fire were often futile gestures. "Lead had scored its old-time victory over steel; the heroic had broken its great heart against the commonplace."

The South came to realize that chivalry, high courage, and fine horsemanship—despite their effect in the novels of Sir Walter Scott—were not warrants for victory. For all the gallantry of Ashby or Fitzhugh Lee, the grim machine of Grant crunched its way to grinding triumph. John Esten Cooke admitted in 1867, ". . . in modern war, when men are organized in masses and converted into insensate machines, there is really nothing heroic or romantic . . ."

Chivalric standards died. So did the belief in personal freedom. The volunteer soldier had to learn that an army could only operate by strict obedience and discipline. Perhaps the most difficult lesson for a democratic populace to learn was the icy military ethic that commanded the individual to submerge himself and his desires into the mass. Discipline was a sobering fact of life, taught by the iron necessities of war.

The Union, too, had to face the shock of disillusionment. Stupid leadership, inadequate planning, lost opportunities plagued the administration of the war. The New York draft riots made a sharp contrast to the earlier rush of volunteers to the colors. Profiteers, bounty jumpers, pillagers, deserters—over 200,000 of them—helped to break the old dream of "the pomp and circumstance of glorious war."

Americans at the conflict's start were prepared to believe the old motto, "Dulce et decorum est pro patria moritur." It seemed sweet and proper to offer one's life for one's country. But citizens became aware of the anguish of Andersonville and Fort Delaware. Soldiers learned that there was nothing sweet and proper about lingering death from festering wounds in filthy army hospitals. There was no glory in the hunger that led men to eat mule meat. Most of all, there was no relief from the interminable waiting, followed by action, then more waiting, and still no conclusion. The war reached into the homes and stomachs of half a nation. Ideologies gave way, grudgingly, to practicalities. War was a matter of supply rather than glorious resolves. After discovering these ugly realities, the American was ready to agree with Sherman's dictum that war was surely hell.

And so it went. A soldier, an army, a nation changed its frame of reference during the war from a complacent belief in honor and courage to a grim realization of expediency and economics.

Slowly the theme of four years of American life emerged as the theme of a body of war fiction. The facts of war became essential parts of American culture and American literature. The key emotional event of United States history, the Civil War, was a watershed in the development of a national consciousness. The heritage of the war was Reconstruction and wooden legs, industrial growth and Memorial Days. Although vestiges of trust in honor and glory remained, for the most part heartiness and optimism gave way to nostalgia and pessimism. The writers of war fiction turned this national experience into art.

IV

Nineteenth-century Civil War fiction reflected the war-taught actualities and helped to provide subject matter for the more realistic literary techniques of the 1890's. As the Civil War had taught that battle was a serious matter, so the war fiction became more serious and sophisticated. Authors moved from an emphasis on combat as a great adventure to a view of war as a necessary horror. In contrast to American action writing earlier in the century, Civil War fiction was not casual and abstract. The war stories and novels of De Forest, Bierce, and Crane, for example, substituted harsh and bitter irony for cool and uninvolved narrative.

Even more emotional writers, like Page or Lanier, while regretting the lost cause, avoided bathos and portrayed a powerful feeling for the dash and glory that had met defeat. Southern war fiction found in defeat a theme of dignity and strength. And realists like Mark Twain and Hamlin Garland, different as their approaches might be, used the military background effectively. The Civil War was a proper subject for serious fiction.

V

Many of these Civil War stories that appeared from 1863 to 1898 have fallen out of print. Some tales were published only in journals and magazines of the day; others came out as a single war story in a general collection. Romantic and sentimental plots buried brilliant battle passages in Cooke's *Mohun,* Lanier's *Tiger-Lilies,* and Kirkland's *The Captain of Company K.* Despite the conventions of mysterious legacies, sinister villains, disguised heroes, and tormented heroines, the books contain marvelous treatments of the war's moods and events.

This anthology sets forth three groupings of Civil War fiction. The first section samples five authors who saw active service in the war and wrote about the romantic glories with which the realities of war harshly clashed. In the next section appear four authors who wrote out of their extreme rejection of the war they also experienced at first hand. Finally, I have represented seven nineteenth-century writers who, although they did not actually take part in the Civil War, transmuted tales and events close to them into the materials of fiction.

All the writers sought to make vivid a war that had marked the lives and thoughts of a generation of Americans. The conception of the Civil War as a deep psychological experience, terrifying yet stimulating, irrational yet inevitable, overwhelming yet endurable, called for an intensification of realistic technique by the authors who sought to depict the essence of the war in their fiction. In these stories the Civil War comes alive and fresh as it was for the authors when they were creating their tales. Here, then, is the way the Civil War appeared to writers of fiction who lived during the period when the struggle still retained its immediacy.

E. S.

1

The Romantic Quest

from Mohun

JOHN ESTEN COOKE (1830–1886), VIRGINIAN NOVELIST AND HISTORIAN, HAD ALREADY achieved a large measure of literary success by the time the Civil War broke out. Two of his novels, *The Virginia Comedians* and *Henry St. John,* were best sellers in the 1850's. Cooke was a fierce secessionist. He served through the entire war, first on the staff of General J. E. B. Stuart—his nephew—and then with Lee until Appomattox.

Cooke rose through the ranks from private to captain. Stuart put him in for a majority, but the Confederate Senate did not confirm the promotion, probably because Cooke strongly recommended leaving Richmond to its fate at the hands of the Union armies and carrying on the war elsewhere.

In addition to his three novels dealing with the Civil War—*Surry of Eagle's Nest, Hilt to Hilt,* and *Mohun*—Cooke collected his reminiscences and military essays in two unjustly neglected volumes, *Wearing of the Grey* and *Hammer and Rapier.* He also wrote a military biography of General Robert E. Lee. Cooke continued to turn out historical novels until his death.

Mohun (1869) typifies Cooke's approach to war fiction, an uneasy amalgam of brilliantly realistic military description and outrageously melodramatic romance. The plot is a mélange of picturesque heroes, intriguing villains, secret sins. This absurd story, however, is overshadowed by the real aim of the novel, to elegize the gallant armies of the Confederacy. The plot, the narrator, even the nominal hero, all sink into oblivion in comparison to the genuine heroes of *Mohun,* General Jeb Stuart and the Army of Northern Virginia.

Cooke recaptures the romantic dash and splendor of a cavalry foray; he catches the scope and excitement of a full-scale battle. These selections from Cooke's novel include one of the finest extant descriptions of the action at Gettysburg and excellent accounts of the action at Fleetwood, Warrenton, Spottsylvania Court-House, and Yellow Tavern. The special quality of Cooke's war fiction comes from the poignant note of nostalgia for the dead past, for the glamor of combat, for the comradeship of bivouac, and for the old, lost feelings of hope and victory. *Mohun* is a monument to the dream of chivalric combat that was crushed by the machine of modern warfare.

The Cavalry Review

ON A BEAUTIFUL DAY OF JUNE, 1863, THE plains of Culpeper, in Virginia, were the scene of an imposing pageant.

Stuart's cavalry was passing in review before Lee, who was about to commence his march toward Gettysburg.

Those of my readers who were fortunate enough to be present, will not forget that scene. They will remember the martial form of Stuart at the head of his *sabreurs;* how the columns of horsemen thundered by the great flag; how the multitude cheered, brightest eyes shone, the merry bands clashed, the gay bugles rang; how the horse artillery roared as it was charged in mimic battle—while Lee, the gray old soldier, with serene carriage, sat his horse and looked on.

Never had the fields of Culpeper witnessed a spectacle more magnificent. The sunshine darted in lightnings from the long line of sabres, lit up beautiful faces, and flashed from scarfs, and waving handkerchiefs, rosy cheeks, and glossy ringlets. All was life, and joy, and splendor. For once war seemed turned to carnival; and flowers wreathed the keen edge of the sword.

Among the illustrious figures gazed at by the crowd, two were the observed of all the observers—those of Lee and Stuart.

Lee sat his powerful horse, with its plain soldierly equipments, beneath the large flag. He was clad in a gray uniform, almost without mark of rank. Cavalry boots reached nearly to his knees; as usual he wore no sword; over his broad brow drooped a plain brown felt hat, without tassel or decoration. Beneath, you saw a pair of frank and benignant, but penetrating eyes, ruddy cheeks, and an iron gray mustache and beard, both cut close. In the poise of the stately head, as in the whole carriage of his person, there was something calm, august and imposing. This man, it was plain, was not only great, but good;—the true type of the race of gentlemen of other times.

Stuart, the chief of cavalry of the army, was altogether different in appearance. Young, ardent, full of life and abandon, he was the true reproduction of Rupert, said to be his ancestor. The dark cavalry feather; the lofty forehead, and dazzling blue eyes; his little "fighting jacket," as he called it, bright with braid and buttons, made a picture. His boots reached to the knee; a yellow silk sash was about his waist; his spurs, of gold, were the present of some ladies of Maryland; and with sabre at tierce point, extended over his horse's head, he led the charge with his staff, in front of the column, and laughing, as though the notes of the bugle drove him forward.

In every movement of that stalwart figure, as in the glance of the blue eyes, and the laughter curling the huge mustache, could be read youth and joy, and a courage which nothing could bend. He was called a "boy" by some, as Coriolanus was before him. But his Federal adversaries did not laugh at him; they had felt his blows too often. Nor did the soldiers of the army. He had breasted bullets in front of infantry, as well as the sabre in front of cavalry. The civilians might laugh at him—the old soldiers found no fault in him for humming his songs in battle. They knew the man, and felt that he was a good soldier, as well as a great general. He would have made an excellent private, and did not feel "above" being one. Never was human being braver, if he did laugh and sing. Was he not brave? Answer, old sabreurs, whom he led in a hundred charges! old followers of Jackson, with whom he went over the breastworks at Chancellorsville!

Some readers may regard this picture of Stuart as overdrawn; but it is the simple truth of that brave soul. He had his faults; he loved praise, even flattery, and was sometimes irascible—but I have never known a human being more pure, generous and brave.

At sunset the review was over. The long columns of cavalry moved slowly back to their camps. The horse artillery followed; the infantry who had witnessed the ceremony sought their bivouacs in the woods; and the crowd, on foot, on horseback, or in carriages, returned toward the Court-House, whose spires were visible across the fields.

Stuart had approached the flag-staff and, doffing his plumed hat, had saluted Lee, who saluted in return, and complimented the review. After a few moments' conversation, they had then saluted a second time. Lee, followed by his staff, rode toward his quarters; and Stuart set out to return to his own.

How I Became a Member of General Stuart's Staff

If the reader has done me the honor to peruse the first volume of my memoirs, I indulge the vanity of supposing that he will like to be informed how I became a member of General Stuart's staff.

When oaks crash down they are apt to prostrate the saplings growing around them. Jackson was a very tall oak, and I a very humble sapling. When the great trunk fell, the mere twig disappeared. I had served with Jackson from the beginning of the war; that king of battle dead at Chancellorsville, I had found myself without a commander, and without a home. I was not only called upon in that May of 1863, to mourn the illustrious soldier, who had done me the honor to call me his friend; I had also to look around me for some other general; some other position in the army.

I was revolving this important subject in my mind, when I received a note from General J. E. B. Stuart, Jackson's friend and brother in arms. "Come and see me," said this note. Forty-eight hours afterward I was at Stuart's headquarters, near Culpeper Court-House.

When I entered his tent, or rather breadth of canvas, stretched beneath a great oak, Stuart rose from the red blanket upon which he was lying, and held out his hand. As he gazed at me in silence I could see his face flush.

"You remind me of Jackson," he said, retaining my hand and gazing fixedly at me.

I bowed my head, making no other reply; for the sight of Stuart brought back to me also many memories; the scouting of the Valley, the hard combats of the Lowland, Cold Harbor, Manassas, Sharpsburg, Fredericksburg, and that last greeting between Jackson and the great commander of the cavalry, on the weird moonlight night at Chancellorsville.

Stuart continued to gaze at me, and I could see his eyes slowly fill with tears.

"It is a national calamity!" he murmured. "Jackson's loss is irreparable!"*

He remained for a moment gazing into my face, then passing his hand over his forehead, he banished by a great effort these depressing memories. His bold features resumed their habitual cheerfulness.

Our dialogue was brief, and came rapidly to the point.

"Have you been assigned to duty yet, my dear Surry?"

"I have not, general."

"Would you like to come with me?"

"More than with any general in the army,

* His words.

since Jackson's death. You know I am sincere in saying that."

"Thanks—then the matter can be very soon arranged, I think. I want another inspector-general, and want *you*."

With these words Stuart seated himself at his desk, wrote a note, which he dispatched by a courier to army head-quarters; and then throwing aside business, he began laughing and talking.

For once the supply of red tape in Richmond seemed temporarily exhausted. Stuart was Lee's right hand, and when he made a request, the War Office deigned to listen. Four days afterward, I was seated under the canvas of a staff tent, when Stuart hastened up with boyish ardor, holding a paper.

"Here you are, old Surry,"—when he used the prefix "old" to any one's name, he was always excellently well disposed toward them, —"the Richmond people are prompt this time. Here is your assignment—send for Sweeney and his banjo! He shall play 'Jine the Cavalry!' in honor of the occasion, Surry!"

*   *   *

Lee's "Old War Horse"

Stuart was sitting his horse beside Davenant's guns, which from the slope grinned defiance at the enemy, when hoof-strokes were heard from the direction of the village of Paris, in his rear, and a party of horsemen ascended the mountain.

In front rode a personage of heavy figure, but soldierly bearing. He was clad in an old gray uniform, almost without decorations; wore a black-round head hat; his beard was long, matted and brown, like the full mus-

tache: and the expression of the countenance was calm, almost phlegmatic.

Such was the appearance of Lieutenant-General Longstreet, called by Lee "My Old War Horse."

Longstreet advanced slowly, at the head of a party of officers. Beside him rode a superb looking old cavalier of about sixty. He wore the uniform of a brigadier-general of infantry, and sat as erect as an arrow. The firm lips were covered by a heavy mustache, gray like his hair: his bearing was full of a courtly elegance; this man was evidently one of the old race of Virginians—a cavalier of the cavaliers.

Let me add a brief outline of one other figure. Behind the old cavalier came a sort of mouse on horseback; an urchin of about twelve, blue eyes, auburn hair, long and curling like a girl's, and an air of warlike pride. The mouse wore a braided jacket, a little jaunty cap, a floating feather, and beautiful gauntlets probably worked by his mother, as he seemed much too small to possess a sweetheart. He rode jauntily among the officers, exchanging jests with each and all: and it was easy to see that the youth was a favorite and a privileged character.

Longstreet halted beside Stuart, and grasping his hand, conversed with him for some moments. I afterward knew that the heavy firing had been heard over the mountain, and Longstreet, arresting his march, had occupied Ashby's Gap. From our lofty position, indeed, we could see the bayonets of his infantry glittering in the gorge.

All at once, Longstreet turning to the gray-headed officer, with a brief apology for his remissness, introduced him to Stuart as "General Davenant."

Stuart saluted, and exchanged a pressure of the hand with the courtly old officer.

"Your son, Will, has fought like a hero to-day, general," he said.

The old cavalier bowed.

"Those words are worth another grade of rank, general," he replied.

As he spoke, Will Davenant came up and greeted his father with blushing pleasure. Before he could speak, however, the urchin in the braided jacket spurred forward, and threw his arms around the young man's neck.

"How are you, Willie!" he exclaimed, "have you had a good fight? We were waiting yonder to help you if you were driven back, old fellow!"

Longstreet smiled. Will Davenant laughed, and said:—

"Glad to hear it, Charley."

"We don't think much of the cavalry, you know," said the urchin, *sotto voce,* "it takes the infants to do the work—but old Stuart is a trump!"

And Charley curled an imaginary mustache as his brother turned to speak to his father.

Half an hour afterward Stuart and Longstreet had finished their conversation, and exchanging a grasp of the hand, separated—the latter to return to Ashby's Gap.

Charley Davenant followed last, with evident regret.

"Well, good-bye, Willie," he said, throwing his arm around his brother again, "take care of yourself, old fellow, and if you are hard pressed call upon us. You will find the infants ready!"

"All right, Charley!"

"And I say, Willie"—

"What, Charley?"

"Remember that lieutenancy you promised me. I am a Davenant you know—and the Davenants are born to command! My motto is, 'Victory or Death,' old fellow!"

With which words the mouse waved his hand, put spur to his pony, and went at a gallop down the mountain.

Mosby Comes to Stuart's Assistance

Sore and restive at the reverse which had come to balance his victory of Fleetwood, Stuart bivouacked near Paris, that night, and made every preparation to attack at dawn.

At daylight he was in the saddle, and spurred to the high ground commanding Upperville.

All at once he checked his horse. The enemy had disappeared.

Stuart's blue eye flashed, and half an hour afterward he was advancing at the head of his cavalry. Not a foe was visible. Pressing on through Upperville, and over the trampled fields beyond, he continued to advance upon Middleburg, and near that place came up with the rear of the enemy. They showed little fight, however, and were driven beyond the place. The gray troopers pursued them with shouts and cheers—with which were mingled cries of rejoicing from the people of Middleburg.

An hour afterward the lines were re-established in triumph.

Stuart returned to his former head-quarters amid a drenching rain; and this recalls an incident very honorable to the brave soldier. As night descended, dark and stormy, Stuart gazed gloomily at the torrents of rain falling.

"My poor fellows!" he said, with a sigh, "they will have a hard time to-night."

Then suddenly turning to his servant, he added:—

"Spread my oil-cloth and blankets under that apple tree yonder. I will keep them dry enough when I once get into them."*

* His words.

"You are not going to sleep out on such a night, general!" exclaimed a staff officer.

"Certainly I am," was his reply, "I don't intend to fare better than my men!"*

And an hour afterward Stuart was asleep under the apple tree, with a torrent pouring on him.

That was the act of a good officer and soldier, was it not, reader?

Before sunrise Stuart was up, and walking uneasily to and fro. As the day wore on, he exhibited more and more impatience. All at once, at the appearance of an officer, approaching rapidly from the front, he uttered an exclamation of pleasure.

"Here is Mosby at last!" he said.

And he went to meet the new-comer. It was the famous chief of partisans whose name by this time had become a terror to the enemy. He wore a plain gray uniform, a brace of revolvers in a swaying belt, rode a spirited gray mare, and I recognized at once the roving glance, and satirical smile which had struck me on that night when he rescued Farley and myself in Fauquier.

Stuart rapidly drew him into a private apartment; remained in consultation with him for half an hour; and then came forth, with a smile of evident satisfaction.

Mosby's intelligence must have pleased him. It at least dispelled his gloom.

An hour afterward his head-quarters had disappeared—every thing was sent toward the mountains. Stuart set out apparently to follow them—but that was only a ruse to blind busybodies.

A quarter of a mile from head-quarters he leaped a fence, and doubled back, going in the direction now of Manassas.

At daylight on the next morning he had forced his way through the Bull Run mountain.

Two hours afterward he had made a sudden attack on the enemy's infantry. It was the rear of Hancock's corps, which was the rear of Hooker's army, then retiring toward the Potomac.

The Supper Near Bucklands

Stuart's fight near Haymarket, here alluded to, was a gay affair; but I pass over it, to a scene still gayer and decidedly more pleasant.

The fighting continued throughout the day, and at dusk a heavy rain came on. We were all tired and hungry—the general no less so than his staff—and when an invitation was sent to us by a gentleman near Bucklands, to come and sup with him, we accepted it with fervor, and hastened toward the friendly mansion.

A delightful reception awaited us. The house was full of young ladies, passionately devoted to "rebels," and we were greeted with an enthusiasm which passed all bounds. Delicate hands pressed our own; bright eyes beamed upon us; rosy lips smiled; musical voices said "welcome!"—and soon a savory odor, pervading the mansion, indicated that the wants of the inner man were not forgotten.

An excellent supper was plainly in preparation for the bold Stuart and his military family; and that gay and gallant cavalier, General Fitz Lee having also been invited, the joy of the occasion was complete! The house rang with clashing heels, rattling sabres, and clanking spurs. A more charming sound still, however, was that made by jingling keys and rattling china, and knives and forks. All was joy and uproar: jests, compliments and laughter. Young ladies went and came; the odors grew more inviting. In ten minutes the door of a large apartment opposite the drawing-room was thrown open, and a magnificent, an enthralling spectacle was revealed to every eye.

Not to be carried away, however, by enthusiasm, I will simply say that we saw before us a long mahogany table covered with the most appetizing viands—broils, roasts, stews, bread of every variety, and *real* coffee and tea in real silver! That magical spectacle still dwells in my memory, reader, though the fact may lower me in your good opinion. But alas! we are all "weak creatures." The most poetical grow hungry. We remember our heroic performances in the great civil war— but ask old soldiers if these recollections are not the most vivid!

An incident connected with the repast made it especially memorable. The servants of the house had deserted to their friends in blue; and as there was thus a deficiency of attendants, the young ladies took their places. Behind every chair stood a maiden—their faces wreathed with smiles. We were shown to our seats, amid joyous laughter. The comedy evidently afforded all engaged in it immense enjoyment —and the cavaliers humoring the angelic maid-servants, gravely advanced toward the table.

Stuart threw his plumed hat upon a chair, and drew near the foot of the table. The light fell full on the ruddy face, the heavy beard and mustache, and brilliant fighting jacket. He looked round with a gay smile. "Was any one absent," asked the kind lady of the house, as she saw the glance. Stuart made a low bow, and said:—

"All are here, madam!"

All at once, however, a voice at the door responded:—

"I think you are mistaken, general!"

And he who had uttered these words advanced into the apartment.

He was a young man, about twenty-three, of medium height, graceful, and with a smile of charming good humor upon the lips. His hair was light and curling: his eyes blue: his lips shaded by a slender mustache. His uniform was bran new, and decorated with the braid of a lieutenant. Yellow gauntlets reached his elbow, he wore a shiny new satchel, and in his hand carried a brown felt hat, caught up with a golden star.

Stuart grasped his hand warmly.

"Here you are, old fellow!" he exclaimed.

And turning to the company, he added:—

"My new aid-de-camp, Lieutenant Herbert, ladies. A fop—but an old soldier. Take that seat by Colonel Surry, Tom."

And every one sat down, and attacked the supper.

I had shaken hands with Tom Herbert, who was far from being a stranger to me, as I had met him frequently in the drawing-rooms of Richmond before the war. He was a fop, but the most charming of fops, when I first knew him. He wore brilliant waistcoats, variegated scarfs, diamond studs, and straw-colored kid gloves. In his hand he used to flourish an ivory-headed whalebone cane, and his boots were of feminine delicacy and dimensions. Such was Tom at that time, but the war had "brought him out." He had rushed into the ranks, shouldered a musket, and fought bravely. So much I knew—and I was soon to hear how he had come to be Stuart's aid.

The supper was charming. The young girls waited on us with mock submission and delighted smiles. Tom and I had fallen to the lot of a little princess with golden ringlets; and Miss Katy Dare—that was her name—acquitted herself marvellously. We supped as though we expected to eat nothing for the next week—and then having finished, we rose, and waited in turn on the fair waiters.

Behind every chair now stood an officer in uniform.

Bright eyes, rosy cheeks, jewelled hands, glossy curls—there was the picture, my dear reader, which we beheld as we "waited" at that magical supper near Buckland.

When we wrapped our capes around us, and fell asleep on the floor, the little maidens still laughed in our dreams! *

An Honest Fop

Stuart moved again at dawn. The scene of the preceding evening had passed away like a dream. We were in the saddle, and advancing.

Riding beside Lieutenant Tom Herbert, I conversed with that worthy, and found the tedious march beguiled by his gay and insouciant talk.

His "record" was simple. He had volunteered in the infantry, and at the battle of Cold Harbor received a wound in the leg which disqualified him for a foot-soldier thenceforward. His friends succeeded in procuring for him the commission of lieutenant, and he was assigned to duty as drill master at a camp of instruction near Richmond.

"Here I was really in clover, old fellow," said Tom, laughingly, "no more toils, no more hardships, no bullets, or hard tack, or want of soap. A snowy shirt every day—kid gloves if I wanted them—and the sound of cannon at a very remote distance to lull me to repose, my boy. Things had changed, they had indeed! I looked back with scorn on the heavy musket and cartridge-box. I rode a splendidly groomed

* A real incident.

horse, wore a new uniform shining with gold braid, a new cap covered with ditto, boots which you could see your face in, a magnificent sash, and spurs so long and martial that they made the pavement resound, and announced my approach at the distance of a quarter of a mile! I say the pavement; I was a good deal on the pavement—that of the fashionable Franklin street being my favorite haunt. And as the Scripture says, it is not good for man to be alone, I had young ladies for companions. My life was grand, superb—none of your low military exposure, like that borne by the miserable privates and officers in the field! I slept in town, lived at a hotel, mounted my horse after breakfast, at the Government stables near my lodgings and went gallantly at a gallop, to drill infantry for an hour or two at the camp of instruction. This was a bore, I acknowledge, but life cannot be all flowers. It was soon over, however—I galloped gallantly back—dined with all the courses at my hotel, and then lit my cigar and strolled up Franklin. I wore my uniform and spurs on these promenades—wild horses tearing me would not have induced me to doff the spurs! They were so martial! They jingled so! They gave a military and ferocious set-off to my whole appearance, and were immensely admired by the fair sex! Regularly on coming back from my arduous and dangerous duties at camp, I brushed my uniform, put on my red sash, and with one hand resting with dignity on my new sword belt, advanced to engage the enemy—on Franklin street."

Tom Herbert's laugh was contagious; his whole bearing so sunny and *riante* that he was charming.

"Well, how did you awake from your *dolce far niente?*" I said.

"By an effort of the will, old fellow—for I

really could not stand that. It was glorious, delightful—that war-making in town; but there was a thorn in it. I was ashamed of myself. 'Tom Herbert you are not a soldier, you are an imposter,' I said; 'you are young, healthy, as good food for powder as anybody else, and yet here you are, safely laid away in a bomb-proof, while your friends are fighting. Wake, rouse yourself, my friend! The only way to regain the path of rectitude is to go back to the army!' "

"I said that, Surry," Tom continued, "and as I could not go back into the infantry on account of my leg, I applied for an assignment to duty in the cavalry. Then the war office had a time of it. I besieged the nabobs of the red tape day and night, and they got so tired of me at last that they told me to find a general who wanted an aid and they would assign me."

"Well, as I was coming out of the den I met General Jeb. Stuart going in. I knew him well, and he was tenth cousin to my grandmother, which you know counts for a great deal in Virginia."

"What's the matter, Tom?" he said.

"I want a place in the cavalry, general."

"What claim have you?"

"Shot in the leg—can't walk—am tired of drilling men in bomb-proof."

"Good!" he said. "That's the way to talk. Come in here."

"And he dragged me along. I found that one of his aids had just been captured—he wanted another, and he applied for me. A month afterward his application was approved—short for the war office. That was five days ago. I got into the saddle,—pushed for the Rapidan—got to Middleburg—and arrived in time for supper."

"That's my history, old fellow, except that I have just fallen in love—with the young angel who waited on me at supper, Miss Katy Dare. I opened the campaign in a corner last night—and I intend to win her, Surry, or perish in the attempt!"

Stuart Grazes Capture

As Tom Herbert uttered these words, a loud shout in front startled us.

Stuart had ridden on ahead of his column, through the immense deserted camps around Wolf Run Shoals, attended only by two or three staff officers.

As I now raised my head quickly, I saw him coming back at headlong speed, directing his horse by means of the halter only, and hotly pursued by a detachment of Federal cavalry, firing on him as they pressed, with loud shouts, upon his very heels.

"Halt!" shouted the enemy. And this order was followed by "bang! bang! bang!"

Stuart did not obey the order.

"Halt! halt!"

And a storm of bullets whistled around our heads. I had drawn my sword, but before I could go to Stuart's assistance, Tom shot ahead of me.

He came just in time. Two of the enemy had caught up with Stuart, and were making furious cuts at him. He parried the blow of one of the Federal cavalry-men—and the other fell from the saddle, throwing up his hands as he did so. Tom Herbert had placed his pistol on his breast, and shot him through the heart.

But by this time the rest had reached us. A sabre flashed above Tom's head; fell, cutting him out of the saddle nearly; and he would have dropped from it, had I not passed my arm around him.

In another instant, all three would have

been killed or captured. But the firing had given the alarm. A thunder of hoofs was heard: a squadron of our cavalry dashed over the hill: in three minutes the enemy were flying, to escape the edge of the sabre.

Stuart led the charge, and seemed to enjoy it with the zest of a fox-hunter. He had indeed escaped from a critical danger. He had pushed on with a few of his staff, as I have said, to Fairfax Station, had then stopped and slipped his bridle to allow his horse to eat some "Yankee oats," and while standing beside the animal, had been suddenly charged by the party of Federal cavalry, coming down on a reconnaissance from the direction of the Court-House. So sudden was their appearance that he was nearly "gobbled up." He had leaped on the unbridled horse; seized the halter, and fled at full speed. The enemy had pursued him; he had declined halting—and the reader has seen the sequel.*

Stuart pressed the party hotly toward Sanxter's, but they escaped—nearly capturing on the way, however, a party of officers at a blacksmith's shop. The general came back in high good humor. The chase seemed to have delighted him.

"Bully for old Tom Herbert!" he exclaimed. "You ought to have seen him when they were cutting at him, and spoiling his fine new satchel!"

Tom Herbert did not seem to participate in the general's mirth. He was examining the satchel which a sabre stroke had nearly cut in two.

"What are you looking at?" asked Stuart.

"This hole, general," replied Tom, uttering a piteous sigh.

"Well, it is a trifle."

"It is a serious matter, general."

"You have lost something?"

* Real.

"Yes."

"What?"

"A joint of my new flute."

And Tom Herbert's expression was so melancholy that Stuart burst into laughter.

"You may have lost your flute, Tom," he said, leaning on his shoulder, "but you have won your spurs at least, in the cavalry!"

Drowsyland

At daylight, on the next morning, Stuart had crossed the Potomac into Maryland.

He had advanced from Wolf Run Shoals to Fairfax Court-House, where the men rifled the sutlers' shops of tobacco, figs, white gloves, straw hats, and every edible and wearable:— then the column pushed on toward Seneca Falls, where the long wavering line of horsemen might have been seen hour after hour crossing the moonlit river, each man, to prevent wetting, holding above his head a shot or shell taken from the caissons. Then the artillery was dragged through: the panting horses trotted on, and the first beams of day saw the long column of Stuart ready to advance on its perilous pathway to the Susquehanna, by the route between the Federal army and Washington.

The word was given, and with the red flags fluttering, Stuart moved toward Rockville, unopposed, save by a picket, which was driven off by the advance guard. Without further incident, he then pushed on, and entered the town in triumph.

A charming reception awaited him. The place was thoroughly Southern; and the passage of the cavalry was greeted with loud cheers. Unbounded was the delight, above all, of a seminary of young girls. Doors and windows were crowded: bright eyes shone; red lips laughed; waving handkerchiefs were seen everywhere; and when Stuart appeared in person, he was received with wild rejoicing.

He bowed low, removing his plumed hat, but suddenly intelligence came which forced him to push on. A long train of "government" wagons had come up from Washington, and on discovering our presence, returned toward the city at a gallop. But the ferocious rebels were after them. Stuart led the charging column—the warlike teamsters were soon halted—the trains became our spoil—and with countless kicking mules driven onward in droves before them, the cavalry, escorting the captured wagons, continued their way toward Pennsylvania.

Moving all that night, Stuart came to Westminster, where Fitz Lee, the gallant, drove the enemy's cavalry from their camp, and the town fell into the hands of Stuart.

Here scowls instead of smiles greeted us. Every face was glum and forbidding, with a few exceptions. So we hastened to depart from that "loyal" town, and were soon on the soil of Pennsylvania.

Approaching Hanover we suddenly waked up the hornets. Chambliss, leading Stuart's advance, pushed ahead and drove in a picket. Then that brave soldier rushed on, and seemed intent on taking the place, when I was sent by Stuart to order him "not to go too far."

I came up with Chambliss as he was charging, but had scarcely given him the order, when he was charged in turn by a heavy force and driven back.

The enemy rushed on, firing volleys, and the road was full of tramping horsemen. To avoid being carried away with them, I diverged into a field, when all at once Stuart appeared, retreating at full gallop before a party who were chasing him.

It was a serious matter then, but I laugh now, remembering that "good run."

Stuart and myself retreated at a gallop, boot to boot; leaped ditches and fences; and got off in safety.

A few moments afterward his artillery opened its thunders. From the lofty hill, that hardy captain of the horse artillery, Breathed, roared obstinately, driving them back. Hampton's guns on the right had opened too—and until night, we held the heights, repulsing every advance of the enemy.

It was truly a fine spectacle, that handsome town of Hanover as I looked at it, on the afternoon of the fair June day. In front extended green fields; then the church spires rose above the roofs of the town; behind, a range of mountains formed a picturesque background. It is true, the adjuncts of the scene were far from peaceful. The green fields were full of blue sharp-shooters; in the suburbs were posted batteries; down the mountain road behind, wound a long compact column of cavalry.

Breathed fought hard that day. From the waving field of rye on the upland his guns thundered on—in the face of that fire, the enemy could not, or would not, advance.

So the night came on, and Stuart's great train moved.

Those wagons were a terrible encumbrance to us on the march. But Stuart determined not to abandon them, and they were dragged on— a line stretched to infinity!

Thenceforth, dear reader, the march was a sort of dream to me. How can I relate my adventures—the numerous spectacles and events of the time? I know not even now if they were events or mere dreams, seeing that, all the long way, I was half asleep in the saddle! It was a veritable Drowsyland that we moved through on horseback! The Dutchmen, the "fraus," the "spreading," the sauer-kraut—the conestogas, the red barns, the guttural voices, the strange faces—were these actual things, or the mere fancies of a somnambulist? Was I an officer of real cavalry making a real march; or a fanciful being, one of a long column of phantoms?

I seem dimly to remember a pretty face, whose owner smiled on me—and a faint memory remains of a supper which she gave me. If I am not mistaken I was left alone in the town of Salem—hostile faces were around me—and I was falling asleep when Hampton's cavalry came up.

I think, then, I rode on with him—having been left to direct him. That we talked about horses, and the superiority of "blood" in animals; that at dawn, Hampton said, "I am perishing for sleep!" and that we lay down, side by side, near a haystack.

All that is a sort of phantasmagoria, and others were no better than myself. Whole columns went to sleep, in the saddle, as they rode along: and General Stuart told me afterward, that he saw a man attempt to climb over a fence, half succeed only, and go to sleep on the top rail!

Some day I promise myself the pleasure of travelling in Pennsylvania. It possesses all the attractions to me of a world seen in a dream!

But after that good sleep, side by side with the great Carolinian, things looked far more real, and pushing on I again caught up with Stuart.

He advanced steadily on Carlisle, and in the afternoon we heard artillery from the south.

I looked at my military map, and calculated the distance. The result was that I said:—

"General, those guns are at a place called Gettysburg on this map."

"Impossible!" was his reply. "They can not be fighting there. You are certainly wrong."

But I was right.

Those guns were the signal of the "First day's fight at Gettysburg."

Carlisle By Firelight

It can not be said that we accomplished very enormous results at Carlisle. The enemy defended it bravely.

Stuart sent in a flag, demanding a surrender: this proposition was politely declined; and for fear that there might possibly remain some doubts on the subject, the Federal commander of the post opened with artillery upon the gray cavalry.

That was the signal for a brisk fight, and a magnificent spectacle also.

As soon as the enemy's response to the flag of truce had been received, Stuart advanced his sharp-shooters, replied with his artillery to their own, and dispatched a party to destroy the extensive United States barracks, formerly used as cantonments for recruits to the army.

In ten minutes the buildings were wrapped in flames; and the city of Carlisle was illumined magnificently. The crimson light of the conflagration revealed every house, the long lines of trees, and made the delicate church spires, rising calmly aloft, resemble shafts of rose-tinted marble.

I recall but one scene which was equally picturesque—the "doomed city" of Fredericksburg, on the night of December 11, 1862, when the church spires were illumined by the burning houses, as those of Carlisle were in June, 1863.

So much for this new "Siege of Carlisle." Here my description ends. It was nothing—a mere picture. An hour afterward Stuart ceased firing, the conflagration died down; back into the black night sank the fair town of Carlisle, seen then for the first and the last time by this historian.

The guns were silent, the cavalry retired; and Stuart, accompanied by his staff, galloped back to a great deserted house where he established his temporary head-quarters.

On the bold face there was an expression of decided ill-humor. He had just received a dispatch, by courier, from General Lee.

That dispatch said, "Come, I need you urgently here," and the "here" in question, was Gettysburg, at least twenty miles distant. Now, with worn-out men and horses, twenty miles was a serious matter. Stuart's brows were knit, and he mused gloomily.

Suddenly he turned and addressed me.

"You were right, Surry," he said, "those guns were at Gettysburg. This dispatch, sent this morning, reports the enemy near there."

I bowed; Stuart reflected for some moments without speaking. Then he suddenly said:—

"I wish you would go to General Lee, and say I am coming, Surry. How is your horse?"

"Worn-out, general, but I can get another."

"Good; tell General Lee that I will move at once to Gettysburg, with all my force, and as rapidly as possible!"

"I will lose no time, general."

And saluting, I went out.

From the captured horses I selected the best one I could find, and burying the spurs in his sides, set out through the black night.

*　　*　　*

Gettysburg

I came in sight of Gettysburg at sunrise.

Gettysburg!—name instinct with so many tears, with so much mourning, with those sobs which tear their way from the human heart as the lava makes its way from the womb of the volcano!

There are words in the world's history whose very sound is like a sigh or a groan; places which are branded "accursed" by the moaning lips of mothers, wives, sisters, and orphans. Shadowy figures, gigantic and draped in mourning, seem to hover above these spots: skeleton arms with bony fingers point to the soil beneath, crowded with graves: from the eyes, dim and hollow, glare unutterable things: and the grin of the fleshless lips is the gibbering mirth of the corpse torn from its cerements, and erect, as though the last trump had sounded, and the dead had arisen. No fresh flowers bloom in these dreary spots; no merry birds twitter there; no streamlets lapse sweetly with musical murmurs beneath the water-flags or the drooping boughs of trees. See! the blighted and withered plants are like the deadly nightshade—true flowers of war, blooming, or trying to bloom, on graves! Hear the voices of the few birds—they are sad and discordant! See the trees—they are gnarled, spectral, and torn by cannon-balls. Listen! The stream yonder is not limpid and mirthful like other streams. You would say that it is sighing as it steals away, soiled and ashamed. The images it has mirrored arouse its horror and make it sad. The serene surface has not given back the bright forms of children, laughing and gathering the summer flowers on its banks. As it sneaks like a culprit through the scarred fields of battle, it washes bare the bones of the dead in crumbling uniforms—bringing, stark and staring, to the upper air once more, the blanched skeleton and the grinning skull.

Names of woe, at whose utterance the heart shudders, the blood curdles! Accursed localities where the traveller draws back, turning away in horror! All the world is dotted with them;

everywhere they make the sunlight black. Among them, none is gloomier, or instinct with a more nameless horror, than the once insignificant village of Gettysburg.

I reached it on the morning of July 2, 1863.

The immense drama was in full progress. The adversaries had clashed together. Riding across the extensive fields north of the town, I saw the traces of the combat of the preceding day—and among the dying I remember still a poor Federal soldier, who looked at me with his stony and half-gazed eye as I passed; he was an enemy, but he was dying and I pitied him.

A few words will describe the situation of affairs at that moment.

Lee had pressed on northward through the valley of the Cumberland, when news came that General Meade, who had succeeded Hooker, was advancing to deliver battle to the invaders.

At that intelligence Lee arrested his march. Meade menaced his communications, and it was necessary to check him. Hill's corps was, therefore, sent across the South Mountain, toward Gettysburg; Ewell, who had reached York, was ordered back; and Lee made his preparations to fight his adversary as soon as he appeared.

The columns encountered each other in the neighborhood of Gettysburg—a great centre toward which a number of roads converge, like the spokes of a wheel toward the hub.

The head of Hill's column struck the head of Reynolds's—then the thunder began.

The day and scene were lovely. On the waving wheat-fields and the forests in full foliage, the light of a summer sun fell in flashing splendor. A slight rain had fallen; the wind was gently blowing; and the leaves and golden grain were covered with drops which the sunshine changed to diamonds.

Over the exquisite landscape drooped a beautiful rainbow.

Soon blood had replaced the raindrops, and the bright bow spanning the sky was hidden by lurid smoke, streaming aloft from burning buildings, set on fire by shell.

I give but a few words to this first struggle, which I did not witness.

The Federal forces rushed forward, exclaiming:—

"We have come to stay!"

"And a very large portion of them," said one of their officers, General Doubleday, "never left that ground!"

Alas! many thousands in gray, too, "came to stay."

Hill was hard pressed and sent for assistance. Suddenly it appeared from the woods on his left, where Ewell's bayonets were seen, coming back from the Susquehanna.

Rodes, the head of Ewell's corps, formed line and threw himself into the action.

Early came up on the left; Rodes charged and broke through the Federal centre. Gordon, commanding a brigade then, closed in on their right flank, and the battle was decided.

The great blue crescent was shattered, and gave way. The Confederates pressed on, and the Federal army became a rabble. They retreated pellmell through Gettysburg, toward Cemetery Hill, leaving their battle-flags and five thousand prisoners in our hands.

Such was the first day's fight at Gettysburg. Lee's head of column had struck Meade's; each had rapidly been re-enforced; the affair became a battle, and the Federal forces were completely defeated.

That was the turning point of the campaign. If this success had only been followed up—if we could only have seized upon and occupied Cemetery Hill!

Then General Meade would have been compelled to retire upon Westminster and Washington. He would doubtless have fought somewhere, but it is a terrible thing to have an army flushed with victory "after" you!

Cemetery Range was not seized that night. When the sun rose the next morning, the golden moment had passed. General Meade was ready.

From right to left, as far as the eye could reach, the heights bristled with blue infantry and artillery. From every point on the ridge waved the enemy's battle flags. From the muzzles of his bronze war-dogs, Meade sent his defiant challenge to his adversary to attack him.

"Come on!" the Federal artillery seemed to mutter fiercely.

And Lee's guns from the ridge opposite thundered grimly in reply,

"We are coming!"

The Army

Alas!—

That is the word which rises to the lips of every Southerner, above all to every Virginian, who attempts to describe this terrible battle of Gettysburg.

The cheeks flush, the voice falters, and something like a fiery mist blinds the eyes. What comes back to the memory of the old soldiers who saw that fight is a great picture of heroic assaults, ending in frightful carnage only,—of charges such as the world has rarely seen, made in vain,—of furious onslaughts, the only result of which was to strew those fatal fields with the dead bodies of the flower of the Southern race.

And we were so near succeeding! Twice the enemy staggered; and one more blow—only one more! promised the South a complete victory!

When Longstreet attacked Round Top Hill, driving the enemy back to their inner line, victory seemed within our very grasp—but we could not snatch it. The enemy acknowledge that, and it is one of their own poets who declares that

> "The century reeled
> When Longstreet paused on the slope of the hill."

Pickett stormed Cemetery Heights, and wanted only support. Five thousand men at his back would have given him victory.

There is a name for the battle of Gettysburg which exactly suits it—"The Great Graze!"

You must go to the histories, reader, for a detailed account of this battle. I have not the heart to write it, and aim to give you a few scenes only. In my hasty memoirs I can touch only upon the salient points, and make the general picture.

The ground on which the battle was fought, is familiar to many thousands. A few words will describe it. Cemetery Ridge, where General Meade had taken up his position, is a range of hills running northward toward Gettysburg, within a mile of which place it bends off to the right, terminating in a lofty and rock-bound crest.

This crest was Meade's right. His line stretched away southward then, and ended at Round Top Hill, the southern extremity of the range, about four miles distant.

From one end to the other of the extensive range, bayonets glistened, and the muzzles of cannon grinned defiance.

Opposite the Cemetery Range was a lower line of hills, called Seminary Range. Upon this Lee was posted, Ewell holding his left, A. P. Hill his centre, and Longstreet his right.

Between the two armies stretched a valley, waving with grain and dotted with fruit-trees, through which ran the Emmettsburg road, on the western side of a small stream. The golden grain waved gently; the limpid water lapsed away beneath grass and flowers; the birds were singing; the sun was shining—it was the strangest of all scenes for a bloody conflict.

I rode along the line of battle, and curiously scanned the features of the landscape. There is a frightful interest connected with ground which is soon going to become the arena of a great combat. A glance told me that the enemy's position was much the stronger of the two. Would Lee attack it?

From the landscape I turned to look at the army. Never had I seen them so joyous. It would be impossible to convey any idea of the afflatus which buoyed them up. Every man's veins seemed to run with quicksilver, instead of blood. Every cheek was glowing. Every eye flashed with superb joy and defiance. You would have supposed, indeed, that the troops were under the effect of champagne or laughing gas. "I never even imagined such courage," said a Federal officer afterward; "your men seemed to be drunk with victory when they charged us!"

That was scarce an exaggeration. Already on the morning of battle they presented this appearance. Lying down in line of battle, they laughed, jested, sang, and resembled children enjoying a holiday. On the faces of bearded veterans and boy-soldiers alike was a splendid pride. The victories of Fredericksburg, and Chancellorsville had electrified the troops. They thought little of a foe who could be so easily driven; they looked forward to victory as a foregone conclusion—alas! they did not remember that *they* held the heights at Fredericksburg; and that Meade on Cemetery Hill was an adversary very different from Hooker in the Spottsylvania Wilderness!

Such was the spectacle which I witnessed, when after delivering my message to General Lee, I rode along the Southern line. I think the great commander shared in some measure the sentiment of his troops. His bearing was collected; in his eye you could read no trace of excitement; the lips covered by the gray mustache were firm and composed; and he greeted me with quiet courtesy:—but in the cheeks of the great soldier a ruddy glow seemed to betray anticipated victory.

I confess I shared the general sentiment. That strange intoxication was contagious, and I was drunk like the rest with the thought of triumph. That triumph would open to us the gates of Washington and bring peace. The North scarcely denied that then—though they may deny it to-day. The whole country was completely weary of the war. There seemed to be no hope of compelling the South to return to the Union. A victory over Meade, opening the whole North to Lee, promised a treaty of peace. The day had arrived, apparently when the army of Northern Virginia, musket in hand, was about to dictate the terms of that document.

"Lee has only to slip the leash," I thought, as I gazed at the army, "and these war-dogs will tear down their prey!"

Alas! they tore it, but were torn too! they did all at Gettysburg that any troops could do.

What was impossible, was beyond even their strength.

The Wrestle for Round Top Hill

From the morning of the second of July to the evening of the third, the fields south of Gettysburg were one great scene of smoke, dust, uproar, blood; of columns advancing and returning; cannon thundering; men shouting, yelling, cheering, and dying; blue mingled with gray in savage and unrelenting battle.

In that smoke-cloud, with the ears deafened, you saw or heard little distinctly. But above the confused struggle rose two great incidents, which on successive days decided every thing.

The first of them was Longstreet's assault on the enemy's left wing, in front of Round Top Hill.

Lee had displayed excellent soldiership in determining upon this movement, and it will be seen that it came within an inch of success. Standing upon Seminary Range, near his centre, he had reconnoitered General Meade's position through his field-glass, with great attention; and this examination revealed the fact that the Federal line was projected forward in a salient in front of Round Top Hill, a jagged and almost inaccessible peak, near which rested General Meade's extreme left.

If this weak point could be carried, "it appeared" said Lee, "that its possession would give facilities for assailing and carrying the more elevated ground and crest beyond."

As to the importance of that crest—namely Round Top Hill—hear General Meade:—

"If they had succeeded in occupying that, it would have prevented me from holding any of the ground which I subsequently held to the last."

Lee determined to attack the salient, making at the same time a heavy demonstration— or a real assault—upon the Federal right, opposite Ewell.

All his preparations were not made until the afternoon. Then suddenly, Longstreet's artillery opened its thunders.

At that moment the spectacle was grand. The heights, the slopes, the fields, and the rugged crest opposite, were enveloped in smoke and fire from the bursting shell. The sombre roar ascended like the bellowing of a thousand bulls, leaped back from the rocks, and rolled away, in wild echoes through the hills. All the furies seemed let loose, and yet this was only the preface.

At four in the evening the thunder dropped to silence, and along the lines of Hood and McLaws, which formed the charging column, ran a wild cheer, which must have reached the ears of the enemy opposite.

That cheer told both sides that the moment had come. The word was given, and Longstreet hurled his column at the blue line occupying a peach-orchard in his front.

The blow was aimed straight at the salient in the Federal line, and in spite of a brave resistance it was swept away; McLaws advancing rapidly toward the high ground in its rear. At one blow the whole left wing of General Meade's army seemed thrown into irretrievable confusion, and Hood pressing forward on McLaw's right, hastened to seize upon the famous Round Top, from which he would be able to hurl his thunder upon the flank and rear of the Federal line of battle.

The scene, like the conflict which now took place, was wild and singular. The crest of Round Top Hill was a mass of rock, which rose abruptly from the rough and jagged slope. It was unoccupied—for the sudden overthrow of the force in front of it had not been anticipated—and one headlong rush on the part of Hood alone seemed necessary to give him possession of the real key of the whole position.

Hood saw that at a glance, and dashed up the slope at the head of his men. It was scarcely an order of battle which his troops presented at this moment. But one thought burned in every heart. The men swarmed up the hill-side; the woods gave back the rolling thunder of their cheers; already the Southern battle-flags carried by the foremost were fluttering on the crest.

The mass rushed toward the red flags; for an instant the gray figures were seen erect upon the summit—then a sudden crash of musketry resounded—and a mad struggle began with a Federal brigade which had hastened to the spot.

This force, it is said, was hurried up by General Warren, who finding the Federal signal-officers about to retire, ordered them, to remain and continue waving their flags to the last; and then, seizing on the first brigade he could find, rushed them up the slope to the crest.

They arrived just in time. Hood's men were swarming on the crest. A loud cheer arose, but all at once they found themselves face to face with a line of bayonets, while beyond were seen confused and struggling masses, dragging up cannon.

What followed was a savage grapple rather than an ordinary conflict. Only a small part of Hood's force had reached the summit, and this was assailed by a whole brigade. The fight was indescribable. All that the eye could make out for some moments in the dust and smoke, was a confused mass of men clutching each other, dealing blows with the butt-ends of muskets, or fencing with bayonets—men in blue and gray, wrestling, cursing, falling, and dying, in the midst of the crash of small-arms, and the thunder of cannon, which clothed the crest in flame.

When the smoke drifted, it was seen that the Confederates had been repulsed, and driven from the hill. Hood was falling back slowly, like a wounded tiger, who glares at the huntsman and defies him to the last. The slope was strewed with some of his bravest. The Federal cannon roaring on Round Top Hill, seemed to be laughing hoarsely.

McLaws, too, had fallen back after nearly seizing upon the crest in his front. The enemy had quickly re-enforced their left, with brigades, divisions, and corps, and the Confederates had been hotly assailed in their turn. As night descended, the whole Southern line fell back. The pallid moonlight shone on the upturned faces of the innumerable dead.

Longstreet sat on a fence, cutting a stick with his penknife, when an English officer near him exclaimed:—

"I would not have missed this for any thing?"

Longstreet, laughed grimly.

"I would like to have missed it very much!"* he said.

The Charge of The Virginians

Lee's great blow at the enemy's left had failed. He had thrown his entire right wing, under Longstreet, against it. The enemy had been driven; victory seemed achieved;—but suddenly the blue lines had rallied, they had returned to the struggle, their huge masses had rolled forward, thrown Longstreet back in turn, and now the pale moon looked down on the battlefield where some of the bravest souls of the South had poured out their blood in vain.

Lee had accomplished nothing, and one of his great corps was panting and bleeding. It was not shattered or even shaken. The iron fibre would stand any thing almost. But the sombre result remained—Longstreet had attacked and had been repulsed.

What course would Lee now pursue? Would he retire?

Retire? The army of Northern Virginia lose

* His words.

heart at a mere rebuff? Lee's veteran army give up the great invasion, after a mere repulse? Troops and commander alike shrunk from the very thought. One more trial of arms—something—an attack somewhere—not *a retreat!*

That was the spirit of the army on the night of the second of July.

A flanking movement to draw the enemy out of their works, or a second attack remained.

Lee determined to attack.

Longstreet and Ewell had accomplished nothing by assailing the right and left of the enemy. Lee resolved now to throw a column against its centre—to split the stubborn obstacle, and pour into the gap with the whole army, when all would be over.

That was hazardous, you will say perhaps to-day, reader. And you have this immense argument to advance, that it failed. Ah! these arguments *after the event!* they are so fatal, and so very easy.

Right or wrong, Lee resolved to make the attack; and on the third of July he carried out his resolution.

If the writer of the South shrinks from describing the bloody repulse of Longstreet, much more gloomy is the task of painting that last charge at Gettysburg. It is one of those scenes which Lee's old soldiers approach with repugnance. That thunder of the guns which comes back to memory seems to issue, hollow and lugubrious, from a thousand tombs.

Let us pass over that tragedy rapidly. It must be touched on in these memoirs—but I leave it soon.

It is the third of July, 1863. Lee's line of battle, stretching along the crest of Seminary Ridge, awaits the signal for a new conflict with a carelessness as great as on the preceding day. The infantry are laughing, jesting, cooking their rations, and smoking their pipes. The ragged cannoneers, with flashing eyes, smiling lips, and faces blackened with powder, are standing in groups, or lying down around the pieces of artillery. Near the centre of the line a gray-headed officer, in plain uniform, and entirely unattended, has dismounted, and is reconnoitering the Federal position through a pair of field-glasses.

It is Lee, and he is looking toward Cemetery Heights, the Mount St. Jean of the new Waterloo—on whose slopes the immense conflict is going to be decided.

Lee gazes for some moments through his glasses at the long range bristling with bayonets. Not a muscle moves; he resembles a statue. Then he lowers the glasses, closes them thoughtfully, and his calm glance passes along the lines of his army. You would say that this glance penetrates the forest; that he sees his old soldiers, gay, unshrinking, unmoved by the reverses of Longstreet, and believing in themselves and in him! The blood of the soldier responds to that thought. The face of the great commander suddenly flushes. He summons a staff officer and utters a few words in calm and measured tones. The order is given. The grand assault is about to begin.

That assault is going to be one of the most desperate in all history. Longstreet's has been fierce—this will be mad and full of headlong fury. At Round Top blood flowed—here the earth is going to be soaked with it. Gettysburg is to witness a charge recalling that of the six hundred horsemen at Balaklava. Each soldier will feel that the fate of the South depends on him, perhaps. If the wedge splits the tough grain, cracking it from end to end, the axe will enter after it—the work will be finished—the red flag of the South will float in triumph over a last and decisive field.

Pickett's division of Virginia troops has

been selected for the hazardous venture, and they prepare for the ordeal in the midst of a profound silence. Since the morning scarce a gunshot has been heard. Now and then only, a single cannon, like a signal-gun, sends its growl through the hills.

Those two tigers, the army of Northern Virginia and the army of the Potomac, are crouching, and about to spring.

At one o'clock the moment seems to have arrived. Along the whole front of Hill and Longstreet, the Southern artillery all at once bursts forth. One hundred and forty-five cannon send their threatening thunder across the peaceful valley. From Cemetery Heights eighty pieces reply to them; and for more than an hour these two hundred and twenty-five cannon tear the air with their harsh roar, hurled back in crash after crash from the rocky ramparts. That thunder is the most terrible yet heard in the war. It stirs the coolest veterans. General Hancock, the composed and unexcitable soldier, is going to say of it, "Their artillery fire was most terrific; . . . it was the most terrific cannonade I ever witnessed, and the most prolonged. . . . It was a most terrific and appalling cannonade, one possibly hardly ever equalled."

For nearly two hours Lee continues this "terrific" fire. The Federal guns reply—shot and shell crossing each other; racing across the blue sky; battering the rocks; or bursting in showers of iron fragments.

Suddenly the Federal fire slackens, and then ceases. Their ammunition has run low,* or they are silenced by the Southern fire. Lee's guns also cease firing. The hour has come.

The Virginians, under Pickett, form in double line in the edge of the woods, where Lee's centre is posted. These men are ragged

* This was the real reason.

and travelworn, but their bayonets and gun-barrels shine like silver. From the steel hedge, as the men move, dart lightnings.

From the Cemetery Heights the enemy watch that ominous apparition—the gray line of Virginians drawn up for the charge.

At the word, they move out, shoulder to shoulder, at common time. Descending the slope, they enter on the valley, and move steadily toward the heights.

The advance of the column, with its battle-flags floating proudly, and its ranks closed up and dressed with the precision of troops on parade, is a magnificent spectacle. Old soldiers, hardened in the fires of battle, and not given to emotion, lean forward watching the advance of the Virginians with fiery eyes. You would say, from the fierce clutch of the gaunt hands on the muskets, that they wish to follow; and many wish that.

The column is midway the valley, and beginning to move more rapidly, when suddenly the Federal artillery opens.

The ranks are swept by round shot, shell, and canister. Bloody gaps appear, but the line closes up, and continues to advance. The fire of the Federal artillery redoubles. All the demons of the pit seem howling, roaring, yelling, and screaming. The assaulting column is torn by a whirlwind of canister, before which men fall in heaps mangled, streaming with blood, their bosoms torn to pieces, their hands clutching the grass, their teeth biting the earth. The ranks, however, close up as before, and the Virginians continue to advance.

From common time, they have passed to quick time—now they march at the double-quick. That is to say, they run. They have reached the slope; the enemy's breastworks are right before them; and they dash at them with wild cheers.

They are still three hundred yards from the Federal works, when the real conflict commences, to which the cannonade was but child's play. Artillery has thundered, but something more deadly succeeds it—the sudden crash of musketry. From behind a stone wall the Federal infantry rise up and pour a galling fire into the charging column. It has been accompanied to this moment by a body of other troops, but those troops now disappear, like dry leaves swept off by the wind. The Virginians still advance.

Amid a concentrated fire of infantry and artillery, in their front and on both flanks, they pass over the ground between themselves and the enemy; ascend the slope; rush headlong at the breastworks; storm them; strike their bayonets into the enemy, who recoil before them, and a wild cheer rises, making the blood leap in the veins of a hundred thousand men.

The Federal works are carried, and the troops are wild with enthusiasm. With a thunder of cheers they press upon the flying enemy toward the crest.

Alas! as the smoke drifts, they see what is enough to dishearten the bravest. They have stormed the first line of works only! Beyond, is another and a stronger line still. Behind it swarm the heavy reserves of the enemy, ready for the death-struggle. But the column can not pause. It is "do or die." In their faces are thrust the muzzles of muskets spouting flame. Whole ranks go down in the fire. The survivors close up, utter a fierce cheer, and rush straight at the second tier of works.

Then is seen a spectacle which will long be remembered with a throb of the heart by many. The thinned ranks of the Virginians are advancing, unmoved, into the very jaws of death. They go forward—and are annihilated. At every step death meets them. The furious fire of the enemy, on both flanks and in their front, hurls them back, mangled and dying. The brave Garnett is killed while leading on his men. Kemper is lying on the earth maimed for life. Armistead is mortally wounded at the moment when he leaps upon the breastworks:— he waves his hat on the point of his sword, and staggers, and falls. Of fifteen field officers, fourteen have fallen. Three-fourths of the men are dead, wounded, or prisoners. The Federal infantry has closed in on the flanks and rear of the Virginians—whole corps assault the handful—the little band is enveloped, and cut off from succor—they turn and face the enemy, bayonet to bayonet, and die.

When the smoke drifts away, all is seen to be over. It is a panting, staggering, bleeding remnant only of the brave division that is coming back so slowly yonder. They are swept from the fatal hill—pursued by yells, cheers, cannon-shot, musket-balls, and canister. As they doggedly retire before the howling hurricane, the wounded are seen to stagger and fall. Over the dead and dying sweeps the canister. Amid volleys of musketry and the roar of cannon, all but a handful of Pickett's Virginians pass into eternity.

The Great Moment of a Great Life

I was gazing gloomily at the field covered with detachments limping back amid a great whirlwind of shell, when a mounted officer rode out of the smoke. In his right hand he carried his drawn sword—his left arm was thrown around a wounded boy whom he supported on the pommel of his saddle.

In the cavalier I recognized General Davenant, whom I had seen near the village of Paris, and who was now personally known to me. In the boy I recognized the urchin, Charley, with the braided jacket and jaunty cap.

I spurred toward him.

"Your son—!" I said, and I pointed to the boy.

"He is dying I think, colonel!" was the reply in a hoarse voice. They gray mustache trembled, and the eye of the father rested, moist but fiery, on the boy.

"Such a child!" I said. "Could *he* have gone into the charge?"

"I could not prevent him!" came, in a groan, almost from the old cavalier. "I forbade him, but he got a musket somewhere, and went over the breastworks with the rest. I saw him then for the first time, and heard him laugh and cheer. A moment afterward he was shot—I caught and raised him up, and I have ridden back through the fire, trying to shield him—but he is dying! Look! his wound is mortal, I think—and so young—a mere child—never was any one braver than my poor child—!"

A groan followed the words: and bending down the old cavalier kissed the pale cheek of the boy.

I made no reply; something seemed to choke me.

Suddenly a grave voice uttered some words within a few paces of us, and I turned quickly. It was General Lee—riding calmly amid the smoke, and re-forming the stragglers. Never have I seen a human being more composed.

General Davenant wheeled and saluted.

"We are cut to pieces, general!" he said, with something like a fiery tear in his eye. "We did our best, and we drove them!—but were not supported. My brigade—my brave old brigade is gone! This is my boy—I brought him out—but he is dying too!"

The hoarse tones and fiery tears of the old cavalier made my heart beat. I could see a quick flush rise to the face of General Lee. He looked at the pale face of the boy, over which the disordered curls fell, with a glance of inexpressible sympathy and sweetness. Then stretching out his hand, he pressed the hand of General Davenant, and said in his deep grave voice:—

"This has been a sad day for us, general—a sad day, but we cannot expect always to gain victories. Never mind—all this has been *my* fault. It is *I* who have lost this fight, and you must help me out of it in the best way you can."*

As he uttered these measured words, General Lee saluted and disappeared in the smoke.

General Davenant followed, bearing the wounded boy still upon his saddle.

Ten minutes afterward, I was riding to find General Stuart, who had sent me with a message just before the charge.

I had gloomy news for him. The battle of Gettysburg was lost.

*   *   *

The Game A-Foot

It was a magnificent morning of October.

Stuart leaped to saddle, and, preceded by his red flag rippling gayly in the wind, set out from his head-quarters in the direction of the mountains.

He was entering on his last great cavalry campaign—and it was to be one of his most successful and splendid.

The great soldier, as he advanced that morning, was the beau ideal of a cavalier. His black plume floated proudly; his sabre rattled; his eyes danced with joy; his huge mustache curled with laughter; his voice was gay, sono-

* His words.

rous, full of enjoyment of life, health, the grand autumn, and the adventurous and splendid scenes which his imagination painted. On his brow he seemed already to feel the breath of victory.

It was rather an immense war-machine, than a man which I looked at on that morning of October, 1863. Grand physical health, a perfectly fearless soul, the keenest thirst for action, a stubborn dash which nothing could break down—all this could be seen in the face and form of Stuart, as he advanced to take command of his column that day.

On the next morning at daylight he had struck the enemy.

Their outposts of cavalry, supported by infantry, were at Thoroughfare Mountain, a small range above the little village of James City. Here Stuart came suddenly upon them, and drove in their pickets:—a moment afterward he was galloping forward with the gayety of a huntsman after a fox.

A courier came to meet him from the advance guard, riding at full gallop.

"Well!" said Stuart.

"A regiment of infantry, general."

"Where?"

"Yonder in the gap."

And he pointed to a gorge in the little mountain before us.

Stuart wheeled and beckoned to Gordon, the brave North Carolinian, who had made the stubborn charge at Barbee's, in 1862, when Pelham was attacked, front and rear, by the Federal cavalry.

"We have flushed a regiment of infantry, Gordon. Can you break them?"

"I think I can, general."

The handsome face of the soldier glowed— his bright eyes flashed.

"All right. Get ready, then, to attack in front. I will take Young, and strike them at the same moment on the right flank!"

With which words Stuart went at a gallop and joined Young.

That gay and gallant Georgian was at the head of his column; in his sparkling eyes, and the smile which showed the white teeth under the black mustache, I saw the same expression of reckless courage which I had noticed on the day of Fleetwood, when the young Georgian broke the column on the hill.

Stuart explained his design in three words:—

"Are you ready?"

"All ready, general!"

And Young's sabre flashed from the scabbard.

At the same instant the crash of carbines in front, indicated Gordon's charge.

Young darted to the head of his column.

"Charge!" he shouted.

And leading the column, he descended like a thunderbolt on the enemy's flank.

As he did so, Gordon's men rushed with wild cheers into the gorge. Shouts, carbine-shots, musket-shots, yells resounded. In five minutes the Federal infantry, some three hundred in number, were scattered in headlong flight, leaving the ground strewed with new muskets, whose barrels shone like burnished silver.

"Good!" Stuart exclaimed, as long lines of prisoners appeared, going to the rear, "a fair beginning, at least!"

And he rode on rapidly.

The Chase

The cavalry pressed forward without halting and reached the hills above James City— a magniloquent name, but the "city" was a small affair—a mere village nestling down amid an amphitheatre of hills.

On the opposite range we saw the enemy's cavalry drawn up; and, as we afterward learned, commanded by General Kilpatrick.

They presented a handsome spectacle in the gay autumn sunshine; but we did not attack them. Stuart's orders were to protect the march of Ewell from observation; and this he accomplished by simply holding the Federal cavalry at arm's-length. So a demonstration only was made. Skirmishes advanced, and engaged the enemy. The whole day thus passed in apparent failure to drive the Federals.

A single incident marked the day. Stuart had taken his position, with his staff and couriers, on a hill. Here, with his battle-flag floating, he watched the skirmishers,—and then gradually, the whole party, stretched on the grass, began to doze.

They were to have a rude waking. I was lying, holding my bridle, half asleep, when an earthquake seemed to open beneath me. A crash like thunder accompanied it. I rose quickly, covered with dust. A glance explained the whole. The enemy had directed a gun upon the tempting group over which the flag rose, and the percussion-shell had fallen and burst in our midst.

Strangest of all, no one was hurt.

Stuart laughed, and mounted his horse.

"A good shot!" he said, "look at Surry's hat!" which, on examination, I found covered half an inch deep with earth.

In fact, the shell had burst within three feet of my head—was a "line shot," and with a little more elevation, would have just reached me. Then, exit Surry! in a most unmilitary manner, by the bursting of a percussion-shell.

At nightfall the enemy was still in position, and Stuart had not advanced.

We spent the night at a farm-house, and were in the saddle again at dawn.

The hills opposite were deserted. The enemy had retreated. Stuart pushed on their track down the Sperryville road, passed the village of Griffinsburg, and near Stonehouse Mountain came on, and pushed them rapidly back on Culpeper Court-House.

All at once quick firing was heard on our right.

"What is that?" Stuart asked.

"An infantry regiment, general!" said Weller, one of our couriers, galloping quickly up.

The words acted upon Stuart like the blow of a sword. A wild excitement seemed to seize him.

"Bring up a squadron!" he shouted—for we were riding ahead without support; "bring up the cavalry! I am going to charge! Bring me a squadron!"

And drawing his sword, Stuart rushed at full gallop, alone and unattended, toward the Federal infantry, whose gun-barrels were seen glittering in the woods.

Never had I seen him more excited. He was plainly on fire with the idea of capturing the whole party.

The staff scattered to summon the cavalry, and soon a company came on at full gallop. It was the "Jefferson Company," under that brave officer, Captain George Baylor.

"Charge, and cut them down!" shouted Stuart, his drawn sword flashing as he forced his horse over fallen trees and the debris of the great deserted camp.

A fine spectacle followed. As the Federal infantry double-quicked up a slope, Baylor charged.

As his men darted upon them, they suddenly halted, came to a front-face, and the long line of gun-barrels fell, as though they were parts of some glittering war-machine.

The muzzles spouted flame, and the cavalry received the fire at thirty yards.

It seemed to check them, but it did not. They had come to an impassable ditch. In another moment, the infantry broke, every man for himself, and making a detour, the cavalry pursued, and captured large numbers.

For the second time Stuart had charged infantry and broken them. Pushing on now through the great deserted camps of Stonehouse Mountain, he descended upon Culpeper.

The enemy's cavalry retreated, made a stand on the hills beyond, with their artillery; and seemed to have resolved to retreat no further.

Suddenly the thunder of artillery came up from the Rapidan. I was sitting my horse near Stuart and Gordon. They were both laughing —indeed, Stuart seemed laughing throughout the campaign.

"That is Fitz Lee!" he said; "he has crossed and driven them."

And turning round,—

"I wish you would go to General Lee, Surry —you will find him toward Griffinsburg—and tell him we are driving the enemy, and Fitz Lee seems to be coming up."

I saluted, and left the two generals laughing as before.

In half an hour I had found General Lee. He was in camp on the Sperryville road, and was talking to Ewell.

It was a singular contrast. Lee, robust, ruddy, erect, with his large frank eye—Ewell, slight, emaciated, pale, with small piercing eyes, and limping on his crutch.

"Thank you, colonel," General Lee said, with his grave but charming courtesy; "tell General Stuart to continue to press them back toward the river."

And turning to Ewell:—

"You had better move on with your command, general," he said, in his measured voice.

Ewell bowed and turned to obey—I returned to Stuart.

He was pushing the Federal cavalry "from pillar to post." Driven back from the hill, where they had planted their artillery, they had retreated on Brandy; Stuart had followed like a fate; Gordon, sent round to the left, struck their right flank with his old sabreurs; Fitz Lee, coming up on the right, thundered down on their left—and in the woods around Brandy took place one of those cavalry combats which, as my friends, the novelists say, "must be seen to be appreciated!" If the reader will imagine, in the dusk of evening, a grand hurly-burly made up of smoke, dust, blood, yells, clashing swords, banging carbines, thundering cannon, and wild cheers, he will have a faint idea of that "little affair" at Brandy.

A queer circumstance made this fight irresistibly comic.

Fitz Lee had repulsed Buford on the Rapidan; followed him on his retreat, harassing him at every step—when, just as Buford reached Brandy, with Fitz Lee at his heels, Kilpatrick descended on Fitz Lee's rear by the Sperryville road, and Stuart thundered down on *his!*

Thus Fitz Lee was pursuing Buford; Kilpatrick, Fitz Lee; and Stuart, Kilpatrick! It was a grand and comic jumble—except that it came very near being any thing but comic to that joyous cavalier, "General Fitz," as we called him—caught as he was between Generals Buford and Kilpatrick!

General Fitz was the man for a "tight place," however—and "his people," as he called his cavalry, soon cut through to Stuart.

It was a tough and heavy fight.

"Old Jeb cut off more than he could *chaw*, that time!" said a veteran afterward, in describing the fight. And at one time it seemed that the enemy were going to hold their ground.

Fleetwood, beyond, was lined with bayonets, and every knoll was crowned with cannon: when night fell, however, the whole force had retreated and crossed the Rappahannock, leaving the ground strewed with their dead and wounded.

In the dusky woods near Brandy, Stuart sat his horse, looking toward the Rappahannock, and laughing still. He was talking with brave Fitz Lee, whose stout figure, flowing beard, and eyes twinkling with humor, were plain in the starlight. I shall show you that gallant figure more than once in this volume, reader. You had but to look at him to see that he was the bravest of soldiers, and the best of comrades.

So night fell on a victory. Stuart had driven the enemy at every step. He had charged their infantry, cavalry, and artillery, routing all,—and he was once more in sight of Fleetwood Hill, where he had defeated them in the preceding June.

Singular current of war! It used to bear us onward; but be taken with a sudden fancy to flow back to the old spots! See Manassas, Fredericksburg, Cold Harbor, Chancellorsville!

Fleetwood takes its place with them—twice bloody and memorable. In sight of it took place two of Stuart's hardest combats—and both were victories.

The Ruse

By sunrise Stuart was pushing rapidly up the bank of the Rappahannock toward Warrenton Springs.

Meade had retreated from Culpeper, and was falling back rapidly. Lee was pressing on to cut him off in the vicinity of Auburn.

A hot fight took place at Jeffersonton, a little village beyond Hazel River; and here the enemy fought from house to house, but finally retreated.

Stuart followed, and came up with their rear retreating over the bridge at Warrenton Springs.

On the northern bank the Federal sharpshooters were posted in double line.

Stuart turned, and saw, not far from him, the Jefferson Company who had charged so gallantly at Stonehouse Mountain. A movement of his hand, and they were charging over the bridge.

Suddenly they recoiled. The head files had stopped,—the horses rearing. The flooring in the centre of the bridge had been torn up—it was impossible to cross.

The men wheeled and came back under a hot fire of sharp-shooters. Stuart's face was fiery.

"To the ford!" he shouted.

And placing himself in front of the men, sword in hand, he led them through the ford, in face of a heavy fire, charged up the opposite slope, and the Federal skirmishers scattered in wild flight.

The Twelfth Virginia Cavalry followed them, and they were cut down or captured.

As the column moved on, Stuart galloped along the line toward the front.

He had just faced death with these men, and at sight of him they raised a cheer.

"Hurrah for old Jeb!" rose in a shout from the column.

Stuart turned: his face glowed: rising in his stirrups, he took off his hat and exclaimed:—

"Bully for the old Twelfth!"

The words were unclassic, it may be, reader, but they raised a storm.

"I felt like I could die for old Jeb after that," one of the men said to me.

Stuart disappeared, followed by tumultuous cheers, and his column continued to advance upon Warrenton ahead of the army.

He had ridden on for a quarter of an hour, when he turned to me, and said:—

"I am getting uneasy about things at Culpeper. I wish you would ride back to Rosser, who is there with two hundred men, and tell him to call on Young, if he is pushed."

I turned my horse.

"You know where Young is?"

"On the Sperryville road."

"Exactly—Rosser can count on him. I am going on toward Warrenton."

And the general and myself parted, riding in opposite directions.

I returned toward Hazel River; passed that stream, and the long rows of army wagons; and as the sun was sinking, drew near Culpeper.

As I pressed on, I heard the long thunder of cannon coming up from the direction of Brandy.

What could that sound mean? Had the enemy again advanced and assailed the small force of cavalry there?

Going on now at full speed, I heard the cannon steadily approaching Culpeper Court-House. All at once, as I drew near the village, I heard a tremendous clatter in the streets; a column of cavalry was advancing to the front —soon the crack of carbines was heard beyond the town.

A short ride brought me to the field, and all was explained. Colonel Rosser had been attacked by a whole corps of Federal infantry, and two divisions of cavalry—while his own force was about two hundred men, and a single gun.

He had offered an obstinate resistance, however, fallen back slowly, and when about to be driven into the town, Young had come to his aid.

Then followed one of the gayest comedies of the war. Young was the author of it. You laugh sometimes still, do you not, old comrade, at the trick you played our friends on that October evening?

Young threw himself into the fight with the true cavalry *élan*. Dismounting his whole brigade, he opened a rapid fire on the advancing enemy; and this obstinate resistance evidently produced a marked effect upon their imaginations. They had been advancing— they now paused. They had been full of audacity, and now seemed fearful of some trap. It was evident that they suspected the presence of a heavy force of infantry—and night having descended, they halted.

This was the signal for the fifth act of the comedy. Young kindled camp-fires along two miles of front; brought up his brass band and played "The Bonnie Blue Flag," and "Dixie." It was obvious to the enemy that at least a corps of Lee's infantry was there in their front, ready to renew the action at dawn!

The finale was comic—I shared the blankets of the gallant Georgian that night—when we rose the enemy's whole force had disappeared.

Such had been the result of the ruse, and I always regarded the affair as one of the gayest incidents of the war.

When I left the brave Young, he was laughing in triumph.

If your eye meets this page, old comrade, it may give you another laugh—and laughter is something in this dull epoch, is it not?

But whether you laugh or sigh, and wher-

ever you may be, health and happiness attend
you!

In the afternoon, I was at Warrenton.

Stuart Caught in the Trap

I found the general moving toward Auburn, on a reconnaissance.

Meade had been delayed much by uncer-
tainty as to his adversary's designs—had
scarcely advanced beyond the Rappahannock
—and the object of Stuart was to discover his
position and intentions.

That was the work always assigned to the
"Eyes and Ears" of the army—Stuart's cavalry;
and the stout cavalier, now at the head of his
column, was on for the railroad, along which
the enemy must retreat.

Another comedy was to follow—which
came near being a tragedy.

Stuart steadily advanced, and about sunset
had passed Auburn, when, as he was riding at
the head of his column, a messenger rode up
hastily from Gordon, holding the rear.

"Well!" said Stuart.

"The enemy are in your rear, general!"

"Impossible!"

"General Gordon sent me to say so."

Stuart turned and galloped back. Gordon
came to meet him.

"The Yankee army are in our rear, general,"
said Gordon. "Come, and I will show you."

And riding to an eminence he pointed out
across the fields, in the gathering gloom, long
lines of infantry and artillery moving toward
Manassas.

Stuart gazed at them keenly. As he sat looking toward them, a staff officer from the front
came up rapidly.

"Well, captain!"

"The enemy are in front, general."

"Infantry?"

"Yes, with artillery."

Stuart looked at Gordon.

"A real trap," he said coolly, knitting his
brows.

"Have they seen you, Gordon?" he asked.

"I think not, general."

"Well, so far all is well. There is nothing to
do but to lay low, and take the chances of getting out."

Stuart's voice was never cooler. He looked
quietly at the huge column cutting off his retreat.

"A splendid chance to attack them!" he all
at once exclaimed.

And tearing a leaf out of his dispatch-book,
he wrote a hasty note to General Lee. I afterward knew what it contained. Stuart described
his situation, and proposed that Rodes, then
near Warrenton, should attack at dawn—
when he would open with his artillery, charge
with his horsemen, and cut his way out.

"A good man in blue uniform now, Gordon."

Gordon sent off an aid, and the man soon
appeared. From top to toe he was of irre-
proachable blue; and he listened keenly to his
instructions.

Five minutes afterward he had dismounted,
given his horse to a comrade, and was stealing
on foot through the thicket toward the Federal
column. A moment afterward he had mingled
with their column and disappeared.

Other messengers, also in Federal uniform,
were dispatched: the whole force of cavalry
was massed, and concealed in the woods: then
darkness descended; and the long night of anxiety began.

The situation was not agreeable. Stuart was
caught in a veritable trap. On both sides—in

his rear and his front—were passing heavy corps of Federal infantry; their numerous artillery; and their long-drawn columns of cavalry. Discovery was destruction; the only hope was that the enemy would not suspect our proximity. If we were once known to be lurking there, good-bye to Stuart and his men!

So the long night commenced. The hours passed on, and still we were not discovered. It seemed miraculous that some noise did not betray Stuart's hiding-place; but an Unseen Eye seemed to watch over him, and an Unseen Hand to guard him.

More than once the neigh of a horse rang out on the air of night; and two or three times the discordant bray of a mule attached to the artillery startled the silence of the woods. But these sounds were unheeded. They evidently attracted no attention from the enemy.

Leaning down in their saddles, the men, half overcome by sleep, but afraid of a rough waking, passed sleepless hours, looking for the dawn.

Stuart was never cooler. On his horse, at the head of his men, he betrayed no emotion. You would not have known, except for his subdued tones when speaking to some one, that he and his command were in a veritable "tight place." Cool and resolute, he was equal to any event. Certain capture or destruction of his whole force was imminent.

Thus the night glided away. We had not been discovered. Over the trees was seen the yellow streak of dawn.

I looked round. The men's faces were haggard from want of sleep. But they evidently felt perfect confidence in Stuart.

He hastened to justify it.

No sooner had light come than he placed his artillery in position. As it grew and broad-ened, the enemy were seen just on a hill in front of us, busily cooking their breakfasts.

Suddenly a single cannon sent its long thunder, dull and reverberating, through the woods, from the direction of Warrenton.

Stuart rose erect in his saddle, and looked in the direction of the sound, his eyes glowing.

Another followed; then another; then a long, continuous bellow of artillery, making the hills echo.

There was no longer any doubt about the fate of the messengers. Lee had received the dispatches; Rodes had opened on the Federal columns, attacking as that good soldier knew how to attack.

Stuart darted to his guns. On his countenance was a grim smile.

"Attention!" he exclaimed.

The cannoneers ran to their posts, a cheer rose, the next instant the guns spouted flame; shell after shell in rapid succession screamed through the woods—and bursting in the midst of the blue groups, threw them into the wildest disorder.

Stuart did not allow the panic to subside. His sharp-shooters opened at the same instant a determined fire; the great cavalier went at full speed to the head of his column:—then rushing like an avalanche, troopers and artillery, charged the column in front, burst through, trampling it as he went, and at a gallop the gray horsemen, with guns following, broke out; and were again free.

Stuart was out of the trap. From one of the "tightest places" that a commander was ever in he had extricated his whole command.

Once in safety, he turned like a wild boar on his enemies. In ten minutes his artillery had taken a new position—its thunders had opened—its roar told the army, that his feather still floated, his star was still in the ascendant.

Such was that queer affair of Auburn. Few more curious incidents occurred in the war.

A brave officer of the infantry had accompanied us as an amateur.

"I've got enough of the cavalry," he said, laughing; "I am going back to the infantry. It is safer!"

* * *

The Unseen Death

The morning of the 6th of May was ushered in with thunder.

The battle of the preceding day had been a sort of "feeler"—now the real struggle came.

By a curious coincidence, Grant and Lee both began the attack and at the same hour. At five o'clock in the morning the blue and gray ranks rushed together, and opened fire on each other. Or rather, they fired when they heard each others' steps and shouts. You saw little in that jungle.

I have already spoken more than once of this sombre country—a land of undergrowth, thicket, ooze; where sight failed, and attacks had to be made by the needle, the officers advancing in front of the line with drawn—compasses!

The assaults here were worse than night fighting; the combats strange beyond example. Regiments, brigades, and divisions stumbled on each other before they knew it; and each opened fire, guided alone by the crackling of steps in the bushes. There was something weird and lugubrious in such a struggle. It was not a conflict of men, matched against each other in civilized warfare. Two wild animals were prowling, and hunting each other in the jungle. When they heard each others' steps, they sprang and grappled. One fell, the other fell

upon him. Then the conqueror rose up and went in pursuit of other game—the dead was lost from all eyes.

In this mournful and desolate country of the Spottsylvania Wilderness, did the bloody campaign of 1864 begin. Here, where the very landscape seemed dolorous; here, in blind wrestle, as at midnight, did 200,000 men, in blue and gray, clutch each other—bloodiest and weirdest of encounters.

War had had nothing like it. Destruction of life had become a science, and was done by the compass.

The Genius of Blood, apparently tired of the old common-place mode of killing had invented the "Unseen Death," in the depths of the jungle.

On the morning of May 6th, Lee and Grant had grappled, and the battle became general along the entire line of the two armies. In these rapid memoirs I need only outline this bitter struggle—the histories will describe it.

Lee was aiming to get around the enemy's left, and huddle him up in the thicket—but in this he failed.

Just as Longstreet, who had arrived and taken part in the action, was advancing to turn the Federal flank on the Brock road, he was wounded by one of his own men; and the movement was arrested in mid career.

But Lee adhered to his plan. He determined to lead his column in person, and would have done so, but for the remonstrances of his men.

"To the rear!" shouted the troops, as he rode in front of them; "to the rear!"

And he was obliged to obey.

He was not needed.

The gray lines surged forward: the thicket was full of smoke and quick flashes of flame: then the woods took fire, and the scene of carnage had a new and ghastly feature added to it. Dense clouds of smoke rose, blinding and choking the combatants: the flames crackled, soared aloft, and were blown in the men's faces; and still, in the midst of this frightful array of horrors, the carnival of destruction went on without ceasing.

At nightfall, General Lee had driven the enemy from their front line of works—but nothing was gained.

What *could* be gained in that wretched country, where there was nothing but thicket, thicket!

General Grant saw his danger, and, no doubt, divined the object of his adversary,—to arrest and cripple him in this tangle-wood, where numbers did not count, and artillery could not be used.

There was but one thing to do—to get out of the jungle.

So, on the day after this weird encounter, in which he had lost nearly 20,000 men, and Lee about 8,000, Grant moved toward Spottsylvania.

The thickets of the Wilderness were again silent, and the blue and gray objects in the undergrowth did not move.

The war-dogs had gone to tear each other elsewhere.

Breathed and His Gun

In the din and smoke of that desperate grapple of the infantry, I have lost sight of the incessant cavalry combats which marked each day with blood.

And now there is no time to return to them. A great and sombre event drags the pen. With one scene I shall dismiss those heroic fights —but that scene will be superb.

Does the reader remember the brave Breathed, commanding a battalion of the Stuart horse artillery? I first spoke of him on the night preceding Chancellorsville, when he came to see Stuart, at that time he was already famous for his "do-or-die" fighting. A Marylander by birth, he had "come over to help us": had been the right-hand man of Pelham; the favorite of Stuart; the admiration of the whole army for a courage which the word "reckless" best describes;—and now, in this May, 1864, his familiar name of "Old Jim Breathed," bestowed by Stuart, who held him in high favor, had become the synonym of stubborn nerve and *élan*, unsurpassed by that of Murat. To fight his guns to the muzzles, or go in with the sabre, best suited Breathed. A veritable bulldog in combat, he shrank at nothing, and led everywhere. I saw brave men in the war— none braver than Breathed. When he failed in any thing, it was because reckless courage could not accomplish it.

He was young, of vigorous frame, with dark hair and eyes, and tanned by sun and wind. His voice was low, and deep; his manners simple and unassuming; his ready laugh and off-hand bearing indicated the born soldier; eyes mild, friendly, and full of honesty. It was only when Breathed was fighting his guns, or leading a charge, that they resembled red-hot coals, and seemed to flame.

To come to my incident. I wish, reader, to show you Breathed; to let you see the whole individual in a single exploit. It is good to record things not recorded in "history." They are, after all, the real glory of the South—of which nothing can deprive her. I please myself, too, for Breathed was my friend. I loved and admired him—and only a month or two before, he had made the whole army admire— and laugh with—him too.

See how the memory leads me off! I am

going to give ten words, first, to that incident which made us laugh.

In the last days of winter, a force of Federal cavalry came to make an attack on Charlottesville—crossing the Rapidan high up toward the mountains, and aiming to surprise the place. Unfortunately for him, General Custer, who commanded the expedition, was to find the Stuart horse artillery in winter quarters near. So sudden and unexpected was Custer's advance, that the artillery camps were entirely surprised. At one moment, the men were lying down in their tents, dozing, smoking, laughing—the horses turned out to graze, the guns covered, a profound peace reigning—at the next, they were running to arms, shouting, and in confusion, with the blue cavalry charging straight on their tents, sabre in hand.

Breathed had been lounging like the rest, laughing and talking with the men. Peril made him suddenly king, and, sabre in hand, he rushed to the guns, calling to his men to follow.

With his own hands he wheeled a gun round, drove home a charge, and trained the piece to bear upon the Federal cavalry, trampling in among the tents within fifty yards of him.

"Man the guns!" he shouted, in his voice of thunder. "Stand to your guns, boys! You promised me you would never let these guns be taken!"*

A roar of voices answered him. The bulldogs thrilled at the voice of the master. Suddenly the pieces spouted flame; shell and canister tore through the Federal ranks. Breathed was everywhere, cheering on the cannoneers. Discharge succeeded discharge; the ground shook: then the enemy gave back, wavering and losing heart.

* His words.

Breathed seized the moment. Many of the horses had been caught and hastily saddled. Breathed leaped upon one of them, and shouted:—

"Mount!"

The men threw themselves into the saddle—some armed with sabres, others with clubs, others with pieces of fence-rail, caught up from the fires.

"Charge!" thundered Breathed.

At the head of his men, he lead a headlong charge upon the Federal cavalry, which broke and fled in the wildest disorder, pursued by the ragged cannoneers, Breathed in front, with yells, cheers, and cries of defiance.

They were pursued past Barboursville to the Rapidan, without pause. That night Stuart went after them: their officers held a council of war, it is said, to decide whether they should not bury their artillery near Stannardsville, to prevent its capture. On the day after this, they had escaped.

In passing Barboursville, on their return from Charlottesville, one of the Federal troopers stopped to get a drink of water at the house of a citizen.

"What's the matter?" asked the citizen.

"Well, we are retreating."

"Who is after you?"

"Nobody but old Jim Breathed and his men, armed with fence-rails."*

Such was one of a dozen incidents in Breathed's life. Let me come to that which took place near Spottsylvania Court-House.

Grant had moved, as we have seen, by his left flank toward that place. General Fitzhugh Lee opposed him on the way, and at every step harassed the head of the Federal column with his dismounted sharp-shooters and horse artillery. Near Spottsylvania Court-House, it was the stand made by Fitz Lee's cavalry that saved the position, changing the aspect of the whole campaign.

Sent by Stuart with a message to the brave "General Fitz," I reached him near Spottsylvania Court-House, at the moment when he had just ordered his cavalry to fall back slowly before the advancing enemy, and take a new position in rear.

Two guns which had been firing on the enemy were still in battery on a hill; upon these a heavy Federal skirmish line was steadily moving: and beside the guns, Breathed and Fitzhugh Lee sat their horses, looking coolly at the advancing line.

"Give them a round of canister, Breathed!" exclaimed General Fitz Lee.

Breathed obeyed, but the skirmish line continued bravely to advance. All at once, there appeared in the woods behind them, a regular line of battle advancing, with flags fluttering.

To remain longer on the hill was to lose the guns. The bullets were whizzing around us, and there was but one course left—to fall back.

"Take the guns off, Breathed!" exclaimed the general; "there is no time to lose! Join the command in the new position, farther down the road!"

Breathed looked decidedly unwilling.

"A few more rounds, general!"

And turning to the men, he shouted:—

"Give them canister!"

At the word, the guns spouted flame, and the canister tore through the line of skirmishers, and the Federal line of battle behind; but it did not check them. They came on more rapidly, and the air was full of balls.

"Look out for the guns, Breathed! Take them off!" exclaimed the general.

Breathed turned toward one of the pieces, and ordered:—

"Limber to the rear!"

The order was quickly obeyed.

"Forward!"

The piece went off at a thundering gallop, pursued by bullets.

"Only a few more rounds, general!" pleaded Breathed; "I won't lose the guns!"

"All right!"

As he spoke, the enemy rushed upon the single gun.

Breathed replied by hurling canister in their faces. He sat his horse, unflinching. Never had I seen a more superb soldier.

The enemy were nearly at the muzzle of the piece.

"Surrender!" they were heard shouting; "surrender the gun!"

Breathed's response was a roar, which hurled back the front rank.

Then, his form towering amid the smoke, his eyes flashing, his drawn sabre whirled above his head, Breathed shouted,—

"Limber up!"

The cannoneers seized the trail; the horses wheeled at a gallop; the piece was limbered up; and the men rushed down the hill to mount their horses, left there.

Then around the gun seemed to open a volcano of flame. The Federal infantry were right on it. A storm of bullets cut the air. The drivers leaped from the horses drawing the piece, thinking its capture inevitable, and ran down the hill.

In an instant they had disappeared. The piece seemed in the hands of the enemy—indeed, they were almost touching it—a gun of the Stuart horse artillery for the first time was to be captured!

That thought seemed to turn Breathed into

a giant. As the drivers disappeared, his own horse was shot under him, staggered, sunk, and rolled upon his rider. Breathed dragged himself from beneath the bleeding animal, rose to his feet, and rushing to the lead horses of the gun, leaped upon one of them, and struck them violently with his sabre to force them on.

As he did so, the horse upon which he was mounted fell, pierced by a bullet through the body.

Breathed fell upon his feet, and, with the edge of his sabre, cut the two leaders out of the traces. He then leaped upon one of the middle horses—the gun being drawn by six—and started off.

He had not gone three paces, when the animal which he now rode fell dead in turn. Breathed rolled upon the ground, but rising to his feet, severed the dead animal and his companion from the piece, as he had done the leaders.

He then leaped upon one of the wheel-horses—these alone being now left—struck them furiously with his sabre—started at a thundering gallop down the hill—and pursued by a hail-storm of bullets, from which, as General Lee says in his report, "he miraculously escaped unharmed," carried off the gun in safety, and rejoined the cavalry, greeted by a rolling thunder of cheers.

Such was the manner in which Breathed fought his artillery, and the narrative is the barest and most simple statement of fact.

Breathed came out of the war a lieutenant-colonel only. Napoleon would have made him a marshal.

My Last Ride with Stuart

More than one stirring incident marked those days of desperate fighting, when, barri-

cading all the roads, and charging recklessly, Stuart opposed, at every step, Grant's advance toward the Po.

But I can not describe those incidents. They must be left to others. The pen which has paused to record that exploit of Breathed, is drawn onward as by the hand of Fate toward one of those scenes which stand out, lugubrious and bloody, from the pages of history.

From the moment when Grant crossed the Rapidan, Stuart had met the horsemen of Sheridan everywhere in bitter conflict; and the days and nights had been strewed all over with battles.

Now, on the ninth of May, when the two great adversaries faced each other on the Po, a more arduous service still was demanded of the great sabreur. Sheridan had been dispatched to sever General Lee's communications, and, if possible, capture Richmond. The city was known to be well nigh stripped of troops, and a determined assault might result in its fall. Sheridan accordingly cut loose a heavy column, took command of it in person, and descended like a thunderbolt toward the devoted city.

No sooner, however, had he begun to move, than Stuart followed on his track. He had no difficulty in doing so. A great dust-cloud told the story. That cloud hung above the long column of Federal cavalry, accompanied it wherever it moved, and indicated clearly to Stuart the course which his adversary was pursuing.

If he could only interpose, with however small a force, between Sheridan and Richmond, time would be given for preparation to resist the attack, and the capital might be saved. If he failed to interpose, Sheridan would accomplish his object—Richmond would fall.

It was a forlorn hope, after all, that he

could arrest the Federal commander. General Sheridan took with him a force estimated at 9,000. Stuart's was, in all, about 3,000; Gordon, who was not in the battle at Yellow Tavern, included. That action was fought by Fitz Lee's division of 2,400 men all told. But the men and officers were brave beyond words; the incentive to daring resistance was enormous; they would do all that could be done.

Such was the situation of affairs on the 9th of May, 1864.

Stuart set out at full gallop on his iron gray, from Spottsylvania Court-House, about three o'clock in the day, and reached Chilesburg, toward Hanover Junction, just as night fell.

Here we found General Fitz Lee engaged in a hot skirmish with the enemy's rear-guard; and that night Stuart planned an attack upon their camp, but abandoned the idea.

His spirits at this time were excellent, but it was easy to see that he realized the immense importance of checking the enemy.

An officer said in his presence:—

"We won't be able to stop Sheridan."

Stuart turned at those words; his cheeks flushed; his eyes flamed, and he said:—

"No, sir! I'd rather die than let him go on!"*

On the next morning, he moved in the direction of Hanover Junction; riding boot to boot with his friend General Fitz Lee. I had never seen him more joyous. Some events engrave themselves forever on the memory. That ride of May 10th, 1864, was one of them.

Have human beings a presentiment, ever, at the near approach of death? Does the shadow of the unseen hand ever reveal itself to the eye? I know not, but I know that no such presentiment came to Stuart; no shadow of the coming event darkened the path of the great cavalier.

* His words.

On the contrary, his spirits were buoyant beyond example, almost; and, riding on with General Fitz Lee, he sang in his gallant voice his favorite ditties "Come out of the Wilderness!" and "Jine the Cavalry!"

As he rode on thus, he was the beau ideal of a cavalier. His seat in the saddle was firm; his blue eyes dazzling; his heavy mustache curled with laughter at the least provocation. Something in this man seemed to spring forward to meet danger. Peril aroused and strung him. All his energies were stimulated by it. In that ride through the May forest, to attack Sheridan, and arrest him or die, Stuart's bearing and expression were superbly joyous and inspiring. His black plume floated in the spring breeze, like some knight-errant's; and he went to battle humming a song, resolved to conquer or fall.

Riding beside him, I found my eyes incessantly attracted to his proud face; and now I see the great cavalier as then, clearly with the eyes of memory. What a career had been his! what a life of battles!

As we went on through the spring woods, amid the joyous songs of birds, all the long, hard combats of this man passed before me like an immense panorama. The ceaseless scouting and fighting in the Shenandoah Valley; the charge and route of the red-legged "zouaves" at Manassas; the falling back to the Peninsula, and the fighting all through Charles City; the famous ride around McClellan; the advance and combats on the Rapidan and Rappahannock, after Cedar Mountain; the night attack on Catlett's, when he captured Pope's coat and papers; the march on Jackson's flank, and the capture of Manassas; the advance into Maryland; the fights at Frederick, Crampton's, and Boonsboro', with the hard rear-guard work, as Lee retired to Sharpsburg; his splendid handling of artillery on the left wing of the army there; the retreat, covered by his cavalry; the second ride around McClellan, and safe escape from his clutches; the bitter conflicts at Upperville and Barbee's, as Lee fell back; the hard fighting thereafter, on the banks of the Rappahannock; the "crowding 'em with artillery," on the night of Fredericksburg; the winter march to Dumfries; the desperate battle at Kelly's Ford; the falling back before Hooker; the battle of Chancellorsville, when he succeeded Jackson; the stubborn wrestle of Fleetwood; the war of giants below Upperville; the advance across Maryland into Pennsylvania, when the long march was strewed all over with battles, at Westminster, Hanover, Carlisle, Gettysburg, where he met and repulsed the best cavalry of the Federal army; the retreat from Gettysburg, with the tough affair near Boonsboro'; guarding the rear of the army as it again crossed the Potomac; then the campaign of October, ending with Kilpatrick's route at Buckland; the assault on Meade's head of column, when he came over to Mine Run; the bold attack on his rear there; and the hard, incessant fighting since Grant had come over to the Wilderness; —I remembered all these splendid scenes and illustrious services as I rode on beside Stuart, through the fields and forests of Hanover, and thought, "This is one of those great figures which live forever in history, and men's memories!"

To-day, I know that I was not mistaken, or laboring under the influence of undue affection and admiration. That figure has passed from earth, but still lives!

Stuart is long dead, and the grass covers him; but there is scarce a foot of the soil of Virginia that does not speak of him. He is gone, but his old mother is proud of him—is she not?

Answer, mountains where he fought—lowlands, where he fell—river, murmuring a dirge, as you foam through the rocks yonder, past his grave!

"Soon with Angels I'll be Marching"

Let me rapidly pass over the events of the tenth of May.

Gordon's little brigade had been ordered to follow on the rear of the enemy, while Fitz Lee moved round by Taylorsville to get in front of them.

Stuart rode and met Gordon, gave the brave North Carolinian, so soon to fall, his last orders; and then hastened back to Fitz Lee, who had continued to press the enemy.

They had struck the Central railroad, but the gray cavaliers were close on them. Colonel Robert Randolph, that brave soul, doomed like Gordon, charged them furiously here, took nearly a hundred prisoners, and drove them across the road.

At this moment Stuart returned, and pushed forward toward Taylorsville, from which point he intended to hasten on and get in their front.

About four in the afternoon we reached Fork church, and the command halted to rest.

Stuart stretched himself at full length, surrounded by his staff, in a field of clover; and placing his hat over his face to protect his eyes from the light, snatched a short sleep, of which he was very greatly in need.

The column again moved, and that night camped near Taylorsville, awaiting the work of the morrow.

At daylight on the 11th, Stuart moved toward Ashland. Here he came up with the enemy; attacked them furiously, and drove them before him, and out of the village, killing, wounding, and capturing a considerable number.

Then he put his column again in motion, advanced rapidly by the Telegraph road toward Yellow Tavern, a point near Richmond, where he intended to intercept the enemy—the moment of decisive struggle, to which all the fighting along the roads of Hanover had only been the prelude, was at hand.

Stuart was riding at the head of his column, looking straight forward, and with no thought, apparently, save that of arriving in time.

He was no longer gay. Was it the coming event; was it the loss of sleep; the great interest at stake; the terrible struggle before him? I know not; but he looked anxious, feverish, almost melancholy.

"My men and horses are tired, jaded, and hungry, but all right," he had written to General Bragg, from Ashland.

And these words will serve in large measure to describe the condition of the great commander himself.

I was riding beside him, when he turned to me and said, in a low tone:—

"Do you remember a conversation which we had at Orange, Surry, that night in my tent?"

"Yes, general."

"And what I said?"

"Every word is engraved, I think, upon my memory."

"Good. Do not let one thing ever escape you. Remember, that I said what I say again to-day, that 'Virginia expects every man to do his duty!'"

"I will never forget that, general."

He smiled, and rode on. For half a mile he was silent. Then I heard escape from his lips, in a low, musing voice, a refrain which I had never heard him sing before—

"Soon with angels I'll be marching!"*

I know not why, but that low sound made me shiver.

Yellow Tavern, May 11, 1864

Yellow Tavern! At the mention of that name, a sort of tremor agitates me even to-day, when nearly four years have passed.

In my eyes, the locality is cursed. A gloomy cloud seems ever hanging over it. No birds sing in the trees. The very sunshine of the summer days is sad there.

But I pass to my brief description of the place, and the event which made it one of the black names in Southern history.

Yellow Tavern is an old dismantled hostelry, on the Brook road, about six miles from Richmond. Nothing more dreary than this desolate wayside inn can be imagined. Its doors stand open, its windows are gone, the rotting floor crumbles beneath the heel, and the winds moan through the paneless sashes, like invisible spirits hovering near and muttering some lugubrious secret. "This is the scene of some deed of darkness!" you are tempted to mutter, as you place your feet upon the threshold. When you leave the spot behind you, a weight seems lifted from your breast—you breathe freer.

Such was the Yellow Tavern when I went there in the spring of 1864. Is it different to-day? Do human beings laugh there? I know not; but I know that nothing could make it cheerful in my eyes. It was, and is, and ever will be, a thing accursed!

For the military reader, however, a few words in reference to the topographical features of the locality are necessary.

* Real.

Yellow Tavern is at the forks of the Telegraph and Mountain roads, six miles from Richmond. The Telegraph road runs north and south—over this road Stuart marched. The Mountain road comes into it from the northwest. By this road Sheridan was coming.

Open the left hand, with the palm upward; the index finger pointing north. The thumb is the Mountain road; the index-finger the Telegraph road; where the thumb joins the hand is the Yellow Tavern in open fields; and Richmond is at the wrist.

Toward the head of the thumb is a wood. Here Wickham, commanding Stuart's right, was placed, his line facing the Mountain road so as to strike the approaching enemy in flank.

From Wickham's left, or near it, Stuart's left wing, under Lomax, extended along the Telegraph road to the Tavern—the two lines thus forming an obtuse angle.

On a hill, near Lomax's right, was Breathed with his guns.

The object of this disposition of Stuart's force will be seen at a glance. Lomax, commanding the left, was across the enemy's front; Wickham, commanding the right, was on their flank; and the artillery was so posted as to sweep at once the front of both Stuart's wings.

The enemy's advance would bring them to the first joint of the thumb. There they would receive Lomax's fire in front; Wickham's in flank; and Breathed's transversely. The cross fire on that point, over which the enemy must pass, would be deadly. Take a pencil, reader, and draw the diagram, and lines of fire. That will show Stuart's excellent design.

Stuart had reached Yellow Tavern, and made his dispositions before the arrival of Sheridan, who was, nevertheless, rapidly advancing by the Mountain road. Major McClel-

lan, adjutant-general, had been sent to General Bragg, with a suggestion that the latter should attack from the direction of the city, at the moment when the cavalry assailed the Federal flank. All was ready.

It was the morning of May 11th, 1864.

Never was scene more beautiful and inspiring. The men were jaded, like their horses; but no heart shrank from the coming encounter. Stretching in a thin line from the tavern into the woods on the right of the Mountain road, the men sat their horses, with drawn sabres gleaming in the sun; and the red battle-flags waved proudly in the fresh May breeze, as though saluting Stuart, who rode in front of them.

Such was the scene at Yellow Tavern. The moment had come. At about eight, a stifled hum, mixed with the tramp of hoofs, was heard. Then a courier came at a gallop, from the right, to Stuart. The enemy were in sight, and advancing rapidly.

Stuart was sitting his horse near Yellow Tavern when that intelligence reached him. He rose in his saddle, took his field-glasses from their leathern case, and looked through them in the direction of the woods across the Mountain road.

Suddenly, quick firing came on the wind—then, loud shouts. Stuart lowered his glasses, shut them up, replaced them in their case, and drew his sabre.

Never had I seen him present an appearance more superb. His head was carried proudly erect, his black plume floated, his blue eyes flashed—he was the beau ideal of a soldier, and as one of his bravest officers* afterward said to me, looked as if he had resolved on "victory or death." I had seen him often

* Breathed.

aroused and strung for action. On this morning he seemed on fire, and resembled a veritable king of battle.

Suddenly, the skirmish line of the enemy appeared in front of the woods, and a quick fire was opened on Stuart's sharp-shooters under Colonel Pate, in the angle of the two roads; Stuart hastened to take the real initiative. He posted two guns on a rising ground in the angle, and opened a heavy fire; and galled by this fire, the enemy suddenly made a determined charge upon the guns.

Stuart rose in his stirrups and gazed coolly at the heavy line advancing upon him, and forcing Pate's handful back.

"Take back the guns!" he said.

They were limbered up, and went off rapidly.

At the same moment Colonel Pate appeared, his men obstinately contesting every foot of ground as they fell back toward the Telegraph road, where a deep cut promised them advantage.

Colonel Pate was a tall, fair-haired officer, with a ready smile, and a cordial bearing. He and Stuart had bitterly quarrelled, and the general had court-martialed the colonel. It is scarcely too much to say that they had been deadly enemies.

For the first time now, since their collision, they met. But on this day their enmity seemed dead. The two men about to die grasped each other's hands.

"They are pressing you back, colonel!" exclaimed Stuart.

"Yes, general, I have but three skeleton squadrons! and you see their force."

"You are right. You have done all that any man could. Can you hold this cut?"

"I will try, general."

Their glances crossed. Never was Stuart's face kinder.

"If you say you will, you will do it! Hold this position to the last, colonel."

"I'll hold it until I die, general."*

With a pressure of the hand they parted.

Fifteen minutes afterward, Pate was dead. Attacked at once in front and on both flanks in the road, his little force had been cut to pieces. He fell with three of his captains, and his handful were scattered.

Stuart witnessed all, and his eyes grew fiery.

"Pate has died the death of a hero!"* he exclaimed.

"Order Wickham to dismount his brigade, and attack on the right!" he added to Lieutenant Garnett, aid-de-camp.

Twenty minutes afterward, Wickham's men were seen advancing, and driving the enemy before them. This relieved the left, and Wickham continued to push on until he struck up against a heavy line behind rail breastworks in the woods.

He then fell back, and each side remained motionless, awaiting the movement of the other.

Such was the preface to the real battle of Yellow Tavern,—the species of demonstration which preluded the furious grapple.

Stuart's melancholy had all vanished. He was in splendid spirits. He hastened back his artillery to the point from which it had been driven, and soon its defiant roar was heard rising above the woods.

At the same moment a courier galloped up.

"What news?"

"A dispatch from Gordon, general."

Stuart took it and read it with high good humor.

* His words.

"Gordon has had a handsome little affair this morning," he said; "he has whipped them."

And looking toward the northwest—

"I wish Gordon was here,"* he said.

The guns continued to roar, and the enemy had not again advanced. It was nearly four o'clock. Night approached.

But the great blow was coming.

Stuart was sitting his horse near the guns, with Breathed beside him. Suddenly the edge of the woods on the Mountain road swarmed with blue horsemen. As they appeared, the long lines of sabres darted from the scabbards; then they rushed like a hurricane toward the guns.

The attack was so sudden and overpowering, that nothing could stand before it. For a short time the men fought desperately, crossing sabres and using their pistols. But the enemy's numbers were too great. The left was driven back. With triumphant cheers, the Federal troopers pressed upon them to drive them completely from the field.

Suddenly, as the men fell back, Stuart appeared, with drawn sabre, among them, calling upon them to rally. His voice rose above the fire, and a wild cheer greeted him.

The men rallied, the enemy were met again, sabre to sabre, and the field became a scene of the most desperate conflict.

Stuart led every charge. I shall never forget the appearance which he presented at that moment; with one hand he controlled his restive horse, with the other he grasped his sabre; in his cheeks burned the hot blood of the soldier.

"Breathed!" he exclaimed.

"General!"

* His words.

"Take command of all the mounted men in the road, and hold it against whatever may come! If this road is lost, we are gone!"*

Breathed darted to the head of the men and shouted:—

"Follow me!"

His sword flashed lightning, and digging the spur into his horse, he darted ahead of the column, disappearing in the middle of a swarm of enemies.

A superb sight followed. Breathed was seen in the midst of the Federal cavalry defending himself, with pistol and sabre, against the blows which were aimed at him on every side.

He cut one officer out of the saddle; killed a lieutenant with a pistol ball; was shot slightly in the side, and a sabre stroke laid open his head. But five minutes afterward he was seen to clear a path with his sabre, and reappear, streaming with blood.**

The momentary repulse effected nothing. The enemy re-formed their line, and again charged the guns, which were pouring a heavy fire upon them. As they rushed forward, the hoofs of their horses shook the ground. A deafening cheer arose from the blue line.

Stuart was looking at them, and spurred out in front of the guns. His eyes flashed, and, taking off his brown felt hat, he waved it and cheered.

Then he wheeled to take command of a column of Lomax's men, coming to meet the charge.

They were too late. In a moment the enemy were trampling among the guns. All but one were captured, and that piece was saved only by the terror of the drivers. They lashed their horses into a gallop, and rushed toward the

** This incident, like all here related as attending this battle, is rigidly true.

Chickahominy, followed by the cannoneers who were cursing them, and shouting:—

"For God's sake, boys, let's go back! They've got Breathed! Let's go back to him!"*

That terror of the drivers, which the cannoneers cursed so bitterly, ended all. The gun, whirling on at wild speed, suddenly struck against the head of the column advancing to meet the enemy. A war-engine hurled against it could not have more effectually broken it. Before it could re-form the enemy had struck it, forced it back; and then the whole Federal force of cavalry was hurled upon Stuart.

His right, where Fitz Lee commanded in person, was giving back. His left was broken and driven. The day was evidently lost; and Stuart, with a sort of desperation, rushed into the midst of the enemy, calling upon his men to rally, and firing his pistol in the faces of the Federal cavalrymen.

Suddenly, one of them darted past him toward the rear, and as he did so, placed his pistol nearly on Stuart's body, and fired.

As the man disappeared in the smoke, Stuart's hand went quickly to his side, he reeled in the saddle, and would have fallen had not Captain Dorsay, of the First Virginia Cavalry, caught him in his arms.

The bullet had passed through his side into the stomach, and wounded him mortally. In its passage, it just grazed a small Bible in his pocket. The Bible was the gift of his mother—but the Almighty had decreed that it should not turn the fatal bullet.

Stuart's immense vitality sustained him for a moment. Pale, and tottering in the saddle, he still surveyed the field, and called on the men to rally.

"Go back," he exclaimed, "and do your

* Their words.

duty, as I have done mine! And our country will be safe!"**

A moment afterward he called out again to the men passing him:—

"Go back! go back! I'd rather die than be whipped!"**

The old lightning flashed from his eyes as he spoke. Then a mist passed over them; his head sank upon his breast; and, still supported in the saddle, he was led through the woods toward the Chickahominy.

Suddenly, Fitzhugh Lee, who had been stubbornly fighting on the right, galloped up, and accosted Stuart. His face was flushed, his eyes moist.

"You are wounded!" he exclaimed.

"Badly," Stuart replied, "but look out, Fitz! Yonder they come!"

A glance showed all. In the midst of a wild uproar of clashing sabres, quick shots, and resounding cries, the Federal cavalry were rushing forward to overwhelm the disordered lines.

Stuart's eye flashed for the last time. Turning to General Fitzhugh Lee, he exclaimed in a full, sonorous voice:—

"Go ahead, Fitz, old fellow! I know you will do what is right!"**

This was the last order he ever gave upon the field. As he spoke, his head sank, his eyes closed, and he was borne toward the rear.

There was scarcely time to save him from capture. His wound seemed to have been the signal for his lines to break. They had now given way everywhere—the enemy were pressing them with loud shouts. Fighting with stubborn desperation, they fell back toward the Chickahominy, which they crossed, hotly pressed by the victorious enemy.

Stuart had been placed in an ambulance and borne across the stream, where Dr. Randolph

** His words.

and Dr. Fontaine made a brief examination of his wound. It was plainly mortal—but he was hastily driven, by way of Mechanicsville, into Richmond.

His hard fighting had saved the city. When Sheridan attacked, he was repulsed.

But the capital was dearly purchased. Twenty-four hours afterward Stuart was dead.

The end of the great cavalier had been as serene as his life was stormy. His death was that of the Christian warrior, who bows to the will of God, and accepts whatever His loving hand decrees for him.

He asked repeatedly that his favorite hymns should be sung for him; and when President Davis visited him, and asked:—

"General, how do you feel?"

"Easy, but willing to die," he said, "if God and my country think I have fulfilled my destiny, and done my duty."*

As night came, he requested his physician to inform him if he thought he would live till morning. The physician replied that his death was rapidly approaching, when he faintly bowed his head, and murmured:—

"I am resigned, if it be God's will. I should like to see my wife, but God's will be done."*

When the proposed attack upon Sheridan, near Mechanicsville, was spoken of in his presence, he said:—

"God grant that it may be successful. I wish I could be there."*

Turning his face toward the pillow, he added, with tears in his eyes, "but I must prepare for another world."*

Feeling now that his end was near, he made his last dispositions.

"You will find in my hat," he said to a member of his staff, "a little Confederate flag, which a lady of Columbia, South Carolina, sent me, requesting that I would wear it on my horse in battle, and return it to her. Send it to her."*

He gave then the name of the lady, and added:—

"My spurs—those always worn in battle—I promised to give to Mrs. Lily Lee, at Shepherdstown. My sabre I leave to my son."*

His horses and equipments were then given to his staff—his papers directed to be sent to his wife.

A prayer was then offered by the minister at his bedside: his lips moved as he repeated the words. As the prayer ended he murmured:—

"I am going fast now—I am resigned. God's will be done!"*

As the words escaped from his lips, he expired.

* His words.

from Tiger-Lilies

POET, MUSICIAN, SCHOLAR, SIDNEY LANIER (1842–1881) INTERRUPTED HIS STUDIES AT OGLE-thorpe University in April of 1861 to enlist in the Macon Volunteers, the first company to move out from Georgia to Virginia. Lanier fought through the Seven Days at Chickahominy and at Malvern Hill. In '63 and '64 he was a mounted scout along the James River, then a signal officer on blockade runners, and finally a prisoner for four months at Point Lookout, Maryland. Lanier's only novel, *Tiger-Lilies* (1867), grew out of these wartime experiences.

Writing to Bayard Taylor, Lanier summarized the rest of his life as "merely not dying." He was poor and tubercular. Lanier achieved some success as a musician; he eventually became first flautist in the Peabody Orchestra of Baltimore. His studies of Elizabethan literature and versification received recognition in 1879 when Johns Hopkins appointed him a lecturer. Lanier's poetry shows him to be a brilliant technician. Some of his best poems—"Symphony," "Sunrise," "The Marshes of Glynn," for example—are equal to the finest American lyric verse of the century.

The greater part of *Tiger-Lilies* is in a metaphysical style that echoes the German romantics Novalis and Richter or the Herman Melville of *Pierre.* Much of the novel depicts an unreal pre-war Southern intellectual society where Byronic mountain-climbers and distraught German beauties roam dreaming and philosophizing through the lush landscape. The second section of the novel, however, intersperses among its arch pages some genuinely realistic and powerful war scenes. Lanier's savage anti-war symbolism is strangely effective. Here Lanier treats in highly colored fashion the repulse of General Ben Butler's Army of the James before Petersburg as well as the discomforts of a Yankee prison.

THE EARLY SPRING OF 1861 BROUGHT TO bloom, besides innumerable violets and jessa-mines, a strange, enormous, and terrible flower.

This was the blood-red flower of war, which grows amid thunders; a flower whose freshen-ing dews are blood and hot tears, whose shadow chills a land, whose odors strangle a people, whose giant petals droop downward, and whose roots are in hell.

It is a species of the great genus, sin-flower, which is so conspicuous in the flora of all ages and all countries, and whose multifarious leafage and fruitage so far overgrow a land that the violet, or love-genus, has often small chance to show its quiet blue.

The cultivation of this plant is an expensive business, and it is a wonder, from this fact alone, that there should be so many fanciers of it. A most profuse and perpetual manuring with human bones is absolutely necessary to keep it alive, and it is well to have these powdered, which can be easily done by hoofs of cavalry-horses and artillery-wheels, not to speak of the usual method of mashing with cannon-balls. It will not grow, either, except in some wet place near a stream of human blood; and you must be active in collecting your widows' tears and orphans' tears and mothers' tears to freshen the petals with in the mornings.

It requires assiduous working; and your labor-hire will be a large item in the expense, not to speak of the amount disbursed in preserving the human bones alive until such time as they may be needed, for, I forgot to mention, they must be fresh, and young, and newly-killed.

It is, however, a hardy plant, and may be grown in any climate, from snowy Moscow to hot India.

It blooms usually in the spring, continuing to flower all summer until the winter rains set in: yet in some instances it has been known to remain in full bloom during a whole inclement winter, as was shown in a fine specimen which I saw the other day, grown in North America by two wealthy landed proprietors, who combined all their resources of money, of blood, of bones, of tears, of sulphur and what not, to make this the grandest specimen of modern horticulture, and whose success was evidenced by the pertinacious blossoms which the plant sent forth even amid the hostile rigors of snow and ice and furious storms. It is supposed by some that seed of this American specimen (now dead) yet remain in the land; but as for this author (who, with many friends, suffered from the unhealthy odors of the plant), he could find it in his heart to wish fervently that these seed, if there be verily any, might perish in the germ, utterly out of sight and life and memory and out of the remote hope of resurrection, forever and ever, no matter in whose granary they are cherished!

But, to return.

It is a spreading plant, like the banyan, and continues to insert new branch-roots into the ground, so as sometimes to overspread a whole continent. Its black-shadowed jungles afford fine cover for such wild beasts as frauds and corruptions and thefts to make their lair in; from which, often, these issue with ravening teeth and prey upon the very folk that have planted and tended and raised their flowery homes!

Now, from time to time, there have appeared certain individuals (wishing, it may be, to disseminate and make profit upon other descriptions of plants) who have protested against the use of this war-flower.

Its users, many of whom are surely excellent men, contend that they grow it to protect themselves from oppressive hailstorms, which destroy their houses and crops.

But some say the plant itself is worse than any hailstorm; that its shades are damp and its odors unhealthy, and that it spreads so rapidly as to kill out and uproot all corn and wheat and cotton crops. Which the plant-users admit; but rejoin that it is cowardly to allow hailstorms to fall with impunity, and that manhood demands a struggle against them of some sort.

But the others reply, fortitude is more manly than bravery, for noble and long endurance wins the shining love of God; whereas brilliant bravery is momentary, is easy to the enthusiastic, and only dazzles the admiration of the weak-eyed since it is as often shown on one side as the other.

But then, lastly, the good war-flower cultivators say, our preachers recommend the use of this plant, and help us mightily to raise it in resistance to the hailstorms.

And reply, lastly, the interested other-flower men, that the preachers should preach Christ; that Christ was worse hailed upon than anybody, before or since; that he always refused to protect himself, though fully able to do it, by any war-banyan; and that he did, upon all occasions, not only discourage the resort to this measure, but did inveigh against it more earnestly than any thing else, as the highest and heaviest crime against Love—the Father of Adam, Christ, and all of us.

Friends and horticulturists, cry these men, stickling for the last word, if war was ever right, then Christ was always wrong; and war-flowers and the vine of Christ grow different ways, insomuch that no man may grow with both!

But these sentiments, even if anybody could have been found patient enough to listen to them, would have been called sentimentalities, or worse, in the spring of 1861, by the inhabitants of any of those States lying between Maryland and Mexico. An afflatus of war was breathed upon us. Like a great wind, it drew on and blew upon men, women, and children.

Its sound mingled with the solemnity of the church-organs and arose with the earnest words of preachers praying for guidance in the matter. It sighed in the half-breathed words of sweethearts conditioning impatient lovers with war-services. It thundered splendidly in the impassioned appeals of orators to the people. It whistled through the streets, it stole in to the firesides, it clinked glasses in barrooms, it lifted the gray hairs of our wise men in conventions, it thrilled through the lectures in college halls, it rustled the thumbed book-leaves of the schoolrooms.

This wind blew upon all the vanes of all the churches of the country, and turned them one way—toward war. It blew, and shook out, as if by magic, a flag whose device was unknown to soldier or sailor before, but whose every flap and flutter made the blood bound in our veins.

Who could have resisted the fair anticipations which the new war-idea brought? It arrayed the sanctity of a righteous cause in the brilliant trappings of military display; pleasing, so, the devout and the flippant which in various proportions are mixed elements in all men. It challenged the patriotism of the sober citizen, while it inflamed the dream of the statesman, ambitious for his country or for himself. It offered test to all allegiances and loyalties; of church, of state; of private loves, of public devotion; of personal consanguinity; of social ties. To obscurity it held out eminence; to poverty, wealth; to greed, a gorged maw; to speculation, legalized gambling; to patriotism, a country; to statesmanship, a government; to virtue, purity; and to love, what all love most desires—a field wherein to assert itself by action.

The author devoutly wishes that some one else had said what is here to be spoken—and said it better. That is: if there was guilt in any, there was guilt in nigh all of us, between Maryland and Mexico; that Mr. Davis, if he be termed the ringleader of the rebellion, was so not by virtue of any instigating act of his, but purely by the unanimous will and appointment of the Southern people; and that the hearts of the Southern people bleed to see how their own act has resulted in the chaining of Mr. Davis, who was as innocent as they, and in the pardon of those who were as guilty as he!

All of us, if any of us, either for pardon or for punishment: this is fair, and we are willing.

*   *   *

At two o'clock on the morning of May 5th, 1864, Philip Sterling relieved John Briggs on guard. The morning was clear and still, the Bay was fast asleep, the stars were in an ecstasy, the enchanted trees seemed to fear that a stir would insult the night and prevent the day from coming.

"It's beautiful, Phil, beautiful, beautif—beaut"—and John Briggs was asleep. He had accomplished it in one time and three motions, as the tactics say. He had spread out a blanket, fallen down on it, and slept. His comrades were sleeping soundly in all wonderful attitudes, as they lay under a magnificent oak close to the edge of the bluff.

The spot was a few yards from the niche which has been described. The scouts had chosen it as a night-post, since it offered a fair view of the Bay, and presented a sward clear of undergrowth, along which the sentinel could pace and relieve the tedious vigil of the night. As Philip Sterling walked back and forth, a large and luminous star appeared rising over the low point at Newport News. He glanced at it and sighed, and fell to dreaming

of another star that had risen upon him when Ottilie came wounded to Thalberg.

Half an hour later, his attention was suddenly attracted to this star, he knew not why. He watched it closely. It had not ascended, but was now shining *between* him and the dim line of trees at Newport News. It had become triple; three stars shone like illuminated globes in front of a pawnbroker's shop.

Behind these his eye caught another golden light, then a red one, then golden and red ones, close together as dots on a page, stretching in a long curve around Newport News and appearing on the other side of it, until the land rising inland hid them from sight. It was as if a glittering crown of stars had fallen down out of the generous heavens and encircled the dark land. It was as if an interminable serpent, with golden and red scales, lay in an infinite coil upon the top of the sea, and was slowly unwinding his folds and stealthily ringing himself about the earth.

The fascination of these silent lights which moved so rapidly yet so insensibly, which shone so serenely in the tranquil water, which had sprung up so magically out of the darkness, kept Philip Sterling for some moments in a dream. Rather by some instinct of a scout, than with any definite idea, he stooped down over Flemington and shook him.

"Get up, Flem," said he. "Queen Mab's coming up the river!"

"Ah—ah—ugh—umph!" observed Flemington, yawning fearfully. "Phil," he continued, without opening his eyes, "present my complim—that is, if the enemy's not within a few inches give him the bayo—I mean, wait till you can see the white of his—Yes, Phil, wait till then—I'm a little sleepy—umph"—and he fell back and snored.

Philip shook more vigorously.

"Get up, Flem. No fun, boy. The Bay's full of gunboats!"

Flemington caught the last word and sprang to his feet. He glanced down the Bay.

"Butler, Phil, by the Rood! Butler at last!" Flemington could scarcely restrain a shout. Down in the river, there, silently approached the danger which he and his men had been sent here to announce.

Cain Smallin's long legs lay extended promiscuously along the sward. Flemington placed himself between them, as between the shafts of a wheelbarrow, and, seizing hold of the feet for knobs, dragged the living machine furiously round amongst the sleepers, and ran over and crushed four dainty, childlike dreams. The wheelbarrow creaked.

"Thunder and lightnin' and—hello!" growled the mountaineer, sitting upon the sward, breathless, and gazing with wide eyes at the thousand lights in the water below. "I thought, Bi'gemini, a b'ar had me an' was a-rollin' me down old Smoky Mount'in for pastime!"

"Whillikens!" groaned Aubrey, in a voice that came as if from afar, he writhing under Rübetsahl and John Briggs piled across him in a miscellaneous mass of humanity. "Briggs, which of these numerous legs—which I don't see, but am conscious of—is mine? Wish you'd just feel along, old fellow, and find out which is my leg; one will do—I merely want to use it to get up with!"

"Phil," said Flemington, who had been scanning the line with his glass, and counting the lights, "mount, and ride to Petersburg in a hurry. I see the signal-men up the river yonder are sending up the news, but a fog might stop 'em, or something. It'll be better to go yourself. Briggs, ride with him; it'll be lonesome. Saddle up, boys; and don't mind about

killing your horses; ride 'em till they drop and then 'press' some more. Tell the general that forty vessels were in sight when you left, and that I'll send another courier with details in the morning, soon as I can see by daylight a little. The signal-line will be broken up of course, but I'll keep him posted with couriers. Wait a minute till I make another count." He swept down the line of lights with his glass. "Forty-five of 'em, now; can't swear to it, it's so dark, but one or two monitors, I think, in front. Off, boys! Good-by, and come back as quick as you can. We'll have some lively times down here!"

In ten minutes Philip Sterling and John Briggs were spurring lustily towards Petersburg.

The foremost lights had now passed the spot where Flemington and his comrades lay, and were far on their way towards a bold bend in the river, fifteen miles above, which sweeps around the long projection of Hog Island, and incloses the water-view. Fifteen miles above and fifteen miles below—there were thirty miles of lights, and still new ones kept rapidly gliding into view from behind the dim shore-line far down the river.

"Paul, it looks as if somebody had roused all the *Ignes Fatui* in the world, and they were all going on a pilgrimage to some vast marsh in the west," said Flemington, meditatively gazing on the slow-passing lights.

"Or like a stately Polonaise, with flames for the dancers of it," added Rübetsahl.

"I was just imagining," said Aubrey, "a hundred angels, each with his star on forehead, floating in a wavy file behind General Michael yonder, in front, triple-starred; executing, perhaps, a brilliant flank movement on old Lucifer and his army in the black bend up there!"

"Waal, now," interposed the sturdy mountaineer, "I cain't find it in my heart to look on them bloody Yankee gunboats, an' call 'em angels 'ith stars upon ther heads. To me, now, hit 'pears more like they was a hundred devils, an' every man of 'em was totin' a piece o' brimstone in his hand, ready sot a-fire, for to blow up Richmond and Petersburg with!"

"You see, Cain," said Flemington, "if the Yankees, even in the act of attacking us, show us a pretty sight, why, in Heaven's name, let's take it!—even if we don't say thank'ee, gentlemen; nor fight any the less for this unintentional beneficence! Indeed, I don't like the gift any more than you: 'timeo Danaos'—if you'll excuse me, but it's *too* pat! I fear Beauregard hasn't reached Petersburg yet; likely as not Butler will gobble it up before he *can* reach there!"

"Nary time, gobble it up!" sturdily rejoined the moutaineer. "Ef Beauregard don't git thar in time, God A'mighty will! *He*'ll hold 'em in check untwell Beauregard does come up; and 'ith *them two* together, hit 'pears to me likely 'at we kin about tan out anything the Yanks kin bring up Jeems's River!"

In the early morning of May 7th, John Briggs and Philip Sterling lay sleeping peacefully in No. 78 of that charming old Virginia hotel which stands like a reservoir to receive the stream of passengers flowing into it from the great channel of the Petersburg and Weldon railroad.

Simultaneously entered into this room two visitors, one from heaven and the other from the hotel-office.

These were a sun-ray which flashed in through the window, and a black waiter who opened the door half-way and inserted his dark and dignified phiz therethrough.

The sun-ray, retaining its *penchant* for win-dows, continued its course and entered into Philip Sterling's soul by the windows of it. It shone on his eyes, passed through, and produced upon the soul inside some vague impression that darkness was gone and light was about; under which impression Philip Sterling threw open the shutters of his soul-windows. The black waiter, on the contrary, true to his instincts, retained his *penchant* for doors,—since, if eyes be the windows, surely ears are the doors, of the soul.

"Glad to see you sleep so comfuttable, sah! Compliment to de house, sah! Bin knockin' ten minutes or mo, sah! Note for you; gemplim waitin' at de door on de hoss send compliments, an' tell de boys he in a hell of a hurry, sah!"

Philip placed his mouth at the ear of John Briggs and blew strenuously. In his sleep the blowee was straightway nightmared with the dream that all the winds of heaven had drawn to a focus in his ear, where they did yell and hound him on through the world.

"Get up, John. Note from the major. Wants us to ride with him immediately, before breakfast. Horses saddled, at the door," said Philip, reading from the note.

As John Briggs was pulling on his right sock, his eyes fell on the open note lying on the table.

"I see," said he, laughing, "the major retains his affectionate propensity for calling us pet names, Phil. Did you notice the sweet term of endearment wherewith he commences his yepistle? *'You damned lazy hounds,'* quoth he, *'I want you!'* &c., &c."

Oh that I had but time, while these boys are dressing, to submit a little dissertation upon *"Individual Character as displayed in pulling on socks and breeches o' mornings, together with a View of Humanity at the Moment of*

Emergence from the general Couch of Slumber," but who hath time to say aught while a Confederate soldier was dressing,—a matter of two minutes and less! Moreover the horses wait down-stairs and Major M— is fuming, being the most restless of mortals. Yet, oh that I had time!

"Mount, boys!" cried the major, as the two young men descended the steps. "Haygood's out on the railroad, and he's going to have a devilish hard time of it this morning."

As they rode down the street, John Briggs whistled long, like a boatswain i' the calm.

"Phe-ee-ee-w!" observed he. "Phil, I'm hungry! I could eat dog. I could masticate adamant. I could deglutite a fortress, or a chain-shot, or the major's conscience, there,— and I'll stop, for that's the hardest simile extant. Methinks I see the early pies, borne on the heads of the daughters of Afric. Hast in thy purse, my friend, aught wherewithal a gentleman might buy—a pie?"

"That have I," said Philip proudly,—"and thereby hangs a tale. I drew two months' wages t'other day. It was twenty-two dollars. I met three friends, and we four drank: one gill, of *such* whiskey, apiece. Four drinks at five dollars *per* drink, is twenty-dollars. The residuum and sweet overplus of my two months' wages thou beholdest there!" he said, and flaunted a two dollar bill like a triumphal flag upon the breeze.

"Here, Dinah," quoth Briggs, "give us a pie. Dinah, these be pale and feeble pies,— how much for one of 'em?"

"Two dollars, sah!"

"Now an I had had Golconda in my pocket, she had surely said Golconda was the price of a pie: which is, in the vernacular, she would 'size my pile!' What, Dinah! This large bill, this most rare and radiant sweet bill, with

the pathetic inscription thereupon! *'Six months after the ratification of a treaty of peace, I promise to pay!'* quotha! As who should say, ten days after death I will disburse! —Here, Relentless! receive the pathetic inscription! and give me a pie: and now my money is gone, my future is black as thou, Dinah—till pay-day."

In silence they rode on. "Methinks," presently said Briggs, meditatively biting into the last half of his pie,—"methinks I see within this pie"—

"What is it, John; a fly, or a cockroach?" tenderly inquired the major.

"Or a lock of hair?" suggested Phil.

"Gentlemen, it is a most monstrous thing— it is worse than flies and larger than cockroaches and it strangleth more chokingly than hair: for it is—the degeneracy and downfall of my country! Hear me! Philip Sterling, do you remember, oh, do you remember how, when we passed herethrough two years ago, you and I did straggle into Ledbetter's bakery, and sat down at a marble-topped table and took a pie and a glass of milk? Compare that time with this! Sir,"—appealing to the major as he rose into the pathetic-sublime,—"the crust of that pie (at Ledbetter's two years ago) was dark with richness! The crust of it was short, ladies and gentlemen; short as—as the major's nose, there; short as rations; short as life compared with eternity; in short, it was as short as a pie-crust. It did melt upon the tongue sweetly; languidly dissolving into a vague deliciousness, as the sweet day dissolves into mysterious twilight. Moreover, between these dainty crusts our am'rous tongues discovered liberal largesse of th' integrant fruit,— peach, and other the like confections, sugared and spiced, which with the creamy milk did mingle and marry—in rarely, patly, like 'two souls with but'—and so forth; like 'perfect music set to noble words'; like dreamy starlight shimmering into dreamy dawnlight i' the early morn. Thinking of those pies I have much contempt for Apicus, Heliogabalus & Co.

"But alas, and woe is me, Alhama!

"I contrast this pie with those pies.

"I observe with pain and smearing, that molasses, otherwise sorghum, hath entirely superseded sugar.

"I observe that this crust hath a weakly-white and wan aspect, and a familiar tang it leaveth as it departeth, admonisheth my secret soul of bacon-fat that went to the making of it, *vice* lard, deceased.

"And as for the spices, they have shared the doom of Ilium and of the buried past; *fuit;* they are not.

"And I do remember that those large pies were vended to the happy at the rate of twenty-five cents each, whereas these small pies bring two dollars: stated generally, the price proceedeth upon the inverse ratio to the size.

"Sir, and gentlemen of the jury! aside, my lords, from the moral degradation evinced by this low pass to which the once pure pie is come,—how can men be raised to fight upon such villainous coward's-pabulum as this?

"Is this, O ye delegates of the diet of worms, is *this*"—holding up the last ragged mouthful between finger and thumb—"to be the sweet reward and guerdon of the battle-grimed veteran, just come from the big wars? Forbid it, Mars!—which is to say, cook better ones, mothers!" concluded the speaker, and meekly, in absence of mind, swallowed the last piece.

"*Eheu, Pius Eneas!* I"—

"Hold your gab, boys! Listen!" interposed the major.

Stopping the horses a moment, they heard the sound of a cannon booming in the direc-tion of Richmond. Another and another followed. Presently came a loud report which seemed to loosen the battle as a loud thunder-peal releases the rain, and the long musketry-rattle broke forth.

"Haygood's having a rough time of it. Let's get there, hearties! It'll be three more of us, anyhow," said the major, sticking spurs to his horse.

They approach the outskirts of the storm of battle.

There lies a man, in bloody rags that were gray, with closed eyes. The first hailstone in the advancing edge of the storm has stricken down a flower. The dainty petal of life shrivels, blackens: yet it gives forth a perfume as it dies; his lips are moving,—he is praying.

The wounded increase. Here is a musket in the road: there is the languid hand that dropped it, pressing its fingers over a blue-edged wound in the breast. Weary pressure, and vain,—the blood flows steadily.

More muskets, cartridge-boxes, belts, greasy haversacks, strew the ground.

Here come the stretcher-bearers. They leave a dripping line of blood. "Walk easy as you kin, boys," comes from a blanket which four men are carrying by the corners. Easy walking is desirable when each step of your four carriers spurts out the blood afresh, or grates the rough edges of a shot bone in your leg.

The sound of a thousand voices, eager, hoarse, fierce, all speaking together yet differently, comes through the leaves of the under-growth. A strange multitudinous noise accompanies it,—a noise like the tremendous sibla-tion of a mile-long wave just before it breaks. It is the shuffling of two thousand feet as they march over dead leaves.

"Surely that can't be reserves; Haygood didn't have enough for his front! They must be falling back: hark! there's a Yankee cheer. Good God! Here's three muskets on the ground, boys! Come on!" said the major, and hastily dismounted.

The three plunge through the undergrowth. Waxen May-leaves sweep their faces; thorns pierce their hands; the honey-suckles cry "Wait!" with alluring perfumes; guarded oak-twigs wound the wide-opened eyes.

It is no matter.

They emerge into an open space. A thousand men are talking, gesticulating, calling to friends, taking places in rank, abandoning them for others. They are in gray rags.

"Where's Haygood?"

He is everywhere! On right flank cheering, on left flank rallying, in the centre commanding: he is ubiquitous; he moves upon the low-sweeping wing of a battle genius: it is supernatural that he should be here and yonder at once. His voice suddenly rings out,—

"Form, men! We'll run 'em out o' that in a second. Reinforcements coming!"

"What's the matter with the Yanks? Look, Phil!" says Briggs.

The Federals, having driven the small Confederate force from the railroad, stop in their charge as soon as they have crossed the track. Behind their first is a second line. As if on parade this second line advances to the railroad, and halts. "Ground arms!" Their muskets fall in a long row, as if in an armory rack. The line steps two paces forward. It stoops over the track. It is a human machine with fifty thousand clamps, moved by levers infinitely flexible. Fifty thousand fingers insert themselves beneath the stringers of the road. All together! They lift, and lay over, bottom upwards, a mile of railroad.

But, O first line of Federals, you should not have stopped! The rags have rallied. Their line is formed, in the centre floats the cross-banner, to right and left gleam the bayonets like silver flame-jets, unwavering, deadly; these, with a thousand mute tongues, utter a silent yet magnificent menace.

"Charge! Steady, men!"

The rags flutter, the cross-flag spreads out and reveals its symbol, the two thousand sturdy feet in hideous brogans, or without cover, press forward. At first it is a slow and stately movement; stately in the mass, ridiculous if we watch any individual leg, with its knee perhaps showing through an irregular hole in *such* pantaloons!

The step grows quicker. A few scattering shots from the enemy's retiring skirmishers patter like the first big drops of the shower.

From the right of the ragged line now comes up a single long cry, as from the leader of a pack of hounds who has found the game. This cry has in it the uncontrollable eagerness of the sleuth-hound, together with a dry harsh quality that conveys an uncompromising hostility. It is the irresistible outflow of some fierce soul immeasurably enraged, and it is tinged with a jubilant tone, as if in anticipation of a speedy triumph and a satisfying revenge. It is a howl, a hoarse battle-cry, a cheer, and a congratulation, all in one.

They take it up in the centre, they echo it on the left, it swells, it runs along the line as fire leaps along the rigging of a ship. It is as if some one pulled out in succession all the stops of the infernal battle-organ, but only struck one note which they all speak in different voices.

The gray line nears the blue one, rapidly. It is a thin gray wave, whose flashing foam is the glitter of steel bayonets. It meets with a swell in the ground, shivers a moment, then rolls on.

Suddenly thousands of tongues, tipped with red and issuing from smoke, speak deadly messages from the blue line. One volley? A thousand would not stop them now. Even if they were not veterans who know that it is safer at this crisis to push on than to fall back, they would still press forward. They have forgotten safety, they have forgotten life and death: their thoughts have converged into a focus which is the one simple idea,—to get to those men in blue, yonder. Rapid firing from the blue line brings rapid yelling from the gray.

But look! The blue line, which is like a distant strip of the sea, curls into little waves; these dash together in groups, then fly apart. The tempest of panic has blown upon it. The blue uniforms fly, flames issue from the gray line, it also breaks, the ragged men run, and the battle has degenerated to a chase.

John Briggs and Philip had started side by side. But the swaying line, the excitement of the chase in which the fastest man, either pursuing or pursued, was the happiest also, had drawn them asunder.

Briggs overtook a color-sergeant.

"Surrender!"

"B'lieve I will. Got me!"

"Hurr—!" It is probable that John Briggs finished this exclamation with a sigh of ineffable delight. For he was at this moment, in the Jean Paul sense, promoted. A random bullet entered his mouth; and, with that eagerness to escape which argues the soul's great contempt for the body, through this small aperture leaped out John Briggs' ascending spirit. Philip was not near to congratulate him upon this heavenly brevet, conferred purely for gallantry on the world's field. But when the day of separated friends comes, then what shakings of the hand, then what felicitations poured on fine John Briggs, that he won his bay so well and with so much less pain of life than we!

Philip was wild with the fascination of vic-

tory. It was an enchantment that urged him on. He saw nothing, knew nothing, to right or left; a spell in front drew him forward. He was far ahead of the line. Something behind a smoke called out,—

"Surrender!"

Philip raised his gun. His left arm suddenly felt paralyzed and he was half-blind with pain. The next moment a form which loomed before his hot eyes like a blue mountain, lifted a musket to what seemed an immeasurable height in the sky, which dazzled him like an infinite diamond. The musket descended with a sidewise deflection and fell upon his eye as if a meteor had crashed into it. He felt himself falling, and fainted.

Philip Sterling attempted to open his eyes. One of them unclosed, but the other refused to do him that good turn: it had swollen fearfully.

"John," said he faintly, without turning his head, "believe I'm hurt a little."

"Humph?" replied a gruff voice.

Slowly and wearily, Philip turned upon his side. A Federal soldier stood near him. Through an opening he saw strange trees and hills whirling past him in a wild gigantic dance. As his eye moved from point to point, his slow ideas gradually shaped themselves into the conclusion that he was lying upon the deck of a steamer in rapid motion.

The surprise of this idea stimulated him. He rose to a sitting posture, remained so a moment, then caught hold of a stanchion and assisted himself to stand. The delicious breeze of the May-morning blew upon his fevered head, cooled him, and strengthened him.

To Philip, a tree was always equal to a dream; a hill was but a surface that slanted his soul upwards; a dell was only a vase that brought forth its own flowers, and every stream held truth, white-bosomed, like a naiad, in its depths. To-day he had all these. The hours flew past him as rapidly as the trees on the banks. At four o'clock they rounded the curve which leads into Burwell's Bay. Philip watched the shore with intense yet furtive eagerness. He wished to discover some trace of his comrades; but he feared to attract the attention of the officers standing about the deck lest they also should discover some sign of the hostile scouts on the shore.

Presently the face of the continuous bluff grew familiar to him. At this moment an officer who had been also curiously regarding the shore, called out,—

"Lend me your glass a minute, quartermaster!"

The quartermaster aye-aye'd-sir, handed him the glass, touched his hat, and resumed his beat.

"Thought I saw a man dodging about amongst those trees over yonder," said the officer, adjusting the glass to his eye. He looked steadily towards the shore for some moments.

"Well, by old Gideon!" exclaimed he, without taking the glass from his eye; "a cosy spying-nook as ever I saw, and be damned to 'em!"

"What is it, chief?" inquired several voices.

"A real Johnny Reb over there, stuck in the face of the bluff like a sand-martin, bi-God, in a hole! Got his spy-glass and all, too, and gazing away at us as if he was reading a newspaper! Let's give him the news, what d'ye say?"

He ran to the gun on the starboard quarter.

"Bear a hand; we'll run her out ourselves. How's she charged?"

"Shell, sir; two seconds."

"Too much. Run in a grape-pill over it. 'Tisn't four hundred yards from here to the impudent rascal yonder. Now then. Let me aim her. So."

"Fire!"

Philip's heart thrilled and sickened.

The channel makes inward at this point. It is not more than a quarter of a mile from the shore. The shell and the grape-shot howled and screamed in an agony of delight, like bloodhounds long held and just unleashed when a few springs bring them on the victim.

The chief raised his glass.

"Damned if he isn't gone up," said he, "or gone down, more likely. Can't see anything of him."

"Good God!" thought Philip, "who's killed? Was it Flem, or Paul Rübetsahl, or honest Cain, or Aubrey?"

Vague ideas ran through his mind. They were something like this; life—death—friendship—strange—how does God have the heart to allow it—don't understand—insane if I think—wait—wait!

The steamer touched at Newport News wharf. Two passengers came aboard, of whom one was in blue and the other in dirty gray. This was all that Philip noticed as he glanced at them and fell back into his sorrowful reflections. If he had looked more closely, he would have discovered that the man in gray looked at him twice, the last time with a grin of triumph which soon darkened into an expression of hatred and revenge.

Philip must needs moralize.

"The skies," said he to himself, "smile, no matter who frowns. They are unmindful of men. And so are the waters. Two years ago these very waves floated our *Merrimac* proudly; there are the masts of the frigate she sunk that day. Now they float, full as proudly, the hostile keels of our enemies.

"Ah, Nature has no politics. She'll grow a

rose as well for York as Lancaster; and mayhap beat both down next minute with a storm!

"She has no heart; else she never had rained on Lear's head.

"She has no eyes; for, seeing, she never could have drowned that dainty girl, Ophelia.

"She has no ears; or she would hear the wild Sabian hymns to Night and prayers to Day that men are uttering evermore.

"O blind, deaf, no-hearted Beauty, we cannot woo thee, for thou silently contemnest us, we cannot force thee, for thou art stronger than we; we cannot compromise with thee, for thou art treacherous as thy seas: what shall we do, we, unhappy, that love thee, coquette Nature?"

This inquiry of Philip Sterling's received immediate answer,—from the lips of a dead man. For at this moment he heard someone saying in a low voice,—

"Toes up, boys!"

He looked towards the sound. A wounded prisoner had just died. Philip stepped to his cot.

Winged victory, in the likeness of a smile, dwelt upon the dead man's face. This still smile contained the ineffable repose of a marble statue, and something more, namely, the potential energy and smooth irresistible activity of a victorious soul. Spiritual force, confident, calm, untrammelled,—this is the meaning of such a smile on such a face.

Philip perceived it.

He stood at the bow of the boat looking seaward until she ran alongside the wharf at Fortress Monroe.

At a wooden building which bore sign "Provost Marshal's Office," our prisoner sat down in midst of some frightened-looking men, and one or two women, who seemed to be following similar instructions to those given to Philip by his guard:—

"Wait here till you hear your name called."

The guard stepped into a room adjoining the ante-chamber where the prisoners sat, delivered a written paper, and retired after a short colloquy with the clerk at the desk.

Philip was evidently to be shortly disposed of; his turn came first.

"Philip Sterling!" called out the clerk. *Mein Himmel,* Federal conquerors, how greasy, sleek, and complacent was the voice of this clerk in your provost's office there! It was the tone of the spider *after* the fly has walked into his little parlor.

"That your name?" inquired the greasy voice, as Philip stood up.

"Yes."

Without further ado, a spruce attendant in citizen's dress, unarmed, stepped from the next room, politely (aye, politely; he was a good man—that spruce attendant—let him here receive benedictions!) requested Philip to walk with him, and led the way along a plank sidewalk, which divided an irregular, crooked street from a line of crooked, irregular buildings. Philip's impression, as he walked, was a miscellaneous idea of grayish sand, of whitewash, and of the want of it, of granite bastions, of earthworks of a casemate,—through whose one embrasure peered a cannon like an *ennuyée* prisoner through his window,—of parapets over which also peeped black cannon-faces, as if the cannon had climbed there to see over, and were holding on by their hands and knees,—of a wilderness of smoke-stacks and masts,—of a strange gassy odor. He turned once to look back. Chesapeake smiled to him, like a maiden inviting him to stay. He disregarded the invitation, as in duty bound, and followed his guide through a sally-port. They emerged from the inner mouth of the dark passage into a brick-paved court. A tall grenadier, in blue with red trimmings, stood at the angle of the wall, bearing at his belt an immense key.

With a half-smile, Philip's conductor made a sign silently. The red-trimmed faced about, turned a key which was in the lock of a wooden door opening out from the wall, and disclosed a huge iron grating which he unfastened with the key at his belt. It creaked open wide enough to admit a man.

"Step in!" growled the key-bearer.

Philip stepped in.

Instantly the iron grating clanged, the sound reverberated through the brick-walled court, the wooden door came to with a heavy thud, and Philip found himself in darkness, amidst a Babel of oaths, songs, groans, chain-clankings, jars, unmeaning cries, and intermingling echoes.

He had closed his eyes in order to accustom them more quickly to the darkness. When he opened them he saw at first a semicircular line of sparkles gathered around him. A moment elapsed before he perceived that these were human eyes, the shadowy forms of whose owners he could barely trace at the distance of a few feet from him. The noises had suddenly ceased. The occupants of the cell had discovered the newcomer and were peering curiously into his face.

Suddenly a furious clanking and rolling of heavy metal issued from a low-arched corridor, which communicated between the main cell and some subterranean recess. The dusky crowd around Philip opened. Through the opening appeared a tall, thin man, with long hair and beard, and glimmering cat-like eyes. He was dancing a progressive jig toward Philip; his saltatory performances being ap-

parently little impeded by a chain which connected both his legs to a large cannon-ball, that darted about in all kinds of gyratory movements by reason of the vigorous and eccentric jerks of the legs about which its chain was wound. As he approached, his arms and hands lashed the air with fierce and threatening gestures.

Suddenly he made a bound which placed him immediately in front of the new prisoner. Philip was in the act of drawing back to defend himself, when he saw the strange dancer place his hand on his heart and bend in a profound bow, until his peaked face almost touched the floor.

"Sir," said the shadow, "permit me to inquire if you intend to remain in this house for some time?"

"I must confess, I think it extremely likely," replied Philip.

"Ah! Then I hope that I shall be able to offer you better accommodations than is possible to-night. You perceive,"—with a stately apologetic wave of the hand—"how crowded I am at present. My guests come faster than they go; but I hope I may do better for you to-morrow. For this time, at least, allow me to point out to you what I consider the softest bed in the establishment. Walk this way, sir!" The host stepped a pace toward the wall.

"There, sir!" he continued, with a magnificent gesture of one hand, while he pointed to the dirty bricks of the floor with the other. "I, myself, having a constitutional aversion to sleeping with the whole Democratic party, have retired to an inner apartment. But you will find these bricks good bricks, soft bricks as ever you slept on in your life, sir. I have tried them. You will repose in the honored consciousness of sleeping, sir, where *I* have slept!"

In this cell the sweet light was niggard of her cheer. Day dawned there about noon, glimmered an hour or two, and the night came on before sunset.

Philip was weary. He stretched himself upon the soft spot indicated by his singular landlord, and clasped his hands under his head for a pillow. But he could not sleep yet. The noises recommenced with their pristine fury. A man would rise and start across the floor. Suddenly he would yell like a fiend, and, as if the inspiration of a howling dervish had rushed upon him, would set up a furious jig in which feet, arms, legs, and head strove in variety and wild energy of movement. To this the invariable accompaniment was the rattle of chains connecting ankles or wrists, or dragging balls,—sometimes both. A double shuffle and a terrible oath would complete the performance, and the man would proceed upon his errand across the room. It was as if some infernal deity had his altar in the centre of the floor, at which each must perform his hideous devotions before he could pass.

Upon each side of Philip a man lay stretched along the floor. The face of one, in which the eyes rolled restlessly, was turned towards him.

"Who was the man that danced up to me just now?" said Philip to the eyes.

"Oh, hell! he's a fellow that's been in here some time."

The eyes looked down, and Philip following the direction, saw two legs elevated at an angle of forty-five degrees. The ankles were linked together by a chain.

"Them things," continued Philip's companion, while the feet dangled to and fro so as to rattle the chain-links, "is apt to make a feller sorter how-come-you-so 'bout the head, if a feller wears 'em too long. He"—jerking one

foot toward the corridor into which the host had retired, "he's dam nigh crazy."

"You are not Confederate soldiers?"

"No, not much. Yanks, all of us. Don't you see the blue blouses? But you ain't got owl-eyed yet!"

"Why in the world do they confine you so rigidly? It is worse than their prisoners fare!"

"Oh, we're extra fellers. Bounty-jumpin', stealin', fightin', murderin', desertin', and so foth! That feller with the brass buttons there, he's a paymaster; 'counts not square, or the like o' that. Jugged him. The feller inside that skeered you, he's been waitin' some time for 'em to take him out and shoot him. Sentenced!"

Philip remained quietly watching the dusky figures that stormed about the cell. Gradually the noises receded, the shadows flitted silently, the coarse web of the darkness lightened into an airy scarf that inclosed him, and day dawned for Philip in a peaceful dream.

*   *   *

To go into a prison of war is in all respects to be born over. For, of the men in all the prisons of the late war, it might be said, as of births in the ordinary world,—they came in and went out naked. Into the prison at Point Lookout, Maryland, were born, at a certain time, of poor and probably honest parents, twelve thousand grown men. Their inheritance with which they had to begin life *de novo* was the capability of body or soul wherewith each happened to be endowed at the moment of this second birth. And so, in this far little world, which was as much separated from the outer world as if it had been in the outer confines of space, it was striking to see how society immediately resolved itself into those three estates which invariably constitute it elsewhere.

For there were here, first, the aristocrats,

who lived well but did not labor; second, the artisans, who lived well by laboring; and third, the drones, who starved by not laboring. Moreover one could find here all the sub-divisions of these great classes which occur in the regions of crowded civilization. For instance, of the aristocrats, there were the true-gentlemanly sort, the insulating-obtrusive sort, the philanthropic sort, the fast sort; of the artisans, there were the sober-citizenly sort, the mind-your-own-business-and-I-mine sort, the gloomy, brooding-over-oppression sort, the cheerful workers, the geniuses, together with those whose labor was spiritual, such as the teachers of French, and arithmetic, and music, including those who lived by their wits in the bad sense; and of the drones, the kind who swear that the world owes them a living, but who are too lazy to collect the debt; the sentimental-vulgar kind, whose claims are based upon a well-turned leg or a heavy mustache, and are consequently not appreciated by a practical world; the self-deprecatory sort, who swear that Nature has been unkind in endowing them, and who then *must* starve for consistency's sake or forswear themselves; and lastly, the large class of out-and-out unmitigated drones, who, some say, serve the mere purpose of inanimate clay chinked into the cracks of this great log-cabin which we all inhabit, and who, poor men! must endure much bad weather on the wrong side of the house.

Was there then no difference between life in the prison and life in the world?

It is to be answered,—none, generically; the difference was one of degree merely.

For instance, if our every-day world had a catechism, its first question, What is the chief end of man? might be answered, "The chief end of man is either end of Pennsylvania Avenue." Whereas this question in the prison-

world catechism would be answered, "The chief end of man is the West End";—which at Point Lookout was (for the pleasure of the paradox-loving) at the eastern extremity of the Peninsula.

In the one case the aim was to be President or Congressman, with honor and luxury; in the other, the aim was to get into a cracker-box cabin, where rain and vermin were not free of the house, as they were in the tents in which ten out of the twelve thousand resided.

So, the stature of the men and the burning of their passions remained the same inside the prison as out of it, only the objects of these passions and exertions were immeasurably diminished in number and dignity. To Philip Sterling this was the terrible feature in the prison-changed behaviour of his old army friends. They did not crowd to shake joyful hands with him and hear the news from outside, but met him with smiles that had in them a sort of mournful greasiness, as if to say: Ah, old boy, mighty poor eating in here! Their handshakes were not vigorous, their souls did not run down and meet Philip's at the finger-tips. How could they? These same souls were too busy in devising ways and means to quiet the stomachs and intestines,—a set of dependents who show their born inferiority to the soul by always crying out to it when they are in distress, and by always endeavoring to dethrone it when they have waxed fat on its labor.

Some such thoughts crossed Philip's mind, as on the loveliest morning of May, a few days after his night in the cell at Fortress Monroe, he found himself inside the great gate of the prison at Point Lookout. He had recognized and spoken to some friends as they passed by, but had not yet left the rank in which his squad of seventy fellow-captives had been drawn up after being marched into the prison.

A Federal sergeant told them off into smaller squads. Philip stood in the last.

—"Four, five, six, seven, eight," finished the sergeant. "Plenty o' room in eleventh division. Corporal, Eleventh!"

"Here, sir."

"Here's your squad. March 'em down."

"Forward," said the corporal, placing himself with the front file.

Passing a row of small A tents presently, the corporal looked at his book.

"Tent fifteen; think there's four men in it. Let's see." He thrust his head into the low opening. "How many in here?"

" 'Bout a million, countin' lice and all!" responded a voice, whose tone blent in itself sorrow, anger, hunger, and the sardonic fearlessness of desperation.

"Guess *they* want another man in, if *you* don't," said the corporal, with a pleasant smile. "You, Number Four, what's your name?"

"Philip Sterling."

"Bunk here. Rest, forward,"—and the corporal passed on with his squad, writing, as he went, the name in his book.

A long, cadaverous man sat outside the door of Philip's tent, sunning himself. He was bare to the middle, but held a ragged shirt on his knees, toward which he occasionally made gestures very like those of a compositor setting type.

" 'Fords me a leetle amusement," said he, looking up with a sickly smile toward Philip. "Jest gittin' well o' the feever: cain't git about much yet!"

Sick at heart, Sterling made no reply, but entered the tent. Just inside the entrance stood a low bench, which held a rat-tail file, a beef-bone, a half-dozen gutta-percha buttons, a piece of iron barrel-hoop, two oyster shells, and a pocket-knife. Cross-legged on the ground

before it, sat a huge individual, who was engaged in polishing, with a rag and the grease of bacon, a gutta-percha ring which he held with difficulty on the tip of his little finger.

For this man's clothes, those three thieves, grease, dirt, and smoke, had drawn lots; but not content with the allotment, all three were evidently contending which should have the whole suit. It appeared likely that dirt would be the happy thief.

"Wash 'em!" said this man one day when the Federal corporal had the impudence to refer to the sacred soil on his clothes—"wash 'em? corp'ral! I'm bound to say 'at you're a dam fool! That mud's what holds 'em together; sticks 'em fast,—like! Ef you was to put them clo's in water they'd go to nothin' jest like a piece o' salt!"

As inside of these clay-clothes a stalwart frame of a man lived and worked, so, inside this stalwart clay-frame lived and worked a fearless soul, which had met death and laughed at it, from the Seven-days to Gettysburg, but which was now engaged in superintending a small manufactory of bone trinkets and gutta-percha rings, the sale of which brought wherewithal to eke out the meagre substance of the prison ration.

Sterling threw down his blanket.

"This corner occupied?"

"Wa'al—yes, a leetle, you may say. I should judge thar was about some sebben or eight thousand livin' thar now. You needn't mind *them* tho'; they won't keer ef you sleep thar," observed the huge ring-maker.

"They are very kind, indeed."

"Sorry I cain't offer you a cheer; jest now loaned out all the cheers."

Sterling squatted tailor-wise upon his blanket, placed his chin in his hand, and prepared to go into a terrible sentimental review of the utter loneliness of his position. Suddenly, how-ever, the ludicrous phase of the situation came over him. He smiled, then chuckled, and at last burst into a long, uproarious laugh.

The eye of the ring-maker twinkled. His lip quivered. He thrust his head through the open-ing of the tent and ejected from his mouth a surprising quantity of tobacco-juice. It was his manner of laughing. Beyond this he made no sign.

"Hello, Sterling, where are you?" shouted a cheery voice outside.

Philip showed a merry face through the door, and recognized an old "Ours."

"By the poker, but you are merry for a man that's just come to Point Lookout! As a general thing we may say here,

My cue is villainous melancholy.

And of all men in the world *you,* who were always a sort of melancholy Jacques! Have you, like him, heard a fool moralling on the times?" he continued, shaking Philip's hand, and directing their walk toward the head of the division.

"Aye, that have I," replied Sterling.

"We must get you out o' that hole in the 11th div. some way. Let's see; I think I saw an advertisement yesterday on the bulletin-board yonder, of a fellow in the 3d that wanted to sell out. Let's walk up and see."

The bulletin-board was surrounded by a thick crowd, to whom a lucky man on the in-side was reading, in a loud voice, a long list of names from a paper tacked to a plank.

"Letters from Dixie," said Sterling's friend.

They placed themselves on the outer edge of the circle, and gradually moved in toward the centre.

"Do you notice a man over on the other side of the crowd yonder, pushing and struggling this way, with his gaze fixed on you?" said Sterling, to his friend. "His eye has a sneaky glare in it. He hasn't lost sight of you for ten minutes. Got something against you, hasn't he?"

"He is my Nemesis. Every morning at nine o'clock, I come to the bulletin-board. Every morning at nine o'clock he meets me here, and demands of me a"—

"What?"

"A chew of tobacco! He commenced it two months ago. He has not missed a morning since. One day I attempted to dodge him. I sought cover behind every tent successively in the en-campment. My meanderings must have been between five and ten miles in length. I thought I had succeeded. Breathless, but with a proud smile of triumph on my countenance, I walked slowly down the street, when he emerged dig-nifiedly from behind the next tent, and with disdainful composure inquired if I had ary chaw of terbacker about my clo'es. Since then I have resigned myself. He is a fate!"

"The Fates, then, have learned to chew tobacco, also! *eheu!* what would Pius Aeneas have said to see them using spitoons in Hades?"

They were now at the board. It was covered with a thousand strips of paper, bearing in all manner of chirographies a thousand items of information. Mr. A. had changed his residence from No. 3, 4th division, to No. 7, 10th divi-sion; Mr. B. had a corner to let in his shop, "splendid stand for the unwanted bean-soup trade"; J. Shankins had a blanket "which he would swop it fur a par of britches, pleese caul at," &c; the negro minstrels, in big red letters, announced "an entire change of programme, at 5 o'clock, G.M. Admission 10 cents. No Confederate money received at the door"; L.

Crabbe advertised to meet the eye of his brother, M. Crabbe, who, if in the prison, would call at, &c; Jaines Haxley inquired "ef any gentleman in the 64th regiment seed his son with his own eyes killed at the Sharpsburg fite"; a facetious individual, blushing to reveal his name, and therefore writing over Anonymous, perpetrated the enormous joke of "Help wanted, to assist me in eating my rations. None need apply except with the unexceptionable reference"; to which was appended the replies of a hundred different applicants for the situation; a sardonic gentleman inquired "if Dixie and the Yanks was still a-havin' high words. Let dogs delight," &c., &c.; J. Shelpole had drawed a par of shues, but one of thum was number six an' wun was No. 10, and "wished to know ef enny gentleman had a shue, size number 10, pleese call at," &c., &c.

"Here it is at last!" said Sterling. The legend ran, "Fur privit reesons," (—"to wit," interposed Phil's companion, "a plug of tobacco, or the equivalent thereof in bread, bean-soup, cash, or other commodities,") "the undersined will swop places, fur a little boot, with eny gentleman in the 11th division. Pleese call at, &c., 3d, division. Call soon and git a bargain.

"Sined

J. THREEPITS"

"He's your man, Phil. Let's go right up and see him."

"But how do you do it? when my corporal calls the roll"—

"All you've got to do is to answer to the euphonious appelation of Threepits, while Mr. T. will respond to the call for Sterling. The corporal won't know the difference. I can't deny but Mr. Threepits, in the matter of names, will slightly get the advantage in the swap. But it's a very good thing here to have two names; inasmuch as you stand two chances, when the exchange-lists are read out, to go back to Dixie. You must take care, however, that both of you don't answer to the same name,—a circumstance which has several times occurred, and caused no little pleasure to the sharp-witted authorities, as affording a pretext to remand the disappointed prisoner back to his hole."

The Military Ball at Goulacaska

EVEN WAR HAS ITS LIGHTER MOMENTS. ONE OF THE RARE HUMOROUS ACCOUNTS OF A "battle," "The Military Ball at Goulacaska" appeared in the *Atlantic Monthly* in 1870. The story was written by Charles Ledyard Norton (1837–1909). Norton left his studies at the Yale Scientific School when the Civil War started. For the first year of the war he served as a private in the 7th New York National Guard. In 1862 Norton was a captain in the 25th Connecticut Volunteers, and in 1863 he became Colonel of the 78th U.S. Colored Troops. After his release from the army in 1866, Norton took up a career of journalism in New York. His work included a number of boys' novels such as *A Medal of Honor Man* and *A Soldier of the Legion*.

The fairly heavy air of condescension makes "The Military Ball at Goulacaska" a period piece. Still, the accumulation of realistic garrison details and sidelights on officers' social lives makes the tale a fascinating commentary on more obscure aspects of the Civil War.

MILITARY BALLS HAVE BORNE THEIR PART in song and story ever since that memorable night, recorded in Holy Writ, when Belshazzar the king drank wine before a thousand of his lords, and saw, it is to be feared with blurred vision, the prophetic handwriting on the wall. That the entertainment in question partook largely of a military character I think there can be no reasonable doubt, for it behooved the king to provide good cheer for his generals when the Medes and Persians were advancing their parallels within short canister range of the Babylonish outworks, and when, as we may fairly assume, the Persian and Chaldean archers were exchanging morning papers, and swapping jackknives, even as our own pickets used to do, a few years ago, along the advanced line in Virginia and Tennessee. The resemblance between Belshazzar's little entertainment and the ball whose history and untimely end I propose to relate ceases with their military character; for the palm-dotted plains of Mesopotamia bore as little resemblance to the bayous and prairies by which we were surrounded as did the old plantation-house, with its wide verandas, to the massive colonade of the royal palace in Babylon.

There was something of a garrison at Goulacaska in those days, for it was an important outpost on the border of a vast territory of swamp, savannah, and bayou, through which from time to time armies moved or chased one another, according to the varying fortunes of war. Our force was divided, the main body, composed exclusively of white troops, being stationed on the most important side of the wide river and bay, in a well-fortified position, while we, that is to say, two regiments of colored troops, with a few pieces of artillery, occupied a large *tête-du-pont,* so called, on the opposite side.

On the islands and along the bayous of the vicinity lived the sparse remains of local aristocracy, composed for the most part of ladies, with a few old men and boys, unfit for service in the field, and whom the rigid conscription had not yet reached. Sons, brothers, and husbands who could or would carry musket or sword were away in the army.

Black regiments were then at the height of their unpopularity, officers and all sharing in the disfavor with which the organizations were regarded. For a time we felt rather keenly the coolness with which our brother officers across the river treated us; but by the end of the summer these little prejudices wore off, and we were on excellent terms.

Life in both camps was monotonous, of course. Socially the head-quarters side of the river was preferable. A long period of inactivity on the part of the Confederate forces had led many of the officers to send for their wives as winter came on, and quite a little party of ladies could upon occasion be assembled from the various regiments and batteries which composed the command. On our side we had the excitement of occasional skirmishes with the enemy's cavalry, and if a foraging-party ventured out of sight of the picket-line it was tolerably certain of a lively time before getting back. So we called it an even thing, and considered it a great privilege to have leave of absence for an evening across the river, while they, on the other hand, envied us the excitements of our more exposed position.

The long period of military inactivity and the constant presence of good-looking young fellows in blue had caused the memory of absent cavaliers in gray to fade somewhat in the minds of our fair Southern neighbors, who, although unswerving in their allegiance to the Confederate cause, could not bring themselves utterly to refuse masculine adulation, even when it was bound in blue and gold.

We of the colored troops found, however, that as soon as our corps was announced, an immediate cooling off ensued on the part of our Southern sisters, and we considered ourselves lucky if we were not treated with undisguised scorn or given the cut direct, if an opportunity occurred.

Our Post Commandant was an old Regular Army officer, holding a brigadier commission in the volunteers. He and his wife occupied part of the old plantation-house aforementioned, and ruled with stern but beneficent tyranny respectively over our military and social world. Garrison society in the volunteer army was apt to contain elements so incongruous that an utter lack of harmony often existed, but the General's wife was a woman who had seen the world, and was so completely mistress of the situation that no one of her female subordinates ever attempted to set up a rival claim to social supremacy.

Of course it was no more than natural that secesh society should have a queen of its own, and Madame Presbourg, the wife of a Confederate general, occupied the throne by virtue of her husband's rank, and bore aloft the somewhat bedraggled escutcheon of local upper-tendom. Her two pretty daughters were Rebels to the tips of their fingers, but were so deeply imbued with the native coquetry of Southern maidens that they could not forego the temptation of society, and so by some unknown diplomacy had persuaded their mamma to permit calls from approved Federals. It is to be feared that certain officers, yielding to feminine blandishments, forwarded sundry notes and letters across the lines to Confederate territory which would have hardly reached their destination by other channels. However, no harm appears to have been done, although untold disaster might easily have followed such youthful rashness.

The late Southern fall with its charming days was turning the cypresses brown, and bringing myriads of water-fowl from the far north to swim in the sheltered lagoons which surrounded our encampment. The rank and file of our colored regiments as they sat around their camp-fires were beginning to recall half regretfully memories of bygone Christmas holidays in old plantation times, when it was rumored that a ball was to be given on Christmas eve at post head-quarters. The report was at first disbelieved; but about two weeks before that festival an orderly was observed making the rounds of our officers' quarters, bearing in his hand a package of unofficial-looking envelopes, which proved to be manuscript notifications to the effect that General and Mrs. Mars would be at home on Christmas eve at half past seven o'clock in the evening. Similar documents were sent by the General's body-servant to various secesh families in the neighborhood, part of the General's creed being to cultivate the social virtues so far as was consistent with the good of the service, and no further.

Of course this break in the monotony of our life was looked forward to with pleasure by everybody who was concerned, and it was understood on all sides that for once the hatchet should be buried, and that the memory of the absent should be pledged alike by North and South, thus laying a foundation for a merrier Christmas and a happier New Year in the days to come.

I regret to say that this charming dream of social reconstruction was not destined to attain a perfect realization. In a few days a rumor arose, no one knew whence, that the secesh ladies had accepted their invitations only on condition that no officers of colored troops were to attend the ball. Of course this proviso was not embodied in the written notes of acceptance; but it is well understood that ladies have ways of making known such decisions, without forwarding documents through the regular official channels.

Here was a dilemma, and the faces of our garrison ladies grew visibly longer as the threatened danger assumed definite proportions. The General would probably have solved the difficulty by remarking, with honest indignation, that they might stay away and be hanged; and his wife would have expressed the same idea in ladylike phrase. This, however, would practically have broken up the ball, so it became necessary to manage the affair independently of head-quarters, and the whole responsibility fell upon the garrison ladies at large, some of whom, as the result proved, were willing to stoop that they might conquer, and who, sad to relate, found "officers and gentlemen" willing to aid in their unpatriotic schemes.

On our side of the river we had a sort of public hall where we were wont to meet in the evening, and where such papers and periodicals as came to hand were deposited for the common good. This hall, not to call it a shanty, was built of boards, found, as Sherman's bummers used to say, in the woods more than a mile from any house, and was an institution which I recommend to all officers of United States troops on detached stations. Officers of other nations have mess-rooms and tents furnished by their respective governments, and therefore need not scour the neighboring forest in search of casual boards.

A few evenings before the ball, such of us as were off duty were sitting as usual in our hall engaged in the various innocent amusements characteristic of such gatherings, when the door opened and in came two officers from the other side. It was a rare thing to receive such a visit in the evening, but this was apparently only a friendly call, and we endeavored to make the occasion an agreeable one by sending to the sutler's for a bottle or two of his best soda-water, with which to drink the health of our unexpected guests. After a while the talk turned on the coming ball, and the last news was demanded concerning the progress of preparations. "Why," said Captain Linn, the most self-possessed of our guests, "haven't you heard that the idea of a ball has been given up, and we are to have simply a reception, which the garrison ladies only will attend."

This change of programme excited general surprise, and various were the speculations concerning the cause. Our guests kept discreetly silent or evaded our questions for some minutes, till at length the Captain, shifting rather uneasily in his seat, broke out as follows, in reply to a direct appeal from one of our number:—

"I didn't mean to say anything about it, but the fact is that we owe the affair to you fellows on this side of the river."

"To us!" "What do you mean?" was queried on all sides; and the Captain, gaining courage, went on:—

"Well, you know it has been rumored that the secesh girls, not to mention their mammas, would not attend the ball in case you officers of colored troops went. Everybody thought they would be glad enough to come anyhow, and were only talking so as to make a show of loyalty to the Rebel cause; but at last it came out that they had actually decided to stand by their principles and stay away altogether, unless assured that they should not meet the nig— the officers of colored troops. So there you are. I didn't mean to tell you of it, for of course it is disagreeable to feel that you are depriving the rest of us of a good time; but you made me tell, so it can't be helped."

We looked at on another in mute indignation for a few seconds, and then mutterings of wrath indicated the sense of the meeting. In the course of ten minutes or so the question was proposed,—by whom we never could find out,—whether or no we should magnanimously stay away so that the ball might come off as at first proposed. The proposition was greeted with scorn, and even our guests joined us in agreeing that this would be an unbecoming concession to rebeldom. The question was, however, discussed, and presently Captain Tybale, who had been quietly listening to the talk and taking observations, raised his voice so as to arrest the hum of general conversation. Now the Captain was one of our acknowledged leaders, first in war, first in peace, etc., and his words always commanded respect.

"Well, gentlemen," said he, "in my opinion, it is a piece of confounded secesh impudence, and I'm no more disposed than any of you to yield to it; but if Southern girls don't appreciate us, we can't help it. It is very evident to any disinterested observer that they are the losers, so I think our best way is to keep still and take our pay out of the masculine Rebs next time we meet 'em. You see we 'colored officers' number only about fifty men all told, and probably not more than thirty could be allowed leave of absence to attend the ball, while those fellows on the other side will turn out at least seventy-five or a hundred pairs of shoulder-straps. I move that we don't spoil the fun of the majority. Let us just stay away and let them have their old ball to themselves. And, Linn," turning towards our guests, "you may present my compliments to Miss Le C—, and tell her that I have already had two chances to shoot that gray-coated cousin of hers, and didn't because I had a slight acquaintance with herself. Tell her there is no knowing what may happen another time."

The Captain ceased, and at once communicated with two or three of us privately, urging us to second his motion. The result was that in half an hour our guests departed authorized to say that, as a body, we would not attend the ball. Tybale escorted them to their boat, and we broke up to attend tattoo roll-call. Soon after "taps" Tybale's servant brought word to me that the Captain wished to see me, and going over to his quarters we spent an hour talking over certain plans which shall be laid before the reader as my tale proceeds.

It is sufficient to say here that, from certain facts in Tybale's possession, it was made evident to all who were admitted to his confidence, that a few of the garrison ladies had conspired to keep us away from the ball, so that the tender feelings of their secesh acquaintance should not be harrowed by meeting officers of colored troops on a social equality.

The two officers whose visit to us I have just described were secret emissaries from this female cabal, sent over to pave the way for a voluntary consent, on our part, to stay away from the entertainment. The next day the affair was more generally talked of, the greatest secrecy being observed with regard to the discovered conspiracy. The field and staff officers, with others who had not been present on the previous evening, approved our action. The Colonel of our regiment, who, being senior officer, commanded on our side the river, agreed with us, but said that it was necessary for him to pay his respects to the General in an official way on the evening of the ball, and that he would take one of his staff with him for form's sake.

So it was all quietly settled, and everything went on with the usual clock-like regularity of military routine.

At this epoch of my story I beg leave to introduce a letter from Harry Wistar, at that time our Adjutant. A day or two after the ball he was commissioned in a Regular regiment then stationed in the far West, and, starting at once to join his command, he heard none of the stories which were soon in circulation concerning events at Goulacaska. His letter shows the view taken by the outside public, and I certify on honor that the following is a true and correct copy of the original epistle.

ADJUTANT WISTAR'S ACCOUNT

Terminus Pacific Railway,
August 29, 1868.

My Dear Tom,—Ever since the arrival of your letter I have been trying in vain to discover why, at this late day, you want a particular account of that luckless ball at Goulacaska and its untimely end. The request for such a narrative is, however, a modest one, considering the source; so here it is, exactly as I recollect it.

You know the history of the affair as well as I do up to 6.30 P.M. on Christmas eve. 1863, when the Colonel and I, arrayed in our best uniforms, embarked in the yawl, and were pulled away through the gathering darkness toward the twinkling lights of the east side. When we were some fifty yards from the landing the Colonel, who had until that time maintained a reflective silence, suddenly ordered the men to avast pulling, and, turning to me as he crowded the tiller to starboard, "Adjutant," said he, "I'm very certain that the devil is to pay somewhere to-night, and I've a good notion to step ashore and send you with my excuses to the General."

The boat swung slowly round, bobbing up and down on the sea which the ebb tide was making, and we both sat in the stern-sheets looking back at the lights and fires which marked the camp. Everything bore its ordinary appearance. I reminded the Colonel that Jones was officer of the day, and that Major Thomas was sober, which latter rather exceptional state of things, together with the fact that all was quiet outside the pickets, had the reassuring effect which I intended, and the Colonel, still shaking his head somewhat dubiously, ordered the men to give way, and brought the boat's head round once more toward the opposite shore. A steady pull of an hour brought us to the opposite side, and during the voyage we had some further conversation on the subject of the suspicions which, when we were half-way across, I admitted were shared by myself. We concluded that our forebodings had no sufficient foundation, and were only caused by our simultaneous absence from camp, which was an event of rare occurrence.

At about a quarter before eight we reached head-quarters, and found, as we anticipated, that only the loyal part of the company had as yet arrived. The Colonel and I made our bow without serious discomfort, and, leaving him in conversation with our host and hostess, I proceeded to make myself agreeable to any one whom I could get to talk with me.

I soon found it expedient to confine my attentions to my own sex, for as the hour for the expected arrival of the secesh contingent drew near the feminine intellect became so intensely preoccupied in watching for that event that it was impossible to engage any of the ladies present in rational conversation. From this sweeping assertion I wish, however, to except Mrs. General Mars, who rose superior to all such weakness, and was just her ordinary charming self.

Soon after eight o'clock the expected guests began to arrive. Far be it from me to cast ridicule upon the poverty which fell upon so many once wealthy Southern families during those days; but when I saw the old tumbledown relics of former grandeur,—once elegant carriages, drawn to the door by such animals as had been left behind after successive occupations by the hostile armies, and driven by such decrepit darkies as still remained faithful to "de ole place,"—I may be pardoned if the ludicrous side of the picture caught my eye before its sadder moral sobered my thoughts. It was curious to see these Southern ladies enter the rooms arrayed in the forgotten fashions of years past. Many dresses were rich and elegant, and some of them seemed, to my uncultivated eye, far more graceful than the modern costumes worn by our garrison ladies, which observation aroused a suspicion in my mind, since confirmed, that every succeeding fashion is not necessarily more tasteful and beauteous than its predecessor. Most of the Southern ladies, some thirty in number, came without any escort save the drivers of their respective vehicles. A few old men and young boys, however, were made to do duty, but they attracted comparatively little attention, and a pleasant hum of conversation began to diffuse itself through the parlors. Mrs. Mars had, with her usual taste and skill, draped the rooms with flag, for which purpose all the bunting possessed by the land and naval forces of the Union, then stationed at Goulacaska, had been borrowed. Among the naval signals the sharp eyes of some of our fair Southern guests soon detected a pennant of red, white, and red, with a "lone star," near one corner. This was at once seized upon as a recognition of Southern rights, and much good-humored talk ensued, amid which the General was repeatedly thanked for his courtesy in thus giving a place to the colors of the "new nation."

"Ladies," said he, as a bevy of his guests tendered him their thanks,—"ladies, you are very welcome, but your new nation is, I think, only an imagination."

So the talk went on, and society was fast being reorganized on an excellent basis of good fellowship, when interruption number one came in the shape of the party from St. Jean's. You remember Madame Presbourg, Tom, with her two lovely daughters, of course? Why, we used to joke you about one of them. Well, after everybody was there and in good spirits, at forty-five minutes past eight precisely by the Post Adjutant's clock, I beheld Madame Presbourg in the doorway leaning on the arm of a good-looking, dark-complexioned man of thirty or thereabout, and followed at easy supporting distance by the two young ladies. In this order the party passed without wincing under the cross battery-guidons over the door, and advanced resolutely upon the big garrison flag that hung across the end of the parlor, in front of which our hosts stood to receive their onset. The ladies were simply and tastefully dressed, and looked their loveliest, but all eyes were concentrated upon the male escort whose presence and bearing so enhanced the effect of this very successful *entré*. Who could he be? No able-bodied Southern man of his stamp had been seen, at least during Federal occupancy, in that vicinity since 1861. Was he a Confederate officer in disguise, or an emissary from Richmond, or only a distinguished foreigner? Speculation was rife as the party moved through the not very full rooms, and saluted the General and his wife with a dignity which said as plainly as words could have done, "We are Rebels, every one of us. We have come to your ball, but are not conciliated by any means."

I watched the General curiously. There was a slight elevating of his gray eyebrows as the stranger appeared, then a searching glance at him from head to foot, but nothing betrayed his suspicions if he had any. Those of the company who stood nearest the General heard Madame Presbourg say, as she introduced her escort, "My nephew, Presley Creighton of Virginia. He arrived quite unexpectedly to-day, and I have taken the liberty of availing myself of his escort."

"Most happy to see him, madame," was the General's reply; and a short commonplace talk followed, ending with the earnestly expressed hope from Madame Presbourg, reiterated by the young ladies, that no serious interruption should occur to mar the festivities of the evening.

At nine o'clock the orchestral troupe entered and made their way to the lower end of the rooms, whence forthwith proceeded the shriekings consequent upon the adjustment of stringed instruments. The orchestra was composed of a bass-viol, three fiddles, and two banjos, all in the hands of musical members of the colored troops, and of similarly gifted freedmen from the neighboring plantations.

The Colonel during all this time showed no disposition to leave, as I expected, and everything went on serenely, notwithstanding our presence. At half past ten the dancing was at its height (and Southern girls do dance better than Northern ones, although they are not near so pretty or clever), when suddenly I became conscious of a cessation in the hum of talk, and of a movement among the non-dancing part of the company towards windows and doors. As the music did not stop, the dancing continued, but in a few seconds more there came through the windows the crack-crack of rifles up the river. The sound was too palpable for any mistake. The first fiddle rolled the whites of his eyes toward the window and missed two notes, then turned purple and broke down, carrying with him the whole sable orchestra, just as the rattling crash of a solid volley echoed down the river, and shook the sashes in their frames, while the last figures of the cotillon melted into a crowd which now hurried toward the gallery. By this time the long roll was beating, the troops were falling in, and we could hear the first sergeants hurrying up the laggards and forming their companies. At this moment the General called out in his military tone, "Stations, gentlemen, stations," and away went the masculine portion of the assembly. At this point I repress a strong desire to quote a certain apropos verse from Childe Harold, but if, as I half suspect, you are going to print this yarn, I won't deprive you of the pleasure which I know arises from an apt quotation.

As the Colonel and I were rushing out with the rest, the General stopped us. "You cannot reach your command," said he, "in time to be of any service. This affair will be over, one way or the other, before you could get there. I want you two to stay here, and don't let a soul leave this house. I'm afraid that nephew of the Presbourgs has escaped already; but if he has not, don't let him. I'll send a guard at once." The General went off toward his horse, and the Colonel sent me immediately to guard the back gallery. The house was built, like many Southern mansions, with a broad gallery in front and rear at the height of the second story, where were the parlors, etc. A single flight of stairs led from each of these galleries to the ground. The Colonel stationed himself at the head of the front stairs, while I mounted guard, revolver in hand, at the rear ones. My stairs were fortunately provided with a swinging gate, which when closed rendered my position impregnable to any feminine assault.

The Colonel was less lucky, and was obliged single-handed to keep the stairhead against a threatened attack, which might well have caused Horatius himself to quail. As soon as the first moments of confusion had passed, the feminine crowd on the gallery resolved itself into two elements, to wit, loyal and rebel. The latter had the advantage in point of numbers, and very soon announced its intention of going home; then it was that the Colonel and myself were discovered at our posts.

Madame Presbourg at once assumed command of the Confederate forces, by virtue of seniority, and, making a stately farewell to our hostess, swept into the ladies' dressing-room, followed by her daughters and by nearly all of the secesh contingent. A wide hall opened through the house, so that I had a clear view, and could even hear most of the conversation. A few moments served to complete the plan of operations, and Madame Presbourg, at the head of her force, moved out from the dressing-room intrenchments in a two-rank formation, which deployed into line as the gallery was reached. The male escort was not visible, and had not been since the firing commenced. Meanwhile the skirmishing up stream had slackened into a dropping fire, which seemed to draw slowly nearer. Madame Presbourg, without a moment's hesitation, led the forlorn hope of her two daughters to the assault, while the rest of her command halted at supporting distance to await the result. Never shall I forget the superb air of indifference which the party assumed as they drew near the stairs and made as if they would walk past or over the Colonel. It was as if the honor of the whole Confederacy rested upon their individual shoulders. The Colonel's soldierly figure looked more dignified than ever as he quietly placed his hand upon the post at his side, so that his arm barred the way, and addressed the party in perfectly respectful tones:—

"Ladies, it is my painful duty to inform you that I am directed by the General commanding to prevent your leaving this house until further orders."

Madame Presbourg halted, and with the most cutting hauteur in her accents answered: "This, then, is your Northern hospitality, to invite defenceless women to your camp and then imprison them." Just at this moment the dropping fire on the skirmish-line swelled into an irregular volley nearer than before, and a faint yell was borne to our ears, as if the assaulting party had made a determined advance.

"Madame," said the Colonel, "that sound is a sufficient reason for your detention."

The Confederate leader doubtless saw the force of the Colonel's logic, but not one whit did her magnificence abate. Turning to her reserve troop she spoke:—

"Ladies, there are occasions when it is proper and womanly for us to lay aside our gentler nature and acquire by force what we cannot gain by more moderate means. This is one of those occasions, and I call upon you as Southern women to aid me in forcing a passage to our husbands and sons, whose voices we but now—"

"Halt! order arms!" came from the darkness outside and the but-plates of twenty rifles rang on the flagging below. In another moment a brace of sentries with fixed bayonets was posted at each exit, and a sergeant with a squad of men was searching the house for the missing male escort, who, by the way, was never seen more. Madame Presbourg, however, was equal to the emergency, and remarked, in tones loud enough for all to hear:—

"Pray be seated, ladies; we can afford to wait a few minutes until our friends are in possession of the post, and then, perhaps," she added, "the ball may be continued under different management, and Southern gentlemen may be your partners, ladies, instead of this Northern *canaille.*"

Such was Madame's last withering remark as the Colonel and I hastened off to report to the General for further orders. The firing had by this time nearly ceased, the General had sent out supports to the pickets, who were straggling in through the bushes in a state of utter demoralization, bringing accounts of an overwhelming force of Rebels; the gunboats were shelling the woods, and everything bore a pleasing aspect of efficient readiness.

We were ordered to return to our camp, which we did with all possible expedition, reaching it in time to prevent the Major from opening fire on the gunboat with grape and canister.

Now I have always suspected that there was something about the events of that night which my transfer to the Regulars prevented my finding out, and I wish you would let me know what it is.

Yours as ever,
HENRY C. WISTAR

I now resume the history of the ball at Goulacaska, or rather of Christmas eve, 1863, as the events which occurred thereon were observed by myself. Soon after the Colonel and his companion left the wharf, as related by Adjutant Wistar, and darkness had settled down over camp and river, a careful observer might have suspected, as the Colonel did, that "the devil was to pay somewhere." The little flotilla of half a dozen scows in front of the Colonel's quarters had been mysteriously reduced to two, which were the smallest and most unserviceable of all. Stranger still, the sharp-eyed sentry of the wharf, one of whose duties it was to watch these boats, had given no notice of their disappearance. A further investigation would have revealed the fact that the missing boats were moored just back of Captain Tybale's tent, and that from six to ten rifles were stowed away in each one. Moreover, each boat was furnished with oars,—a remarkable fact, as our flotilla was notoriously deficient in those necessary implements.

Other quiet but unusual movements were to be detected in and about the line officers' quarters, but elsewhere everything kept the even tenor of its way. The Major and Quartermaster sat over their whiskey-toddy, and bewailed their inability to taste the General's sherry, the rank and file sat about the cook-fires or danced noisily in the company streets, striving, with but partial success, to realize something like the careless jollity of ante-war times; and so the evening wore away.

At length the drum-corps rattled off tattoo, roll-call was over, the officer of the day reported at the Major's quarters, "All present or accounted for." "Very true, me boy," replied that officer, who was dozing after his fourth tumbler, and becoming indifferent to the General's sherry. The camp-fires burned low, lights were extinguished, and at 9.30 P.M. silence reigned supreme.

Immediately after "taps" officers began to gather at the rear of Tybale's tent, where the boats were moored. Each one wore a waist-belt and cartridge-box, and each was dressed in his most undressy clothes. Silently they gathered on the shore under the over-hanging bank. Tybale called off in a whisper the names of the crew and detail for each boat,—thirty names all told, just the number which could be spared, as Tybale said, to attend the ball. Silently as each boat was filled it was shoved clear of the shore and held in position by the bow oarsman. Taking charge of the largest boat, Tybale signalled to shove off, and, following his lead, the four boats moved off into the darkness of mid-channel. The tide had now turned, the wind had fallen, and we fancied that we could hear strains of music from head-quarters, telling us that the dancing had begun and that our fellow-officers of the more favored white regiments were enjoying the smiles of beauty, thoughtless of our shameful exclusion.

Pulling with great care, we safely passed the river picket on our side and then drew in shore, in order to avoid the patrol-boat, and run less risk of challenge from the pickets of the main detachment. Silence was now less imperatively necessary, and we were becoming quite merry in a stifled way, when suddenly "Boat ahoy!" split the darkness ahead of us. "Ay, ay," answered Tybale, adding, *sotto voce,* "There's that infernal patrol-boat."

"Come alongside," said the same voice; and Tybale reluctantly turned the boat's head to the sound, the other boats meanwhile resting on their oars in utter silence. Presently a dim something loomed ahead, we could hardly see it at all, but sailor eyes made out our numbers and a sharp voice ordered, "Starn all! or I'll fire into you."

We checked our headway willingly enough, and then a parley ensued. Tybale tried various means to get away, but without avail, and so at last he made a clean breast of it and appealed to sailor generosity. Fortunately the non-commissioned officer in charge of the boat was a volunteer, and the love of fun which dwells in the heart of Jack Tar proved stronger than his sense of duty, so we were suffered to go on our way, while the man-of-war's men, after solemnly promising inviolable secrecy, lay on their oars as our four boats pulled past.

In half an hour more we landed just as the distant gunboat struck five bells. The disembarkation was effected without noise, and, leaving one man in each boat with orders to drop down stream, keeping just behind us, so as to be ready in case of accident, we walked down the river-bank without any regular formation, simply keeping well together. Tybale had studied the ground, and presently, halting the whole party, sent me with a squad of ten men to station myself in a clump of trees a quarter of a mile off, and near, as he informed me, to the bayou picket on that side, while he with the main body waited at the river-bank within a few hundred yards of the reserve guard, and a still shorter distance of the picket-line. My orders were to open fire as soon as I

ascertained the position of the picket on the bayou, and if possible drive them in on the reserve. Fortune favors the brave, and so she had on this occasion caused the detail for picket to be made from a green short-term regiment, which the government in its wisdom had raised at a maximum cost to do a minimum of fighting.

The unmilitary reader should know that a picket-line was at that time usually composed of successive posts of three men each, stationed within easy sight and hail of each other. One man on each post must always be on the alert. At the most important part of the line a reserve of some thirty or forty men is posted, and the detached posts are often ordered to fall back at once on the reserve, in case of a determined night attack. Such we knew were the orders in the present case.

On reaching the clump of trees I crawled forward to reconnoitre, and soon discovered the pickets comfortably smoking their pipes around the smouldering remains of a fire, all which was exactly contrary to their orders. We were soon in position behind trees, and, taking a careful sight so that my bullet should pass a foot or two above the group, I fired. The rest of the party followed my example, and, lying close, we reloaded. Precaution, however, was needless; only one of the party had the pluck to return our fire; the others obeyed orders with the most exemplary promptitude, and fell back on the reserve at the top of their speed, followed at once by our plucky man, who evidently did not consider it his duty to remain on picket alone. We gave chase at a respectable distance, loading and firing as we advanced, and making all the noise we could in the underbrush. The panic spread along the line, scattering shots were delivered, and we could hear men crashing through the bushes as we walked back towards our party along the line just abandoned by our short-term friends.

Presently I stumbled over something which gave a groan. I stopped in horror, fearing that a chance shot had killed some poor fellow, and the rashness of our adventure flashed upon me as it had not before done. Stooping down I placed my hand on the dimly visible form. It winced at my touch.

"O for God's sake," said a pitiful voice, "don't kill me!"

"Are you wounded?" said I.

"Yes, I believe so; no, I ain't, but the bullets were flying around so thick that I thought I'd better lay down."

The true state of the case began to dawn upon me. Seizing him by the collar, I jerked him to his feet! something clanked on the ground. Could this be an officer? I laid my hand on his shoulder, and there, sure enough, were the straps of a lieutenant.

"What's your name?" said I.

"Elkanah Duzenbury," was the reply. "Gentlemen," he added, "I didn't expect to have to fight when I came out,—I didn't, indeed."

My reply was at least patriotic. I jerked his sword from its scabbard, and whacked him soundly over the shoulders, admonishing him between the strokes not to fight Southerners again. Then with a parting kick I precipitated him into the swamp, and flung his sword beyond him, and then we resumed our advance.

This little episode occupied not more than three minutes, and soon after we recommenced firing it became evident that the reserve had turned out and was making a stand. Bullets began to be uncomfortably plentiful, and we took to cover, firing blank cartridge from behind our logs. Tybale's silence puzzled us, but he had seen a chance to render the discomfiture of our friends complete. The fact

of the case was that an attack from this direction from a considerabe hostile force was well-nigh impossible, and the General had allowed the Post Quartermaster to pasture his surplus and disabled mules on the upper part of the promontory. Tybale had discovered these mules huddled together, and in a moment of inspiration caused them to be driven quietly down toward the reserve. As soon as it became evident that the men were turned out and formed across the road, which was just after our castigation of Duzenbury, Tybale drove his mules into the road, headed them towards camp, fired a volley of blank cartridge right among them, and at the same moment everybody gave a regular Rebel yell. The intentions of the reserve were good, but it must be remembered that they were fresh from home, and had never smelt powder before; at any rate, when the Quartermaster's broken-winded, wheezing, terrified mules charged, snorting with fear, down the road, followed by a rattling volley and the yells of a score of throats, the reserve broke ranks and took the double-quick toward camp without any particular orders, while we reassembled our scattered forces to the sound of the long-roll beaten in both camps, fired a few parting shots, and embarked just as shells from the gunboat began to burst in the woods behind us.

We arrived without further adventure, and found the Major full of fight, but entirely ignorant of the fact that more than half his officers had been absent without leave. Jones, the officer of the day, was in our confidence, and had managed everything admirably, so that our absence was as little noticed as possible. Of course we slept under arms all night, but that was a cheap price to pay for our fun.

It only remains for me to explain that mysterious male escort whose appearance and disappearance at the ball caused the sensation described by Adjutant Wistar.

It so happened that early in the fall the regiment of which my brother was colonel was ordered to a station a few miles east of Goulacaska. We of course exchanged visits; and while with him I had become acquainted with one of his officers, between whom and myself something of an intimacy had sprung up. His family and history were entirely unknown in his regiment, except to my brother, who, after the war was over, told me his story. The poor fellow was killed before Petersburg, so that secrecy was no longer necessary. He was the son of one of Virginia's proudest families, and yet he had no parents. Born as it was possible to be in slave times, he had been brought up as one of the planter's legitimate children, until misfortune had compelled his sale. Natural abilities of a high order had received an impulse by such education as had been given him in boyhood; and after a year or two in the far South he had effected his escape, and had lived as he could, at last getting upon the stage and winning his bread as an actor. He had improved himself by study and reading, and when the war broke out had won for himself at least a name. No one would for a moment suspect that negro blood flowed in his veins, and he had enlisted as a private in my brother's regiment. In the course of two years he had by sheer merit earned a commission. When my brother sent for him and told him that his name had been forwarded for confirmation as second lieutenant, the poor fellow broke down, and, as in honor bound, told my brother his story, evidently expecting to be kicked out of the regiment. My brother, who is not over partial to the negro, hesitated but a moment, then, grasping his hand, addressed him pathet-ically as follows: "See here; what are you boohooing at? You just go to Captain Gray's tent and report for duty."

While we were planning for the *coup* of Christmas eve, the idea entered my head that this young actor might play a part in our drama. No one in our two detachments knew him, so I sent a special messenger for him to come down at once as secretly as possible, giving him a hint as to what was wanted of him. His histrionic instincts were at once awakened on hearing the details of our plan. At that time I little suspected what motives of private revenge led him the more willingly to give us his aid.

He was to personate a relative of the Presbourgs, Presley Creighton, who was actually serving in the Virginia army, and whom they had not seen since his early boyhood. Corwin (for such was his name on the regimental rolls) knew the Creighton family only too well, and anticipated none of the difficulties which we, ignorant of his history, warned him against. We fitted him out with a tattered gray uniform, and on Christmas eve he presented himself at Madame Presbourg's as their cousin, having been kept in close concealment, so that not a soul save those of us who were in the secret had seen him.

He told the Presbourgs that an attack was to be made that night on the Federal lines, and that his object was to get inside their camp, and blow up the magazine soon after the attack commenced. It was naturally decided that he should act as their escort to the ball, be introduced under his own name, so as to secure him, if possible, against the fate of a spy, should he be taken, watch his opportunity to leave the house, and so accomplish his purpose.

Of course the patriotism of the whole Presbourg family was deeply stirred by the arrival of the handsome, ragged young Confederate officer. The young ladies kissed him, and called him "dear Cousin Presley." They dressed him up in some of General Presbourg's old clothes, and were as proud as possible of their adventurous cousin, until a few days after what Madame Presbourg considered the unaccountable repulse of the Confederate forces, when she received a neat package containing her husband's clothes, and enclosing the following note:—

MADAME,—Permit one whom you have called nephew, and whom your charming daughters have treated with cousinly intimacy, to return the garments which you were so kind as to provide for his use.

The former slave of ————— of Virginia did not anticipate so early a recognition from his father's family. Thanking you and my cousins for your kindness,

I remain,
Your nephew,

The note was signed with the name by which Corwin was once known at his father's house, and the consternation produced by its receipt at the St. Jean plantation must be imagined, for it cannot be described.

We had a narrow escape from a searching military investigation into the proceedings of that night, for a few days later some of our Jack Tar friends "sprung aleak," as the boatswain expressed it, and a story was soon in circulation to the effect that the Christmas attack was a sham one. The report presently reached the General's ears, but by good fortune the old soldier had taken a fancy to me, and had detailed me on his staff. When I saw that he was bent on an investigation, I thought the matter over, and told him the whole story one day after dinner, with such success that he nearly went into an apoplectic fit.

The only court-martial which resulted was in the case of Elkanah Duzenbury, who was easily convicted of cowardice, and had his shoulder-straps cut off and his sword broken in the presence of the whole command.

The only life lost in the fight at the picket-line was that of one poor broken-down army mule, shot dead in his tracks by a bullet from the reserve while gallantly leading the charge that broke up the military ball at Goulacaska.

The Brothers

LOUISA MAY ALCOTT (1832–1888) IS CELEBRATED FOR HER EVOCATIONS OF THE JOYS AND sorrows of childhood. Her own story is well known: as the devoted daughter of the unworldly philosopher Bronson Alcott, she tried to support her family by sewing, teaching, and writing. In 1868 *Little Women,* the novel of life in the Alcott household, brought great literary fame and financial success and led the way to a series of best-selling children's books.

The later years of her life were uneventful. But during the Civil War Miss Alcott had served as a volunteer nurse in the Union military hospital at Georgetown. Like the poet Walt Whitman who was a male nurse, she had the opportunity to see for herself the grim, heart-searing results of war. Her letters to her family were first published in the *Commonwealth* and put out in book form in 1863 under the title of *Hospital Sketches.* These strong pieces conveyed the essence of her touching experiences among the wounded and dying.

In 1863 Miss Alcott also published "The Brothers" in the *Atlantic Monthly.* The plot of the short story is to some extent melodramatic and contrived; yet her war experiences provided the author with a saving vein of realism. The account has remarkable power. "The Brothers" certainly differs in style from *Little Men* or *Jo's Boys,* and this early piece of war fiction preserves the agony and tension of a war between brothers.

DOCTOR FRANCK CAME IN AS I SAT SEWING up the rents in an old shirt, that Tom might go tidily to his grave. New shirts were needed for the living, and there was no wife or mother to "dress him handsome when he went to meet the Lord," as one woman said, describing the fine funeral she had pinched herself to give her son.

"Miss Dane, I'm in a quandary," began the Doctor, with that expression of countenance which says as plainly as words, "I want to ask a favor, but I wish you'd save me the trouble."

"Can I help you out of it?"

"Faith! I don't like to propose it, but you certainly can, if you please."

"Then give it a name, I beg."

"You see a Reb has just been brought in crazy with typhoid; a bad case every way; a drunken, rascally little captain somebody took the trouble to capture, but whom nobody wants to take the trouble to cure. The wards are full, the ladies worked to death, and willing to be for our own boys, but rather slow to risk their lives for a Reb. Now you've had the fever, you like queer patients, your mate will see to your ward for a while, and I will find you a good attendant. The fellow won't last long, I fancy; but he can't die without some sort of care, you know. I've put him in the fourth story of the west wing, away from the rest. It is airy, quiet, and comfortable there. I'm on that ward, and will do my best for you in every way. Now, then, will you go?"

"Of course I will, out of perversity, if not common charity; for some of these people think that because I'm an abolitionist I am also a heathen, and I should rather like to show them, that, though I cannot quite love my enemies, I am willing to take care of them."

"Very good; I thought you'd go; and speaking of abolition reminds me that you can have a contraband for servant, if you like. It is that fine mulatto fellow who was found burying his Rebel master after the fight, and, being badly cut over the head, our boys brought him along. Will you have him?"

"By all means,—for I'll stand to my guns on that point, as on the other; these black boys are far more faithful and handy than some of the white scamps given me to serve, instead of being served by. But is this man well enough?"

"Yes, for that sort of work, and I think you'll like him. He must have been a handsome fellow before he got his face slashed; not much darker than myself; his master's son, I dare say, and the white blood makes him rather high and haughty about some things. He was in a bad way when he came in, but vowed he'd die in the street rather than turn in with the black fellows below; so I put him up in the west wing, to be out of the way, and he's seen to the captain all the morning. When can you go up?"

"As soon as Tom is laid out, Skinner moved, Haywood washed, Marble dressed, Charley rubbed, Downs taken up, Upham laid down, and the whole forty fed."

We both laughed, though the Doctor was on his way to the dead-house and I held a shroud on my lap. But in a hospital one learns that cheerfulness is one's salvation; for, in an atmosphere of suffering and death, heaviness of heart would soon paralyze usefulness of hand, if the blessed gift of smiles had been denied us.

In an hour I took possession of my new charge, finding a dissipated-looking boy of nineteen or twenty raving in the solitary little room, with no one near him but the contraband in the room adjoining. Feeling decidedly more interest in the black man than in the white, yet remembering the Doctor's hint of his being "high and haughty," I glanced furtively at him as I scattered chloride of lime about the room to purify the air, and settled matters to suit myself. I had seen many contrabands, but never one so attractive as this. All colored men are called "boys," even if their heads are white; this boy was five-and-twenty at least, strong-limbed and manly, and had the look of one who never had been cowed by abuse or worn with oppressive labor. He sat on his bed doing nothing; no book, no pipe, no pen or paper anywhere appeared, yet anything less indolent or listless than his attitude and expression I never saw. Erect he sat, with a hand on either knee, and eyes fixed on the bare wall opposite, so rapt in some absorbing thought as to be unconscious of my presence, though the door stood wide open and my movements were by no means noiseless. His face was half averted, but I instantly approved the Doctor's taste, for the profile which I saw possessed all the attributes of comeliness belonging to his mixed race. He was more quadroon than mulatto, with Saxon features, Spanish complexion darkened by exposure, color in lips and cheek, waving hair, and an eye full of the passionate melancholy which in such men always seems to utter a mute protest against the broken law that doomed them at their birth. What could he be thinking of? The sick boy cursed and raved, I rustled to and fro, steps passed the door, bells rang, and the steady rumble of army-wagons came up from the street, still he never stirred. I had seen colored people in what they call "the black sulks," when, for days, they neither smiled nor spoke, and scarcely ate. But this was something more than that; for the man was not dully brooding over some small grievance; he seemed to see an all-absorbing fact or fancy recorded on the wall, which was a blank to me. I wondered if it were some deep wrong or sorrow, kept alive by memory and impotent regret; if he mourned for the dead master to whom he had been faithful to the end; or if the liberty now his were robbed of half its sweetness by the knowledge that some one near and dear to him still languished in the hell from which he had escaped. My heart quite warmed to him at that idea; I wanted to know and comfort him; and, following the impulse of the moment, I went in and touched him on the shoulder.

In an instant the man vanished and the slave appeared. Freedom was too new a boon to have wrought its blessed changes yet, and as he started up, with his hand at his temple and an obsequious "Yes, Ma'am," any romance that

had gathered round him fled away, leaving the saddest of all sad facts in living guise before me. Not only did the manhood seem to die out of him, but the comeliness that first attracted me; for, as he turned, I saw the ghastly wound that had laid open cheek and forehead. Being partly healed, it was no longer bandaged, but held together with strips of that transparent plaster which I never see without a shiver and swift recollections of the scenes with which it is associated in my mind. Part of his black hair had been shorn away, and one eye was nearly closed; pain so distorted, and the cruel sabre-cut so marred that portion of his face, that, when I saw it, I felt as if a fine medal had been suddenly reversed, showing me a far more striking type of human suffering and wrong than Michel Angelo's bronze prisoner. By one of those inexplicable processes that often teach us how little we understand ourselves, my purpose was suddenly changed, and though I went in to offer comfort as a friend, I merely gave an order as a mistress.

"Will you open these windows? this man needs more air."

He obeyed at once, and, as he slowly urged up the unruly sash, the handsome profile was again turned toward me, and again I was possessed by my first impression so strongly that I involuntarily said,—

"Thank you, Sir."

Perhaps it was fancy, but I thought that in the look of mingled surprise and something like reproach which he gave me there was also a trace of grateful pleasure. But he said, in that tone of spiritless humility these poor souls learn so soon,—

"I a'n't a white man, Ma'am, I'm a contraband."

"Yes, I know it; but a contraband is a free man, and I heartily congratulate you."

He liked that; his face shone, he squared his shoulders, lifted his head, and looked me full in the eye with a brisk—

"Thank ye, Ma'am; anything more to do fer yer?"

"Doctor Franck thought you would help me with this man, as there are many patients and few nurses or attendants. Have you had the fever?"

"No, Ma'am."

"They should have thought of that when they put him here; wounds and fevers should not be together. I'll try to get you moved."

He laughed a sudden laugh,—if he had been a white man, I should have called it scornful; as he was a few shades darker than myself, I suppose it must be considered an insolent, or at least an unmannerly one.

"It don't matter, Ma'am. I'd rather be up here with the fever than down with those niggers; and there a'n't no other place fer me."

Poor fellow! that was true. No ward in all the hospital would take him in to lie side by side with the most miserable white wreck there. Like the bat in Aesop's fable, he belonged to neither race; and the pride of one, the helplessness of the other, kept him hovering alone in the twilight a great sin has brought to overshadow the whole land.

"You shall stay, then; for I would far rather have you than my lazy Jack. But are you well and strong enough?"

"I guess I'll do, Ma'am."

He spoke with a passive sort of acquiescence,—as if it did not much matter, if he were not able, and no one would particularly rejoice, if he were.

"Yes, I think you will. By what name shall I call you?"

"Bob, Ma'am."

Every woman has her pet whim; one of mine was to teach the men self-respect by treating them respectfully. Tom, Dick, and Harry would pass, when lads rejoiced in those familiar abbreviations; but to address men often old enough to be my father in that style did not suit my old-fashioned ideas of propriety. This "Bob" would never do; I should have found it as easy to call the chaplain "Gus" as my tragical-looking contraband by a title so strongly associated with the tail of a kite.

"What is your other name?" I asked. "I like to call my attendants by their last names rather than by their first."

"I've got no other, Ma'am; we have our master's names, or do without. Mine's dead, and I won't have anything of his about me."

"Well, I'll call you Robert, then, and you may fill this pitcher for me, if you will be so kind."

He went; but, through all the tame obedience years of servitude had taught him, I could see that the proud spirit his father gave him was not yet subdued, for the look and gesture with which he repudiated his master's name were a more effective declaration of independence than any Fourth-of-July orator could have prepared.

We spent a curious week together. Robert seldom left his room, except upon my errands; and I was a prisoner all day, often all night, by the bedside of the Rebel. The fever burned itself rapidly away, for there seemed little vitality to feed it in the feeble frame of this old young man, whose life had been none of the most righteous, judging from the revelations made by his unconscious lips; since more than once Robert authoritatively silenced him, when my gentler hushings were of no avail, and blasphemous wanderings or ribald camp-songs made my cheeks burn and Robert's face assume an aspect of disgust. The captain was a gentleman in the world's eye, but the contraband was the gentleman in mine;—I was a fanatic, and that accounts for such depravity of taste, I hope. I never asked Robert of himself, feeling that somewhere there was a spot still too sore to bear the lightest touch; but, from his language, manner, and intelligence, I inferred that his color had procured for him the few advantages within the reach of a quick-witted, kindly treated slave. Silent, grave, and thoughtful, but most serviceable, was my contraband; glad of the books I brought him, faithful in the performance of the duties I assigned to him, grateful for the friendliness I could not but feel and show toward him. Often I longed to ask what purpose was so visibly altering his aspect with such daily deepening gloom. But I never dared, and no one else had either time or desire to pry into the past of this specimen of one branch of the chivalrous "F.F.Vs."

On the seventh night, Dr. Franck suggested that it would be well for some one, besides the general watchman of the ward, to be with the captain, as it might be his last. Although the greater part of the two preceding nights had been spent there, of course I offered to remain,—for there is a strange fascination in these scenes, which renders one careless of fatigue and unconscious of fear until the crisis is passed.

"Give him water as long as he can drink, and if he drops into a natural sleep, it may save him. I'll look in at midnight, when some change will probably take place. Nothing but sleep or a miracle will keep him now. Good night."

Away went the Doctor; and, devouring a whole mouthful of gapes, I lowered the lamp, wet the captain's head, and sat down on a hard stool to begin my watch. The captain lay with his hot, haggard face turned toward me, filling the air with his poisonous breath, and feebly muttering, with lips and tongue so parched that the sanest speech would have been difficult to understand. Robert was stretched on his bed in the inner room, the door of which stood ajar, that a fresh draught from his open window might carry the fever-fumes away through mine. I could just see a long, dark figure, with the lighter outline of a face, and, having little else to do just then, I fell to thinking of this curious contraband, who evidently prized his freedom highly, yet seemed in no haste to enjoy it. Doctor Franck had offered to send him on to safer quarters, but he had said, "No, thank yer, Sir, not yet," and then had gone away to fall into one of those black moods of his, which began to disturb me, because I had no power to lighten them. As I sat listening to the clocks from the steeples all about us, I amused myself with planning Robert's future, as I often did my own, and had dealt out to him a generous hand of trumps wherewith to play this game of life which hitherto had gone so cruelly against him, when a harsh, choked voice called,—

"Lucy!"

It was the captain, and some new terror seemed to have gifted him with momentary strength.

"Yes, here's Lucy," I answered, hoping that by following the fancy I might quiet him,—for his face was damp with the clammy moisture, and his frame shaken with the nervous tremor that so often precedes death. His dull eye fixed upon me, dilating with a bewildered look of incredulity and wrath, till he broke out fiercely,—

"That's a lie! she's dead,—and so's Bob, damn him!"

Finding speech a failure, I began to sing the

quiet tune that had often soothed delirium like this; but hardly had the line,

"See gentle patience smile on pain,"

passed my lips, when he clutched me by the wrist, whispering like one in mortal fear,—

"Hush! she used to sing that way to Bob, but she never would to me. I swore I'd whip the Devil out of her, and I did; but you know before she cut her throat she said she'd haunt me, and there she is!"

He pointed behind me with an aspect of such pale dismay, that I involuntarily glanced over my shoulder and started as if I had seen a veritable ghost; for, peering from the gloom of that inner room, I saw a shadowy face, with dark hair all about it, and a glimpse of scarlet at the throat. An instant showed me that it was only Robert leaning from his bed's-foot, wrapped in a gray army-blanket, with his red shirt just visible above it, and his long hair disordered by sleep. But what a strange expression was on his face! The unmarred side was toward me, fixed and motionless as when I first observed it,—less absorbed now, but more intent. His eye glittered, his lips were apart like one who listened with every sense, and his whole aspect reminded me of a hound to which some wind had brought the scent of unsuspected prey.

"Do you know him, Robert? Does he mean you?"

"Lord, no, Ma'am; they all own half a dozen Bobs: but hearin' my name woke me; that's all."

He spoke quite naturally, and lay down again, while I returned to my charge, thinking that this paroxysm was probably his last. But by another hour I perceived a hopeful change, for the tremor had subsided, the cold dew was gone, his breathing was more regular, and

Sleep, the healer, had descended to save or take him gently away. Doctor Franck looked in at midnight, bade me keep all cool and quiet, and not fail to administer a certain draught as soon as the captain woke. Very much relieved, I laid my head on my arms, uncomfortably folded on the little table, and fancied I was about to perform one of the feats which practice renders possible,—"sleeping with one eye open," as we say: a half-and-half doze, for all senses sleep but that of hearing; the faintest murmur, sigh, or motion will break it, and give one back one's wits much brightened by the brief permission to "stand at ease." On this night, the experiment was a failure, for previous vigils, confinement, and much care had rendered naps a dangerous indulgence. Having roused half a dozen times in an hour to find all quiet, I dropped my heavy head on my arms, and, drowsily resolving to look up again in fifteen minutes, fell fast asleep.

The striking of a deep-voiced clock woke me with a start. "That is one," thought I, but, to my dismay, two more strokes followed; and in remorseful haste I sprang up to see what harm my long oblivion had done. A strong hand put me back into my seat, and held me there. It was Robert. The instant my eye met his my heart began to beat, and all along my nerves tingled that electric flash which foretells a danger that we cannot see. He was very pale, his mouth grim, and both eyes full of sombre fire,—for even the wounded one was open now, all the more sinister for the deep scar above and below. But his touch was steady, his voice quiet, as he said,—

"Sit still, Ma'am; I won't hurt yer, nor even scare yer, if I can help it, but yer waked too soon."

"Let me go, Robert,—the captain is stirring,—I must give him something."

"No, Ma'am, yer can't stir an inch. Look here!"

Holding me with one hand, with the other he took up the glass in which I had left the draught, and showed me it was empty.

"Has he taken it?" I asked, more and more bewildered.

"I flung it out o' winder, Ma'am; he'll have to do without."

"But why, Robert? why did you do it?"

"Because I hate him!"

Impossible to doubt the truth of that; his whole face showed it, as he spoke through his set teeth, and launched a fiery glance at the unconscious captain. I could only hold my breath and stare blankly at him, wondering what mad act was coming next. I suppose I shook and turned white, as women have a foolish habit of doing when sudden danger daunts them; for Robert released my arm, sat down upon the bedside just in front of me, and said, with the ominous quietude that made me cold to see and hear,—

"Don't yer be frightened, Ma'am; don't try to run away, fer the door's locked an' the key in my pocket; don't yer cry out, fer yer'd have to scream a long while, with my hand on yer mouth, before yer was heard. Be still, an' I'll tell yer what I'm goin' to do."

"Lord help us! he has taken the fever in some sudden, violent way, and is out of his head. I must humor him till some one comes"; in pursuance of which swift determination, I tried to say, quiet composedly,—

"I will be still and hear you; but open the window. Why did you shut it?"

"I'm sorry I can't do it, Ma'am; but yer'd jump out, or call, if I did, an' I'm not ready yet. I shut it to make yer sleep, an' heat would do it quicker 'n anything else I could do."

The captain moved, and feebly muttered,

"Water!" Instinctively I rose to give it to him, but the heavy hand came down upon my shoulder, and in the same decided tone Robert said,—

"The water went with the physic; let him call."

"Do let me go to him! he'll die without care!"

"I mean he shall;—don't yer interfere, if yer please, Ma'am."

In spite of his quiet tone and respectful manner, I saw murder in his eyes, and turned faint with fear; yet the fear excited me, and, hardly knowing what I did, I seized the hands that had seized me, crying,—

"No, no, you shall not kill him! it is base to hurt a helpless man. Why do you hate him? He is not your master?"

"He's my brother."

I felt that answer from head to foot, and seemed to fathom what was coming, with a prescience vague, but unmistakable. One appeal was left to me, and I made it.

"Robert, tell me what it means? Do not commit a crime and make me accessory to it. There is a better way of righting wrong than by violence;—let me help you find it."

My voice trembled as I spoke, and I heard the frightened flutter of my heart; so did he, and if any little act of mine had ever won affection or respect from him, the memory of it served me then. He looked down, and seemed to put some question to himself; whatever it was, the answer was in my favor, for when his eyes rose again, they were gloomy, but not desperate.

"I *will* tell you, Ma'am; but mind, this makes no difference; the boy is mine. I'll give the Lord a chance to take him fust; if He don't, I shall."

"Oh, no! remember, he is your brother."

An unwise speech; I felt it as it passed my lips, for a black frown gathered on Robert's face, and his strong hands closed with an ugly sort of grip. But he did not touch the poor soul gasping there behind him, and seemed content to let the slow suffocation of that stifling room end his frail life.

"I'm not like to forget that, Ma'am, when I've been thinkin' of it all this week. I knew him when they fetched him in, an' would 'a' done it long 'fore this, but I wanted to ask where Lucy was; he knows,—he told to-night,—an' now he's done for."

"Who is Lucy?" I asked hurriedly, intent on keeping his mind busy with any thought but murder.

With one of the swift transitions of a mixed temperament like this, at my question Robert's deep eyes filled, the clenched hands were spread before his face, and all I heard were the broken words,—

"My wife,—he took her"——

In that instant every thought of fear was swallowed up in burning indignation for the wrong, and a perfect passion of pity for the desperate man so tempted to avenge an injury for which there seemed no redress but this. He was no longer slave or contraband, no drop of black blood marred him in my sight, but an infinite compassion yearned to save, to help, to comfort him. Words seemed so powerless I offered none, only put my hand on his poor head, wounded, homeless, bowed down with grief for which I had no cure, and softly smoothed the long neglected hair, pitifully wondering the while where was the wife who must have loved this tender-hearted man so well.

The captain moaned again, and faintly whispered, "Air!" but I never stirred. God forgive me! just then I hated him as only a woman thinking of a sister woman's wrong could hate. Robert looked up; his eyes were dry again, his mouth grim. I saw that, said, "Tell me more," and he did,—for sympathy is a gift the poorest may give, the proudest stoop to receive.

"Yer see, Ma'am, his father,—I might say ours, if I warn't ashamed of both of 'em,—his father died two years ago, an' left us all to Marster Ned,—that's him here, eighteen then. He always hated me, I looked so like old Marster: he don't,—only the light skin an' hair. Old Marster was kind to all of us, me 'specially, an' bought Lucy off the next planta-tion down there in South Car'lina, when he found I liked her. I married her, all I could, Ma'am; it warn't much, but we was true to one another till Marster Ned come home a year after an' made hell fer both of us. He sent my old mother to be used up in his rice-swamp in Georgy; he found me with my pretty Lucy, an' though young Miss cried, an' I prayed to him on my knees, an' Lucy run away, he wouldn't have no mercy; he brought her back, an'—took her, Ma'am."

"Oh! what did you do?" I cried, hot with helpless pain and passion.

How the man's outraged heart sent the blood flaming up into his face and deepened the tones of his impetuous voice, as he stretched his arm across the bed, saying, with a terribly expressive gesture,—

"I half murdered him, an' to-night I'll fin-ish."

"Yes, yes,—but go on now; what came next?"

He gave me a look that showed no white man could have felt a deeper degradation in remembering and confessing these last acts of brotherly oppression.

"They whipped me till I couldn't stand, an'

then they sold me further South. Yer thought I was a white man once;—look here!"

With a sudden wrench he tore the shirt from neck to waist, and on his strong brown shoulders showed me furrows deeply ploughed, wounds which, though healed, were ghastlier to me than any in that house. I could not speak to him, and, with the pathetic dignity a great grief lends the humblest sufferer, he ended his brief tragedy by simply saying,—

"That's all, Ma'am. I've never seen her since, an' now I never shall in this world,—maybe not in t' other."

"But, Robert, why think her dead? The captain was wandering when he said those sad things; perhaps he will retract them when he is sane. Don't despair; don't give up yet."

"No, Ma'am, I guess he's right; she was too proud to bear that long. It's like her to kill herself. I told her to, if there was no other way; an' she always minded me, Lucy did. My poor girl! Oh, it warn't right! No, by God, it warn't!"

As the memory of this bitter wrong, this double bereavement, burned in his sore heart, the devil that lurks in every strong man's blood leaped up; he put his hand upon his brother's throat, and, watching the white face before him, muttered low between his teeth,—

"I'm lettin' him go too easy; there's no pain in this; we a'n't even yet. I wish he knew me. Marster Ned! it's Bob; where's Lucy?"

From the captain's lips there came a long faint sigh, and nothing but a flutter of the eyelids showed that he still lived. A strange stillness filled the room as the elder brother held the younger's life suspended in his hand, while wavering between a dim hope and a deadly hate. In the whirl of thoughts that went on in my brain, only one was clear enough to act upon. I must prevent murder, if I could,—but

how? What could I do up there alone, locked in with a dying man and a lunatic?—for any mind yielded utterly to any unrighteous impulse is mad while the impulse rules it. Strength I had not, nor much courage, neither time nor wit for stratagem, and chance only could bring me help before it was too late. But one weapon I possessed,—a tongue,—often a woman's best defence; and sympathy, stronger than fear, gave me power to use it. What I said Heaven only knows, but surely Heaven helped me; words burned on my lips, tears streamed from my eyes, and some good angel prompted me to use the one name that had power to arrest my hearer's hand and touch his heart. For at that moment I heartily believed that Lucy lived, and this earnest faith roused in him a like belief.

He listened with the lowering look of one in whom brute instinct was sovereign for the time,—a look that makes the noblest countenance base. He was but a man,—a poor, untaught, outcast, outraged man. Life had few joys for him; the world offered him no honors, no success, no home, no love. What future would this crime mar? and why should he deny himself that sweet, yet bitter morsel called revenge? How many white men, with all New England's freedom, culture, Christianity, would not have felt as he felt then? Should I have reproached him for a human anguish, a human longing for redress, all now left him from the ruin of his few poor hopes? Who had taught him that self-control, self-sacrifice, are attributes that make men masters of the earth and lift them nearer heaven? Should I have urged the beauty of forgiveness, the duty of devout submission? He had no religion, for he was no saintly "Uncle Tom," and Slavery's black shadow seemed to darken all the world to him and shut out God. Should I have warned him of penalties, of judgments, and the potency of law? What did he know of justice, or the mercy that should temper that stern virtue, when every law, human and divine, had been broken on his hearthstone? Should I have tried to touch him by appeals to filial duty, to brotherly love? How had his appeals been answered? What memories had father and brother stored up in his heart to plead for either now? No,—all these influences, these associations, would have proved worse than useless, had I been calm enough to try them. I was not; but instinct, subtler than reason, showed me the one safe clue by which to lead this troubled soul from the labyrinth in which it groped and nearly fell. When I paused, breathless, Robert turned to me, asking, as if human assurances could strengthen his faith in Divine Omnipotence,—

"Do you believe, if I let Marster Ned live, the Lord will give me back my Lucy?"

"As surely as there is a Lord, you will find her here or in the beautiful hereafter, where there is no black or white, no master and no slave."

He took his hand from his brother's throat, lifted his eyes from my face to the wintry sky beyond, as if searching for that blessed country, happier even than the happy North. Alas, it was the darkest hour before dawn!—there was no star above, no light below but the pale glimmer of the lamp that showed the brother who had made him desolate. Like a blind man who believes there is a sun, yet cannot see it, he shook his head, let his arms drop nervelessly upon his knees, and sat there dumbly asking that question which many a soul whose faith is firmer fixed than his has asked in hours less dark than this,—"Where is God?" I saw the tide had turned, and strenuously tried to keep this rudderless life-boat from slipping back

into the whirlpool wherein it had been so nearly lost.

"I have listened to you, Robert; now hear me, and heed what I say, because my heart is full of pity for you, full of hope for your future, and a desire to help you now. I want you to go away from here, from the temptation of this place, and the sad thoughts that haunt it. You have conquered yourself once, and I honor you for it, because, the harder the battle, the more glorious the victory; but it is safer to put a greater distance between you and this man. I will write you letters, give you money, and send you to good old Massachusetts to begin your new life a freeman,—yes, and a happy man; for when the captain is himself again, I will learn where Lucy is, and move heaven and earth to find and give her back to you. Will you do this, Robert?"

Slowly, very slowly, the answer came; for the purpose of a week, perhaps a year, was hard to relinquish in an hour.

"Yes, Ma'am, I will."

"Good! Now you are the man I thought you, and I'll work for you with all my heart. You need sleep, my poor fellow; go, and try to forget. The captain is still alive, and as yet you are spared that sin. No, don't look there; I'll care for him. Come, Robert, for Lucy's sake."

Thank Heaven for the immortality of love! for when all other means of salvation failed, a spark of this vital fire softened the man's iron will until a woman's hand could bend it. He let me take from him the key, let me draw him gently away and lead him to the solitude which now was the most healing balm I could bestow. Once in his little room, he fell down on his bed and lay there as if spent with the sharpest conflict of his life. I slipped the bolt across his door, and unlocked my own, flung up the window, steadied myself with a breath of air, then rushed to Doctor Franck. He came; and till dawn we worked together, saving one brother's life, and taking earnest thought how best to secure the other's liberty. When the sun came up as blithely as if it shone only upon happy homes, the Doctor went to Robert. For an hour I heard the murmur of their voices; once I caught the sound of heavy sobs, and for a time a reverent hush, as if in the silence that good man were ministering to soul as well as sense. When he departed he took Robert with him, pausing to tell me he should get him off as soon as possible, but not before we met again.

Nothing more was seen of them all day; another surgeon came to see the captain, and another attendant came to fill the empty place. I tried to rest, but could not, with the thought of poor Lucy tugging at my heart, and was soon back at my post again anxiously hoping that my contraband had not been too hastily spirited away. Just as night fell there came a tap, and, opening, I saw Robert literally "clothed and in his right mind." The Doctor had replaced the ragged suit with tidy garments, and no trace of that tempestuous night remained but deeper lines upon the forehead and the docile look of a repentant child. He did not cross the threshold, did not offer me his hand, —only took off his cap, saying, with a traitorous falter in his voice,—

"God bless you, Ma'am! I'm goin'."

I put out both my hands, and held his fast.

"Good bye, Robert! Keep up good heart, and when I come home to Massachusetts we'll meet in a happier place than this. Are you quite ready, quite comfortable for your journey?"

"Yes, Ma'am, yes; the Doctor's fixed everything; I'm goin' with a friend of his; my papers are all right, an' I'm as happy as I can be till I find"——

He stopped there; then went on, with a glance into the room,—

"I'm glad I didn't do it, an' I thank yer, Ma'am, fer hinderin' me,—thank yer hearty; but I'm afraid I hate him jest the same."

Of course he did; and so did I; for these faulty hearts of ours cannot turn perfect in a night, but need frost and fire, wind and rain, to ripen and make them ready for the great harvest-home. Wishing to divert his mind, I put my poor mite into his hand, and, remembering the magic of a certain little book, I gave him mine, on whose dark cover whitely shone the Virgin Mother and the Child, the grand history of whose life the book contained. The money went into Robert's pocket with a grateful murmur, the book into his bosom with a long look and a tremulous—

"I never saw *my* baby, Ma'am."

I broke down then; and though my eyes were too dim to see, I felt the touch of lips upon my hands, heard the sound of departing feet, and knew my contraband was gone.

*   *   *

When one feels an intense dislike, the less one says about the subject of it the better; therefore I shall merely record that the captain lived,—in time was exchanged; and that, whoever the other party was, I am convinced the Government got the best of the bargain. But long before this occurred, I had fulfilled my promise to Robert; for as soon as my patient recovered strength of memory enough to make his answer trustworthy, I asked, without any circumlocution,—

"Captain Fairfax, where is Lucy?"

And too feeble to be angry, surprised, or insincere, he straightway answered,—

"Dead, Miss Dane."

"And she killed herself, when you sold Bob?"

"How the Devil did you know that?" he muttered, with an expression half-remorseful, half-amazed; but I was satisfied and said no more.

Of course, this went to Robert, waiting far away there in a lonely home,—waiting, working, hoping for his Lucy. It almost broke my heart to do it; but delay was weak, deceit was wicked; so I sent the heavy tidings, and very soon the answer came,—only three lines; but I felt that the sustaining power of the man's life was gone.

"I thought I'd never see her any more; I'm glad to know she's out of trouble. I thank yer, Ma'am; an' if they let us, I'll fight fer yer till I'm killed, which I hope will be 'fore long."

Six months later he had his wish, and kept his word.

Every one knows the story of the attack on Fort Wagner; but we should not tire yet of recalling how our Fifty-Fourth, spent with three sleepless nights, a day's fast, and a march under the July sun, stormed the fort as night fell, facing death in many shapes, following their brave leaders through a fiery rain of shot and shell, fighting valiantly for "God and Governor Andrew,"—how the regiment that went into action seven hundred strong came out having had nearly half its number captured, killed, or wounded, leaving their young commander to be buried, like a chief of earlier times, with his bodyguard around him, faithful to the death. Surely, the insult turns to honor, and the wide grave needs no monument but the heroism that consecrates it in our sight; surely, the hearts that held him nearest see through their tears a noble victory in the seeming sad defeat; and surely, God's benediction was bestowed, when this loyal soul answered, as Death called the roll, "Lord, here am I, with the brothers Thou has given me!"

The future must show how well that fight was fought; for though Fort Wagner still defies us, public prejudice is down; and through the cannon-smoke of that black night the manhood of the colored race shines before many eyes that would not see, rings in many ears that would not hear, wins many hearts that would not hitherto believe.

When the news came that we were needed, there was none so glad as I to leave teaching contrabands, the new work I had taken up, and go to nurse "our boys," as my dusky flock so proudly called the wounded of the Fifty-Fourth. Feeling more satisfaction, as I assumed my big apron and turned up my cuffs, than if dressing for the President's levee, I fell to work on board the hospital-ship in Hilton-Head harbor. The scene was most familiar, and yet strange; for only dark faces looked up at me from the pallets so thickly laid along the floor, and I missed the sharp accent of my Yankee boys in the slower, softer voices calling cheerily to one another, or answering my questions with a stout, "We'll never give it up, Ma'am, till the last Reb's dead," or, "If our people's free, we can afford to die."

Passing from bed to bed, intent on making one pair of hands do the work of three, at least, I gradually washed, fed, and bandaged my way down the long line of sable heroes, and coming to the very last, found that he was my contraband. So old, so worn, so deathly weak and wan, I never should have known him but for the deep scar on his cheek. That side lay uppermost, and caught my eye at once; but even then I doubted, such an awful change had come upon him, when, turning to the ticket just above his head, I saw the name, "Robert Dane." That both assured and touched me, for, remembering that he had no name, I knew that he had taken mine. I longed for him to speak to me, to tell how he had fared since I lost sight of him, and let me perform some little service for him in return for many he had done for me; but he seemed asleep; and as I stood reliving that strange night again, a bright lad, who lay next him softly waving an old fan across both beds, looked up and said,—

"I guess you know him, Ma'am?"

"You are right. Do you?"

"As much as any one was able to, Ma'am."

"Why do you say 'was,' as if the man were dead and gone?"

"I s'pose because I know he'll have to go. He's got a bad jab in the breast, an' is bleedin' inside, the Doctor says. He don't suffer any, only gets weaker 'n' weaker every minute. I've been fannin' him this long while, an' he's talked a little; but he don't know me now, so he's most gone, I guess."

There was so much sorrow and affection in the boy's face, that I remembered something, and asked, with redoubled interest,—

"Are you the one that brought him off? I was told about a boy who nearly lost his life in saving that of his mate."

I dare say the young fellow blushed, as any modest lad might have done; I could not see it, but I heard the chuckle of satisfaction that escaped him, as he glanced from his shattered arm and bandaged side to the pale figure opposite.

"Lord, Ma'am, that's nothin'; we boys always stan' by one another, an' I warn't goin' to leave him to be tormented any more by them cussed Rebs. He's been a slave once, though he don't look half so much like it as me, an' I was born in Boston."

He did not; for the speaker was as black as the ace of spades,—being a sturdy specimen, the knave of clubs would perhaps be a fitter representative,—but the dark freeman looked at the white slave with the pitiful, yet puzzled expression I have so often seen on the faces of our wisest men, when this tangled question of Slavery presents itself, asking to be cut or patiently undone.

"Tell me what you know of this man; for, even if he were awake, he is too weak to talk."

"I never saw him till I joined the regiment, an' no one 'peared to have got much out of him. He was a shut-up sort of feller, an' didn't seem to care for anything but gettin' at the Rebs. Some say he was the fust man of us that enlisted; I know he fretted till we were off, an' when we pitched into old Wagner, he fought like the Devil."

"Were you with him when he was wounded? How was it?"

"Yes, Ma'am. There was somethin' queer about it; for he 'peared to know the chap that killed him, an' the chap knew him. I don't dare to ask, but I rather guess one owned the other some time,—for, when they clinched, the chap sung out, 'Bob!' an' Dane, 'Marster Ned!'— then they went at it."

I sat down suddenly, for the old anger and compassion struggled in my heart, and I both longed and feared to hear what was to follow.

"You see, when the Colonel—Lord keep an' send him back to us!—it a'n't certain yet, you know, Ma'am, though it's two days ago we lost him—well, when the Colonel shouted, 'Rush on, boys, rush on!' Dane tore away as if he was goin' to take the fort alone; I was next him, an' kept close as we went through the ditch an' up the wall. Hi! warn't that a rusher!" and the boy flung up his well arm with a whoop, as if the mere memory of that stirring moment came over him in a gust of irrepressible excitement.

"Were you afraid?" I said,—asking the

question women often put, and receiving the answer they seldom fail to get.

"No, Ma'am!"—emphasis on the "Ma'am," —"I never thought of anything but the damn' Rebs, that scalp, slash, an' cut our ears off, when they git us. I was bound to let daylight into one of 'em at least, an' I did. Hope he liked it!"

"It is evident that you did, and I don't blame you in the least. Now go on about Robert, for I should be at work."

"He was one of the fust up; I was just behind, an' though the whole thing happened in a minute, I remember how it was, for all I was yellin' an' knockin' round like mad. Just where we were, some sort of an officer was wavin' his sword an' cheerin' on his men; Dane saw him by a big flash that come by; he flung away his gun, give a leap, an' went at that feller as if he was Jeff, Beauregard, an' Lee, all in one. I scrabbled after as quick as I could, but was only up in time to see him git the sword straight through him an' drop into the ditch. You needn't ask what I did next, Ma'am, for I don't quite know myself; all I'm clear about is, that I managed somehow to pitch that Reb into the fort as dead as Moses, git hold of Dane, an' bring him off. Poor old feller! we

said we went in to live or die; he said he went in to die, an' he's done it."

I had been intently watching the excited speaker; but as he regretfully added those last words I turned again, and Robert's eyes met mine,—those melancholy eyes, so full of an intelligence that proved he had heard, remembered, and reflected with that preternatural power which often outlives all other faculties. He knew me, yet gave no greeting; was glad to see a woman's face, yet had no smile wherewith to welcome it; felt that he was dying, yet uttered no farewell. He was too far across the river to return or linger now; departing thought, strength, breath, were spent in one grateful look, one murmur of submission to the last pang he could ever feel. His lips moved, and, bending to them, a whisper chilled my cheek, as it shaped the broken words,—

"I would have done it,—but it's better so,— I'm satisfied."

Ah! well he might be,—for, as he turned his face from the shadow of the life that was, the sunshine of the life to be touched it with a beautiful content, and in the drawing of a breath my contraband found wife and home, eternal liberty and God,

from Southern Soldier Stories

GEORGE CARY EGGLESTON (1839–1911) HAS NOT BEEN ACCORDED RECOGNITION IN HIS-
tories of American literature. An occasional reference to him usually mentions, in passing, that he
was a brother of Edward Eggleston, the author of *The Hoosier Schoolmaster*. Nevertheless,
Eggleston's neglected little volume entitled *Southern Soldier Stories* (1898) includes some of the
most trenchant vignettes of the Civil War.

Eggleston, a close friend of John Esten Cooke, also served from the start of the war under Stuart
and then under the dashing Fitzhugh Lee. Eggleston became the sergeant-major of a battery of
Longstreet's artillery and in 1864 was in charge of a mortar fort throughout the savage and
protracted siege of Petersburg.

After the war, Eggleston became an outstanding journalist; he was literary editor of the New
York *Post* and later one of Joseph Pulitzer's chief editorial writers on the *World*. He wrote ten
novels, many juveniles and biographies, and a history of the war. His reminiscences of the war
appeared in the *Atlantic Monthly* in 1874 under the title of *A Rebel's Recollections* and have
recently been reprinted.

Eggleston's version of what he called the Confederate War resembles that of the other Southern
novelists. He hails the departed glory of a lost cause, the gallantry of the defeated armies, the
bravery of Rebel womanhood. But the short pieces of *Southern Soldier Stories* differ markedly
from contemporary war stories. In the first place, Eggleston concentrates on the enlisted man. He
does not balk at giving examples of cowardice, betrayal, and death. He is one of the first American
writers to follow the hints of Tolstoy and Crane and delve into the psychology of the harassed
individual under fire. Though these stories, dealing mostly with the trench warfare around Petersburg, may seem casual if compared to the similarly short tales of Ambrose Bierce, Eggleston's tight,
at times ironic, stories catch the tragic overtones of war.

Joe

JOE WAS VERY MUCH IN EARNEST AT POCO-taligo, South Carolina, where a great little battle was fought on the 22d of October, 1862.

That is to say, Joe was not quite seventeen years old, was an enthusiastic soldier, and was as hot headed as a boy well can be.

We had two batteries and a few companies of mounted riflemen—three hundred and fifty-one men all told—to oppose the advance of five thousand. We had only the nature of the country, the impassability of the marshes, and the long high causeways to enable us to make any resistance at all.

Before the battle of Pocotaligo proper began, we went two miles below to Yemassee and there made a stand of half an hour.

Our battery, numbering fifty-four men, received the brunt of the attack.

Joe had command of a gun.

His men fell like weeds before a scythe. Presently he found himself with only three men left with whom to work a gun.

The other battery was that of Captain Elliot of South Carolina; and Captain Elliot had just been designated Chief of Artillery. Elliot's battery was really not in action at all. Joe, seeing Captain Elliot, and being himself full of the enthusiasm which insists upon getting things done, appealed to the Chief of Artillery for the loan of some cannoneers with whom to work his gun more effectively. Captain Elliot declined. Thereupon Joe broke into a volley of vituperation, calling the captain and his battery cowards, and by other pet names not here to be reported.

I, being Joe's immediate chief, as well as his elder brother, commanded him to silence and ordered him back to his gun. There he stood for fifteen minutes astride a dead man and pulling the lanyard himself. At the end of that time we were ordered to retire to Pocotaligo.

Joe was flushed, powder grimed, and very angry; so angry that even I came in for a part of his displeasure. When I asked him, in order that I might make report for the section, how many shots he had fired, he blazed out at me: "How do I know? I've been killing Yankees, not counting shots."

"How many rounds have you left in your limber-chest, Joe?" I asked.

He turned up the lid of the chest, and replied: "Five."

"And the chest had fifty, hadn't it, when you went into action?"

"Of course."

"Then you fired forty-five, didn't you?"

"Oh, I suppose so, I don't know! Confound these technicalities, anyhow! I'm *fighting*, not counting! Do your own arithmetic!"

It wasn't a very subordinate speech for a sergeant to make to the commander of his section, but Joe was my brother, and I loved him.

At Pocotaligo he fought his gun with superb devotion and effect. But he remained mad all over and clear through till two o'clock that night. At that hour I was able to persuade him that he had been indiscreet in his remarks to the Chief of Artillery.

"Maybe I was," he said, grasping my hand; "but you're not to worry, old fellow; I'll stand the consequences, and you're the best that ever was."

Nevertheless I did worry, knowing that such an offence was punishable without limit in the discretion of a court-martial. It was scarcely sunrise the next morning when I appeared at Captain Elliot's headquarters. I had ridden for half an hour, I suppose, my mind all the time recalling a certain military execution I had seen; but this morning I imagined Joe in the role of the victim. I had not slept, of course, and my nerves were all on edge.

I entered headquarters with a degree of trepidation which I had never felt before.

Captain Elliot was performing his ablutions as well as he could, with a big gourd for basin. He nodded and spoke with his head in the towel.

"Good fight, wasn't it? We have a lot of those fellows to bury this morning. Pretty good bag for three hundred and fifty-one of us, and it was mainly your battery's canister that did it."

I changed feet and said, "Y—e—s."

I thought to myself that that was about the way *I* should take to "let a man down easy" in a hard case.

The captain carefully removed the soap from his ears, then turning to me said: "That's a *fighter*, that brother of yours."

"Yes," I replied; "but, captain, he is very young, very enthusiastic, and very hot-tempered; I hope—I hope you'll overlook—his—er—intemperateness and—"

"THUNDER, MAN, DO YOU SUPPOSE I'VE GOT ANY GRUDGE AGAINST A FELLOW THAT FIGHTS LIKE THAT?" roared the gallant captain.

As I rode back through the woods, it seemed to me about the brightest October morning that I had ever seen, even in that superb Carolina climate.

Around the Camp-Fire

It was a kind of off-night, the 23d of October, 1862 twenty-four hours after the battle of Pocotaligo, on the South Carolina coast.

We had to stop over there until morning, because the creek was out of its banks, and we couldn't get across without daylight. There were only about a dozen of us, and we had to build a camp-fire under the trees.

After supper we fell to talking, and naturally we talked of war things. There wasn't anything else to talk about then.

There was the long-legged mountaineer, with the deep voice, and the drawl in his speech which aided the suggestion that he kept his voice in his boots and had to pump it up when anything was to be said. Opposite him was the alert, rapid-speaking fellow, who had come in as a conscript and had made a superb volunteer,—a fellow who had an opinion ready made on every subject that could be mentioned, and who was accustomed to wind up most conversations with a remark so philosophical as to seem strangely out of keeping with the rest of the inconsequent things that he had said. Then there were the two mountaineers who never said anything because they never had anything to say. They had reached that point of intellectual development where the theory is accepted that there ought to be thought behind every utterance; and under this misapprehension they abstained from utterance.

Joe was there, but Joe wasn't talking that night. Joe was surly and sullen. He had had to kill his horse at Pocotaligo the day before, and all the honors he had harvested from that action had not reconciled him to the loss. The new horse he had drawn was, in his opinion, "a beast." Of course all horses are beasts, but that isn't precisely what Joe meant. Besides, he had received a letter from his sweetheart just before we left camp,—she's his wife now, and the mother of his dozen or more children,—in which that young woman had expressed doubts as to whether, after all, he was precisely the kind of man to whom she ought to "give her life." Joe was only seventeen years of age at that time, and he minded little things like that. Still again, Joe had the toothache. Besides that, we were hungry after our exceedingly scant meal of roasted sweet potatoes. Besides that, it was raining.

All the circumstances contributed to make us introspective and psychological in our conversation.

The long-legged mountaineer with the deep voice was telling some entirely inconsequent story about somebody who wasn't known to any of us, and none of us was listening. After a while he said: "He was that sort of a feller that never felt fear in his life."

From Joe: "There never was any such fellow."

The long mountaineer: "Well, that's what he *said,* anyhow."

From Joe: "He lied, then."

"Well," continued the long-legged mountaineer, "that's what he said, and he sort o' lived up to it. If he had any fear, he didn't show it till that time I was tellin' you about, when he went all to pieces and showed the white feather."

"There," growled Joe, "what did I tell you? He was lying all the time."

The postscript philosopher on the other side of the fire broke in, saying: "Well, maybe his breakfast went bad on him that morning. An overdone egg would make a coward out of the Duke of Wellington."

Joe made the general reflection that "some people locate their courage in their transverse colons."

"What's a transverse colon?" asked one of the mountaineers. Joe got up, stretched himself, and made no answer. Perhaps none was expected.

"Well," asked the long-legged mountaineer, "ain't they people that don't feel no fear?"

The glib little fellow quickly responded: "Let's find out. Let's hold an experience meeting. I suppose we're a pretty fairly representative body, and I move that each fellow tells honestly how he feels when he is going into battle; for instance, when the skirmishers are at work in front, and we know that the next two minutes will bring on the business."

"Infernally bad," growled Joe; "and anybody that pretends to feel otherwise lies."

The postscript philosopher replied: "I never saw *you* show any fear, Joe."

"That's because I'm too big a coward to show it," said Joe.

Even the two reticent mountaineers understood that.

One of them was moved to break the silence. At last he had, if not a thought, yet an emotion to stand sponsor for utterance.

"*I* always feel," said he, "as though the squegees had took hold of my knees. There ain't anything of me for about a minute—exceptin' a spot in the small of my back. I always wish I was a woman or a baby, or dead or something like that. After a while I git holt of myself and I says to myself, 'Bill, you've got to stand up to the rack, fodder or no fodder.' After that it all comes sort of easy like, you know, because the firin' begins, and after the firin' begins you're doin' somethin', you see, and when you're fightin' like, things don't seem so bad. I s'pose you've all *noticed* that."

From Joe: "In all the works on psychology it has been recognized as a universal principle, that the mind when occupied with a superior consideration is able to free itself from considerations of a lesser sort."

The mountaineer looked at him helplessly and said nothing.

The postscript philosopher began: "I shall never forget my first battle. It wasn't much of a battle either, but it was lively while it lasted.

Unfortunately for me it was one of those fights where you have to wait for the enemy to begin. I was tender then. I had just left home, and every time I looked at the little knick-knacks mother and the girls had given me to make camp life comfortable,—for bless my soul they thought we *lived* in camp,—every time I looked at these things I grew teary. There oughtn't to be any bric-à-brac of that kind given to a fellow when he goes into the army. It isn't fit. It worries him."

He was silent for a minute. So were the rest of us. We all had bric-à-brac to remember. He resumed:

"We were lying there in the edge of a piece of woods with a sloping meadow in front, crossed by a stone wall heavily overgrown with vines. At the other edge of the meadow was another strip of woods. The enemy were somewhere in there. We knew they were coming, because the pickets had been driven in, and we stood there waiting for them. The waiting was the worst of it, and as we waited I got to feeling in my pockets and—pulled out a little, ole three-cornered pincushion. Conscience knows I wouldn't have pulled out that pincushion at that particular minute to have won a battle. I've got it now. I never had any use for a pincushion because I never could pin any two things together the way a woman can, but a man can't make his womenkind believe that: I've kept it all through the war, and when I go back home—if it suits the Yankees that I ever go back at all—I'm going to give it as a souvenir to the little sister that made it for me. And I'm going to tell her that it was that pincushion, little three-cornered thing that it is, that made a man out of me that day.

"My first thought as I pulled it out was that I wanted to go home and give the war up; but then came another kind of a thought. I said, 'The little girl wouldn't have given that pin-cushion to me if she hadn't understood that I was going off to fight for the country.' So I said to myself, 'Old boy, you've got to stand your hand pat.' And now whenever we go into battle I always brace myself up a little by feeling in my breeches pocket and sort of shaping out that pincushion."

From Joe: "It's a good story, but the rest of us haven't any pincushions. Besides that, it's raining." I couldn't help observing that Joe drew that afternoon's letter out of his pocket and fumbled it a little, while the long-legged mountaineer was straightening out his limbs and his thoughts for his share in the conversation. He said in basso profundo: "The fact is I'm always so skeered just before a fight that I can't remember afterwards how I did feel. I know only this much, that that last three minutes before the bullets begin to whistle and the shells to howl, takes more out of me than six hours straightaway fightin' afterwards does."

From Joe: "There must be a lot in you at the start, then."

There were still two men unheard from in the experience meeting. Some one of us called upon them for an expression of opinion.

"I dunno. I never thought," said one.

"Nuther did I," said the other.

"Of course you didn't," said Joe.

Then the postscript philosopher, rising and stretching himself, remarked: "I reckon that if any man goes into a fight without being scared, that man is drunk or crazy."

Then we all lay down and went to sleep.

A Family That Had No Luck

There were two instances of supreme heroism in the Civil War. One was upon the one side, the other upon the other.

One was the charge of Pickett's Southerners

at Gettysburg. The other was the heroic series of assaults, made by the Northern troops on Marye's Heights, at Fredericksburg.

General Lee's works in the last-named battle were high up on the hill. Crossing the field in front of them was a sunken road—a perfect breastwork already formed. The main body of the army was in the works above; but a multitude of us were thrown forward into the sunken road.

The enemy knew nothing of this geographical peculiarity. But their first advance revealed the impossibility of breaking Lee's lines at that point. The column that advanced was swept away as with a broom before it got within firing distance of the works it supposed itself to be attacking. The men knew what that meant. Wiser than their general, they saw the necessity of selecting some other point of attack. Nevertheless when their commander persisted, they six times came unflinchingly to an assault which every man of them knew to be hopeless. This may not have been war, but it was heroism.

We who faced them there honored it as such.

Just as we tumbled into the sunken road, an old man came in bearing an Enfield rifle and wearing an old pot hat of the date of 1857 or thereabouts. With a gentle courtesy that was unusual in war, he apologized to the two men between whom he placed himself, saying: "I hope I don't crowd you, but I must find a place somewhere from which I can shoot."

At that moment one of the great assaults occurred. The old man used his gun like an expert. He wasted no bullet. He took aim every time and fired only when he knew his aim to be effective. Yet he fired rapidly. Tom Booker, who stood next to him, said as the advancing

column was swept away: "You must have shot birds on the wing in your time."

The old man answered: "I did up to twenty year ago; but then I sort o' lost my sight, you know, and my interest in shootin'."

"Well, you've got 'em both back again," called out Billy Goodwin from down the line.

"Yes," said the old man. "You see I had to. It's this way: I had six boys and six gells. When the war broke out I thought the six boys could do my family's share o' the fightin'. Well, they did their best, but they didn't have no luck.

"One of 'em was killed at Manassas, two others in a cavalry raid, and the other three fell in different actions—'long the road as you might say. We ain't seemed to had no luck. But it's just come to this, that if the family is to be represented, the old man must git up his shootin' agin, or else one o' the gells would have to take a hand. So here I am."

Just then the third advance was made. A tremendous column of heroic fellows was hurled upon us, only to be swept away as its predecessors had been. Two or three minutes did the work, but at the end of that time the old man fell backward, and Tom Booker caught him in his arms.

"You're shot," he said.

"Yes. The family don't seem to have no luck. If one o' my gells comes to you, you'll give her a fair chance to shoot straight, won't you, boys?"

Youngblood's Last Morning

We were all well used to seeing men shot, but this was different.

It was soft, warm, mellow autumn morning. It was a day suggestive of all gentleness. A purple, Indian-summer haze enveloped the earthworks and the camps. Nature had issued an invitation to peace and repose. The cannon were not at work. Nobody on either side had been tempted to bombard anybody else. Even the mortars and the sharp-shooters were still.

It was not the kind of morning for the bloody work of war.

Yet a young man was to be killed within the hour. He was to be killed deliberately, in cold blood, by sentence of a court-martial, and with great pomp and ceremony; and nobody, even in his heart, could say nay to the justice of the sentence.

For Youngblood had done an infamous thing.

There were many desertions to the enemy about that time. The war was manifestly drawing to a close, and men who lacked self-sacrificing devotion were getting tired of its hardships and privations. In order to stop these desertions, orders had been issued that any soldier arresting another in the act of going to the enemy should have a thirty days' furlough.

Youngblood was on picket one day with another man. He proposed to that other man that they both should desert, and they started together toward the enemy's lines. According to Youngblood's story, it was his purpose to arrest his comrade, and thus earn a furlough at the expense of the other fellow's life. Whether this story was true or not doesn't much matter. The other fellow arrested him.

In any case, he deserved to pay the penalty he did. He was tried, convicted, and sentenced. The sentence was approved by all the authorities, including the war department. This morning it was to be carried out.

It was about ten o'clock, Youngblood's regiment was formed into three sides of a hollow square. Near the entrance to the square, on the right, rested Youngblood's coffin. Beside it was Youngblood's grave.

Presently an ambulance drove up, bearing the prisoner and his attendant guards. As he stepped lightly and lithely from the ambulance, we saw him to be a fine specimen of young manhood. He was twenty-three or twenty-four years of age; tall, well built, and full of elastic vigor. He was handsome, too, and of refined and gentle countenance.

There was no sign of flinching in him: nothing that denoted the coward which his explanation of his crime had shown him to be.

It seemed something more than a pity to put a fellow like that to death.

He took his place in front of the guards and just in the rear of the band, and the dead march began.

He walked alone.

Slowly, and with cadenced step, the procession moved around inside the square. And as it passed me, I was curious to observe the condemned man's behavior. His step was as steady and as firm as that of any man in the guard. I looked at his hands to see if there were any convulsive clutching of the fingers. There was none. I doubt if any man in all that regiment felt so calm in mind or so well poised in nerve as Youngblood looked.

Having completed the seemingly endless march around the three closed sides of the square, the procession turned to the right, and crossed its open end to the point of execution.

There an officer stepped forward and read to Youngblood the findings and sentence of the court which had condemned him, with the formal endorsements approving them and ordering the sentence executed. The guard which had the prisoner in charge divided to the right and left, and Youngblood was left standing alone in front of his coffin, and beside his open grave.

At the word of command he knelt upon the

coffin and folded his arms across his chest. Again at the word of command twelve soldiers stepped out in front of him with guns in their hands. Six of these guns carried ball cartridges, and six were blank. No man in the firing squad was permitted to know whether his gun had a bullet in it or not.

The officer in command spoke scarcely above his breath, but so hushed was the time that his words were audible to the three thousand men there assembled, as he said to each alternate man: "Fire at his head," and to the intervening man: "Fire at his chest." Then turning his back, which was perhaps not an officer-like thing to do, the lieutenant gave in a husky voice the word of command.

"Ready, aim, fire."

There was a sharp crack from twelve rifles fired simultaneously. There was a whirr and whistle of six bullets that had passed through the head or chest of the doomed man, and hurtled off into the fields beyond. Army rifles fire with tremendous force.

The dead man's body rose to its feet and fell limply forward.

Five minutes later all that was left of Youngblood was buried beneath six feet of earth.

There was no merriment in any of the camps that day, or the next, or the next. Even our scant rations were not much relished by those of us who had witnessed this scene.

And yet, as I said at the beginning, we were all well used to seeing men killed.

Griffith's Continued Story

It was early in the summer of 1864. We were in the trenches at Spottsylvania.

It had been raining continuously all day, with now and then a heavy downpour, just to remind us that a little rain ought not to matter to old soldiers. By the use of fragments of fence rail and such other sticks as we could secure to stand upon, we managed to avoid sinking below our ankles into the soft, red, Virginian mud.

It was a little after two o'clock in the morning, but we were all awake and on duty. For it was not General Grant's purpose at that time to allow us much of repose. We had stood in the trenches and in the rain all day, and we must stand in the trenches and in the rain all night, and as much longer as it might please the enemy to keep us there.

The night was one of the blackest I have ever known. There was no possibility of sending couriers anywhere, and all orders had, therefore, to be passed from mouth to mouth up and down the lines.

Every few minutes a great downpour of bucketfuls would come; and, worse still, every now and then the enemy would rush forward in the darkness and come upon us at pistol-shot range without notice.

It was Ulysses S. Grant we were fighting, and that was the line on which he was going to "fight it out, if it took all summer."

We felt the need of entertainment, so somebody called out to a sergeant: "Tell us a story."

"No, no," said Johnny Garrett, "let Griffith tell a story, for he never finishes, and this is a long night."

The suggestion was applauded and insisted upon. Whether Griffith blushed or not, it was much too dark to see; but after a little chaffing he consented to tell the story. Just as he began Billy Goodwin, who always wanted to gamble on everything, offered to bet three to one that he would never finish.

"Shut up, Goodwin," said Johnny Garrett, "and let him begin, anyhow. If he don't get through by the middle of the night, I'll negotiate the bet with you."

Thereupon Griffith began.

"Well, 'taint much of a story—only a bear story."

"Bet two to one he never gets to the bear," said the incorrigible Goodwin.

"Be quiet, will you?" cried some one at the right of the company. The man next to him mistook this adjuration for a command sent down the line; so, to the astonishment of everybody to the left of us, the word was passed from mouth to mouth: "*Be quiet, will you! Be quiet, will you! Be quiet, will you!*"

"Well," said Griffith, " 'twas about six year ago, or maybe seven. No, lemme see—'twas the same year that Jim Coffee married Mirandy Adams. Must have been eight years ago, I s'pose."

Just then came the order down the line: "Perfect silence! Enemy advancing!"

The next minute a line of bayonets broke out of the fog in front of us, and a flaring fire blazed forth in our faces. The charge upon us was a determined one, and for full three minutes it required all our efforts to repel it. After that the artillery silenced all conversation by pouring a shower of shot and shell into the retiring assailants.

"Still ready to make that bet," said Billy Goodwin. But Griffith began again undaunted. He was a phlegmatic person, whose mind was never driven from its not very large purposes by any shock—even that of a shower of canister.

"Well, as I wuz a-sayin', it wuz about six or eight year ago—it don't really matter, I s'pose, how long ago it wuz—"

"No," said Billy Goodwin, "let her rip."

"Well, as I wuz a-sayin'—" Just then the enemy charged again.

Griffith had captured a Henry rifle two days before, in the battle of the Wilderness, and it was loaded with fourteen ball cartridges. With that deliberation which characterized him in everything, he delivered those fourteen shots in the face of the enemy, who by that time had retired. Then he turned and began to fill the magazine of his rifle again, saying: "Well, you see, as I wuz a-sayin', Peter Coffee he taken a cawntract for a bridge over Tye River. Now Peter always pertended that he knew how to lay out bridge work. Of course I knew better. I'd been to Fletcher Massie's school with him, and I knew just how little 'rithmetic he knew. Fletch, he carried me through the rule o' three, and you can't lay out bridge work till you've *bin* through the rule o' three."

The day was dawning, and just then came an order for us to move to the right, the extreme right, four or five miles away. We marched at once. Grant was making his celebrated move by the left flank.

When we got into position, it was necessary to throw up such earthworks as we could with our bayonets, using fence rails for revetments. This occupied us during most of the day, and scattered as we were, we were not able to listen to the remainder of Griffith's story.

That afternoon, to our surprise, we received a ration of three-quarters of a pound of flour to each man. When we had baked it, I happened to go by Tom Booker's position and saw him eating the entire cake. Tom looked at me pitifully as I remonstrated with him for eating three days' rations in advance, and he said with tears in his voice if not in his eyes: "I know it, but I'm go'n' t' fill my stomach once, if I starve for it. I *wish* I was a woman or a baby."

A few minutes later came the order to move; our battery was at that time unhorsed. It had been planned to leave it in the rear, because its guns could not be moved for lack of horses, but with one voice the men had demanded the privilege of taking rifles and going with the battalion as sharp-shooters.

On this march the battalion was the rear guard of the army, and our rifle-armed battery was the rear guard of the battalion.

For fifty-six hours we marched without food or sleep, pausing every fifteen minutes to fight awhile, and then double-quicking to catch up.

There was no chance for Griffith in all this. But when we got to Cold Harbor, and went into the works, Billy Goodwin at a favorable moment insisted that he should resume his story.

"You see I've got three bets on it," said Billy.

Just then a grape-shot passed through George Campbell's foot, and distracted our attention for a time. Then came General Field, who ordered us to burn a barn in front that was full of sharp-shooters. The first two or three shots from the battalion did the business. The sharp-shooters ran with all their might across a thousand yards of space, while we poured upon them the sharpest rifle fire we could deliver. Some of them got to cover, and some of them didn't.

It was not till we moved to Bottom's Bridge that Griffith had a chance to resume his story. There we were all sick from having eaten boiled potato vines, for lack of other food. Being too ill to go to sleep, we demanded a continuation of the story.

"Well, as I wuz a-sayin'," said Griffith, "I'd gone clean through the rule o' three in Fletch Massie's school, and Peter Coffee he knew it. As I told yuh, he'd taken the cawntract to lay out this bridge work; so he got his wife to write to me to come up and do the 'rithmetic. Well, just as I wuz startin' up, Bill Linsey says

to me,—you know he kept a store down there at Arrington, he says to me, says he, 'Griffith, there's a runlet o' cider that's got twenty gallon in it. Can you lif' it?' I says, 'Yes, I can lif' it and drink out o' the bung, if you'll let me drink es much es I please.' I lifted it and took a big swallow of the sweet stuff, then I says, 'I can carry it up the mountain,' says I, and he says, says he, 'On your back?' says he, an' I says, 'Yes, on my back,' says I. An' he says, says he, 'Well, you can have it ef you'll agree to carry it up the mountain on your back, and not to take no lift frum nobody.' "

Just then a battery, three thousand yards away, opened on us, and we had to run to cover, every man of us with his hands on his stomach, in physical memory of the potato vines. Our guns were not in position, and all we could do was to ensconce ourselves behind big trees. As the artillery fire kept up, General Alexander rode to this point of the lines and ordered up three batteries of rifled cannon; by the time they had finished their little controversy with the enemy, we had recovered from the potato tops sufficiently to go to sleep. So Griffith's story was to be "continued in our next."

Our "next" came only after we got to Petersburg. There our battery took charge of the mortars of the enemy. Griffith was one of the men I selected when I asked to volunteer for a particularly perilous mortar service. He might or might not be able to tell a story, but he could stand fire as well as any man I ever knew.

About four o'clock one morning, when we had been engaged in a fierce bombardment all night, the fire ceased for a time, and Billy Goodwin demanded the rest of that bear story.

"You see I've got seven bets on that story," said Billy, "and I don't want to take any man's money unfairly. One bet is that he won't ever get to the bear, and I don't want to take any man's money without givin' him a chance."

"Well, wait a minute," I replied, "till I start up the fire; we've got to have some breakfast."

The fire was out.

"Somebody must go up," I said, "to the next fort and get a chunk of fire. It won't do to get fire by shooting a mortar,"—which was our usual way,—"because if we do that, we'll start this bombardment again."

"I'll go," said Griffith, "and then I'll tell the rest of that story."

There was a fearful hail of bullets between the two forts. The cannon were silent, but the musketry fire was incessant. Griffith started off, crouching as he went up the path so as to expose as little as possible of his person.

That was the last I ever saw of him.

As he was borne off on the litter, he sent word to me that he "hoped I hadn't any bets on that bear story."

Si Tucker—Coward and Hero

I was in command of Fort Lamkin, a mortar fort, in rear of General Bushrod Johnson's lines at Petersburg in 1864.

The fort was named for our immediate commander, from whose command we had been detached for this service.

One day Lamkin himself came to me when I was at his headquarters. He was obviously in trouble.

"This boy, Si Tucker," he said, "is the son of one of the best friends I ever had in the world. The boy is a coward. He literally *lives* in a rat hole. I have repeatedly pulled him out by the legs, only to have him crawl back again the moment I let go of his ankles. I don't know what to do. It's my duty, of course, to prefer charges of cowardice against him; and if I do,

he will certainly be shot—and his father is my best friend."

He paused meditatively, and then said with eagerness in his voice: "Why can't you take him?"

I agreed at once. I told him I would take the boy with me to my pits, and make "either a soldier or a stiff" out of him within the next twenty-four hours. I was under no obligations to his father; I had never even met any of his relatives, and I had seen too many years of service to have much patience with cowardice.

The boy was sent for and ordered to go with me. We walked down towards Blandford church. At the proper point we turned out of the Jerusalem plank road across the fields towards Fort Lamkin. Half-way there and on the top of a little hill, which was especially exposed to the gaze of the sharp-shooters, I made Si Tucker sit down by my side. There we came to an understanding.

I told him that he had been assigned to me to be shot out of hand, or to be court-martialled for cowardice, which at that particular juncture of the war meant very much the same thing. I explained to him that he was about to join a detachment, composed exclusively of men specially selected for their courage—every one of them a volunteer for what was deemed a peculiarly dangerous service.

I explained further that I should require him to do his duty as they did theirs.

"You have managed to make for yourself," I said, "the reputation of a coward. You have now one last chance to redeem yourself. You must do that, or you must die."

The sharp-shooters were, in the meantime, picking at us most uncomfortably as we sat there. My experience as an old soldier strongly suggested to me that we ought to move. The position was of that kind that military men call untenable. Nevertheless, I thought it best to keep Si Tucker there a minute longer, for purposes of observation, if nothing else.

"At our pits," I said, "we have one uniform rule of procedure. When a bombardment begins, the men go to their guns. I take my stand on top of the magazine mound to watch the enemy's fire and direct our own. If I see that a mortar shell is about to fall into one of the gun pits, I call out the pit number, and the men run into the bomb-proof until the explosion is over. No man ever goes into a bomb-proof till this order is given. You must do as the rest do. If you run to a bomb-proof before I have given the order, it will be my imperative duty to shoot you then and there; and I shall certainly discharge that duty. Do you fully understand that, Si?"

He thought he did, and as the sharp-shooters were by this time becoming pestilently personal in their attentions, we resumed our walk.

Half an hour after our arrival at Fort Lamkin, a bombardment began.

I didn't want to shoot that boy. I distinctly preferred to make a soldier rather than a "stiff" out of him. So, instead of taking my customary stand on the mound of earth over the magazine, I ordered Joe to that post, and placed myself in the gun pit to which Si Tucker had been assigned, taking care to stand between him and the mouth of the bomb-proof. I spoke to him as I passed.

"Remember what I told you. If you forget, it is instant death."

He remembered. For nearly two hours he stood there quaking and quivering, but not daring to seek safety by retreat to a bomb-proof.

By the time that the outburst was over, Si Tucker had learned his first lesson in war. He had learned to realize that a man may endure a lot of very savage fire, and yet come out of it alive.

A few hours later, when the guns were at work again, Si was steady enough in his nerves to carry shells to the guns. The next day he was even able during a bombardment to cut fuses —a delicate operation requiring a steady hand.

Within two or three days he had become as good a soldier as we had in all that band of men specially picked for their unflinching courage.

When the great mine explosion occurred a few weeks later, I had occasion to rebuke Si Tucker for a fault quite unrelated to cowardice. We had been ordered to go with our mortars as near as possible to the crater, and to drop a continual rain of shells among the thousands of helpless fellows in that awful pit.

It was cruel, ghastly work. But it was war. And a poet has justly characterized war as a "brain-spattering, windpipe-slitting art." Or as General Sherman once said,—and he knew, —"War is all hell."

We were within sixty yards of the crater. Each one of our mortars was belching from three to five shells a minute into that hole; but Si Tucker's enthusiasm was not satisfied. Having no personal duty to do at the moment, he began plugging shells with long fuses, lighting them, running with them to the margin of the pit, and tossing them in as hand grenades. He was greeted by a tremendous volley of musketry at each repetition of this performance, but he did it three times before we could stop him.

That evening, near the gloaming, he did another thing. The lines had by that time been restored. The men in the crater—those of them who had not been killed—had been driven back to the Federal side. We became aware of the fact that a poor fellow of our own was lying grievously wounded near the Federal side of the fifty yards that separated our works from the enemy's. He had been lying there through all that long, fierce summer day. The explosion at daylight had cast him there.

His groans and his cries for help and for water were piteous in the extreme. We listened to them heartbroken but helpless—all but Si Tucker.

Si began stripping off his clothes; we thought he had gone mad. But when we asked him why he was stripping himself, he replied: "Never you mind."

With that, stripped to the skin, he leaped over the works, ducked his head low, and ran through that hailstorm of bullets to where the wounded man lay. Grasping him quickly, he slung him upon his back like a bag of meal, and ran back with all his might.

As he crossed the works he fell headlong.

The surgeon found three bullets in his body.

Nobody in the battery ever remembered after that, that Si Tucker had once been a coward.

After all, it is perhaps mainly a question of nerves.

2

The Bitterness of Battle

from The Captain of Company K

"I BEGAN TOO LATE." WITH THIS SIMPLE STATEMENT, JOSEPH KIRKLAND (1830–1894) EX-plained the small quantity of his writings. One of the pioneers of middle-western realism, Kirkland published his best novel—which had the quaint title of *Zury: The Meanest Man in Spring County* —when he was fifty-seven. This novel by a man who spent his life in law and business in central Illinois is largely concerned with the wretched toil and misery of the destitute early western settlers.

Kirkland enlisted as a private in the Twelfth Illinois Infantry in 1861 and after three months was elected 2nd Lieutenant of Company C. As an aide-de-camp to General McClellan, Kirkland went through the West Virginia campaign, and as a captain in the Army of the Potomac he took part in the attack on Richmond and the Battle of Williamsburg. Kirkland then became a major on the staff of General Fitz-John Porter, serving through the battles at Hanover Courthouse, Mechanicsville, Gaines' Mill, Malvern Hill, and Antietam. He was on the staff of Porter's suc-cessor, General Buttlefield, long enough to have a horse killed under him at Fredericksburg. When General Porter retired in 1863, Kirkland resigned his commission.

In 1891 Kirkland wrote a novel based on his war observations. *The Captain of Company K,* which won a Detroit *Free Press* literary competition and was serialized in that newspaper, is an uneven performance. The plot of the novel is a genteel romance, superficial and trite. The combat passages are stark and naturalistic.

Kirkland brings out the horror that catches a body of men suddenly faced with the reality of bullets that maim and kill, destroying the glorious image of war carried into battle by simple farm boys. The novel is full of realistic touches, and it provides many solid descriptions of infantry engagements. Kirkland is appalled by a war that erases men's individuality and makes them "food for powder, the mere sport of fate." The book attacks many wretched aspects of war—false news-paper reports, cowardly and inept volunteer officers, public indifference to veterans. Kirkland dedicated his novel to "the surviving men of the firing line, the men who could see the enemy in front of them with the naked eye while they would have needed a field-glass to see the history-makers behind them."

One of the most interesting aspects of *The Captain of Company K* is the way it anticipates the theme and even the main plot device of Stephen Crane's *The Red Badge of Courage*, published four years later. Both novels portray heroes who gain maturity and self-reliance in the crucible of war. The two heroes suffer abstract doubt as to their courage, acute fear immediately before the baptism of fire, unnoticed cowardice in action. They finally achieve the veteran's virtues of confidence and strength. Both William Fargeon and Henry Fleming receive accidental wounds that save them from the accusation of cowardice and confer the appearance of heroism.

Of course, *The Captain of Company K* cannot compare with Crane's novel in symbolism, control of language, and structure. Kirkland's book has one great virtue; the book is an honest attempt to reproduce some of the intense emotions, suffering, and unreason that were part of a terrible conflict. A fine picture of General Grant, the action around Fort Donelson, and the combat of Bloody Shiloh appear in the following excerpts from *The Captain of Company K.*

"MAC, WHY DO YOU KEEP YOUR TENT ALL shut up these hot nights?"

"Well, Captain, because I prefer it, on the whole, to the hospital tent up at Mount City, or the grave-yard close by it."

"Why, isn't fresh air wholesome?"

"Worst thing a man can have."

"The beasts of the field and the fowls of the air take their air raw."

"So they do their rations, but we can't. We need to have 'em cooked, both food and air."

"The boys seem to take theirs raw for choice. Every tent-wall is rolled up to the pole. When I go the grand rounds I think I am making a field-survey of so many acres of naked flesh. Why don't they all die?"

"Well, sir, a good many of them do. And some that don't die have the ague." [This was a sly hit that told.] "And then, perhaps it's true that the mosquito-bites cure malaria—or perhaps there's so much flesh that there isn't enough malaria to go round."

"Fresh air and exercise—a cold bath and a brisk run before breakfast—that's what I was brought up to think we all needed in our business."

"Ya-as," drawled the lieutenant. "Maybe—

in the range of Chicago and Boston, not Richmond and Cairo. In this infernal river-bottom you want to lie still, and breathe through a sponge."

"What's a good fighting weight, Mac?"

"All the flesh I can get and all I can keep."

"Well, some of our brother officers don't look at things your way. Capt'n. Chafferty thinks Company C's men are soft and overweight—thinks 175 pounds is right for a six-footer, and so on down—and he's going to try to train them down to his scale. Colonel Puller agrees with his theory and approves his proposed experiment."

"I know all about that business, Capt'n. Fargeon. A good deal more than you do, I guess."

"What do you know?"

"Chaff is going to have trouble with his men."

"Where and when?"

"Right here in camp, to-morrow."

"To-morrow? Why, good heavens! I'm officer of the day to-morrow."

"Then he'll shoulder off his trouble on you."

"What's he going to do?"

"Order out his company with arms and ac-

coutrements, overcoats, knapsacks and blankets, for a two-mile stretch on the levee at
double-quick; then a halt on the river bank, so
they can go in swimming."

"What will the boys do?"

"As much as they have a mind to, and no
more."

"Company C are good men, Mac."

"Yes; country farmers and farmers' boys
most of them."

"Maybe they'll obey orders, live or die," said
Fargeon, with a gleam of hope.

"But they won't," coolly answered the lieutenant.

"Then what?"

"Then Chaff will call on you, and you'll call
out the guard to disarm the mutineers."

"Guard? Company C is as big as the guard,
and armed the same."

"All right; you can call out the rest of the
regiment, or any part of it. Call out your own
Company K, if you like, with me at the head
of it."

"Will you have our boys load with blank
cartridges?"

"Not a bit of it."

"Won't you even have them fire high if they
have to fire?"

"I'll fire ball cartridges right at their belt-
buckles."

"Mac! what do you mean, when, after all,
the poor boys are in the right of it!"

"I mean business. To-morrow is very likely
a test day—a deciding point for the whole future of the Sixth Illinois. If any man refuses to
lay down his arms when ordered, and succeeds
in his disobedience, then good-bye Sixth."

Will groaned aloud.

"Great Scott! I wish heaven would kindly
remove Chafferty to some brighter sphere, or
that somebody else had the job of backing up

his foolishness with powder and ball—anybody except me!"

"Why, Captain, this is the best luck you
could have! A serious crisis—an armed mutiny
to be put down, by tact or by force, and you
outranking for the day every officer in the
field; commanding the brigade and every man
in it. Why, it's better than a battle for you!"

"All the same, I wish you had it to do instead
of me!"

"It's all right as it is. Less likelihood of
bloodshed than if I had all the responsibility.
You've got the tact which I haven't got. You'll
use it to-morrow, and I'll stand close by you
with the force—you'll wear the glove of velvet, knowing that the hand of iron is right
under it."

"Mac, you're a trump!"

"Captain, you're the joker!"

A sleepless night is much the same everywhere. A monarch tossing on a bed of down
—a fever-stricken patient facing the phantoms
of delirium—a mother longing for her sick
child's final release from pain—a condemned
wretch trying to forget the waiting gallows—
a sentinel on post, in darkness, cold, and wet,
and in deadly peril from unseen foes—a Chi-
nese prisoner sentenced to die of wakefulness
—what is there to choose between them?

These are some of the thoughts that hovered
about the pillow (so-called; in reality a pair of
blanket-wrapped boots) of the captain of
Company K, in the weary hours preceding the
day wherein he expected to have the bitter,
bloody task of subduing, by musketry, a mutiny in his own regiment—to shoot down
good fellows, brothers in arms, who thought
themselves in the right, and whom he considered to be more sinned against than sinning!

He heard, in succession, all the guard reliefs in that long night. Indeed, the only knowledge he had of sleeping at all came from the fact that he had to be wakened to make himself ready for the task. Sadly he donned his uniform, bringing his sash not round his waist as usual, but over his shoulder, to indicate his temporary rank and responsibility—detestable distinction!

Grim was his effort at cool indifference as he joined the mess at breakfast. He could not even command a natural smile when Mark laid beside his plate an oddly-shaped and corded express package bearing his name; nor did he respond in the proper spirit to the curiosity-inspired hints of the others.

"Don't hold back from opening your bale of goods on our account, captain."

"No, captain; we'll excuse you! And, if you're short of time, I'll eat for you while you unpack the parcel."

"Thank you, gentlemen; but (examining the string) it seems to be tied in a remarkably hard knot."

"Now, captain, I am a great hand at untying knots."

Fargeon shook his head.

"The fact is, Morphy," said McClintock, "I guess the captain sees an entanglement in that string that nobody except him can straighten out."

Then the captain changed the subject and began to talk about the trouble in Company C, which they discussed long and seriously, the captain and the first lieutenant taking divergent views, and Mac being much more severe on the men than Will thought just.

Fargeon was dreadfully startled when, after a pause, Mac rose and said with a very grave look:

"I have finally decided on the step I ought to take, and take at once. Orderly, go to my tent and fetch my sword."

"What is it, Mac?"

Mac shook his head in silence, and when Mark brought the sword he drew it from its scabbard and sternly presented the hilt toward his captain.

"What's the matter, Mac? You resign? I decline to accept your resignation! Put up your sword until we talk it over."

"Capt'n. Fargeon, I tender you my sword, and respectfully but firmly insist on your accepting it."

"And I as firmly decline! I would rather leave the service myself! The company—the army can *not* spare *you!*"

The lieutenant stood like a statue, the sword still extended.

"Come, come, Mac! this is not like you! You are not going to desert me in this pinch! What did you promise me yesterday? And how can I maintain good order and military discipline if my own officers won't stand by me?"

No answer. Morphy laid his hand anxiously on Mac's arm, but the latter shook him off.

"Besides, Mac," added Fargeon, "I still hope that with a proper display of force we can bring Company C to reason without bloodshed."

Here a twitching that had been noticeable in Mac's face broke into a full-fledged laugh.

"Resign nobody! Bloodshed nothing! I only meant for you to use the sword to cut the strings of that infernal machine!"

When the laughter had died away Fargeon said:

"I'll forgive you, Mac, if you promise me one thing; that is, that next time you attack me with your sword you come on with it point-foremost. It wouldn't scare me half as much."

Before they had done breakfast there was a loud call for the officer of the day; and Fargeon, merely stopping to toss the package on to the cot in his tent, hurried off to hold a consultation with the colonel and the captain (Chafferty) of Company C regarding the threatened trouble. It was decided not to interfere until there should be an overt act of disobedience—in that case to disarm the mutineers with such force as might be needed (Company K to be called upon if needed)—then to punish them by an extra turn of "police duty," if no more severe measures should be called for. ("Police duty": means the servile tasks of ditching, draining, and cleaning camp.)

After morning parade, Capt'n. Chafferty (instead of the usual drill) had his men don their overcoats, knapsacks, and blankets, and start out for a "training-down", run all according to programme. They obeyed his orders in sullen silence; made the double-quick march along the levee, the sun pouring down volumes of heat on their heads, and the dust rising in a sand-storm from their feet. They threw themselves down on the river bank, declining, to a man, the proffered plunge. Then they marched home to dinner.

Fargeon, through his glass, watched with compassion the moving cloud that marked their run; but he was immensely relieved by their apparent submission. He arrived at mess late for dinner, in high spirits. There he observed, with a laugh, that some one had taken the trouble to bring the mysterious package from his tent and put it beside his plate.

"All our troubles being now over, gentlemen, we will proceed to refresh the inner man, and then—"

He picked up the package with a meaning smile and replaced it in easy reach.

Yet the dinner was far from gay; for Mac ate in grim silence that seemed to say, "Over, are they? Wait and see." He evidently had heard something that lay heavily on his mind. And, to be sure, before they left the table a written message was brought to Fargeon, which he read, first to himself, then aloud:

"Capt'n. Chafferty requests the immediate presence on the parade-ground of the regimental guard to enforce discipline in his command."

Fargeon hurried off. Mac put on his sword and directed Morphy to do likewise, and then gave his orders:

"Fall in, Company K! Fall in, men; fall in!"

The men obeyed, and were marched to their usual place on the color-line. There, in full view of Company C and of the relief-guard, they, at the word of command, deliberately loaded their muskets with ball-cartridge.

Mac scanned his men narrowly as they charged their pieces. His own face was almost unchanged as he gave the successive orders; perhaps showing a slight flush which his men, in after times, learned to recognize as a battle-glow, while his speech took on a slow, cool, half-persuasive deliberateness—a "battle drawl." [We shall all know it well a few pages further on.]

"Handle—cartridge! Tear—cartridge!"

Here he paused and walked along the front of the line, to see that no man bit off the *wrong end* of his cartridge, as reluctant members of firing parties (details for military executions, for instance) have been known to do, removing the bullet, spitting it out, and loading only the powder and wadding.

The men showed various sentiments in their faces. Clinton Thrush was crying quietly—Mac knew he could rely on him. Mark was unmoved and business-like—he, too, could be trusted. Jeff Cobb, George Friend, and Tolliver, the marksman, looked pale and troubled—they probably had not made up their minds. Caleb Dugong was boastful and ferocious—he would fail at the pinch. Well, the lieutenant could calculate on from twelve to twenty shots, and more if the resistance was flagrant, violent, and dangerous, including an appeal by the mutineers to muskets and bayonets.

Here is what had occurred in Chafferty's command. The men, tired as they were, had been mustered after dinner and marched out for a continuance of their "training-down." No sooner were they in column, and the officers giving the marching-time with the usual "Left! Left! Left!" than the men took up the cry with a stentorian "Rest! Rest! Rest! Rest!" that could be heard all over the camp. In vain did the officers command, "Silence in the ranks!" When they were halted they were silent; when they marched they shouted. After Chafferty had tried speech-making, persuasion, and threats, all fruitless, to preserve silence whenever the men were started marching again, he sent off for aid to the officer of the day, as we have already seen.

Fargeon joined him in front of the recalcitrant line of men, standing with arms at shoulder, and the two engaged in a whispered conversation which Fargeon purposely prolonged until he saw Company K take its place and load muskets. Then he and Chafferty turned to Company C, and in a voice loud enough for the men to hear, Fargeon said:

"Capt'n. Chafferty, what lawful order have your men refused to obey?"

"Among others, an order to ground arms."

"Captain, you will please repeat the order in my hearing."

Forward March

"Ground arms!"

Not a man stirred.

Fargeon felt the blood leave his face and surge toward his heart till it seemed full to bursting. He turned slowly toward Company K, and, with a mixture of alarm and relief, saw Mac come running toward him. Was he coming to say that K would not use force against their fellow-soldiers? He walked forward to meet his lieutenant.

"Well, Mac!"

"Why, Captain, don't you see the dam' fool has given an order that cannot be obeyed? Men do not ground arms from shoulder arms! The first command should be to order arms—then ground arms! The men are right in standing still!"

"True enough, Mac! I'll tell Chafferty," and he was starting back when Mac recalled him.

"No, no, Captain! Don't let him try them any more—just tell him you will take the command of his company. You have the right."

Fargeon took the advice.

"Capt. Chafferty, with your permission I will take command of your company."

Both men bowed ceremoniously. Chafferty sheathed his sword, while Fargeon drew his and brought it to his shoulder.

"Attention — Company! ORDER — ARMS!"

Without a moment's hesitation, in admirable time the order was obeyed, each and all the musket-butts striking the earth together.

"GROUND—ARMS!"

Every man stooped forward, advancing and bending the left knee in proper form, laid down his piece, bayonet to the front; and recovered his upright position empty-handed.

"By fours, right FACE! Forward, file right —MARCH!"

He placed himself at their head and conducted them to the quartermaster's tents. There he called for picks and shovels, and ordered every odd-numbered man to take a pick and every even-numbered man a shovel—always looking for the first act of disobedience. Not one showed itself, nor even an instant's hesitation. Next he marched them to the sinks, and set them at the disagreeable job of filling up one and making another.

They went to work with alacrity, even zeal!

Fargeon walked up and down behind these strange "mutineers," pondering much, and feeling his heart warm toward them with every blow they struck and every shovelful they threw. At last he halted, leaning on his sword, near one who was working somewhat apart. The fellow looked up pleasantly, and Fargeon met his look with a slight smile. This was evidently enough to encourage the volunteer to relieve his mind. Never halting in his work, he spoke (the dashes represent shovelfuls of earth thrown out):

"Say, Cap,—do we fellers—look like we was—mutineers?"

"You don't work like it, anyhow."

"No, sir-ree!—Nor we ain't!—There ain't no order—no lawful order—for anythin' that needs to be done—that we don't stand—ready an' willin' to do it!—No, sir-ree!—We come out to fight—an' to drill—an' to dig—an' we'll do it—till hell freezes over!—Yes, sirree!—till the cows come home!—Yew jest try us!" Here he paused for some sign of assent or dissent—which Fargeon dared not trust himself to give. The soldier, however, took encouragement (or obstinancy) from silence, and continued:

"Wha' d' yew s'pose—an' wha' dooz anybody s'pose—we came aout fer?—Fer thirteen dollars a month?—Not by a jug-full!—not by a dam' sight!—Leave aour homes—an' aour farms—an' aour folks—fer boys' wages an' poor-house feed!— **** No! We come t'obey orders—proper orders—live er die—

an' git back home—if we're lucky enough— jest as quick as Goddlemity'll let us—"

Another pause; Fargeon looking far away and winking and blinking rapidly to keep a troublesome moisture out of his eyes. His interlocutor perhaps saw the expression, for his next words were:

"Ye see, Cap,—it ain't every company— has got officers—like Company K has.—Them a tryin'—t' make us—ground arms—from shoulder! Chaff means well—so do the lootenants—an' we're willin' to mind 'em—fer the good o' the service.—But they ain't no call— t' try no dam'—fool notions on us—reg'latin' haow much—flesh we're to carry—on aour own legs!—Aour flesh an' blood—b'longs tew us—till it gits shot away.—When they try t' prescribe—aour fightin' weight—they've bit off more'n they kin chaw—they've cut daown—more'n they kin cock up—afore rain. No sir-ree!—Not fer all the wuthless Chaff— that ever was blowed aout—of all the fannin'-mills in Ellenoy!"

Fargeon turned away and walked the length of the working line, and then back again, saying:

"There, men! Throw out what you've got loose, and square up the sides and bottom." When this was done:

"Fall in, Company K—Company C, I mean." He placed himself on their right, giving the alignment with his sword.

"Right—dress! Front! By fours, right— face! Forward—march!"

He took them to the place for leaving the tools; then to the field where they had laid down their arms; had them resume them, marched them to their place on the color-line; sent for the captain, and prepared to turn over the command to him. As he did so he heard from somewhere in the line:

"Three cheers for—"

"Silence in the ranks!" he shouted; and he was obeyed.

After transferring the command he went to regimental headquarters, and with a very little argument got an order published and posted limiting the hours of drill, and the loads to be placed on the men in drilling, parading, and guard-mounting. The "field and staff" were very glad to get out of their dilemma so easily.

"Mac, would our boys have fired on Company C to kill?"

"They wouldn't have had to, Captain. If the worst came to the worst, all I should have done would be to have K cover them with their muskets while the guard went up and disarmed them. If they'd resisted the guard—why, then, of course—"

"Then would our boys have aimed at their brothers in arms?"

"Some would and some wouldn't. I should have seen that all pieces were properly leveled, but some muzzles would have been dropped when the triggers were pulled. Mark Looney would shoot to kill, because I told him to. Chipstone, Cobb, Tolliver, George Friend, the two Thrushes, and a lot of others would do the same, because they see the necessity of discipline at any cost."

"Well, it's all over now, thank God! And we have nothing to reproach ourselves with. Thanks to you, we did just the right thing at the right time."

"Yes; but Colonel Y. R. Puller has half spoiled our work by a foolish speech he is making to everybody, saying that the boys ought to come straight to him when they have anything to complain of! I always knew he was a

regular *politician*." [What contempt he threw into that last word!]

"But the boys must have some appeal from wrong orders."

"Yes; but it ought to go up through regular channels, as the phrase is; 'Respectfully forwarded, approved' (or 'disapproved,' as the case may be) by company, regimental, brigade, and division officers, clear up to the President himself, if either party desire it."

How delightful were all the duties of the rest of the day! Fargeon's heart was so light he could have sung aloud at every step; and even the steps themselves seemed to be on buoyant air. "Blessed are the peacemakers" rang through his heart unceasingly. Every face he saw was that of a friend and brother. The sun was softly bright, the leaves green, the breeze sweet—in fact, life was very much as it had been while Sara was there to glorify the world with her presence. By the way, there was her present still to be unfolded.

At the mess supper no one had any reason to be sad or glum, and the rebound of spirits made the occasion one of great hilarity. Before long Mac called Fargeon's attention to the express package, which had been again brought out and placed by his plate.

"Ah, yes, Mac; I thank you for reminding me of it—I might never have thought of it again!" And he took it up, scanned it once more with laboriously assumed indifference, and laid it down again.

Morphy ventured a remark:

"It's just the right shape and size for a fine revolver."

"Yes," put in Mac, "but it hasn't the weight."

"We're having the wait," said Morphy.

"I'll tell you what strikes me; it's an infernal

machine, sent down by some rebel sympathizer with murderous intent."

"Yes, Mac; the intent to free the enemy from the three most valuable officers on our side; the three they're most afraid of—the captain, you, and me!"

"Well, we're ready to die. Captain, is there anything we can do to help you solve the mystery?"

"Now, gentlemen, don't you think it would be better that only one of us should perish? Just consider the interests of the Union cause! I ought really to return to my tent and open this alone."

"No!" said Mac stoutly. "Never shall it be said that I owed my promotion to the heroic self-sacrifice of my captain!"

"As for me," said Morphy, "the moment I heard the explosion in your tent I'd blow my brains out! Jine the brass band, I mane, and blow 'em out through me bazoo. But I'll tell you how we can rejuce the risk to a minimum; we'll all crouch down so that only our heads stick up over the edge of the table." [He suited the action to the word.]

"Or, still better," suggested Fargeon, "put our heads down below and let nothing but our feet stick up."

"Oh, come!" cried Mac, "let us say our prayers and die together. Die first and say our prayers afterwards."

"Well, if I had a sword I should certainly proceed at once to cut the Gordian knot."

Instantly both lieutenants sprang for their swords, each striving to get his blade into Will's hand before the other. Both arrived together, and Will took both, carefully tried the edge of each, and asked:

"Are you ready, gentlemen?"

"All ready?" cried the impatient youths.

"Well, then, here goes!" He cut the string

in one place with one, and waited for the explosion; next in another place with the other, and so on alternately until there was not a bit of it left entire. Still no catastrophe. Then with a bow and a smile he returned each sword to its owner, and turning to Mark Looney, handed him the package, and said:

"Be good enough to put that in my tent and not bring it out again until I tell you to. Now, gentlemen, what was it we were talking of before you were so kind as to bring me your swords?"

The laugh was certainly against the lieutenants now—but not for long.

While they were enjoying their first pipes after supper, chaffing each other on the manner in which the captain had turned the laugh on them, lo! the captain himself, puffing away at a handsome meerschaum and pretending to enjoy it. He would put the stem between his lips, fill his mouth with the smoke, remove the pipe, blow out the smoke as quickly as possible, and then repeat the operation—to the great amusement of all beholders. Even the imperturbable Mark was red with suppressed laughter—redder than usual.

"Bravo, Captain!" said Mac. "You take to it like a veteran—just as I did at nine years old. Morphy, how do you think our captain looks with a pipe in his mouth?"

"Well, Mac, if you ask me as a friend, I must say I think he looks like an angel."

"I'm afraid, boys, it's only the fallen angels who smoke—and don't need any pipes even then. No! come to think, there *is* something said in Holy Writ about praising with pipe and tabor."

"Of course! and tabor is Hebrew for tobacker! Might have known it!" [Great laughter.]

"Well, now," said Mac, "if any woman—

any white woman under fifty—were to send me a pipe like that, I'd go and get my leg shot off so I could get discharged, go home and marry her, and live on my pension—twenty dollars a month."

"So would I, Mac," said Barney; "or even if she sent me a needle-case."

Fargeon now sat down with a rather listless air and handed over the pipe to be admired and criticised.

"By the way, Mac, what is it a sign of when you don't know—nor care much—whether you are holding your head up straight or letting it wobble around?"

"Poison, captain! Deadly poison!"

"Humph! And is it generally fatal?"

"Always! A single drop of pure nicotine on the tongue of an elephant kills him in eighteen minutes."

"And on a man—is it slow or quick? How long have I to live?"

"Middling quick. Not one man in ten—feeling the way you look now—not one man in ten lives to be over ninety."

"*Ninety!*" groaned Will.

"But, Captain," cried Morphy, "you don't seem to be very jubilant over the joke you played on us a while ago. Who's ahead now in that affair?"

"Gentlemen," replied Fargeon, with all the sad, weak, bilious bitterness of seasickness, "you are avenged! I am thinking how dreadfully long it will be before I am ninety, and, incidentally, how much it could probably cost me to hire somebody else to smoke that pipe for all those fifty odd years." And he looked with loathing at his beautiful meerschaum.

The nausea wore off, but a nervous, headachy feeling remained, which he felt must be walked away before sleep could be hoped for;

so he wandered through the lightened darkness and busy idleness of evening in a camp of volunteers.

Every tent was wide open, and all were filled with groups of half-dressed men, variously engaged, clustering around candles held in the necks of bottles or in the sockets of bayonets sticking in the ground.

Single men were reading, or writing, or washing and mending clothes. Here was one serving another his hair-cutter; there a little party talking war and politics. Sociable groups were playing cards or draughts and looking on at the games.

Will lingered longest at the tent where Clinton Thrush—he of the fine pale face and natural musical voice—and his brother Aleck were singing (and teaching others to sing) a new patriotic song which Clinton had adapted from an old revival hymn:

> Our God descended from on high
> As blind and heedless we did lie.
> He looked on us with pitying eye,
> And, said, to us as He passed by
> Rise up and save the Union.
>
> I wonder why all saints don't sing
> And praise the Lord up on the wing
> And make the Heavenly Arches ring,
> With loud Hosannas to our King
> Who still preserves our Union.

Will joined in the singing, and many followed his example, so that the fine marching tune could have been heard far, far out over the great rolling river. Then he left them and strayed on and out, passed the line of sentries, climbed the high Mississippi levee and descended its western slope to the very water's edge, stooping and dipping his fingers in to feel the water passing from right to left in its flow to the southward. The stream was so broad that he could only tell it had a farther shore by the slight irregularities in the forest top outlined against the starry sky.

"Reveille" (pronounced *revelee*) is a wild, romantic bugle sound, thrilling to the young soldier. In a large camp the bugler at general headquarters wakes the echoes at some appointed hour in the early dawn or before; and the buglers at other headquarters, division, brigade, and regimental, take it up in succession; each repeating the familiar notes in his own especial key. He wakes the echoes; and he wakes thousands of tired sleepers, unwilling to bid farewell to their short repose.

No use to rebel, no use to protest, no use even to grumble. Good-bye, needful rest; good-bye, forgetfulness of toil, pain, and danger; good-bye, dear dreams of home. Good morrow to hardship. The day has begun—for trying labor; for certain danger; for death to those whom the unseen, unheard messenger of fate has selected during the darkness.

Fargeon failed, for once, to hear reveille and attend morning roll-call, and (by Mac's orders) was allowed to sleep late. His agitating experience as officer of the day, queller of mutiny, apprentice to tobacco-smoking, midnight prowler and scribbler on the banks of the great river, made his morning nap a very welcome luxury, and he was only aroused by wild, wandering cheers, starting, dying away and breaking out afresh all over the camp.

Will sprang from his cot and began his toilet. Mac poked his head through the tent flap, and Will lifted his glowing face from the tin toilet pail and let the water drip, drip, drip from hair, eyebrows, nose, and beard, on the towel spread across his hands, while Mac asked in bantering tones:

"Dressing for the theater, Capt'n. Fargeon?"

"Well, Mac, not that I know of."

"You'd better; you've got to go."

"What do you mean? What theater?"

"Theater of war. The J. R. Graham takes the Sixth, the Aspasia takes the Twelfth, the Memphis takes the Thirty-ninth, and the Ruby takes the battery and the wagon train—all goes, bag and baggage, and three days' cooked rations."

The spread towel continued to catch the drops until there were no more to catch; and then Will buried his face in it, hoping that no perceptible pallor had intervened, and resolute that none should remain when he had done rubbing.

So death was at hand at last!

"Get there? Get where?"

"Nobody knows; but it can't be to the rear. It doesn't need steamboats to carry us there, being there already."

"When do we start?"

"Draw the rations now; cook and distribute 'em as soon as possible; dinner at noon and strike tents by bugle call at one. We ought to steam away by two."

"To the front?"

"Of course. I see two of the gun-boats are getting up steam to go along."

The thought of the gun-boats was comforting. Their huge cannon carry so far!

I can't wake 'em up, I can't wake 'em up,
I can't wake 'em up in the morning; I
can't wake 'em up, I can't wake 'em up,
I can't wake 'em up at all.
Corp'ral's worse than th' private,
Sergeant's worse than th' Corp'ral
L'tenant's worse than th' Sergeant,
and the Captain's worst of all.

The Skirmish

There was rivalry between regiments, and even companies, in the matter of striking camp. The tentpegs were all loosened, and, at the bugle call, the great canvas town sank into nothingness like the baseless fabric of a vision. In twenty-eight seconds by the watch, Company K's men straightened up and looked about them—then burst into a cheer of exultation, for every one of its tents was down and tied fast in its ropes, while no other company in the brigade was within several seconds of the goal.

The baseless fabric of a vision, when it dissolved, left a multitudinous wrack behind, the comfortable paraphernalia which volunteers gather about them wherever they encamped for long. "Pulpits and piano-fortes" Mac called the cumbrous and unmilitary contrivances.

"Looks like the sack of Jerusalem by the Romans, doesn't it, Mac?"

"I guess so—though I wasn't in service at that time."

"What ought to be done about it?"

"Load the tents and the cooking utensils in the wagons, and then muster the men with arms, blankets, knapsacks, and haversacks, and march away."

"Leave all the rest?"

"The whole kit and caboodle!"

It was but a short walk to the boat, however, and the officers allowed the men to load themselves down, even to the floor-boards of the tents being carried by many on their backs under their knapsacks and belts, while their hands and arms were miscellaneously overloaded.

"Now what do things look like, Captain?"

"Well, Mac, a little like the children of Israel starting for the Promised Land, loaded with what they had borrowed from the Egyptians."

Mac chuckled. "Ya-as. Just so. It takes you literary men to state things about right."

To the infinite joy and relief of the rank and file, they had got marching orders "at last." To these heroic, unsoldierly volunteers, three months of drill seemed an unbearable affliction; although it is a space of time about long enough to get an old-world recruit through the awkward squad.

Handling the musket and bayonet, marching, wheeling, facing, ploying, deploying, loading, firing, charging, halting, dressing, skirmishing, saluting, parading, for days and weeks (not to say years); all for the single purpose of bringing men into a double line, shoulder to shoulder, facing the foe; knowing enough (and not too much) to load and fire until they fall in their tracks or the other fellows run away.

To such simple, mechanical, dull, dogged machine-work has the old art of war come down. No more "gaudium certaminis," no more crossing of swords or "push of pike," no more blow and ward, lance, shield, battle-ax, spear, chariot-and-horse; no more of the exhilarating clash of personal contest. *Nothing* left but stern, defenseless, hopeless "stand-up-and-take-your-physic"—fortuitous death by an unseen missile from an unknown hand.

Is not the time coming when the rank and file, the stepping-stones on the road to fame, will call a halt on their own account? When they learn good sense they will cry with one voice: "It is enough. We will have no more of it."

Whenever it shall become the rule that the man who causes a war shall be its first victim, war will be at an end. War flourishes by what

Gen. Scott wittily called "the fury of the non-combatants."

But to the average American brutal battle is better than irksome idleness. This found fresh expression when the men of the Sixth were clustered in groups on the many and spacious decks of the Graham, filling every inch of space where a human being could sit, stand, or lie. The few Mexican war veterans laughed at the impatience of the new volunteers. Said one:

"Why, boys, wha' d'ye mean? Here ye've had it all yer own way. Plenty of grub, camp fixed up like winter quarters—couldn't live better at a county almshouse—nothin' to do but play checkers and draw pay for doin' it! Ye'd orter be'n prayin' Heaven night an' day to have the War Department ferget ye. Yer best luck would be if the card marked Sixth Illinois was to slip out of the pack an' lay on the floor under Uncle Sam's chair till the game was played out."

"Oh, shucks! What in thunder did we come fer if they didn't want us! Might have staid to hum and 'tended to our little biz. 'List for a soldier and spend our time diggin' slippery-ellum stumps out of a Cairo bottom! Idle month after month; two dozen gone to kingdom come, an' goin' on two hundred sick or discharged for disability!"

"That's so, every time! It ain't right. If the head fellers don't know enough to git us to work they'd better resign, and we'll put in somebody that does."

"They want to get a good ready."

"Oh, shucks! They're like the boy that took a run of three miles to jump over a small hill, an' when he got thar he was so tired he couldn't jump over a caterpiller in the road!"

The first speaker disdained to argue. He only drew out his pipe, and, producing a plug of tobacco, proceeded to fill it.

"See that plug o' t'backer? We'll call that the Sixth Illinois."

Then cutting off a bit he added:

"An' that's Company K. Now see what next." He chipped the piece with his knife and ground it between thumb and palm to small fragments. "Now it's gettin' drilled, ye see, ready fer use." Then he poured it carefully into the pipe-bowl. "Now it's loaded onto the J. R. Graham, goin' to the front." He scraped a match on his trouser-leg and lighted the pipe. "An' now it's under fire and wishes it wasn't—wishes it had staid on the farm where it growed."

Loud and long they laughed at this graphic illustration of the fate of the volunteers, but the very laughter showed that they could learn nothing from it. Poor fellows!

Another group fell to discussing their company officers.

"Oh, Cap Fargeon means well. Cap's a good feller, an' a perfect gentleman, too, but he won't never make a soldier, Cap won't."

"No! He's be'n fed on spoon-vittles all his life—can't never learn to stomach bull-beef."

"Thasso! Takes Mac to do the hard chawin'!"

"Cap's fustrate for this camp-trampin' an' book-keepin' business—psalm-singin' an' moral suasion—mark time, present arms, right oblique, tick-tacks, flubdub an' folderol; but whar'll he be come to charge bay'nets an' the enemy in front?"

"Boys," cried Caleb Dugong (a "blowhard" and favorite butt of the quieter men, who saw through him), "would ye believe it, Cap wanted us fellers t'leave our tent-boards behind!"

"Well, Cale," said Jeff Cobb, "ain't you got yourn behind now?"

"Oh, shut up! He wanted us to leave 'em in camp. Said we was a-overloadin' ourselves an' couldn't stan' it. Now mine jest fits my back—kind o' holds me up. Blamed ef I don't believe I kin march better with it than without it."

"Say, Cale," persisted Jeff, "d'ye know what I advise you to do?"

"No; what?"

"Why, whenever ye go into battle, carry that board along an' wear it jest where ye've got it now, an' ye won't never git wounded."

A general guffaw burst out at this "burn" on Caleb, which did not tend to improve his humor. But he was brave, at least among his friends, and not easily bluffed. He turned to Mark Looney as easy prey.

"What do you say, Looney Mark? You'llow you've be'n to battles where Mac was a-fightin' —ain't Mac jest about the right kind of a peanut fer a fight?"

"Oah—the liftin'nt's all roight," replied the discreet veteran.

"Well, how do you say Cap Fargeon'd pan out?"

"The caftain'd turrn as white as a shayt—"

"I'll bet ye!"

"An' he'd shiver an' shake fit to knock the tayth all out av his head—"

"I knowd it!"

"An' he'd shtan' there, pale an' shakin', facin' the music, whilst most av you red-faced divvles'd be out o' soight in the rayr. He wud—oah yis, he wud."

This quaint expression of confidence in their captain was greeted with low laughter and other marks of approval. Caleb tried to turn the tide.

"Tell me a brave man would git pale an' be a-tremblin' like that! Why, the wuss things git,

the madder I git, an' the madder I git the redder my face gits."

"All right, Cale," put in Chipstone. "I'll stand by ye."

"'Course ye will!" said the other, in a gratified tone.

"'Druther stan' by you than by Cap Fargeon."

"That's right, Chips! I ollers knowd ye wuz a friend of mine."

"Well, it ain't that exactly; it's because I guess I'll git to live longer."

Another general laugh at the expense of the helpless Caleb.

"I guess yew fellers must a'found a ha-ha's nest with a tee-hee's eggs in it. Well, laugh all yer a mine ter. I'll bet any man five dollars ye won't never hear my teeth a-chatterin' under fire!"

"No, Caleb; not unless ye're tied there."

"What's the use of a scairt man, anyhow? Cap's chatterin' teeth'd scare the other fellers."

"Oah, whilst his tayth wor a-chatterin', av ye wor a-listenin' ye'd hear em' chatterin', 'Shteady, b'yes, shteady; doa'nt hurry—ye've time a plinty—fire slow an' fire low! Shteady!' That's the how they'd chatter. They wud; oah yis, they wud."

"An' where'd you be all the time, Looney Mark?" asked the angry bully.

"Oah—shtan'in' somewhere's thereabouts; or layin' down on me face takin' it aisy an' quiet-like, through havin' got through me job."

"An' the rest of us'd be all runnin' away, would we? Is that what ye say, ye dam' little split-mouth Mexican Paddy? If I had such a mug as yours I'd lie on it all the time!"

A shocked and angry silence fell upon the group at this brutal assault. Some looked with contempt at the speaker, some with sympathetic curiosity at Mark, to see what he would do. He leaned forward, with his eyes fixed on the ground, and covered his blemish with his hand, while in his disfigured face a look of patient habitual endurance followed the discomposure; a look which might be interpreted, "I bide my time."

"Well!" cried Clinton Thrush, after a moment of thought, "I'd rather be Mark Looney than any man who'd make such a speech as that!"

"That's the talk!" added Chipstone. "Count me in there!"

"Why, fellers! Mark'llowed we was all cowards but him!"

"He never said no such a thing!"

"An' if he had, what you said would go to prove it was true, regarding one of us, an' that's Cale Dugong. It takes a coward to make a break like that!"

Caleb was "squelched"—didn't open his lips for an hour, and was not spoken to again for a day or more.

Proudly and triumphantly, the Sixth disembarked when it reached its destination, with all its comfortable impediments. Gleefully it pitched its camp on the low bluff bank. Stoutly —though with some misgivings—the men took up the march next morning, loaded down with "pulpits and piano-fortes." Before they had gone a mile, however, some began to unburden themselves; Tolliver remarking: "I didn't enlist to be a pack-horse in Foot, Leggit and Walker's line."

If Colonel Puller had asked Mac's advice, the men would have been forbidden to carry anything but the ordinary load of a marching soldier—twenty to thirty pounds under the best circumstances; but no such orders were issued, and all Mac and Fargeon could do '(without causing dissatisfaction, by putting re-

strictions on Company K different from those of other companies) was to tell the men the folly of starting out with a load they would have to drop. This advice was heeded to some extent at starting, and bore more fruit as the day wore on, for before noon there was not a floor-board in the company; and even other burdens were greatly lessened. The consequence was that at night K reached camp entire, not a man missing, after passing, during the afternoon, hundreds of exhausted stragglers from the leading companies, some of which stragglers never reached their destination until after dawn on the following day.

Very creditable was this to Company K, but perhaps not an unmixed blessing, for when the orders came next morning for the Sixth to deploy a company as skirmishers, "to feel the enemy," a very slight examination showed that K was the one best fitted for the job, and K was designated.

Fargeon found time to make a few hasty preparations for "whatever might happen." He wrote a farewell note to Sara—"to be delivered if I fall"—and inclosed it in a sheet containing directions for the disposal of his personal effects and his remains. He donned his oldest suit, so that his best might serve as a burial garb; and then thought of his own face, drawn and ghastly, showing through an open coffin-lid in front of Mr. Penrose's pulpit when the good minister should say, in sad, sonorous tones:

"Friends will now be afforded a last look at our departed brother. Pass up the north aisle, please, and round and out at the south door, where the line will be formed."

As this scene rose before his mind's eye he felt a choking in his throat and moisture on his cheeks. It was all reasonable enough; then why, in later years, did he laugh at himself with shame—keep the weakness secret, and never let it be known to a living soul till now?

To "deploy as skirmishers" (as the Sixth had learned the trick) is to separate the men and dispose of them at intervals of six paces, keeping about a third of them massed in the rear as a reserve. Company K had now about seventy-five men for duty; therefore, twenty-five being in reserve, the remaining fifty covered a front of about 900 feet in extent—about the space occupied by a regiment in "line of battle!" To "advance as skirmishers" is for every second man to kneel, musket at "ready," while the alternate men move forward about twenty paces (keeping the line as nearly straight as may be), and kneel in their turn, while their brothers go forward twenty paces in front of them; and so on until checked by the enemy or halted by command. [In retiring, skirmishers keep the same order—half halting, face toward the foe, while the others get to the rear of them.]

Behold Company K at length on soldierly duty! The men flushed or paled, according to temperament. Sweat trickled down their chests, tickling as it flowed. How their hearts beat! How fast they emptied their canteens! How their hands trembled! As Tolliver afterward described his feelings:

"I couldn't 'a' loaded my gun then to save my life. I couldn't 'a' steered a catteridge into the muzzle of a bushel-basket!"

It was difficult to prevent them from firing whenever they knelt down, albeit there might be no enemy within three miles of them. They had strict orders against it; yet they sometimes fired, and when one did so the contagion was apt to spread along the line. The first offender felt the stinging weight of Mac's curse; and then Fargeon and Morphy, taking their cue from him, and the four sergeants learning their

duty, aided in maintaining the needful discipline.

Listen to Mac, stalking leisurely back and forth and drawling out in a voice clear as a bell:

"Chipstone, don't get so far to the front! Your legs are too long; try fifteen paces. More to the left, Clinton! You're always leaning too much to the right! There! Steady boys! Kneel down! Caleb Dugong, don't let me catch you cocking your piece! You've started the firing once—do it again, and you'll hear me do a gong you won't like."

Fargeon listened to Mac with earnest attention, and tried to go and do likewise. He may make a soldier after all! True, they have not yet seen or heard of a rebel. Well, when that happens we'll hope for the best. He thought to himself:

"Now I ought to be hoping to find the enemy; that's what I'm here for. But I don't hope it—no—I hope I shall not hear or see one all day—or any other day—never while the world stands! I wish there were no enemy; no war; that I were at home where I belong." And a vision of a domestic fireside, a carpeted room, a shaded lamp, a well-spread board, a tea-tray furnished with a bell to call the maid, rose before his mind's eye, and sweet, friendly voices filled his soul. It was a long-forgotten parental tea-table, and his widowed mother sat at the head.

All vanished. Here again was the unfamiliar forest; the loaded, leveled muskets; the enforced seeking for what he feared to find.

Their advance had been through a wood, rather thick with underbrush; now there seemed to be a little light ahead—either a clearing or low ground.

Now listen to Fargeon:

"Forward, second line! Steady! Dugong, I

have got my eye on you! Double-quick to your places, boys! There—not too far—steady—halt and kneel down. Is that a clearing ahead? Now, first line forward! Double-quick! Now down!"

BANG!

"Curse you, Dugong—what do you mean? And you a corporal!"

Had he really said a swear-word for the first time in his life? He hadn't time to make sure whether he had or not, for the trembling culprit spoke.

"Ca-cap! I heard 'em fire on the left."

"That's a lie! Not a man fired till after you did. Is your piece loaded? No? Here—give me your ramrod! now fire again if you can!"

"Sha-shall I go to the rear, Cap? I will, if you say so—go to the guard-tent in arrest."

"No, sir! Go on and learn to behave yourself! What's that—a fence? Halt at the fence—pass the word to halt at the fence!"

"Oh, Cap! Gimme my ramrod, and let me load before I go up to the fence! I'll get killed, sure!"

"Will you behave yourself?"

"Oh, yes, Cap! I won't fire till I see a reb right in range."

"Well, take your ramrod! Hello, Mac! what's the news?"

"Did you say to halt at the fence, Captain?"

"Yes. Let's take a look. Here! what's the use of standing up like that? Get down and let's take a sight. Here seems to be a field of growing corn and woods beyond. What shall we do next?"

"Skirmish right on across the field. I *guess* we shall find some rebs in those woods."

"How far do you think we've come?"

"Oh, three-quarters of a mile, or a little better." [Fargeon would have guessed two miles.]

"No danger of our getting out too far? getting out-flanked and gobbled up?"

"No, I guess not. We must take our chances. Can't drop it this way."

"You think there are rebs in those woods?"

"Shouldn't wonder. We can soon find out by going over there."

"Spoil the man's corn—and perhaps he is a Union man."

Mac either said "Damn the corn," or he thought it so hard that you could hear him think.

Just here a voice seemed to come from the sky.

"Hi! I see 'em. Men movin' in them woods."

It was Ben Town, who had climbed a tree, and whose example was soon followed by several others—so many, in fact, that orders had to be given for all to come down except Ben.

"Well, Captain," said Mac, "will you give us the order to advance? Whenever you're ready, we are."

"Why, Mac, if we go out in the open our men will be all exposed and sure to get hit."

"We've got to go if we want to find out anything."

"Suppose we fire from here, and see if we can't draw them out."

"Oh, they're too sharp for that!"

"Well, why not get a section of artillery and shell the woods?"

"Why, Cap'n Fargeon, we can feel 'em and get done with it long before we could get a gun up here."

"No, sir, never! I should call that a needless waste of life. Keep the men quiet here, and I'll fetch up a gun or two in half an hour."

He started on a run for the camp, and halted to speak to Lieutenant Morphy, commanding the reserves—all of which force was fuming with impatience and curiosity—and reached headquarters in less than ten minutes, much to his surprise, for he could not get rid of the feeling that they had skirmished over many times as much ground as they had really passed.

On reaching Col. Puller's tent Will opened his mouth to speak, and found, to his surprise, dismay, *horror,* that he could not utter a syllable! His mind was clear, his words were ready, but, miraculous to relate, his tongue "clave to the roof of his mouth," and the muscles of his throat refused to act.

"Why, Capt'n Fargeon! Are you wounded? Are you sick? What is the matter? Major, get the captain a glass of whisky."

Will could only manage a ghastly grin and an imbecile chuckle as he sank into a seat. The colonel poured some whisky into a cup. Fargeon took the cup with perfect composure, steadily added a quantity of water, and drank the mixture. He put his hand to his throat, found all apparently in order, tried once more to speak, and succeeded.

"Excuse me, Colonel. I suppose I ran too fast—never felt so before in my life; hope I never shall again."

Poor fellow! Many another citizen soldier has felt so; some as often as they took part in a battle; some only on their first experience.

He made his report and the suggestion as to the aid he would like to have in the shape of a cannon or two. The colonel, being green like himself, thought it an excellent suggestion. [It takes some years of war and the loss of many guns to teach the lesson that artillery is a very poor reconnoitering arm.]

While the colonel went off to brigade headquarters to ask for the guns, Fargeon retired to his tent for a moment to get some food. He fancied that the lightness of his breakfast might account for his extraordinary temporary paralysis of the throat. There he saw Mark Looney, told him of the experiences of the company thus far, and ordered him to help the company's cooks fill two cracker-boxes with food and bring them to the men on the skirmish line as soon as possible.

"Begorra, Caftain—that's the best news I heard since me stef-father's funeral! I was afeared I was goin' to be left out here in the coald! I was—oah, I was!"

"Why," said Will to himself, "I believe he'd rather go than stay here!"

"There," he went on, as he took his way hurriedly to the front, "that shows I am not *frightened.* A man in a panic does not have his wits about him and attend to business like that. Why, I can talk as well as anybody! I can sing." And he sang low, but clear:

"I wonder why all saints don't sing."

"Frightened! Of course I'm not! Only excited. Never felt better in my life! My heart feels warm—glowing."

Then, after a few steps:

"Great Scott! Can this be the whisky? Heavens and earth—I believe it is! Ho-ho! But I don't care! So *this* is what the joy of drink is like, is it? Contented self-conceit! Well, there is something rather pleasant about it—if it only lasted forever!

"Ha! What's that? Firing on our line? Can Mac have disobeyed me and pushed forward? And the guns just coming? Lives lost for nothing! Oh, Mac, I didn't think it of you—I didn't think it of you! My poor boys!

"God! How they rattle! Hark! What's that?" For he heard, far above him, a long, sharp wail, beginning high in the scale and nearly overhead; then lower, lower, as it died away in the distance behind him. "W-e-e-e-e-e-ep," it seemed to say. It was the first hostile bullet he ever heard.

He walked on, but more slowly. He instinctively directed his steps behind trees that stood near where his way led. Then a bullet passed him at his own level—"Whip!" Then another that lodged in a tree—"Hitt!" Then something struck lightly on his kepi—it was only a twig that had been cut off by one of the high-flying balls, but, at the same instant, "Spatt!" a bullet struck the ground at his right, and he rushed up to a tree in front of him and leaned, panting, against it, with both hands on the trunk. It was a white-oak, and the rough gray bark impressed on his staring eyeballs a picture of its long, pointed, diamond-shaped corrugations, which he never forgot.

"Why am I halting here? Because I *cannot* go on! It is settled—the long doubt is over— I am a coward. My poor boys are in front of me; shame and disgrace are behind me—are here with me. Yet I *cannot* quit this shelter. God help me, I cannot! Oh, if I could take a bullet in my hand—my arm—anywhere but in my face!" He thrust his hand out as far as he could reach, absolutely expecting it to be hit.

"Oh, God! Send a bullet through my hand —my arm! Then I could lose a limb and go back home—my dear home—where I belong."

He brought back his hand against the tree trunk; and between his thumbs pressed his forehead hard against the flinty bark, and rolled it from side to side, as if to get a little bodily pain to assuage his mental agony.

"How they screech and scream! Oh, my dear home! I will never marry Sally. I will tell her how unworthy I am—and then bury my shame in solitude.

"What's that? Who said 'Come on, Ed?' Why—there's Mark—poor, simple-hearted little Mark—marching forward as if on pa-

rade, with a cracker-box of provisions on his shoulder, and Ed Ranny behind him! I am saved. Thank God, they did not see me! I must get to the line before they do, or die in my tracks."

He darted past the tree on the side furthest from Mark, put his head down and ran like a racer to the front. The motion, the effort of mind and body, gave him new life. He passed the place where the reserve had stood, and observed that they had moved up to the support of their brothers.

When nearly in sight of the fence he saw— almost stepped on—the body of a man lying on his face behind a log. The soldier's musket lay by his side; a corporal's chevrons were visible on his sleeve; and Will thought he recognized Dugong's stalwart form. Fargeon's heart seemed to stand still; but his legs kept moving and carried him whither his soul impelled. He was still afraid; but panic-stricken ("stampeded") no longer. He remembered Mac's saying: "The ball you hear never hits you; the ball that hits you, you never hear"; and tried, with some success, to gain comfort from it, aided by the wonderful fact that he was still alive.

The enemy had deployed a line of skirmishers and were advancing doggedly across the open, in alternate steps, as has already been described. Our boys were crouching and firing through the fence, with every advantage on their side. Some stood erect, firing coolly over the top of the rail. Mac walked up and down, talking incessantly, in his fighting drawl:

"Steady now, boys—don't waste your shots. Aim! aim now; aim every time, and aim low. Carberry, you fired almost before your gun touched your shoulder; might just as well have fired into the river! There! bully for you, Chip! You fetched him! They won't make another step forward, see if they do! What did I tell you? They are picking him up—that means they're going! Now, when they get started, over the fence, and after 'em! Now's your time! Forward! FORWARD, COMPANY K!"

The Flag of Truce

A wild cheer rose, and Company K swarmed over the barrier, firing and loading on the run as they went. Fargeon was with them, running, shouting, waving his sword, till suddenly he saw one of his men stumble, fall forward, and not get up again. The man next the fallen one dropped his gun and called to another to do the same, and the two, in less time than it takes to tell it, had their hurt comrade raised up between them.

"What are you about?" screamed McClintock with a volley of curses. "Drop that man, * * * and take your guns again!"

"Why, lieutenant—he's wounded—his leg's broke—and he's my brother, De Witt Clinton Thrush."

"I don't care if he's your sister! Drop him and take your gun!"

Poor Aleck obeyed; laid down his burden, tenderly kissed the pale face, rose with tears streaming from his eyes, loaded his piece, crying—still crying, went forward to the firing line, and cried and fought, and fought and cried, as long as there was any fighting to do. Country—duty—glory? Yes; but turning your back on an only brother, a heart's twin, moaning in deep distress and bleeding to death for want of your help!

The advance was tumultuous, yet not rapid, for the brave confederates fought well. With shrieking bullets, scattered puffs of smoke, and sharp reports, now softened by distance, now

near and deafening, the onward surge of Company K carried it some distance beyond where poor Clint Thrush lay moaning. He saw two of his comrades hurrying to the rear, and called to them with all his feeble strength, for help; but they paid no attention; they were nursing wounds of their own.

Mark Looney passed him going toward the fray, and Clinton begged piteously to be carried back.

"Arrah, me bye; tehk me canteen an' gimme yer gun an' yer cathridge-box! I'll jest give them divvles wan or two blessin's in yer oan name; an' thin I'll come back an' carry ye in like a lehdy a-ridin' in a coach an' four." And he too was gone.

An officer from brigade headquarters came to the fence and shouted for Captain Fargeon. Nobody paid any attention to him, so he was forced, against his will, to come on into the melee, making a detour to avoid running over Clinton.

"Captain, I have orders from Gen. Peterkin that you are to halt as soon as you have developed the enemy's position, and retire at your discretion."

Fargeon called McClintock to him and communicated the message. Said Mac:

"Well, that means now. They are firing strongly from the woods; only, their own men being between them and us, they are forced to fire high."

"Very well, sir. You have the general's orders." And the relieved aide darted for the rear. Mac went one way and Fargeon the other, shouting, "Back! back!" and motioning toward the fence; and the excited men reluctantly began their retreat, luckily, before the concealed portion of their foes got a fair chance at them. They brought in the confederate wounded (such as fell into their hands) with as much tenderness as was possible in the haste and confusion. The dead they left as they lay. Fargeon went to poor Clint Thrush, and, with help from Aleck and others, got him to the fence, where the boys quickly laid down a length of rails to pass him through. The transit was not made without some groans, and one cry that was almost a scream. Sharp bone ends were evidently loose in his flesh.

Then all the wounded were clustered together waiting for transportation homeward.

"I wonder if anybody will have sense enough to send us some stretchers! Oh, yes; here they come. Thank God, Dr. McShane knows enough to know that shots call for stretchers."

A feeble voice was heard from near by. It was Clinton's, as he lay by a tree, his head supported by his brother.

"Did we lick 'em, Lieutenant?"

"You bet we did! I counted three stone-dead. And just see our boys fetching in their wounded! One, two, three, four—right where we are."

Company K halted behind the fence and watched the opposite woods while waiting for orders. The pork and crackers brought by Mark and Ed were sparingly dealt out and contentedly munched, the prisoners who were not too badly hurt getting their bite with the rest. Canteens were generally empty before this, and certain men were now allowed to gather from their comrades as many as they could carry and go back to a little ditch they had crossed in their advance, fill them, and distribute them to their thirsty owners. Fargeon noticed Corporal Dugong very active and audible among the workers, so he must have been mistaken in the identity of the dead man.

The captain mingled with the men and ate a bit of cracker with a slice of cold boiled salt pork (sweeter than fresh grass-butter) laid on it; took a pull at one of the canteens newly filled at the ditch (delicious nectar), and, looking round for fresh, new worlds to conquer, accepted the loan of Morphy's pipe, from which he took several cautious whiffs.

"Mac, what day of the week is this?"

"Let's see: we got our orders Wednesday, we sailed Thursday, we landed Friday, we marched Saturday—that's yesterday—to-day's Sunday, by my reckoning."

Captain William Fargeon, Sunday-school superintendent and temperance missionary, smiled grimly, then laughed aloud.

"What's the matter, captain?"

"Oh—nothing much," he answered; then, to himself, he added: "A fight, a swear-word, a drink of liquor, and a pipe—all on Sabbath morning!" and laughed again.

The men are resting gayly, at their ease, some in the shady corners of the worn fence, some under the trees hard by, among whose branches the cicadas are screaming their delight in the hot sunshine. It is scarcely more than twenty minutes since our boys leaped the fence to pursue the retreating foe, yet to some men it is a lifetime, to others the beginning of a long, slow, maimed existence.

In front, the young corn spreads its deep green far and wide, broken and disturbed by the deadly work that went on in and through and over it a little while ago. Somewhere in its expanse, at some unmarked spots, lie three prostrate human figures. Enemies? No; former enemies, now insensate clods, to be neither hated nor feared.

The rest following a small affair, wherein we have had a success, or at any rate no serious loss or disaster, is a delightful interval to those alive and unhurt. One more yawning chasm past, one less deadly peril before us of those marked opposite our names in the illegible book of fate; a hard duty done this day, whether any one except us ever knows it or not; and perhaps a little dearly-loved honor and fame added to our few treasures. Something to talk of in camp; something to write of to the dear home-folks, now further away than ever. Something to remember to the day of death, be it near at hand or dim in the future. A great rebound of spirits from the terrible tension of the ordeal—a hilarity that seems natural even in caring for the suffering wounded or the quiet dead.

"Well, Clinton, old boy! Your turn to-day, mine next time. How do you feel?"

"First-rate, Captain."

"I guess Clint will come out all OK," said Aleck, who now had his arm under his brother's head as it lay on the stretcher, and was wiping off the sweat-drops of pain and weakness as they gathered on his forehead.

"All right? Of course he will! He'll be singing in the quartet again before we know it."

"I wonder if those fellows have any brothers on the other side!" said Clinton, turning his head with difficulty to where the wounded prisoners sat or lay in a row.

"Might be," said Fargeon, while the laugh died from his face. But his blood was flowing too free for long regrets. A smile chased away the pain and he added: "They had no business to be rebels—and then to come out and try to fight Company K!"

"Bully for you! Bully for all!" quavered Clinton. "What became of my gun?"

"Oh, little Mark got it," answered Aleck, "and * * * he used it too!"

Fargeon had taken off his kepi.

"Why, Captain, did you get hit? Your forehead looks as if it had been grazed by a ball."

"No, no!" answered Will hastily, while the abraded forehead flushed up to the roots of his hair. "Brushed against something in passing."

The stretcher-bearers were now told off to help the hospital men, and our wounded carried to camp.

"Set the stretchers down at the hospital tent, and get four more and hurry back for the wounded rebs. Don't wait for these to be unloaded," shouted Mac.

"Four? Why, there are five to go," said Will.

"Oh, there's one who won't need a stretcher."

They went over to where a fine specimen of humanity was lying (and dying), a little apart from the rest. Young, strong, handsome, high-bred—curls, that might have been the pride of a doting mother, clustering round a brow that might have been the hope of an ambitious father. Eyes fit to shine as the heaven of love and trust to some happy bride, the light gone from them forever; the lids drawn back and the balls sunken so that it seemed as if their owner had been born blind. A bullet had torn clean through his lungs, and the breath made a dreadful noise escaping through the wound at every exhalation.

Fargeon wiped away the bloody froth that oozed from the wounded man's lips and over his downy beard, and tried to pour some drops of water into his mouth, but it ran out unswallowed. He asked the others the name of the dying man, and found it to be Huger. [Pronounced Hujee.]

No more "joy of battle" for Captain Fargeon. He walked away along the line, trying to forget the dying boy, and listened to the usual free comments of the private soldier.

"Now, why don't our boys back in camp move up and charge them woods? We've done our part, and now the big-bugs that sent us out ain't ready to follow up our victory!"

"Oh, dry up, Eph! What do you know about war? Ye don't know no more about war than a fish knows about water! War's jest pushin' men out to git killed and then pullin' 'em back to die of old age. Kind o' 'mark-time march'; keep a-steppin' an' never git ahead none."

In spite of the relaxation and repose, watchful eyes were always directed toward the front.

"Hello! They're sending out a flag of truce!"

The cry came from several parts of the line at once; and Fargeon ran to McClintock for advice, as usual.

"Sarg'nt Coggill and Chipstone, leave your guns an' go out—double-quick—halt them where you meet them, and find out what they want. Tell them if they come any nearer we'll fire on them, flag or no flag. One of you stay with 'em—Sarg'nt, you stay with 'em; keep your mouth shut and your eyes and ears open. Chipstone, you bring back the message."

The emissaries started, and our boys began to perch themselves on a fence.

"Down! Git down, all of you, you fools! Do you want to let them know how few there are of us? Let 'em think there's a battery and a whole brigade in line of battle right here, if they want to."

Soon Chipstone came running back.

"They want to see an officer who can treat for a truce to bury dead and care for the wounded."

"What's the rank of the officer with the flag?"

"I—don't know. He had no shoulder-straps."

"No; they don't wear 'em. You go back and find out."

Soon he made the journey out and back.

"A captain and a lieutenant."

"Well, Capt'n Fargeon, you will probably meet the captain, and take either me or Morphy with you."

"Oh, come along, McClintock. We'll see what they want."

"Well, sir, will you instruct Lieut'nt Morphy to take charge of our men—to keep them hidden and watchful in front and on flanks?"

Morphy got his orders, and the others started.

"Mac, could it be that they are moving to cut us off?"

"No, not while the flag of truce is out. They ain't Injins."

As they walked on, he added:

"Same time, this flag of truce is a mere pretense. They want to find out if there's a chance for a rush on us, to retrieve their little repulse of this morning. Now, suppose your two guns were there and only K company to support them, and they found it out by this smart trick, and had a regiment in the edge of those woods—"

"Well, what then?"

"Why, the confederacy would be two guns ahead tonight. Guns without infantry to back them are as helpless as baby-carriages."

They approached the two officers and the sergeant bearing the flag—a handkerchief tied on a gun-rammer. The captain was a tall, pale, rather elderly gentleman, silent and rigidly grave. The lieutenant was the typical southern officer; thin and sallow, smooth-faced except a fringe of mustache over a sharp mouth, long black hair brushed behind his ears and falling to his collar; level brows and black eyes that shone with fierce, untamable light.

The four officers touched their caps as they met. The confederate lieutenant spoke:

"Gentlemen, I make you acquainted with

Capt'n Huger, of the Lou'siana Fire-Eaters. I
am Lieut. Judah, of the same reg'ment."

As the junior officer had spoken, McClintock replied, introducing Captain Fargeon and
himself. Then the southerner went on:

"Gentlemen, as we were ovahmatched—I
would say out numbahed—in our little affaiah
of this morning, we thought best to retiah, and,
in disobedience of the ordahs of Capt'n Huger
and myself, some of ouah dead and wounded
were left on the field."

The northerners bowed.

"Now, sah, Majah Leroy commanding the
fo'ce in your immejate front, sen's his compliments and requests the cou'tesy of a truce fo'
two houahs to cayah fo' ou' wounded and bury
ou' dead."

Fargeon made an inclination to Mac to authorize him to reply, and he did so.

"Lieutenant, we have already cared for your
wounded; and as to your dead, we are willing
to send them over to your line by details of our
men; or, according to rule, to forward your request to our commanding officer."

"Very well, sah. Do you mean that you will
insist that yo' men shall be allowed to bring ou'
dead quite to ou' own lines, sah? Or that we
shall leave them unburied, or come and take
them by fo'ce, sah?"

"As to coming to take them by force, you
know, Lieutenant, you didn't need a flag of
truce to authorize you to do that."

"By God, sah, if I had my way we would
have had no flag of truce, sah! We'd have had
our battle-flag, sah, to recovah ou' dead, sah!"

"We should have been glad to see you, Lieutenant. There's room behind our lines for the
rest of your force."

"By God, sah!—"

But the silent gentleman at his side laid his
hand on the youth's shoulder and quelled him
by a look. Fargeon now interposed.

"Pardon, gentlemen, I think we should feel
authorized to have your dead brought to this
place, and your men allowed unmolested to
take them into your lines."

The elder man, to whom Fargeon had addressed himself, bowed a silent assent to this.

Mac wrote a few lines in his book, and,
tearing out the leaf, gave it to Chipstone to
deliver to Lieut. Morphy. In a few minutes
eight men were seen to leave the fence and begin searching about among the corn-hills. Before long three bodies clad in shabby gray,
dirty and bloodstained, were being slowly
dragged toward the little group, their helpless
heels leveling the corn-plants as they passed,
their hatless heads dropped back, their white
mouths wide open, and their dead eyes staring
hideously toward the pitiless sky.

Captain Huger stood with his back to the
work, but as each corpse was laid down he gave
one quick, searching, agonized glance, and
then turned instantly away.

"That is all, gentlemen."

The old captain heaved a long, deep sigh,
seemingly of relief and hope.

"Are all the six others whom we miss,
wounded and in your hands?"

"We have six in our hands, wounded or
not."

"Are there any prisoners not wounded?"

"One. I have not yet taken his name."

"Can you describe him?" asked the lieutenant. But Captain Huger shook his head, inti-
mating that he knew it was not the man they
had in their minds. So the lieutenant changed
the question.

"Can we obtain him by parole, exchange, or
otherwise?"

"Personally we have nothing to say about parole or exchange."

"If we could lay our hands on him he would be shot at sundown."

"Then of course he can in no case be paroled or exchanged."

The Confederate lieutenant here whispered a few words to his senior, who replied with a nod; then turned his back and stood like a statue.

"There is one man in you' hands, gentlemen, I wish informally to ask about, undah circumstances—"

"Do you mean Private Huger?"

"I do, sah."

"He is wounded in our hands."

"Severely?"

"Mortally."

A dreadful silence fell upon the group. No one knew how to break it. Fargeon, with a question in his look, pointed to the heroic figure beyond; and Judah answered with a nod that seemed to say, "Father and son."

The grief-stricken father never raised his hand to his eyes; but his frame wavered a little, and from time to time he bowed his head and shook it slightly, when one or two scattered drops would shine for an instant in the sun as they fell to the ground.

At last Mac spoke:

"With Capt'n Fargeon's permission, I propose that if Private Huger shall have died before the flag is withdrawn, we shall deliver his body as we have the others."

"Very good, sah. And if not, sah?"

"Then I don't know what more we can say," said Mac; to which Fargeon added:

"Except that we shall treat the rebel wounded as we do our own."

Judah flared up again in an instant.

"I'll thank you, Capt'n Fargeon, not to presume upon the protection affo'ded you by a flag of truce! I'll thank you, sah, to speak of Confederate soldiers befo' Confederate officahs with propah respect, sah!"

"Lieutenant, it was quite accidental. I will repeat the remark in the form I should have given it at first: We shall treat wounded enemies as we would wounded friends."

"Very well, sah. I am moah than satisfied. You speak of us as yo' enemies; I reg-yahd that as the most honorable name you could bestow, sah!"

Fargeon answered with a good-humored smile. How far he was from looking at them as they seemed to look at us!

Said Mac, listlessly plucking a corn-leaf and tearing it into long, thin, green ribbons:

"I need not say that if Private Huger shall live long enough, we shall be glad to favor an exchange for one of our men, if you have one to offer."

"A wounded man, sah?"

"No; a well man."

"Well, sah, I assume to say that that would be an exchange giving you-uns an advantage which Capt'n Huger would decline to give you, sah."

"Then, gentlemen, as we have no more immediate business, we propose to withdraw."

"And how about ouah flag, sah?"

"We shall consider it withdrawn within half an hour after we leave you, unless we in the meantime act under it as proposed."

"Very well, sah! Capt'n Huger, the gentlemen are ready to retiah."

The dignified father turned toward them, his face like that of a stone image. Fargeon impulsively extended his hand, but the other seemed not to see it. He touched his hat, turned on his heel again, and stood motionless while our men retraced their steps, pushing down their sword-hilts so that the scabbards should not drag against the corn-blades.

Our wounded had been sent in and the stretchers brought back for the rebels. All were loaded except Huger, who was still alive, though nearly done with his struggle. Mac went to the stretchers and made a slight examination of the sufferers. Then he said to one of them:

"Get up and walk."

"Oh, Lieutenant, my arm's shot to pieces; I can't travel."

"You don't travel on your arm. Get out of that. I want it for Huger."

"Oh, for Cap Huger's son? Surely I'll get up. Could ye give me suth'n' to tie my arm so it won't hang down?"

"Get up! I ain't here to wait on you," and he made as if he would tip the man off on the ground.

"Oh, hold on!" cried Fargeon. "I can't stand that! Here, boy, let me tie my handkerchief in your buttonhole; now let me slip your wrist through and clasp your hands together—so!"

The fellow submitted in wondering silence, and then got up and sat down on a log, nursing his unlucky arm as if it were a pet dog.

They lifted Huger on the stretcher. Mac looked at him critically.

"Guess we'll call him dead, captain, and give his friends the job of burying him. What do you say?"

"I say yes."

"All right, then. Here, Mark, you and Chipstone and Bob and Coggill carry this body over to the men at the flag. Remember it's a dead man—never anything else—you remember?" And he winked at them individually and collectively.

Fargeon saw them reach the place; saw them lift off the load and come back with the stretcher; saw that there were only two figures instead of three visible at and about the flag; and felt what he could not see—the desolate old man prone among the corn-hills, with his son in his arms. One more embrace, after so many, to the baby, boy, youth and man.

"Now, Mac, what do we do with our dead man? Who was it?"

"One of our men killed? First I've heard of it. Must be out on the flanks somewhere."

"No; right near here. I passed him as I came up. Here—I can find the very log he lay behind, in half a minute."

"Well, let's be quick," said Mac. "I'm expecting some shells over. Of course you noticed that their white flag was tied onto a gun-rammer."

Will was ashamed to confess that he had not noticed anything of the kind.

Bursting Shells

Fargeon and McClintock found the gap in the fence, debated which way from that had been the point where the former had rejoined after his trip to headquarters, started back, and soon came upon the very log. Will approached it with awe-struck seriousness, ready to turn over the corpse and look in the face of a dead friend. There was nothing there.

"No body—nobody!" cried Fargeon, whereat Mac laughed.

"What does it mean?" asked Will, standing on the log and looking about to see if he could be mistaken. No! There in the distance stood the memorable white-oak! Then he got down where the man had lain, and found dim foot-tracks, and marks that might have been made by the toes of boots. Also a dint that might have come from the butt of a musket. Then he cried to Mac to come and look—at not less than a dozen cartridges, partly hidden under the log.

"It means a skulker," said Mac. "A corporal, too, you say? If I can prove it on him, I go for tearing his stripes off in the face of the whole regiment; then having him bucked and gagged, put on police duty for a month and docked of a year's pay! That's a thing that's *got* to be squelched!"

"Why, Mac—is it common?"

"Common? Don't ask me! Every battle is fringed with 'em. The fine fellows get killed and wounded and the skulkers live forever, and their widows draw pensions afterward."

"I guess I can pick him out, Mac. I'll let you know if I succeed."

He strolled off to the line and joined one group of gossipers after another, telling them a little of the scene at the flag of truce, concerning which they were extremely curious.

"Cale Dugong, where were you in the fight?"

"I was right in over yonder, Cap, or a leetle more to the left. I was just telling the boys how I knocked over two of the Johnnies—I shouldn't wonder if one of the wounded men see me aim at him. Maybe not, though. But I know one of the killed did; and it was the last thing he ever did see, too."

"Which two of our men were you between?"

"Oh, I started in between Eph Tolliver an' Tom Looser, didn't I, boys?"

"Yes; that's the way we stood coming up through the woods, an' after we got to the fence, before the rebs come out."

"Well, there's where it was, then. After the reserve jined, I dunno who I was with, I was a-firin' so fast. I bet there ain't a man in the company fired more cartridges than I did!" He opened his cartridge-box, and, to be sure, it was half empty.

"Maybe that's because you fired so often before you were told to fire! Step this way, Caleb: I've got to have a talk with you."

Caleb obeyed, his face turning rapidly from "red as a beet to white as a sheet," the boys said, winking at each other as he disappeared in the wake of the captain.

They walked to the log in grim silence.

"Pick up those cartridges and put them back in your box."

"Why, Cap—"

"Silence, sir! Now throw some leaves over where your toes and the butt of your gun scratched the dirt. Hide your shame!"

Caleb obeyed.

"What ye goin' t' do to me, Cap? I was sick —honest, I was." And he proceeded to give some plausible functional reason for his defection.

When he had done, Fargeon pointed back to his place in the ranks, saying sternly:

"Private Dugong, go back to your duty."

"Ain't I a corp'ral no more, Cap?"

"No. We don't want skulking corporals. If you resign and rip off your stripes, all right; if you don't, it will be done for you. If you are brought before a court-martial, you may be shot for leaving the ranks under fire. Your life depends on your future conduct."

He left Caleb sitting on the log, helpless with fright. The culprit soon braced up, however, and blustered back into his place.

"Well, I won't stand it! I'll go back to the ranks! Any private could make a mistake an' fire without orders, an' nobody'd say a word to him; but let a corp'ral do it wunst and he gits abused like a dog! Yes, sir! You needn't call me Corp'ral Cale no more!" And they did not.

Fargeon told Mac what he'd done, and the latter remarked:

"Well, that's good in one way, anyhow, even

if it's bad in another. It gives us another chance to promote a man. Clinton Thrush is a sergeant; he'll be off for a long time, if he ever comes back. We can promote a corporal to his place and raise two men from the ranks."

"Hard on Clinton."

"No! He ought to be a lieutenant by that time. Lots of vacancies coming; not to speak of new regiments."

"I'd like to see little Mark a corporal, for particular reasons."

"Mark'll be one, of course, though we'll lose him as our orderly. Ought to have been one from the start, knowing as much as he does. How would Clinton's brother Aleck do for a sergeant, and Chipstone for a corporal?"

"Couldn't be better."

Orders now came from headquarters to return to camp at once. [The two guns had been overtaken and turned backward.] Word was passed along the line to come to "attention" and "prepare to retire as skirmishers"; but before the order could be obeyed a flash in the opposite woods sent across the corn-field a slight gleam visible in spite of the sunshine. Soon followed the roar of a distant field-piece, and, almost at the same instant with the sound, the shriek of a near shell passing over their heads; then among the trees behind them there was another great bang as the shell burst; then a humming, as of a hundred gigantic bees, from the fragments of the shell as they flew through the air, hunting the neighborhood for victims.

The men in the immediate vicinity dropped flat down as if they had been struck by lightning. It seemed impossible for human nature to stand up before and beneath the yelling, flying beast. Fargeon dropped among the rest. He felt as if he could not hug mother earth closely enough—he would have liked to dig a hole, with his nails, to hide in. Almost before the echoes of the first shot died away another rang out, with the same series of sounds. The shriek of a shell is more appalling than the scream of an angry horse.

Will knew that something must be done, but what? He wished he could ask Mac. As he framed the wish he heard Mac's drawl above him; raised his head, and there was the bold fellow erect and cool, standing on the top rail of the fence, steadying himself with his left hand on a fence stake, while he peered under his right at the opposite woods.

"Two pieces—that's all. I wish I knew how much infantry they've got! Can't have been much while we were fighting, or they'd have come out and supported their skirmishers. No matter, though. We couldn't venture to go for the guns with only one company. It would take all our men to drag the pieces—allowing for losses before we got hold of 'em. If I had a regiment I'd try it; I would! That is, of course, with your consent, Captain."

Will got up and began to brush the dust off his clothes, but by this time the first gun was reloaded, and again he saw the flash and heard the shriek, the double explosion and the humming—heard them from the ground as before; Mac still perched high above him. The third missile struck in the corn-field, the fertile soil being too mellow for a ricochet.

"They are getting the range," coolly observed Mac. "Let's get back, Captain, whenever you are ready."

"The sooner the better," said Fargeon, now shamed out of his nervousness. "If you'll go to the right I'll go to the left."

"Very well—oh, I thought you said I was to go to the right."

"Do; and I will go to the left."

"Yes, Captain; but you are going to the right now."

"Surely, surely! There; I'll go to the right and you the left. I forgot that I should always talk of right or left as if we were facing the enemy."

The long, straggling, scattered line now worked slowly toward camp, the halting portion of the men always selecting trees, and peering out from behind them as the moving men retired past. The shells still rang merrily, and the tree-tops suffered some damage, but nobody was hurt. Will asked Mac if it wasn't wonderful.

"Naw!" answered Mac contemptuously, true infantryman that he was. "Artillery scares, but doesn't kill. It's only the musket that means business." And he tramped back and forth along the line, talking incessantly, as was evidently his habit in action.

As the sense of danger again wore off, Will's spirits took another rebound, and he moved and talked as Mac did, just as if there were no peril in shells. Then he heard a man near him cry out "Ouch!" and saw him drop his gun and begin squeezing the right hand under his left arm as a boy might who had pounded his thumb with a hammer. One of the buzzing iron bees had evidently stung. Will picked up the gun, and caught a glimpse of the hurt hand as the man hurriedly and anxiously inspected it. It was a mere glimpse, but it showed a broken bone, and bloody skin and flesh both fat and lean. Will told the sufferer to hurry on to camp; and himself resumed his tramping back and forth, carrying the gun and feeling a little nausea.

A new depression seized him; his mind's eye saw only the horrors of the day, and his mind's ears heard only the bubbling escape of air from Private Huger's breast. His fancy pictured this last wounded man going through life with a maimed, misshapen, hideous, useless right hand; a burden to himself and the world. The cannon firing behind them suddenly stopped.

"Now, look out for them, boys!" shouted Mac. "Every man take a tree when he halts, and give 'em 'Hail Columbia' if they're tryin' for a rush."

Will repeated the order, and as Mac didn't take a tree he did not either, but moved back and forth as before.

"Cap Fargeon don't take no tree," he heard one halted man call to his neighbor.

"Cap hain't got no use for no tree," called back the one addressed.

Once more a happy glow filled his heart, and he felt a lump rise in his throat and dew start to his eyes. He loved the men who had praised him. He loved all the men in his company. Then he thought of their being food for powder; the mere sport of fate. "The best fellows get killed; while the skulkers live forever, and their widows draw pensions afterward," Mac had said. Oh, how can a just God permit such things? So did pleasure and pain follow each other across his abnormally excited soul.

No enemy appeared, and soon the movement became a mere scattered tramp to the rear. Fargeon approached McClintock and they walked along together.

"They got their full ration in the cornfield," said Mac.

"Yes—poor devils!"

"If we hadn't met their flag of truce where we did, they would have found out how weak we are, and tried to get back at us, for keeps."

They walked on in silence, Will thinking of Private Huger and his father.

"Oh, Mac! can't this business be stopped?"

"It ought to be. It's a cursed shame."

"Think of that poor old Capt'n Huger!"

"Ya-as. The old cuss ought to know better. But, then, both sides do it when they get a chance."

"Do what, do you mean?"

"Why, use the flag of truce to snoop information."

"Oh! that was not what I had in mind."

"What then?"

"Oh, the whole beastly job—the slaughter, the wounds, the maimings, the bereavements."

"Oh, I see! Well, how can we help them?"

"Just look at it! Take that young Huger, cut off in his prime and promise, shot through the lungs in a corn-field by a man that had nothing against him—Chipstone, as good a fellow as ever lived, without a hard feeling in his heart toward any man on earth; I can see that Chip feels it. He looks like a ghost, and hasn't opened his lips since we picked up the poor boy."

"Oh, Chip'll get over it."

"I hope he will; or I'm afraid he will; I don't know which."

"Let him go and take a good look at Clint Thrush's leg. That'll help him."

"Oh, my God! It makes me sick." Will threw his disengaged hand up toward the unanswering sky.

"Well, how are we going to carry on war if you look at all those things?"

"It ought never to be carried on at all!"

"Oh, of course! Bad the best way you can fix it. But that's none of my business. Our job is to make war; somebody else's job is to make peace."

"I wonder there aren't lots of our fellows poking over to see what the firing is all about."

"Like as not they never heard a thing—except these last cannon-shots."

"What? That fusilade not heard in camp?"

"No. You see the wind is in our faces as we go back. And then the air is dry and thin; that makes a wonderful difference. If it had been rainy they might have heard the muskets in spite of the woods."

"Well, that young aide-de-camp must have told we were engaged."

"Yes, he told it at headquarters of course; and then probably the stretchers were started and the brigade was called out under arms on the color line. No chance for anybody to wander in the woods after that. Still, as you say, there ought to have been messengers constantly going and coming—would have been if headquarters amounted to shucks."

"To be sure, he brought us orders to retire."

"Ya-as, but how did they know we *could* retire in proper order, bringing dead and wounded. Suppose we'd met a regiment, instead of a company, and they'd outflanked us and wrapped us all up!"

"The prisoners we sent in told the story."

"Thanks to our good luck and good fighting, not to their good management."

So they tramped along through the scattered underbrush, spotted with sunshine and shadow.

Meanwhile an unlooked-for glory and pleasure was in store for them.

Honor and Oblivion

"COMPANY—HALT! By the right flank, close intervals—MARCH!"

The skirmishers were coming in sight of camp. They faced into line (fronting toward the enemy, of course), and re-formed, re-counted and re-dressed the ranks disordered by their losses.

The officers drew swords. "By fours, right—FACE! Right shoulder—shift—ARMS! Forward by file right—MARCH! Left—left—left—left."

As they neared the camp they saw that the three regiments of the brigade were under arms on the color line, standing at "rest." [They had been called out, as Mac had guessed they would be, at the sound of the cannon.]

A wild "Heigh!" started spontaneously from the long brigade line when the head of Company K came in sight. Again and again it rose, springing up in one part of the line after another, and always spreading along the ranks from end to end, while the men swung their caps or raised them high in air on the points of their bayonets.

Somewhere in K's rank was heard a strong voice (alas! not Clinton Thrush's!) starting the company song, to which all burst into chorus at the proper time:

"Company K has shown the way.
    BULLY FOR YOU! BULLY FOR ALL!
Your turn's a-coming some other day.
    BULLY FOR YOU! BULLY FOR ALL!"

The other companies of the Sixth took up the song, and then the rest of the brigade caught on in a hearty though desultory and irregular fashion. They paid small attention to words. "Company K! Company K!" was good enough for the song, and "Bully for you! Bully for all!" was always ready when anybody thought it was time for the chorus.

Fargeon was going to lead his men straight in, past the right flank of the brigade, but as he approached he saw the commanding officer (lieutenant-colonel) of the nearest regiment motioning him down toward the left flank. Not knowing just what he would be at, Will changed direction to the right, and soon found that K was to be highly honored.

The lieutenant-colonel brought the regi-

ment to "attention," with arms at shoulder. Then, to the surprise and delight of the homecoming skirmishers, he cried:

"PRESENT—ARMS!"

Fargeon turned to the happy, excited faces of Company K, and called "SHOULDER—ARMS!" [The marching salute was with arms at "shoulder."] Tears of gratified pride rose to his eyes—why, he did not know. The springs of smiles and tears lie close together.

The other regiments in turn were called to "attention," and the salute repeated; and the Sixth, when its turn came, gave three regular cheers and a "tiger" to its distinguished brothers.

At last K reached its tent-street. The coats were old; the caps, once so jaunty, were in all possible shapes of crushed, misshapen disfigurement—the whole uniform was shabby, with various shades of faded blue and various signs of sun and rain, wear and tear; but yet its wearers were clothed with honor and distinction. Company K had fought, suffered, triumphed, and had brought in prisoners and trophies.

"Company — HALT! Break ranks — MARCH!" And with a last "Heigh!" and the usual slapping of musket-stocks, the boys darted into their tents, laid aside their arms and accoutrements, and flung themselves flat on their backs for welcome, grateful rest. They had not known till now how tired they were. The absence of their comrades under arms on the color line, gave them an interval of delicious solitude; utter silence reigned; their eyes closed as if by magic, and some were asleep almost on the instant.

But George Chipstone lay staring at the canvas above him as if he could never sleep again.

Fargeon had noticed that Colonel Puller

was not with the regiment under arms. In fact, all the regiments were in charge of lieutenant-colonels. He went at once to the colonel's tent to report, but learned from an orderly that his commander, with the other colonels, was at brigade headquarters, where some festivity was in progress on the occasion of a sword presentation to the valiant Y. R. Puller, of the Sixth Illinois. A committee from his home district had arrived, which would have taken him greatly by surprise if he had not known all about it beforehand, and now he was entertaining the delegation at headquarters, where speeches were being made, toasts drunk, and a "good time" was enjoyed at a spread given by Colonel Puller to the general, his staff, the visitors, and other invited guests.

Will made his way to brigade headquarters —a neighboring farm-house—and heard, from the open windows, sounds of merriment that jarred on his ears; that festive volubility which is so repulsive to a sad and sober listener. He sent in his name to Colonel Puller; no answer came out for a long time, because the messenger dared not interrupt the speaking; and when word did come it was:

"Colonel Puller sends his compliments to Capt. Fargeon, and requests him to call at his quarters in an hour."

He went back to his own tent sick at heart, the reaction from excitement and tension of nerves taking full possession of soul and body. He threw himself prone along his rude couch and pressed his eyeballs hard with his fingers. "Who am I? Am I Will Fargeon, or am I a Sabbath-breaking, tobacco-smoking, swearing, drinking, murdering ruffian? Who was it storming up and down that man's corn-field, glad to see my friends killing other people's friends? Glad Chipstone's bullet plowed through the lung of that splendid old man's splendid son! Glad my men fired low and sure while theirs fired high and wild! Glad about those corpses with flies sucking the unshed tears from their eye sockets!

"That was just about church-time; when Sally was sitting at the sweet-toned organ, playing soft and low; while the sun was throwing through the stained glass that special ray that always makes her hair look like an aureole. I can hear her voice chanting, 'And on earth peace, good will to men'; while I was screaming through the din, 'Fire low, men! Aim every time!'

"Is it all a horrid nightmare? No—there is the wall of the tent; I can feel the roughness of it with my fingers. What a looking hand! How horribly shabby I am all over! On earth fire low—peace—aim your piece every time. That's a pun, isn't it?" And he fell asleep.

"Hello!" called a vinous voice in spiritous accents. "Hello! Capt'n Fargeon, I believe."

"Ye-es, sir; I believe so too."

"Well, Captain, I represent the 'Fulcrum,' as you may have heard. I just asked Colonel Puller *who* had the honor of commanding our force in the little ruction this morning and he named you." [Silence.] "Now, Cap, I being who I am, and you being who you are, you may readily fancy my object in disturbing your rosy slumbers."

"And what can I do for you, Mr.—?"

"Call me whatever you please, Cap—it's all one—when you talk to me you talk to the 'Fulcrum.' That is, I presume, a sufficient introduction. You had but one company I understand; and I suppose the force you met outnumbered yours two to one, eh? Or was it ten to one this time?"

"Mr.—Mr.—Fulcrum, I may be wrong, but as I understand my duty, it is to make my report in the first instance to my immediate superior, Colonel Puller."

"Oho! Red tape, eh? First lesson in tactics for new beginners is red tape!" [Silence.] "Now, once more, Captain, and for the last time, I ask if you will furnish the public through our columns the details of your alleged skirmish of this morning."

Will slowly rose, slowly pulled aside the tent-flap, pointed in silence toward the outside, and waited till the upstart, with a contemptuous snort, departed.

All was dark, dismal, disgusting, degraded —well-nigh intolerable. Will said to himself:

"Lucky there's no whisky at hand—I should be almost tempted to take some to put me back into that contemptible state of ignoble self-complacency."

Suddenly he bethought himself of his pipe. He found it and filled it; then, looking around for a paper to light at the camp-fire, his eye fell upon the letter to be delivered "if I fall," and he hastened to crumple and burn it, as if it had been something to be ashamed of.

After Fargeon had made his report to Col. Puller, the latter joyfully welcomed the young dispenser of fame, and submitted to the inevitable interview with scarcely disguised gratification, flattering· frankness, and unlimited whisky and cigars.

Fargeon was very glad of this, for he would have been sorry to be the means of depriving his brave fellows of the solace that flows from public mention of public service. As to his personal share in the skirmish, he held it in very humble esteem, and would try not to grieve if the offense he had given should result in his being deprived of anything beyond a bare mention of his name as commanding the fighting force. He knew that some bright eyes would glisten, and some friendly faces would smile

with approval, on merely knowing that he was on hand and had his share in the manly fray.

Then he let his fancy roam a little along the road to fame—so easy for the eyes of the soldier, and so hard for his feet—and read in advance the letters and newspapers that were to reach him through the mails of the next month or two if he should live so long. Sara Penrose? Surely; sweetest and best of all. Her father? Yes; urging that to God should be given the glory. Families of his soldiers? Yes, indeed! Business friends? Probably some; perhaps even one from Mayer Moss-Rosen, his close competitor in the bitter rivalry of trade. How gratifying and consoling *that* would be!

To return to our resting boys: The men of the brigade under arms were relieved from their tiresome confinement on the color-line; not as soon as they might have been, but as soon as the attention of the brigadier-general could be drawn from Puller's hospitable board and turned in their direction. Then the rest of the Sixth swarmed over Company K's quarters and put a speedy end to all repose.

Over and over did the men have to tell of their "baptism of fire." Cale Dugong was perhaps the most graphic and soul-satisfying narrator; George Chipstone the least, for he lay in his tent and scarcely opened his lips.

"Killed a fine young chap," said the others in a whisper, to account for his "horrors."

"Well, what of it? That's what we come out for," said Dugong. "I expect I killed two. Seen 'em drop, anyhow, an' I'm glad of it!"

When Mark brought up the officers' supper he mentioned Chip's predicament to Captain Fargeon, and the captain thought he ought to do something for the good fellow. He had Mark send him up.

"Chipstone, you and Clinton are great friends, aren't you?"

"Yes, Captain," answered the other in a hollow voice.

"Let's go over to the hospital, and cheer him up a little. You get his things together and bring them with you. I'll pass you along."

As they walked Will said: "A Chicago newspaperman is in camp. I suppose our friends at home will get news by day after to-morrow of the good job we did to-day."

No answer.

"Those rebels seem to think they are going to destroy the great United States of America! We have *got* to teach them that it can't be done, while any of us are living. You and I may fall; some other good men will step into our places. The southerners will find they've 'bit off more than they can chaw,' as the country folks say. *They* began it, but *we'll* stay and finish it. Don't you say so?"

"Oh, I suppose it's got to be done by somebody."

"Of course it has! And the bitterer the lessons we give them, the sooner they'll learn the great truth. Did you notice how savage that rebel lieutenant was?"

"Wasn't he!"

"Slave-holding seems to have made those men crazy with pride and foolishness. Now, I haven't got anything against that fellow, but I can see that nothing but blood-letting will give him common sense."

"It's no use to go easy on 'em."

"No. Any kind of half-way fighting would be sheer cruelty. It would be like the fellow who was too soft-hearted to cut his dog's tail off all at once, so he cut it off an inch at a time."

Chipstone gave a half laugh at this illustration, and they reached the hospital—a neighboring barn pressed into the service. Long rows

of cots covered the floor in every direction. They were chiefly occupied with sick men, as the visitors observed as they passed and asked the way to the corner devoted to the wounded.

The great doors at each side of the barn were wide open, the breeze swept through, and the low-descending sun shone kindly in with level rays. Attendants moved about here and there, carrying to the disabled soldiers such rude comforts as a field hospital affords. Pale faces looked at the visitors, and two or three voices called to them:

"Cap, got any newspapers?"

Will was sorry he had no reading matter to relieve their tedium, and made a mental note of what should be his first care on the morrow.

They made straight for the cots devoted to their own companions, and the eyes of the Company K boys lighted up at their approach, and even the wounded confederates seemed to smile at their late antagonists. Familiar voices greeted them: "Hello, Captain! Hello, Chipstone!"

Both gave a hearty hand-clasp to each prostrate comrade. Clinton Thrush was the most seriously wounded, and another—the man who had his hand hurt—sat by his side waving a leafy branch to keep the flies off his exposed and bandaged leg. Clint knew them, but fever had come on, and he talked incessantly and incoherently, in a voice of weakness and excitement.

"Bully for you! Bully for all! Company K in the corn-field. Says Mac, 'Forward, boys!' and I heard him say 'Forward boys!' and I did forward boys! Cap, I'll leave it to you if I didn't forward boys when he sung out 'Forward boys!' First thing I knew I didn't know anything! Give a man all the appellations in the world and take away his consignments, and what'll he offer at next? But *then!* Aleck is my brother. That's nothing against him. Mac had no call to be hard on Aleck for being my brother. Oh, Captain—you'll stand by Aleck, if he *is* my brother, won't you? Don't let Mac hurt him for being my brother. Him an' I are all the boys mother's got—except the girls. Oh, mother! Oh, mother!" And he began to cry in a foolish fashion.

To divert his thoughts, and if possible calm his shattered nerves, Will began in a gentle voice:

"Our God he saw us from on high."

And almost on the instant the poor fellow took up the melody, and in a voice like his own clear tenor, only sublimated, as if made of the breath of Heaven itself, he sang and sang until every other sound was hushed into silence; and still the sweet, touching strain soared aloft and floated out into the fading, dying day. Never afterward, never as long as he lives, can Will sing that strain; nor can he even hear it sung without a choking in his throat and a rush of tears to his eyes.

An attendant brought the sufferer a soothing drink, and he became calm and quiet. Will let go his hand and turned to talk with the surgeon, who was attending the confederate wounded.

"Captain," said the doctor, "I'm glad to see you. The boys are all doing well except Clinton. We are going to try to save his life and maybe his leg, but I don't know about it. If he were at home, in his natural climate and surroundings, he would be all right. But here—blood thinned by hot weather, hard work, and poor food—"

"Why not send him home at once, doctor?"

"Oh, of course we can't send every wounded man home. Ambulances can't be spared, nor attendants provided for individual enlisted men, sick or wounded. They have to be treated together."

"Great heavens! Must the brave boys stay here and die when they might go home and live?"

"Well, how would you fix it?"

"Oh, I don't know! Any way to save lives and limbs. The whole State of Illinois ought to come down for them if necessary!"

"The state won't do it, and can't. If she'll send us well men to take their places when we lose them, that's all we can ask."

"When will you decide about Clinton?"

"In the morning we shall know. We won't amputate if we can save the leg, and we won't amputate if it isn't going to be any use."

"How—any use?"

"Well, if he can't live anyhow. In Mexico we didn't have much luck with large stumps. So much against the patient; so many died of trouble with the stump—they call it blood-poisoning nowadays—that we got to feel as if we might as well let them die without the knife as after it."

"Clinton's brother Aleck ought to be with him."

"Well, why not have him detailed as hospital nurse?"

"The very thing! I'll attend to it to-night."

The doctor smiled enigmatically, but did not say anything more. Fargeon spent the next hour passing from cot to cot; chatting with the men, making memoranda of their little needs and wishes, comforting and encouraging them in every way; his own spirit growing calmer and happier in this congenial task. It was the pleasantest hour of his day, this stormy Sunday.

"Here's where I belong," said he to himself. "Saving life, instead of destroying it; giving comfort and consolation; making peace, instead of war. Blessed are the peacemakers. Oh, how I wish I had such a job as this instead of that other—that infernal corn-field!"

As they walked back, Chip said: "What did the doctor say about Clint?"

"Very doubtful."

"Which, leg or life?"

"Both. If the fever goes off, the leg must probably *come* off; and if they amputate the leg, he'll have a poor chance to get over it."

"Great God! Is that so?"

"Yes. Likely that bullet has silenced Clinton Thrush's singing for good."

"Curse the bullet—and the man that fired it!"

"And those who sent him to fire it," added Fargeon.

As they walked on in silence he said to himself:

"I guess Chip is all right again."

When he spoke to Mac about sending Aleck to serve in the hospital, the lieutenant gave a snort of dissatisfaction.

"Why, Aleck Thrush is one of the best men in the company! If they call on us for a hospital detail we can pick out men who will be no loss; but Aleck Thrush—! The hospital's the place for the trash that haven't got snap enough to fight—the grannies in trousers—but Aleck, he's a *man!*"

"All the same, Company K won't keep him away from his brother while I have anything to say about it." ("But I guess I won't go into the hospital service myself just at present.")

Next morning was rainy, but the requisition in Company K for an enlisted man to serve as hospital attendant came promptly, and Aleck was sent. He carried with him every old newspaper there was in the whole brigade. The The poor fellow's trembling delight was a sight to see. He sang for joy and set off for Clinton's bedside running like a deer.

"See him scoot! Aleck always was the beater to run; he beat us all in a foot-race like we was standing still; but I'll bet this time he's a-beatin' himself!"

Speed uselessly made. Aleck might as well have run in the opposite direction. Before he reached the barn-hospital he met four men carrying a stretcher, using their disengaged hands in restraining the weak, frantic struggles of Company K's first martyr—the brave fellow, the good man, the sweet singer, De Witt Clinton Thrush. His ravings had become a terror and a danger to the other sick and wounded, and he was being carried away out their hearing.

"Christ! Is that my brother? Here, Clint! Old boy, don't ye know Aleck? There, there, there, there!" The soothing tones reached the sufferer's ears and heart, and he threw his arms around Aleck's neck and tried to climb off the stretcher by their help, while the wounded leg bled afresh.

Expelled from the hospital, surrounded by sighing woods through which the rain dropped drearily, no shelter in the world open to him to die in, home and mother and sisters five hundred miles away!

Late the next afternoon Aleck crept back to camp with a piece of board he had somewhere found; and all night he hacked and carved at it until he had made a deep-cut and legible inscription to distinguish his brother's lonely grave. Our forces did not hold this position; and after we retired it is probable that some enemy found the spot and destroyed the simple record, or perhaps the wood-fires burned it, or hogs rooted it up. But what difference did that make? Nobody ever went back to look for it.

* * *

Boat, Bivouac, and Breakfast

"Mac, where have you been?"

"Away out in the bow, Captain."

"On the lookout for rebs?"

"On the listen. Come forward and hark. There; now we're out of the noise of our own boat. Hark!"

Boommm!

Booooommmmm!

"What's that?"

"Gun-boats shelling Fort Donelson."

"Can they take the fort?"

"Naw!" [The *no* contemptuous is *naw*.] "Artillery can destroy, but it's only infantry that can capture."

"Mac, do you know, I half suspect you were born in the infantry." After waiting in vain for a laugh at this poor joke he changed the subject.

"Who is this Grant, anyhow?"

"West Point and Mexico."

"Is he all right?"

"I guess so, if he'll keep straight. He was a bully good company officer; but I hear he went a little wild after he came home from Mexico."

"Will he do any good here?"

"Well, he took Fort Henry the other day with a hurrah, after the gum-boots had tramped it all out of shape. Now he's after bigger game—their whole army and Donelson itself."

At last the Saginaw ran her nose into the muddy bank and the Sixth Illinois disembarked, looking in vain for the Silverheels with the regimental baggage. When they could wait no longer, the men marched along the rear of the earlier comers to their designated camp: alas! no camp! "Foot, Legget and Walker's line again," they said.

As they plodded wearily on, "hunching up" their heavy cartridge-boxes, and changing their heavy muskets from one shoulder to the other, they could hear the novel, thrilling sounds on their left—distant musketry and field artillery, and always the sullen thunder of the fort and the gun-boats.

Weary miles are passed. Night falls, and the gleam of camp-fires lights up the tents of the troops already encamped.

"Say, fellers, ain't we most thar?"

"Never you mind, Johnny, my son. Jest you 'tend to business, an' keep a-puttin' one foot afore the other."

"Ah, yah! Thankee fer nothin', Jeff Cobb. I've been a-doin' that so long I'm tired of it. I b'lieve I'll try puttin' one foot behind the other for awhile." And Johnny turned around and walked backward until the man following him threatened to step on his toes.

"Whar in thunder is our tavern? Blamed if I don't think we must 'a' passed it unbeknownst."

"Nary. We'd 'a' knowed it by the smell of the beefsteak and fried onions they're a-gettin' ready for our supper."

Somebody struck up "The Lord, He saw Us from on High," and for a while the way was lightened with the inspiring music. A melting snow began to fall, and the cheery voice of Mac rang out through the darkness:

"Secure arms! Git yer gunlocks under yer armpits, boys! Ye may not want 'em, but when ye *do* want 'em ye want 'em *bad,* and ye want 'em *dry.*"

A voice called out, "Who's dry in this crowd?" and another answered, "I be—ef ye've got anything in yer flask wuth drinkin'," which raised a low laugh.

The mud was terrible, especially for Company K, which had to tread where the other nine companies had preceded it. Feet floundered and slipped hither and yon. Shoes were loaded and invisible; trousers solid with mire as high as the knees, and plastered up to the waistband, above which coats were spattered to the collar.

Fargeon himself started, "Bully for you, bully for all," and again there was a short space of relief from tedium.

At length they left the soft, slippery road, and halted in a forest of evergreens, where the foliage looked inky black in contrast with the snow that covered the ground and loaded the branches. The night was dark, moonless and starless; and if it had not been for the snow they would have had almost to feel their way. Will groaned in spirit as he thought of the cheer, the moonlit beauty, and the paved streets of Chicago, the floored and roofed houses, the loaded tables, and the lighted fires and lamps.

"Mac, what does this mean?"

"What does what mean, Captain?"

"Why, this; no tents, no blankets, no food, no fire, no axes—no anything but cold and wet and misery!"

"Well, Captain, it means *war;* that's all."

Will kicked the toe of one boot against the heel of the other, alternately, to restore circulation, and then mused aloud:

"It seems incredible! Here am I, a free American citizen, unconvicted of crime, with money in my pocket, and yet I can't leave this —this infernal *purgatory* to get warm and buy a meal of victuals and a night's lodging, to save my life."

Mac smiled grimly for a moment and then rejoined:

"You are not a free citizen. You're a soldier; and you don't come out to save your life, but to spend it—lose it, like enough."

However, a few axes are soon borrowed from a neighboring battery camp, and then how the boys leap and fly to the work! Scarcely is a tree felled before it is stripped of bark and branches by strong hands pulling, twisting, tearing at everything that will come off by help of knives, bayonets, stones, or any other substitute for the friendly ax. The first flames light the choppers to redoubled efforts, and before midnight every company has its fires and its store of fuel laid by for all-night cheer. Even the butt ends of the burning logs hiss and sing almost like the comfortable tea-kettles of home.

Lucky the man who finds himself at last lying upon two sticks of somewhere nearly equal size, which keep his body at least partly clear of the cold snow; his wet feet toward a fire, his musket in the hollow of his arm, his cartridge-box under his head, his haversack spread on his stomach, and its last bits and crumbs finding their way into that long-suffering organ. Those who have no remaining bits and crumbs will know better how to husband their "three-days' cooked rations" on future marches; not throwing away a hard-tack merely because it tastes moldy, or a bit of pork because it smells tainted.

But he who has food is only half blessed if he have not also his tobacco; and he who must fast is not utterly forlorn if he have his tobacco. The luxurious cigar, the comfortable pipe, or even (boldly be it said) the consolatory mouthful! Call it not a "cud," or a "quid"; call it rather a drop of the balm of forgetfulness; a bud of the lotus, which, when Ulysses' fellow-voyagers tasted, they were cured of their homesickness. Spurn, if you will, the churl who has less excuse for resorting to it, but do not begrudge it to the cold, wet, tired, hungry, homesick patriots of Company K.

About midnight some officers pass along the line, calling:

"Fires out! Fires out! General orders says extinguish all fires!"

"What in God's name is that for?"

"The light will draw the enemy's fire."

"Ah, yah! If we can stand it, he can."

"Fires out, I tell you."

"Hell fires out! Nothing out! If General Orders wants our fires put out let him come here and—spit on 'em."

"What regiment is this? I'll report you!"

"The Forty-'leventh Froze-to-death. Give General Orders the compliments of the Forty-'leventh Froze-to-death, and tell him if he'll send us some tents and something to eat we'll put out our fires."

"Where are the officers of this regiment?"

"No officers present, but you. We're all men out here in the snow; and we'll keep our fires till the tents come."

"That's what I call a mutiny!"

"Call it a matinee if you're a min'ter. Only move on about your business."

"Officer of the guard! Where's the guard of this regiment?"

"Out in front, where it belongs, you fool! Out in front, where you don't never go!" (General laughter.)

The *vis inertia* of a great line of prostrate men, half seen by the fitful fire-light, half hidden in the dense darkness of overhanging foliage, was too much for the troublesome emissaries of authority. They could not even say where the voice or voices came from; so they seemed (as in a sense they were) the voice of the regiment at large. They gave one parting threat:

"If these fires aren't out in half an hour the provo' guard will come down and arrest every man that refuses to obey orders."

Then they disappeared, pursued by jeering laughter. The fires were kept going, and the provo' guard did not come.

From one o'clock to four, Capt. Fargeon slept almost constantly, only waking when some man, more uncomfortable than the average, would get up and throw a stick on the fire, rousing clouds of smoke, all alive with sparks, swirling toward the sky, in graceful spirals that died away among the tree-tops.

At about four the first deep slumber gave way to anxious thoughts, and after one or two uneasy lapses into dreams and half-forgetfulness, he found himself broad awake and watching the snow-flakes which had again begun to fall.

With yawns and stretchings he rose from his rigid couch and moved his stiffened joints, feeling so purposeless and spiritless that he wished he could longer have remained oblivious to his painful environments. But the sight of the well-known figures of his own beloved Company K men put from his mind all thought of self, and awakened in him a full, keen sense of his responsibilities. He tramped along the irregular line till he came to the beginning of Company I's men; and then he turned back, hunting for McClintock, his guide, philosopher and friend, his ever-present help in time of need. At length he saw the calm, bronzed face that was always restful to his eyes. Mac was sharing the blanket of two soldiers, each of whom had evidently been so anxious to accommodate the great lieutenant that they had gradually robbed themselves of their precious shelter for his benefit.

Mac was sound asleep. His strong chest rose and fell in slow, rhythmic motion, undisturbed by the slight crackling of the fire, the hissing of the end-logs, and the loud chorus of snores that rose into the still air from the recumbent groups. Will was loth to rouse him, and stood for a long time with his back to the blaze, enjoying the genial warmth and the sight and sound of rest and recuperation all around him.

"Sleep, the leveler! Every one of my poor boys is just as happy as any other sound-asleep man on earth! There is nothing more beautiful —but death."

At length Mac stirred, yawned, turned uneasily, and opened his eyes.

"Good morning, Mac."

"Good morning, Captain. Anything up?"

"Nothing, except me. I'm thinking about the boys' breakfasts."

"That's so," said the other, instantly ready for duty, sitting up and spreading the blanket over his two companions. Then, as he arose, he added: "Of course, the regimental commissary didn't get anything last night, and I don't know where the brigade commissary keeps himself."

"I'd like to beg, borrow, or steal a few rations just now."

"So would I. I guess I'll feel my way back to the artillery camp we passed. The battery boys are always best off. With all their guns, caissons, limbers and one-thing-another, they have more transportation than anybody else."

"Good enough! I'll go too."

"Halt! Who goes there?"

"Friends."

"Advance one friend and give the countersign."

"We haven't the countersign. Please call the officer of the guard."

"OFFICER OF THE GUARD! POST NUMBER FOUR!" The officer came.

"We are from the regiment that got in late last night, and we want some help—the Sixth Illinois."

"What! the Sixth! Come along in, gentlemen! This is Taylor's Battery, right from Chicago, where you belong! What can we do for you?"

All was lovely. There were cooked rations on hand enough to justify the loan of a substantial breakfast for Company K, and there were rested and refreshed men astir ready and willing to "pack" the victuals over. Our lucky friends walked back (after a long, blissful drink of hot, black coffee), munching hardtack and boiled salt pork that "went to the spot," as the phrase goes, and then amused themselves by stealing along the sleeping line of Company K, slipping two biscuits and a bit of pork into every sleeper's haversack; not forgetting the men on post, sleepy, tired, and grateful.

By this time it was almost six o'clock, and, though dark, near enough to dawn to tell which way was east.

Reveille was sounded by bugle at brigade headquarters, and by drum and fife at each regiment. The drum-and-fife tune (as expressed by the words the men had fitted to it) ran thus:

Wake ye lazy soldier, Rouse up and be killed,
Hard tack and salt horse, Git yer gizzard filled:
Then go to fighting, Fire yer forty round;
Go dead and lay there, Buried under ground.

The men began to squirm and yawn and twist and turn; while hoarse coughing, hawking, and other catarrhal sounds bore testimony to the injuries which had resulted from the night's exposure to cold and wet. The more hardy spirits gave vent to their feelings in curses or jokes, as their various dispositions inspired them. Quoth Jeff Cobb:

"Hello, Maria Jane! The baby's pulled all

the clothes off in the night." [He added some imaginary domestic baby infelicities.]

"Tell ye what, fellars, I didn't never in my life feel so old as I dew this minute."

"That's all right, Cy. Don't ye know the reason why? It's 'cause ye never was so old."

"Ice-cream for breakfast, all except the cream part," cried Tolliver.

"Oh, Lord! Darn a volunteer, anyhow, and darn any man who wouldn't git up in the middle of the night to darn a volunteer."

"Gabr'el, blow yer trump! I don't want this world to last any longer."

"If any man names hot griddle-cakes, with butter and honey, shoot him on the spot."

"Ya-as, an' if ye can't hit him on the spot, shoot him in the head."

Fargeon's and Mac's little joke soon began to come to its point.

"Tom Lightner, ye infernal cuss, what ye eatin'?"

"Oh, nothin'. I ain't waked up yet. I'm sound asleep an' dreamin' I'm eatin' a bully good breakfast."

"Why, look a-hyer! I'll swear I eat up every scrap last night the' was in my haversack, an' hyer's pork an' crackers! Seems like the Bible yarn consarnin' the Widder Cruse's oil-jug."

"Say, boys, feel in yer haversacks."

"Great Scott alive!"

"Glory hallelujerum!"

"Ah! that's sweeter than a pretty gal playin' the pieanner with her hands crossways."

The Captain and lieutenant stood, coat-tails in hand and backs to the fire, gazing up into the tree-tops in pretended unconsciousness of the excitement, while man after man made his joyful discovery and expressed his sentiments, until Jim Flynn exhausted the subject and capped the climax of eulogy:

"Tell ye what it is, fellers; it's better than a punch in the eye with a cotton umbrella!"

"Boys!" cried Corporal Chipstone, "that's the kind of officers Company K's got! What ye got to say to our officers?"

A wild "He-igh!" arose on all sides which attracted the attention of the neighboring companies; and K's men were proud of their superiority over the rest, whose fast was not broken for an hour and a half—a weary hour and a half, during which food was got from the brigade commissary and cooked.

"Where did you K men get your grub before the rest of us? That ain't no fair shake."

"Oh, our company officers sat up all night makin' pine cones and spruce gum into good hard-tack and boiled salt pork. *That* ain't no trick at all when you once get the hang of it! If we'd a-slep' an hour longer they'd have finished it up into fricasseed chicken an' punkin pie; but we tol' em we wouldn't wait—we'd take it in pork an' crackers."

"Never mind! We'll ketch K in a tight place some day."

"Hope so—water-tight, anyhow."

Company K took its share of the nine o'clock breakfast, but stored most of it in haversacks, having largely satisfied nature's immediate cravings three hours earlier. At about eleven the drummer beat the "long roll."

"Fall in, men! Roll up your blankets and fall in!"

The long line was soon in place.

"Attention, battalion! Shoulder—ARMS! By fours, right—FACE! By route step, forward—MARCH! Right shoulder shift—ARMS!"

Another hour and a half of marching through the sodden snow brought the Sixth to its destined place beyond the furthest out of the troops who had preceded it.

What next? Where's the enemy? What's before us? What's behind us? What's out there on our exposed right flank?

God knows! A private soldier is like a blind horse in a quarry; a precipice on every side and a lighted blast under his feet; his only comfort the bit in his mouth and the feeling of a human hand holding the reins over his back.

Was it truth, or only an *ex post facto* superstition founded on later events, that Jim Flynn and Harry Planter were gayer than usual—the very life of Company K—this morning?

The Affair on the Right

"Battalion—halt!"

"Close up, men; close up!" and the men, as usual, trotted forward to their places, always "hunching up" their heavy cartridge-belts—haversacks were unluckily very light by this time—and there was a constant sound of musket barrels clashing together as they shouldered each other in the snowy road.

"Front! Right—dress! Front! Order—arms! Stack—arms! Rest!"

"Looks as if we were to form the right of the line," said Mac.

"How do you like our position here?" said Fargeon.

"Here? Thunder! This is no *position* at all —only a trap. It's what we call a 'flank in the air.' No cover and no reserve. Rebs coming in force from the right would have a regular picnic—double us up, one regiment after another, as fast as a man can walk, don't you see?"

"Yes, I see," said Will, looking anxiously toward the unknown right.

"First thing should be to deploy a company as skirmishers to find what there is over there; next, put somebody back in support."

"I guess I'll step over and speak to Col. Puller about it."

"Good enough—if he were a soldier, instead of a politician."

"Can't a soldier be anything else, Mac, besides?"

"Yes; but not a politician."

Will smiled at Mac's well-known dislike of "politicians" (especially his own colonel), as he went over to quote Mac's shrewd counsel—with full credit to Mac—which the colonel forthwith carried to brigade headquarters and repeated as his own ideas.

Within an hour the Sixth was formed "in echelon of companies"—each company thrown back about thirty paces behind its left-hand neighbor—to protect the right of our line; and Company K, its blankets laid aside, was deployed as skirmishers, and pushing out into the unknown wilds to seek a foe. They found a friend instead, in the shape of a swamp practically impassable; but the swamp was some half a mile away from the Sixth, and a road ran along its edge, at right angles with our general line of battle.

Here they halted, scattered in skirmishing order, trying their best to be comfortable. Each man selected some tree or stump, and cleared away the snow behind it to leave him a spot wherein to sit, stand, or lie, or stamp about for warmth and a pretense of drying his soaked and usually ragged shoes.

"Unless old Simon Bolivar Buckner is a fool, he will try a flanking movement by this road," said Mac.

"Where did he learn soldiering?"

"He's a West Pointer, too; and was with us in Mexico."

"How will he go to work if he concludes to try it on?"

"March right down this road, by the flank,

'left in front,' until he meets some force that persuades him to deploy."

"That'll be Company K, as skirmishers, won't it?"

"That's what's the matter."

"And if Company K weren't here—what then?"

"Oh, then Boliver'd have a picnic; get down abreast of our 'flank in the air,' right face into line of battle, and double us up in spite of thunder."

"But we're here, Mac."

"You bet we're here!"

"I hope he won't come."

"Oh, we won't really fight him after he forms line of battle. While he marches by the flank, we'll face him. When he gets deployed, our business is to light out."

"Mac, I guess I'll send word to the colonel, to tell him what we've found out."

"Oh—well—but it's his business to send or come to us for the news."

"Likely he doesn't know enough. Anyhow, he'll be pleased with the attention."

"He'll never be pleased with anything we do."

"Why? Jealous of you, you war-worn old regular army veteran?"

"No; though he may possibly guess what I think of *him*. No; the trouble is the praise the Chicago papers gave Company K for the two Grand Hill skirmishes—leaving him out in the cold."

"Oh, he's forgotten that long ago."

"Forgotten it? Capt'n Fargeon, you just wait and see how much of it he's forgotten."

So Will wrote a few lines to tell Colonel Puller the state of things, and dispatched them to headquarters. He began to hope there would be no fight that day. It was getting well on into the afternoon. Oh, if the day might end in quiet! Some men arrived from the regimental commissary with K's share of the noon rations. They were received with the customary "Heigh! heigh!" which changed to jibes and jeers when the food was found to be uncooked.

"They think we're maggots and can live on raw pork."

Then he watched the efforts of Mark Looney to start a fire. It seemed as if the chilly dampness had infected every particle of matter in the whole region. "Dry leaves" were soaking wet. Match after match was fruitlessly tried.

"Have you plenty of matches, Mark?"

"Yis, Caftain. I'd a box av'em this morrnin'."

"Take care of them! They're precious."

"The' are that, sorr!"

Finally Mac lent a hand. He lighted his pipe and puffed it into a fine glow, then inverted it over a promising mass of splinters, and they, tenderly nursed by Mark's breath, at last consented to blaze. While the fluttering baby flame was growing by the addition of the least refractory stuff they could find, Mark cut and slashed the great slabs of pork into rashers (rations?), and many jack-knives made ready many long twigs whereon the meat was soon sizzling, spreading around the most delicious, appetizing odor a soldier's nostrils can inhale.

Alas! The smell was all the boys were ever to get of that feast; for just now Mac's soldierly instinct was roused to cry out:

"Don't forget what we're here for, boys. Remember the rebs!" And his cry was answered by a shot from the front, the bullet whistling noisily over his head.

Instantly every man was on the alert; even little Mark running to where he left his musket, and peering out from behind his tree, forgetting fire and food.

"Save your fire, boys," said Mac, falling into his usual battle drawl, "and remember your orders. If it's a picket or a skirmish line, stand fast till hell freezes over. If it's a line of battle, give 'em one shot, slow and low, and then skeddadle. No running from skirmishers, and no standing against a line of battle. You hear me?"

Seeing Mac walking boldly over to his post on the left, Will left a friendly tree from which he had been peeping (like the privates), and made his way, hurrying and stooping, but with reasonable coolness, over to his place on the right.

Bang! bang! bang! went the guns of his men near the road, the very point he was making for. A dozen answering reports came from the front, accompanied by the sound of flying bullets, one of which seemed to have been aimed at himself.

"What is it, Tom?"

Tom went on reloading as he answered:

"Looked like a picket guard, Captain—just a squad in the road. One man got hit, and they picked him up and started back."

A dead silence follows this, and Fargeon looks at his watch. Four o'clock. It will be dark in less than an hour—all may yet "blow over."

No. Before 4:15 a rattling fire made itself heard from our own line, far on K's left. It was rapid and simultaneous, and indicated that the enemy was upon them in force—no mere skirmish line. Scarcely had this died away when a roar of confederate musketry from K's front set all doubts at rest. It was certainly a regimental volley. Almost immediately the men at his end of the line caught glimpses that drew their fire, and they were answered by another volley, fired by a full regiment apparently, yet harmless.

"Back men! Back! Double-quick!"

They needed no second order.

Here a dreadful thing happened. The rear companies of the Sixth (in echelon) opened fire, and, careful not to fire on each other, aimed too far to the right and sent a good part of their bullets into the left wing of Company K. Curses filled the air, and Mac and his men, thus taken between two fires, came running from the left over to Will's quarter, whence all, in a confused mob, made for the rear, or the swamp, or any place where they should not be slaughtered by both friend and foe.

"Anybody hurt, Mac?"

"Jim Flynn killed and Harry Planter wounded."

"Where's Harry?"

"The rebs have got him by this time."

"Good God!"

The persistent rattle of musketry and frequent roar of artillery indicated strong fighting along the front of the Union line, and the increasing distance of the sounds made it appear that the enemy was gaining some ground. Time passed and with darkness the cruel noise died away.

Company K was scattered widely through the swamp, without any semblance of order, each man hiding or trying to get farther into the underbrush. Will and Mac were squatting, concealed in a spot whence they had seen the enemy in considerable numbers passing down the road, and none seemed to return. They would have lain down, but the standing water was over shoe-top and level with the snow. When the enemy had passed them and night was near, they were startled by a noise behind them, and Mac hurriedly drew his pistol and cocked it.

"Liftin'nt, wud ye kindly lind me a hand?"

It was Mark Looney who approached, dragging his piece with his right hand, while his left was buried in his breast.

"It's in me lift arrum, liftin'nt. It seems to be blaydin' bad, an' I'd like to jist git a bit o' stuff 'round it." As he lowered his arm the fresh blood trickled from his sleeve.

In the gathering darkness they ministered as well as they could to the poor fellow's needs, while, in spite of himself, his teeth chattered and every limb shook with pain, cold and exhaustion. The blood persisted in drip, drip, dripping, as if an artery had been cut.

"Mac, this poor boy'll die in the water and snow. What shall we do?"

"The road's our only chance. Let's risk it; the enemy is off now for a while at any rate."

"Good enough! Can you walk, Mark?"

"I'll thry, sorr." And he did try, still dragging his musket, until Fargeon insisted on taking it from him.

"Now, Captain," said Mac, "give me the gun, and you and Mark stay back, while I push on toward the rear. I'll whistle and keep whistling all the while, unless I hear or see something. When you don't hear me whistle, you get out of the road."

Mac started off, and Will helped Mark along as best he could, the wounded man's hard breathing growing shorter and harder in a manner that showed that this march of his would be a short one—perhaps his last.

They soon lost the sound of Mac's whistle, and shrank into a fence-corner to wait for the foe. None came, and they concluded that Mac had overestimated their speed and simply walked out of hearing. It was now almost dark; still, they could hardly spend the night there, so they began to stagger slowly down the road once more, and accomplished perhaps another quarter mile before Mark gave up entirely.

"Thankin' ye kindly, Caftain, for all your goodness—I've got to give it uf. Ye'll fush on, av ye flaze; and, caftain, dayr, there's wan or two things in me focket I always kef' ready for whin me time kem. The d'rections is wrote on 'em—ye'll see when ye get to a light."

"Why, Mark, do you think I'd leave you?"

"Oah, yis, Caftain, it wouldn't be right fer ye to be took fris'ner along wid me—an' it'd be no good, nayther. Noa, it wud not."

"Now, Mark, I'll never desert you while I live; and as to being taken prisoners, I'd rather see you and me alive in the enemy's hands than dead out of them. So I am going to light a fire, hit or miss, rebels or no rebels, capture or no capture, sink or swim, live or die, survive or perish; here goes for a fire."

The darkness was now impenetrable, but he scraped away the wet snow, as well as he could, from a sheltered nook, while Mark, with his single hand, tried feebly to get together some moderately dry fence splinters, and picked up a few dead leaves and rubbed them on his clothes.

"Well, my boy, those feel pretty dry. Now, where are your matches?"

"In me focket, Caftain."

"Why—your pocket feels wet. And the match-box feels wet."

"I didn't lay down on that side," wailed the sufferer, who had taken heart of grace at the prospect of a little warmth and light. "Could me wownd have bled onto 'em? Oah, I'm afrehd—I'm afrehd soa."

"I pray God they'll light!"

"Ah-min!"

Will rubbed a patch of fence-rail fiercely with his sleeve to dry it, selected a match and carefully scraped it. No light. But that might be an accident. Another careful scrape—no doubt now but that the chemicals had crumbled off unlighted; he could feel them in his fingers. Another match he tries in the same way, with the same result, while Mark grows sick and sicker with apprehension.

"Thry two to wanst, Caftain," he whispered, vainly trying to steady his voice.

No result.

"I guess I'll try one on the inside of my coat, as men light their pipes in the wind."

Vain again, and vain when he tried a dozen in similar fashion.

"You haven't another box, have you, Mark?"

"Nary a wan at all, Caftain, but the wan."

"Now, Mark, you take these three matches and try them together on the inside of my cap, while I hold it solid with both hands."

"The' moight burrn yer caf, sorr!"

"I hope they will—then we'll have a fire sure enough."

Mark's trembling fingers only made the same desperate effort that so often failed before, and it failed again.

"Av I had me ould musket now—I'd jest break a cattridge—an' lave in a little powdher an' the waddin'—an' shoot 'em into some laves —an' the'd burrn—the' wud—Ochone the' wud—oah the' wud!" [For once Mark's plaintive diminuendo was appropriate to the occasion.]

"Now," said Will, "I think I'll save the rest of the matches and dry them before we risk another trial."

He said it in as cheerful and hopeful a tone as he could command—even unconsciously forcing a false smile in the darkness—all to keep his suffering friend from knowing that there were no more. Those three were the last. The soldier's life-blood had destroyed the means of saving his life. Mark must have suspected that the matches were gone, for he mur-

mured in a broken voice "Ochone—Ochone."

Then Fargeon laid Mark down on his well arm, lay down behind him, and embraced his shivering form, "snuggling spoon-fashion," as the children phrase it. His right arm was under Mark's head; his left strove to make one coat cover them both. As to their soaked and benumbed feet, they were past praying for.

"Caftain, dayr," said the thin voice, grown perceptibly weaker even since it spoke last, "d'ye think it's much afther midnight by this?"

"Oh, a long time!" ("God forgive me— it's not nine yet.")

Will thought the sufferer's weakness had brought on hiccoughs, but soon knew that these were half-suppressed sobs that he heard and felt. When he could disguise them no longer, Mark burst out:

"Caftain, dayr—ye'll not tell the byes that I got kilt with a dommed scratch afther all, comin' from our own min—an' died a-cryin' loike a ba-aby!"

"Never! I'll tell them you got your wound like a soldier and bore it like a man, and got well and wore shoulder-straps, like a hero—as you deserve!"

He beat the poor benumbed body and limbs and hugged the frowsy head; his own spirits rising in this congenial life-saving task—rising in direct proportion to the demands making on them. He could have been gay and happy if it weren't for his feet.

The hours of that night ought, perhaps, to be dismissed without a word; for a chapter or a volume could not depict its length and its misery.

Nature sets a kindly limit to distress, by the interposition of a barrier of insensibility, which says to pain, "Thus far shalt thou go and no further"; and this mercy soon came to Mark's relief and he ceased to suffer, though not to moan "Ochone" and shiver. But Fargeon remained conscious of his wretchedness. A text came to his mind: "In my Father's house is enough and to spare, while I perish with hunger."

A scene rose in his memory; a vision of the warm fireside of Mrs. Penrose's comfortable dining-room; a fire in the grate; whole boxes of matches on the mantel; a bright light shining on Sara's face and on a well-spread tea-table redolent with good things to eat and drink—all warm! warm! His nostrils expanded to inhale the aroma of tea, the comforter, only to find themselves filled by the smell of cold, stale tobacco smoke and other squalid things hanging about poor Mark's hair and clothes.

Grant to the Rescue

All night long, at stated intervals, the long, low thunderous groan of a gunboat cannon came to Will's ears from the distant river. It was almost a comfort—a sign of life in the midst of awful loneliness and desolation.

After midnight the stars came out and the cold grew more bitter. While Will was trying to accustom himself to an endless darkness and a limitless suffering, three figures might have been seen creeping cautiously along the edge of the road, peering sharply into it and into the neighboring shadows. Two carried swords and one a musket. One of the sword-bearers was whistling low and constantly—

"I wonder why all saints don't sing,"

the tune Mac had whistled when he left them last night.

"Oh, Mac! God bless you, Mac! Is that you?"

"Great God, Captain! You here? And alive and able to speak to me?"

McClintock, Morphy, and Chipstone were the angels of succor. But how inadequate are words to do more than dimly suggest the flood of feeling that surged up in their breasts at this meeting! All were visibly moved; even imperturbable Mac showed emotion. All— that is, except poor Mark. He was long past joy or pain. Unconsciousness had dropped the curtain between his nerves and their torturers, and if help had not come it is doubtful if he would ever have felt another pang. Tenderly they disengaged Will from the inanimate Mark, scarcely more helpless than his captain. Joining hands, the two lieutenants raised the little hero between them in the fashion so familiar to soldiers. Corporal Chipstone took his musket on his left shoulder, passed his right arm around Will, and helped him forward until circulation was somewhat restored, so that he could readily keep pace with the rest.

A fire! A blessed fire! A heavenly warmth —to save life and restore benumbed flesh and blood, and bone, and nerve, and brain! How he coughs and sputters the smoke, as he hugs the blaze, and his clothes give off clouds of vapor! No need to offer food; no use to ask questions; no need to talk—nothing but sweet, holy, heavenly warmth now for a long, long time; to be drunk in at every pore, with eyes closed in utter comfort; a whiff or two from the pipe, warm and moist from Mac's lips— and, at last, slumber—even dear, balmy, blessed sleep—steals over the senses, and begins the repair of the most ragged and frayed edges of the sufferer's being.

Yes, it is not another of those false, deceitful dreams. It is a real fire that salutes Will's reopening eyes. *Now* they may give him a toasted bit of biscuit and talk to him slowly and distinctly, asking no questions yet. So Mac tells of his walking and whistling, and his turning back and searching in dismay for the hidden comrades; going on and on until he was challenged by a confederate sentinel; then his return and building a fire, divided between hope that they had got over to their friends, and fear that they had been taken by their foes; then the final effort which had brought the joyful rescue.

Will raised himself sufficiently to look across and see that Chipstone was holding Mark's head in his arms, while his shoes were steaming beautifully in the warmth of the fire.

"Is he alive?"

"Yes," said wide-awake Morphy. "He spoke awhile ago—asked where you were, and then dropped off again with that same little smile you see on his face yet—if you call Mark's smile a smile."

Will a match ever again seem to Will like a simple stick of wood and chemicals? Never! It will always be a "Mark Looney," a humble little red-headed soldier, ready to try to do its duty and perish in the doing.

"What's that light over there, Morphy?"

"Daybreak, by God!"

"That's so!" cried Mac, starting up from a doze. "Come, boys, let's get over toward the regiment."

"Hadn't you better go on ahead, Mac, and see that Company K gets into shape and gets something to eat? I guess most of them have got in."

"Oh, Captain—s'pose you send Barney to do that. I'd rather not leave you and Mark."

So Morphy left them, and they roused Mark sufficiently to get him to eat a bit of biscuit, toasted, and soaked with snow-water into softness.

Will rose with difficulty, and left the blessed fire with regret, a long, strong shudder seizing on him as he faced the morning breeze. He thought the motion made him feel colder than ever! Mac and Chip gripped hands to pass under Mark's knees and gripped elbows to support his chest under his arms.

At the end of a mile or so of difficult walking, they came upon a pleasant scene—Col. Puller and the regimental staff gathered near a fire (a full half-mile to the rear of yesterday's line), and preparing for a breakfast *al fresco,* from which repast a refreshing odor of coffee and fried pork saluted their eager senses. They laid Mark tenderly down, and stretched and rubbed their stiffened arms.

"Good morning, Colonel."

"Good morning, sir."

"We began to think we should never see a friendly face again, or smell that delicious odor of Christian food."

"Where is your company, Capt'n Fargeon, and why are you not with it—you and Lieutenant McClintock!"

"Company K was scattered and driven far to the right by the fire of the enemy in front, and—I am sorry to say it, Colonel—by the fire of your own command in our rear."

"I learned from one of your own men—the same man by whom you sent me a very curt and incomplete report in the afternoon—that your company retired in disorder before the enemy. And now, after a large part of it has straggled into my regiment, *you* appear; you and your first lieutenant bring up the extreme rear—with a cock-and-bull story of having been fired on by your own regiment."

Will stood dumfounded by this assault.

"Lieut. McClintock, have *you* anything to say in explanation of this state of things?"

The lieutenant silently shook his head.

"Both you gentlemen will go to your quarters in arrest."

"What!" cried Will.

"I presume you understand English, Capt'n Fargeon, and that you know your duty under present circumstances."

With an unmoved face and undisturbed voice Mac said:

"You will not object, Colonel, to our carrying Private Looney to brigade hospital before our arrest takes effect?"

Puller turned to consult his adjutant—his monitor in all matters—and then said:

"I have no objection to your caring for Private What's-his-name or any other private business; but you may remove your swords before doing so." Then, turning to Chipstone: "Take the swords and report at your company at once."

Silently the captain and lieutenant took off their swords and handed them to Chipstone. Then they raised unconscious Mark once more and resumed their toilsome, labored march in the direction of the hospital. When they were out of hearing, Mac said quietly:

"Now, what do you think about Col. Puller's memory, Captain?" But Fargeon walked on as if he heard not.

At length they saw before them a large hospital tent. They walked up toward the open door, where sat a short, dark man in plain clothes and a slouch hat, smoking a cigar. Mac began:

"I beg your pardon, sir—why, Captain—General Grant!" and he stopped.

"Good morning, sir. Are you looking for me?"

"No, General, we are looking for the hospital. This is Capt. Fargeon, of the Sixth Illinois. I am Lieutenant McClintock, of the same regiment."

"Ah, McClintock. Yes, yes, Mexico; I thought I knew you. I am glad to see you, Lieutenant, and to know you are again in the service.

"General, this is Mark Looney, whom you may recollect."

"Very well, indeed; very well, indeed. Is Mark badly hurt?"

"Severely, not dangerously—only he has been freezing and starving all night. We were picketing on the extreme right and were driven out by the fire of our own men behind us."

"Ord'ly, is there any of that coffee left? Bring three mugs of it for these gentlemen." He stepped up to where they had laid down Mark. "Mark, do you remember your old lieutenant, Grant?"

Mark nodded and smiled slightly, but did not try to speak.

"Ord'ly, give Dr. Hardy my compliments, and ask him for a stretcher; then get three more men and carry this man to the hospital."

They dipped a bit of biscuit in the coffee and placed it in Mark's mouth, while they blew and sipped their own beverage in luxurious refreshment.

"I haven't heard any intelligent account of the affair on our right. How came you there, and what occurred?"

Will gave a short, lucid statement of the events we have narrated, beginning with giving Mac full credit for the suggestion which led to their being pushed out, and ending with the disaster they had met with. He did not say that they had rendered any especial service, but felt that the older soldier must see that such was manifestly the case. Grant smoked and listened in utter silence; not even an occasional grunt of recognition indicating that he saw the whole scene as it had occurred.

"Where are your swords?"

"As we passed regimental headquarters, Colonel Puller, for reasons best known to himself, placed us both in arrest."

"And had you give him your swords?"

"Not exactly; only send them to our quarters, while we looked out for Mark."

[Puff, puff.] "Well, gentlemen, you know the duty of officers in arrest."

"Yes, General; we are on our way to our quarters."

"Good day, gentlemen!"

"Good day, General."

They departed—but we will remain.

"Ord'ly, give Colonel Puller, of the Sixth Illinois, my compliments, and say that I would like to see him at twelve o'clock."

Then the general strolled over to the hospital and had a talk with Mark, now cared for and comfortable.

Colonel Puller arrived, punctually to the moment, in full regimentals, with sword, sash, and spurs, much excited and pleased by the summons, and primed with a glowing account of his own services of the previous day. He shook hands with the silent, sphinx-like figure sitting on the camp-stool (smoking as usual), and observed that he was glad to see General Grant looking so well.

"Colonel, in advance of regular reports [puff, puff], I should like you to give me an account of the affair of last night."

"Well, General, I am glad to be able to give you one."

[We must abbreviate.] The colonel had observed that our flank was unprotected, and, with the consent of his brigade commander, threw his regiment into echelon of companies, and deployed a company as skirmishers to give warning of any threatened attack. About four o'clock the skirmishers were driven in with some loss, and then the enemy made a most furious and premeditated attack upon that part of the line. For over an hour we withstood the onslaught of vastly superior numbers, repelling one assault after another in the most determined manner, completely decimating their ranks, while our own losses, though considerable, were small by comparison. Finally the enemy retired in confusion, almost decimated. Darkness prevented the pursuit which the colonel had planned, not only to order, but to lead in person.

[Puff, puff.] "What kind of country did you find on your right?"

The colonel had found a road bordered on the far side by a swamp.

"Did you go out to see what your reconnoissance had developed?" The colonel did not.

"Did you send?" No; the commander of the skirmish company had reported very fully.

[Puff, puff.] "Did the enemy use the road in an effort to take us by surprise?" The colonel thought that they had marched nearly their whole force to that point with that purpose.

"What prevented them from succeeding— as the troops that were to fill the gap failed to reach there?" The fire of the skirmishers, which the colonel had placed there for that very purpose, succeeded by the fire of his echelon companies, and, later, by the other regiments of the brigade.

"The skirmishers did well, then?" Up to that point, admirably, in accordance with the colonel's orders. But later, when seriously attacked, they fled in confusion.

"The skirmish line retired before the attack of a line of battle?" The colonel regretted to say that they did.

[Puff, puff.] "When did you learn this?" The colonel was apprised as soon as it transpired.

"Before the engagement began?" At the very beginning of it.

"From whom?" From a member of the skirmishing company.

"The first man of them to report?" The very first. The colonel had felt obliged to place in arrest the captain and first lieutenant.

[Puff, puff.] "Did you so direct the fire of your right flank company as not to injure your own skirmishers?" The colonel had trusted to their own judgment for that.

"Did you tell them where you had placed your skirmishers? Did you give any orders or take any steps to avoid shooting your own men?" The colonel could not quite follow the drift of General Grant's remarks.

[Puff, puff.] "My remarks are not drifting, Colonel Puller. You seem to have sent out a company of skirmishers to reconnoiter, and not to have gone or sent to learn what they found out; then to have left your line of battle uninstructed as to their duty regarding those skirmishers, wherefrom disaster resulted to them; then to have placed two deserving officers under arrest upon the unsupported statement of one skulker."

The silence that followed this was marked—almost obtrusive. The quiet veteran smoked on unmoved.

"Have you anything further to add, sir?"

The unhappy colonel choked and gasped for breath, but was speechless.

"Mr. Badger, one moment, if you please. Be kind enough to write a general order" [Puff, puff]. "'Captain Fargeon and Lieutenant Mc-Clintock, of the Sixth Illinois Volunteer Infantry, having rendered distinguished service in the affair of yesterday, and having been unadvisedly placed in arrest by the colonel of their regiment, are released from arrest and restored to duty.' Have that repeated and sent out at once—or stay. Colonel Puller, should you think proper to demand a court of inquiry on your part in this matter, I will readily grant

your request and make it part of the same order."

"Ge—General Grant—I beg for time to talk with my brother officers."

"Very well, sir. Good morning, sir. Send out the order, Mr. Badger."

The Sixth, still shelterless, had been provided with axes during the day, and was now building for itself a long, double line of "brush-houses," made of boughs supported on poles held up by crotched sticks—a poor camp but better than none; far better, even in case of rain. In front of one of these hovels, at a good fire (for it seemed as if they would nevermore be tired of warming themselves), sat Fargeon and McClintock, brooding over the coals and their own wrongs.

To them arrived Colonel Puller in trembling haste.

"Captain! and Lieutenant!" (extending a hand to each which they failed to notice). "You'll be glad to hear (but not half so glad as I am to say it) that I find that I was entirely misinformed regarding your share in last night's action!—entirely! I ought to have thanked you instead of—doing what I did."

They were as unresponsive as Grant himself.

"Now, I want you to regard those few words as unsaid—forget them as if they had never *been* said. You are relieved from arrest and restored to duty."

After a pause, Mac spoke:

"Thank you, Colonel Puller. I believe we prefer to demand a court of inquiry."

"Oh, Lieutenant—oh, Capt'n Fargeon—don't, I beg and pray, *don't* ruin me! What will be said at home? Where would it place me in the eyes of my congressional district—all for a hasty word or two?"

"Unpremeditated was it, Colonel Puller!"

"Premeditated! My dear lieutenant, what can you mean?"

The colonel laughed uneasily, while an added flush showed that the shot had not missed.

No, the gentlemen did not care to smoke. And they would prefer not to dine with the colonel's mess, under the circumstances. Besides, Captain Fargeon could hardly stand on his feet. Yes, he should be glad of a call from the regimental surgeon.

"To tell you the truth, gentlemen, I have had a little talk with General Grant—a very nice talk on the whole—and he has consented to issue a general order speaking highly of you, and relieving you from arrest."

The others straightened up in their seats, leaned forward, stretched out their arms and shook hands—with each other.

"Now, gentlemen—Lieutenant, you know I am not up in military verbiage as you are— I suppose you can't persist in your own arrest after being relieved in general orders."

"Well, Colonel Puller, we are not officially apprised of our relief until the general order has been read aloud before every regiment at dress-parade."

The colonel departed, very downcast, and forthwith made his own headquarters a little purgatory, and his adjutant temporarily sorry he had ever been born. But the adjutant (who privately hated his colonel) got fully even with him at dress-parade that very afternoon, as the next chapter will show.

The Forlorn Hope

It is not difficult to imagine the deep indignation the men of Company K felt when they learned of the vile treatment meted out to their officers. There were symptoms of a roaring row when Will and Mac dejectedly approached the laboring company. Wild cheers greeted them, followed by resounding groans unmistakably meant for the objectionable colonel. By great effort the arrested officers calmed the tumult, and got the men to give to poor, unoffending Morphy the obedience he had a right to as the commanding officer, and deserved as a good one and a good fellow.

Four o'clock P.M. arrived, and with it dress-parade, and with dress-parade the reading out of general orders. Now came the adjutant's revenge. He read out the expiatory order so that nearly everybody could hear it; then paused for the cheers which he knew would follow. Follow they did, beginning with Company K, and spreading until the whole regiment had taken them up; Company A, which had committed the cruel blunder while in echelon the day before, showing special anxiety to make themselves once more "solid with K."

"Colonel," whispered the adjutant, "it would now be proper to send for the captain and lieutenant before proceeding with the parade."

Colonel Y. R. Puller's curses, "not loud but deep," must be omitted. Fargeon and McClintock were summoned and arrived, the captain leaning heavily on his lieutenant and on a stout stick. Yet both men looked handsome, dignified, and business-like as they were led up to the colonel, who shook their hands with misplaced effusion while the cheers were renewed, K going quite wild when they rejoined its ranks, the men tossing their caps and catching them on bayonet-points in a general scramble.

Puller, as colonel of the Sixth, was essentially "done for." Still he floundered and struggled a good deal. At the headquarters mess that evening he tried the force of eloquence.

"Fellow-comrades, the more I think of the way we've been tampered with by General Grant, the more I don't like it. How are we to maintain any *espirit dee corpse* in our regiment if our best efforts are to be prostituted by having such a stamina put upon them?"

His staff did not know.

"I would suggest," said the lieutenant-colonel, "that you either resign or ask for a court of inquiry." [The lieutenant-colonel was wild to get command of the regiment.]

"Yes," said the major, "that might give Gen. Grant a lesson." [The major wanted to be lieutenant-colonel.]

"And if Grant were out of the way, you ought to get a brigade," put in the adjutant. [He also longed for a step in rank.]

"Well, fellow-comrades," answered the colonel, who fully appreciated the feelings animating his subordinates, "I'll think it over. It might, as you say, give *General* Grant a lesson regarding such high-minded outrages attempting to be put upon volunteer officers by regular officers. I should not be surprised if the matter went to Washington. If the government declines to take it up, Congress could very likely be induced to do so. I know one thing, and that is, that if *I* were in the halls of legislation every volunteer officer in service might be sure of one voice that would never bend the knee, one tongue that would never bow, one hand that would never be silent, where they needed the protection from the overweening, high-minded perturbation of West Point!"

Next day a general advance is made on all parts of the line not already in contact with the enemy's works. The Sixth gets more than a mile forward, and begins a parallel; and the "flank in the air" now rests solidly on the river above (southward of) Fort Donelson, just as the other flank rests solidly on the same river below (northward of) the fort. A semi-circle of converging fire is narrowing about the doomed foe. A confederate battery low down on the river-bank makes sad work with the gun-boats, but still they keep "pegging away," and command the river sufficiently to make the escape of any considerable body impossible; though the confederate Gen. Floyd and a few more do get across, leaving Gen. Buckner to bear alone the burden of defeat and ruin.

Will moves with his company, or at least not far away from it, though his legs and feet are very stiff and painful.

In the advance of the command they find the body of poor Jim Flynn, stripped to his very socks. They bury the hapless martyr; and the burial party, by Mac's orders, refuse to say whether the fatal bullet came to him from the front or rear. Harry Planter has disappeared as utterly as the pork and coffee—and Company K's blankets.

No lack of news along the line on Saturday, February 15, 1862. A flag has come in from Gen. Buckner, bearing proposals for capitulation and asking terms. Grant has named "unconditional surrender," adding, "I propose to move at once upon your works."

During the engagement on the right, Smith's division on the left had dashed in and taken a line of the enemy's outworks; and now the division to which our friends belong has been brought round and massed in that (reversed) entrenchment, in grim preparation for delivering an assault on the main works, if it shall be needful.

Strange to say, this change in what he called "the situation" did not make Colonel Puller any more contented with his lot. Even the rare privilege of leading (that is to say, following) his men up that deadly slope—perhaps underlaid with hidden percussion shells, certainly swept by a storm of missiles—failed to calm his spirit, perturbed by the official snub he had received. But just how to reopen the subject he did not quite see.

His lieutenant-colonel—one Isaacs, a "politician," yet a brave fellow and really a fine officer, who had served in the state militia—saved him the trouble by leading up to it himself.

"Well, Colonel, what did General Grant say?"

"Why, Isaacs, I haven't moved in the matter —yet."

"Now, if I were you, Colonel, I wouldn't hesitate. Go in boldly—heroically, I may say —throw aside all fear of consequences—beard the lion in his den."

The doughty colonel tapped the table with his knife, considering how he could best— that is to say, most reluctantly—follow the advice.

"You know, gentlemen, that I would rather lead that storming party a thousand times— yes, I speak within bounds and mean what I say; would rather lead *one thousand* storming parties—than do what you suggest."

"Oh, we know all about that!" protested Isaacs, with only a scarcely preceptible wink at the major. Then he went on:

"You know, Colonel, this may be your last chance to render this service to your country. A bullet in your body this afternoon wouldn't help the cause a mite, while a word spoken in season might lead to great results."

"It will stir up a good deal of a foment. But if you consider it a matter of duty—"

"Duty before pleasure, every time! Move

on General Grant rather than on Fort Donelson. If the whole volunteer force is to be made into a door-mat for the regulars to wipe their feet on, why, we want to know it!—that's all!"

"I'll do it!" said the colonel, with fierce determination. And he strode forth, courage and self-sacrifice expressed in the very squeak of his boots.

"Maje, my boy! that makes me colonel of the Sixth! And like enough this afternoon will make me an angel, and you the colonel!"

"General Grant, on interviewing my fellow-comrades, I am advised that it is best to take up with your sudgestion, report myself in arrest, and ask a court of inquiry regarding what we consider your very high-minded subvention in the discipline of my regiment."

"Well, Colonel [puff, puff], you can have your court [puff, puff], but I do not insist upon your arrest meanwhile [puff, puff]. You may return to your regiment [puff], and I will order the court." [An infinite succession of puffs.]

"Excuse me, General, but under the stamina of your general order I cannot consistently appear at the head of my regiment."

"Return to duty, Colonel Puller, you are not in arrest."

"General Grant, as a protest against such a stamina as it has been to me to hear that order read at dress-parade, I would rather resign my commission than continue in command pending my justification."

"Let your resignation come up through the proper channels, and I shall act upon it."

The doughty colonel thought all went off pretty well; only once, when he repassed a tent where he had already called, he was disturbed by hearing loud laughter within, scarcely in keeping with the seriousness of the occasion. Then, too, his sensitive ear seemed to detect snorts of merriment as he passed groups of privates of his own Sixth Illinois Regiment, standing, sitting, crouching, lying, or lounging in the wet, muddy, dismal, ill-smelling, deadly earth-work.

"Old Wire-puller knows which side his bread is buttered on. He wants to go home and not wait for any pie."

"I knowed Wire-puller was a politician, quick as I seed how his eyes bug out."

"He reminds me," said Tolliver, perhaps the wittiest man in the regiment, "of a house that's all front door—the minute you lift the latch you're in the back yard."

All laughed. In fact, all were accustomed to laugh whenever Tolliver spoke. As soon as they saw his right eyebrow mount to the roots of his hair, while his left drooped so that the bright glance could be but barely seen through its shadows, they knew "suth'n wuz-a-comin'."

"Ah, yah! Say, fellers, why don't we all resign?"

"I'm only sorry for one thing, an' that is that I never thought to enlist as a major-general, instead of a high private in the front rank. Now thar's ole Grant—ain't it awful easy for him to assault Donelson—'move on your works'—him a-holdin' down a camp-stool, away out of range in the rear?"

"Oh, you dry up, Jeff Cobb! He's in the right place, and the right man in the right place too."

"Well, Chip, I s'pose so. But do you know what I think when I read the papers? I think the folks at home are a-makin' a leetle mistake. They think *he* is where *we* are, and *we* are where *he* is. Now, there's him drawin' steenty-steen thousand a year, on a camp-stool, out of range; and here's me, all the same except the money, the camp-stool, and the range. I can find plenty in print about the brave and heroic Gen. Ulysses S. Grant, but nary a word about the brave and heroic Private Thomas Jefferson Cobb."

"Don't you be scairt, Jeff. Your name'll be in the papers soon enough."

"Ya-as—but it won't be in the head-lines. Them noospaper colyumes is like a coal-shute." [Jeff was a miner.] "The big chunks go thunderin' down on top of the screen whilst the little ones slip down through, 'most out of sight, in the lists of killed an' wounded."

"Wal, its' all one—er will be in a hundred years."

"Ya-as—only there'll be more Grants and fewer Cobbs."

Will got an ambulance to carry him as near to the earth-work as wheels could go; then a couple of men helped him to hobble to his post.

"Captain, you belong in the hospital, not in the assaulting column."

"Yes, Mac, I suppose so. My knees and ankles do feel pretty queer."

"What does the doctor say?"

" 'Inflammatory rheumatism' was the sweet little speech he got off when he made his examination."

"What would he say about your spending the night in a trench—or even in the brush-house?"

"Probably 'fool,' with a past participle before it."

"Well—why don't you go along to the hospital?"

"And give *General* Grant a lesson?"

"Ha, ha! No, not exactly. Give yourself a rest."

"We'll see when the job is done."

And he looked anxiously across the space they would have to charge over.

He was dreadfully frightened. He could not

see how it was possible to live through an advance across that rising ground and reach that horrid inner line of works under a plunging fire of musketry and artillery coming from them and from the fort itself, visible beyond them. True, our artillery had silenced the fire, and could silence it again whenever it broke out; but our artillery must be silent when the assault is made. And then—

Why should he go? He was surely a very sick man; nobody on earth who knew his condition would say it was his duty—nobody except himself.

If he were fearless, like Mac or Mark Looney, he wouldn't go. But now, afraid as he was, he *must*. He dared not stay behind, for fear it should be from the wrong motive.

And then his dear boys—how could he see them leave him and run into that maelstrom of mortality without him? How could he see them go down, one by one, and blot the ground with dreadful little blue heaps, he not even knowing which men were dead and dying? And how explain to the rest of the world why his life was saved when the others fell? He heaved a great sigh:

"I'll be with you, Mac, when you start, anyhow."

"Well, Captain, I s'pose it's no use talking. But promise me one thing; that if we don't assault to-day—and it begins to look as if we shouldn't—you'll go to the hospital for the night."

Will gave a reluctant consent to this, and when it became evident that "it," would not be to-night, he let the ambulance carry him back to the hospital.

"Good enough!" said Mac to Morphy. "Now ten to one the assault will be ordered for daybreak, and be over before Cap knows anything about it."

The men were allowed to go back to their tents and shelters to eat and sleep. Reveille would sound at five (breakfast to be made ready beforehand); the whole army being called to arms to support the assaulting division when it had effected a lodgment, or to receive its bloody fragments if it failed. The division was to be in the outwork at six, field and staff on foot, men in light marching order —no blankets, no knapsacks, no haversacks— nothing but arms, ammunition, and canteens, full of whisky and water if they wished it. They were raw soldiers, but well they knew what all that meant—chosen victims, fatted and decked for sacrifice!

Half the men of the Sixth were writing letters that night. Pens and ink, pencils and paper were borrowed and lent on all sides. Candles stuck in bayonet sockets were flaring everywhere. No guard detail was demanded. Nobody found any fault with anything they did. Surgeons, chaplains, and other friends were burdened with dingy letters and little packages, to be reclaimed to-morrow night or forwarded as addressed. Watches, keepsakes, money, photographs—anything and everything a man does not care to have buried with him or stolen from his body by the foe—were laid out for the dear ones at home. God! If I wanted to magnify the pathos of all this, what could I say that would not belittle it?

It seemed as if almost as soon as the camp had put on its night-quiet the company cooks were at work at the breakfast ration; and not long afterward the bugle at headquarters and the drums and fifes of the doomed regiments sounded the call to the opening of the dreadful Sunday. Then by degrees, yet rapidly, men began to gather around the camp-fires and prepare themselves for the work before them.

"Say, fellers, what's the use of eatin' so

much? Jest wastin' good victuals an' makin' more work for the buryin' squads."

"Oh, yes, Hiram—but I notice you don't hang back from the pot none to speak of! If you'd put all that stuff outside instead of inside, no bullet wouldn't never hurt ye!"

"Well, ye see, Jeff, I'm built like a camel—got three stomachs; one for ornament, one for use, an' one for some other time."

"Ah, yah! Th' ornamental one must be the insidest one of all!"

"Oh, Lord, boys—I wish I was in dad's barn!"

"Wha'd ye want t' be in the barn fer, Jeff?"

"Why, ye see, 't ain't more'n twenty rods from the barn to the house, 'n' I could jest run inter mammy's room an' hide under the bed."

"There's the long roll! Boys, say yer prayers. Somebody say one fer me, so I kin go on eatin'."

"Fall in, Company K! Fall in! Fall in!"

"Oh, yes," cried Jeff Cobb, the irrespressible, "we'll be a-fallin' in in about an hour's time." Then he began to sing in a sentimental treble, "I would I were a boy again."

Jeff's voice was as unmusical as can be possibly imagined. No sooner had he begun to sing than Tolliver interrupted him.

"Say, Jeff; half a minute, please, before you go on. Have you got a house of your own?"

"Not that anybody knows of, so far as heerd from. Why?"

"Why, if I were you, I'd build one—a nice brick house in a nice big lot."

"Some burn of yours, Tolly? Well, my son, drive on about the house and lot."

"Well, Jeff, I'd work it this way. You just go to any vacant spot and begin to sing. Nobody will ever try to serve a warrant on you."

"You won't, Tolly. A man of your size! *You* won't try any such job on *me*—not while you're sober."

"And so, Jeff, you'd have your ground, all OK, don't you see? Now for the bricks. All you've got to do is just go on singing and there'll be enough bricks thrown at you to build a palace!"

Amid the chorus of laughter could be heard Jeff's voice, louder and more raucous than ever:

"I would I were a boy again."

Once more Tolliver interrupted:

"Oh, shucks! What's the use of wouldin' ye was a boy? *I* would *I* were a leetle, teenty-taunty gal-baby!"

Slowly and gropingly the regiments found their way in the dark to the now familiar ditch; lay down, or sat, or squatted, to wait for dawn and the order to advance.

Now, past the reserves, past brigade head-quarters, past the brush houses, past the cooks' fires, past the ambulances and litter-bearers waiting for their sad work, past the intervening space of darkness, comes a little procession—four men carrying, on a litter, a fifth, an officer in uniform with sword and sash. The men stopped chatting and watched with curious eyes the advancing group. The recumbent form raises its head:

"Is this Company K, of the Sixth Illinois?"

It is Fargeon's voice, and a loud-answering "He-igh" is the response.

"Well, Mac, I'm glad to see you."

"Well, Captain, I'm sorry to see you—first time in my life, too."

"Oh, now, Mac, you mustn't be jealous about my commanding K once more. You'll have a chance before noon, like as not."

"I hope, Capt'n Fargeon, you'll command it as long as I'm in it—unless you get promoted and go higher."

"That's what I look for, Mac—a big promotion that'll take me out of your way for good."

They shook hands, and each could see, by the light of Mac's pipe, a loving twinkle about the eyelids of the other.

"Boys, can't you leave the litter here for me to lie on till we start? Yes? That's all right—there'll be work enough for it after I leave it. Now, Mac, let a couple of our men put in their time rubbing my feet and ankles and knees. That's right, Chip—you and Bob will do first-rate. There—hard—oh, ouch; no, don't stop; rub away like fury, no matter if I howl a little. Well, boys, Mark is getting on all right. Wishes he were with us. Oh, Chip—that's right—oh Lordy, Lordy—but rub away. Looks as if it were going to be a fine day. There, there—you may skip the points of my ankles till some other day—after—to-morrow, week—after—next—oh, gee-whillikins! rub underneath my knee instead of on top." And so on.

"Now, boys, I'm going to try my weight on them. Here are my sticks under me—now raise me and let me get them to the ground—there—I guess I can bear my weight. So; now I'm all right." His dangling sword wobbled about his legs and his sticks as he hobbled along the line, nodding to the men, whom he recognized partly from their place in the line and partly from the wintry gray that began to lighten the eastern sky.

"Say, Cap, this is an infantry regiment. We ain't used to marchin' alongside of quadrupeds. I'm afraid you'll beat us all on the charge bay-nets."

"No, Tolliver. But then I'll never run away on my four legs when I once get there." After a few steps more he added: "Perhaps I'd better start now, so we'll be even by and by." Which humorous suggestion was well received.

The gray grew lighter and the men began

to peer into the unknown front, and, as usual, to make remarks.

"Now why in thunder don't the high muk-kemuks start us out? We'd be half-way there before the rebs could get the drop on us."

"Oh, pshaw, John! I wouldn't care if they didn't start us for a month!"

Some of the men talk thus lightly and bandy jests; but the majority are pale, stern, sad, and silent. They are not the ideal soldiers; machines, indifferent to death; fatalists with their "kismet"; pious zealots mumbling prayers and glorying in any sacrifice "for God and Czar." They are common-sense, thrifty American citizens; fathers, brothers, sons, husbands; full of the hopes of peace and prosperity; regretfully though resolutely risking them all at the call of patriotic duty, with the inexplicable self-devotion of the man-at-arms.

Mac mounts the breast-work, field-glass in hand, and peers long and anxiously forward.

"Mac, come down!"

"Shortly, Captain, shortly."

"Lieutenant, I command this company for a while yet, and I order you to come down, and I mean what I say."

Mac slowly obeys, only to walk to another part of the mound and climb again on top of it, again peering into the increasing light, sweeping the field slowly from side to side with his glass.

Will gives it up.

"What do you see, Mac? If you will stick yourself up like a scarecrow to be shot at, you ought to find out something to pay us for the risk."

"I can make out the salient, and I know the flag-staff is just to the left—if the gum-boots haven't shot it away. There; now I've fixed it—the flag is flying."

"What did you expect—that they'd hauled it down?"

Mac's drawl becomes more drawling than ever as he goes on.

What Mac's Field-Glass Showed

The tall lieutenant in his long blue overcoat, both hands supporting his glass and both elbows level with his ears, stands perched on the highest point of the earth-work. His figure relieved against the gray sky in the dim light of misty dawn, seems of gigantic, supernatural height; but his voice has the same old strong, quiet, half-serious, half-playful drawl which his friends—his worshipers—have learned to associate with the flame and roar of battle; with trial and triumph and wounds and death.

"Well, Mac, out with it."

Through the dewy quiet the next words pierce like separate pistol-shots:

"Ye can't—'most always—tell—what—ye may least—expect—specially about—uncertain things—in this world—of chance—and change—the flag's—flying—and it's—a whi-te—fla-ag."

"SURRENDERED!" cries the captain.

"SURRENDERED! SURRENDERED!" shout the men who hear him.

The shout becomes a roar and the roar a yell of frantic joy, triumph, relief, congratulation, thankfulness. Strong men, nerved to die to-day, laugh and cry and sob in each other's arms.

The roar spreads back to other commands, to the headquarters of the stern, stolid commander, to hospitals where sick and wounded take new life at the sound. It flies on the wings of the lightning over the great awakening land —Chicago, Boston, New York, Philadelphia, Washington—cities, towns, and villages by the thousand take it up, and with it awaken the anxious mother and wife; the Wall street gold speculator; the money king; the hopeful, fearful, sadly smiling, burdened President. Fort Donelson, with all its strength and all its men, and all its armament and munitions of war, has fallen into the hands of the Union army!

Oh, what a Sabbath day!

Presently the nearest bands get together; and then, floating on the rays of sunrise, comes the grand, sweet air of "The Star Spangled Banner."

"Oh, say, can you see by the dawn's early light—"

And yet another ineradicable association is engraved on Will's memory.

The national hymn is followed by

"Hail Columbia, happy land!"

And that by a rattling quickstep—

"Yankee Doodle came to town."

The gun-boats catch the news, and over the water from each of them comes the same succession of well-known tunes; not very grand in themselves, but to their hearers always hereafter soul-thrilling with the meaning they express.

*   *   *

The Sixth at the Battle of Shiloh

[SCENE.—*A group of men in K's company street, gathered about a smaller group seated on the ground, playing cards on a blanket spread over their knees. Many are munching the last of their breakfast as they stand.*]

Tolliver (aside to Chipstone and Cobb on his right)—"Now's our chance." (Aloud)—"Say, fellers, I'm tired of euchre. Tell ye what, I'll teach ye a new game. We call it 'Hog' where I come from. Who wants to learn hog?"

All—"We all do."

Tolliver—"Well, I deal the cards round (does so), and then each man passes one card to his left-hand neighbor. Each man picks out his suit, and when we've gone seven times round we show down and see who's got the best hand in any suit." [Passes a card to Cale Dugong on his left, and the game proceeds.]

Dugong (much excited)—"Golly, that runs good! Bet ye I'll lay over the crowd."

Tolliver (after a few moments)—"Thar, boys; that's seven. Now show down."

Dugong—"Hi! What'd I tell ye? Ace, king, jack, an' ten o' di'm'ns and four little ones! Who kin beat that?"

Tolliver—"That's so, Caleb. (Rising.) Boys, that settles it—Dugong is the biggest hog in Company K."

The loud chorus of guffaws at Dugong's expense is mingled with the distant sound of scattered shots. The captain and lieutenants have just finished their breakfast and are enjoying the usual peaceful smoke—at least they are all smoking, and two of them are enjoying it.

"Hello, Mac! What's all this? Somebody else is reconnoitering I guess." For the sharp, untimely musketry persists in making itself heard from the outposts. Mac looks glum and anxious. He hurries up all the morning operations with asperity and profanity not usual with him.

"Eat what you can, boys; dammit, eat a bite and shove the rest into your haversacks. One man from every tent run and loosen the tent-pegs. Get your blankets rolled up quicker'n chain-lightning; do you hear me? Captain, don't you think it would be a good plan to step up to regimental headquarters and get our orders? I'll have your orderly stow your things ready for breaking camp. I suppose we shall get everything into the wagons in short order—we ought to! Musketry as near as that, and we caught with our breeches down!"

Will, taking some food in one hand and a mug of coffee in the other, walks rapidly toward the colonel's tent.

"Only an affair of the outposts, Captain Fargeon," calls Colonel Isaacs as soon as he comes within hearing.

"Well, Colonel, if you'll allow me to say so, there are two whole brigades between us and that firing, so the enemy must be at close quarters already. My men are packing up, expecting the wagons. Lieutenant McClintock feels very uneasy."

"Mac thinks it serious, does he? Well, we'll be on the safe side." Then he orders the regimental quartermaster (much against his will) to have the wagons prepared for instant use; and sends his staff to each company street to hasten the preparations for a move. No orders have come from brigade headquarters, so he hesitates absolutely to strike the tents; short of that everything is put in complete readiness.

The rattle of musketry becomes more and more steady and continuous. Scattered men without muskets begin straggling down the road toward the rear.

"We belong to the —th. The rebs got onto us while we was eating. Our muskets was all stacked on the color line, and we didn't even git to the stacks at all—the Johnnies got thar fust. We just had to scoot. That's the second brigade that's doin' the firin'. We didn't git to fire a shot."

Even while the man talked the road is growing fuller and fuller of fugitives; here and there a wagon or ambulance, but chiefly in-fantry-men walking or running toward the river.

"Strike tents!" shouts Colonel Isaacs; and in little more time than it takes to pen these lines Company K's street ceases to be a street; it is nothing but a flood of wrinkling canvas and flying tent-poles; while in the uncovered homes may be descried pitiful remains of all the usual little devices for comfort and amuse-ment—leafy beds, seats, checker-boards, ex-tempore tables, and so forth. K's wagon is loaded almost as soon as the other streets have fairly fallen to the ground.

A few moments later an aide appears from brigade headquarters and in a consequential tone reports:

"General Blank's compliments, and would thank Colonel Isaacs to say by whose orders he has struck his tents."

"Be kind enough to say to General Blank," replied the quick-witted colonel, "that I am drilling my men in the rapid striking of camp and loading of wagons."

"Very well, sir!" rejoins the pompous aide, and he disappears, seemingly unconscious of the half-smothered laugh that follows him.

Many hundreds of unarmed men have now drifted past the Sixth, all telling the same story. Their officers are with them, but do not try to halt them, unarmed as they are. Now begins to come a different class: men carrying muskets, men who have done some fighting before they gave way; wounded men in ambulances and on foot, and unhurt men helping back the wounded—or, as Mac explains it, wounded men helping back the unhurt, by giving them an excuse (a bad one) for running away.

Still that rising and approaching rattle of musketry; still the utter absence of any orders from general headquarters. The distant sound of cannon has been heard some time; now comes the welcome thunder of a battery which has opened fire from our own side, and a loud "Heigh!" runs along the brigade front.

The next new, noticeable feature is the ap-pearance of stragglers direct from the firing line; not walking on the road, but straggling back through woods, fields, camps—anywhere where panic and cowardice can find a loop-hole of escape. The first one who comes within reach of Company K is seized and hauled away to the regimental guard-house, with the cheer-ful assurance from Mac that he shall be shot at sunset. But a threat to him does not deter others, and they begin to come back in droves.

"Sound the long roll!" calls Isaacs quietly. "Captain Fargeon, deploy your company as skirmishers a hundred paces to the front and halt all unwounded men; make them fall into your skirmish line, and let your reserve shoot down any man who refuses to stay and fight."

As the men gather on the color line in re-sponse to the long roll, they see the other regi-ments in the brigade hurriedly striking tents and scrambling them into wagons as best they can.

Company K "takes intervals on its left file," and spreading along before the face of the rest of the regiment, begins its advance. At every step some wounded man is allowed to pass, and some unwounded man is forced to stop and join the advance. As a general rule they make no objection, and the skirmish line soon be-comes almost a solid rank.

One man refuses to obey Mac's order, say-ing:

"Git out of the way! You ain't no officer of mine!"

Mac whips out his sword. The mutineer lowers his musket (bayonet fixed) and cocks it. Why does Mac hesitate to rush in and kick the piece aside? It isn't like him! The reason is soon evident; he sees Chipstone approaching from behind. Chip clubs his musket and brings down the stock with a crash on the wretch's head and he goes down like a log. Mac calls to Morphy (commanding the reserve) to strap the fellow up to a tree, facing the front, and in that horrible position he recovers his senses; his curses, prayers, and groans fill the air and make the management of other fugitives an easy matter. They all take the hint and join the ranks of the fighters.

But what is the halting of a few score among the vast mass of retreating men who now fill the space? They pass in swarms to right and left of the steady rank of the skirmishers, in a seemingly endless and limitless throng. They all tell the same story.

"The hull rebel army came down on us. We was flanked both sides; an' we fit until they begun to fire onto us from right an' left an' behind."

By this time the road has become a pandemonium of flying forces. Wagons go galloping in the rear in a nearly continuous stream, while *twice* there comes a yet more harrowing sight —the flight of caissons, forge and battery wagon; *but no limbers and no cannon!* The guns are lost—they may be turned on us already, and be swelling that advancing roar; be sending the very shells which we see bursting in the sky, making tiny white cloudlets that spring into sight, so beautiful and so appalling!

K soon finds itself supported on right and left by skirmish lines from the brother regiments of its brigade—an inexpressible comfort, especially as the fugitives now are fewer; they are coming on the run, and not after the manner of skulkers who have fled with scarcely an effort, all of which indicates that the next

people they may expect will be the enemy. Already bullets have made themselves heard and even felt, for one of the fellows who had fallen back, thus far without a scratch, now has a serious wound to justify his going the rest of the way.

"Why, Mark, where's your sling?"

"In me focket, Caftain. I can hould me fiece fretty fair, ye see, on me elbow."

"Oh, well, my boy—you needn't have come out to-day."

"I didn't intind to, Caftain, but when I sor ye start—" A nod, silent but expressive, fills out the speech with a thrilling eloquence.

The last Union men are coming in now, chiefly helping badly wounded officers and soldiers whom they have not the heart to leave to the tender mercies of the foe.

Fargeon has the right flank, Mac the left, and Morphy the reserve.

"Mac!" calls Will, "you'll feel 'em first. What will you do, and what do you want us to do? Give your orders—have 'em passed along, and we'll fall in with 'em."

"All right, Captain Fargeon," comes back in Mac's cheerful, sonorous, reassuring drawl. "We could take care of a whole regiment with this line of men, but we'll just fire one volley and then give the rest of the army a chance. We don't want to be hoggish!"

A laughing "Heigh!" greets this quip, and Mac goes on:

"Now, men, when you see 'em coming, fire one shot apiece, then run back. Don't stop again; get back to your place in our own line as fast as Goddlemity'll let ye. Recollect, the regiment can't fire till you get out of the way."

Suddenly firing begins in the Union line far to the left of K's position, and rapidly extends in its direction. Mac's place is the most ticklish;

and high above the din can be heard that well-known drawl:

"Let the Forty-fifth boys shoot at nothing all they've a mind to! We'll show 'em that Company K can hold its water! No man fire till I give the word. You hear me?"

So the firing from our side extends up to where Mac stands and there stops for a considerable time, while dead silence reigns all along the front of Company K and its forced allies. Fargeon stands in miserable suspense waiting for a word from Mac, and peering into the impenetrable leafage before him. Ha! What is that? A swaying of the bushes? Why doesn't Mac open fire? Shall *he* do it without waiting? Where *is* Mac, anyway? Why, that is Mac out in front! He has been reconnoitering, and now is backing slowly and softly toward the kneeling line, which parts to let him through, and he resumes his place on the left.

"Hang you, Mac! We might have shot you to pieces!"

"Oh, the boys knew I was there. I went out on purpose to hold them steady."

Now the wild yell of the enemy is audible, beginning far away on the left and spreading toward them. Now it is directly in front, and Mac speaks—drawls out:

"When I give the word, fire low—fire at their knees—you hear me?" (All he says is passed along the line.)

The yell becomes nearer and more plain; but the enemy is saving his powder. A movement in the underbrush is perceptible, a glimpse of butternut shows here and there, three of four scattering shots are heard, and the bullets go whizzing by.

"FIRE!"

More than a hundred muskets ring out their death-dealing cry (fully half of them being in the hands of the forced "recruits"), and the yell in their immediate front suddenly stops. The enemy has something else to think of, and probably imagines that this level, deliberate, destructive volley comes from a line of battle, not from a mere skirmish-line.

"Back, boys!" (No drawl now). "Stoop down and run for your lives! But don't leave any wounded! Pick up every man that gets hit; you hear me?"

An irregular volley comes in response to theirs, mostly passing over their heads. One man (a stranger) goes down, but he is killed, and they leave him. The strapped-up mutineer falls to begging again for his life.

"Oh, Lieutenant—for God's sweet sake don't leave me here! I didn't mean nothing. My gun wasn't loaded—there it lays—you can see for yourself!"

"Will you behave yourself?"

"I'll fight for you as long as there's breath left in my body if you'll *only* take me along."

Mac, after glancing at the musket and seeing that it was not capped, loosens the belt that held the fellow and tells him to pick up his cap and gun and fall in with the rest. As soon as his hand is free he begins to rub the lump on his head—tries to put on his cap—gives it up and puts it in his haversack instead.

Bullets have been dropping among Morphy's men, and two have to be helped back. Soon all are in their places on the color line, Company K taking more room than it had ever filled before since it came out. Isaacs comes down the line and congratulates Will and the rest, and gleans what news they have to give. When they ask him about things in the rear, he only answers by an expressive shake of the head. Then they are once more alone.

One of the strangers leaves the line and runs toward the road. Mac draws his pistol and fires a snap shot after him—the fellow gives a yell of either pain or triumph, and runs faster than ever.

"I'll drop the next one!" said Mac, audibly but quietly; and no next one tried the experiment.

The interval of quiet is so long that the captain and first lieutenant, passing along the rear of their line, stop a moment together.

"Captain, what would you think of a little breast-work along about now?"

"Well, Mac, I was once worth a good deal over a hundred thousand dollars; and if I had it now, I would give every cent of it for a ditch two feet deep with a bank two feet high on the far side."

"A hundred dollars a foot is a good deal of money for a little thing we might just as well have had for nothing; but it would be worth it."

The ground is mostly clear of trees for a quarter mile or more in front of the color line, and across this space and into the woods beyond all eyes are anxiously looking.

Just now some movement is noticeable on the right rear of the Sixth. A battery of artillery swings grandly into position there and unlimbers for action—six fierce muzzles pointing terribly toward the foe. The horses are quickly unhitched and trotted clattering out of sight to the rear.

Will sees Mac look at the battery with unusual interest, finally using his field-glass to examine its guidons and other distinguishing features.

"What is it, Mac?"

"Captain Fargeon, those are re   hat is a battery of the Fourth United Sta   rtillery—and I feel as if I ought to raise my hat as I name the regiment."

Suddenly, from the woods in front, come puffs of smoke and a second later the reports of muskets, mingled with the shrill whistle of bullets.

"Now watch the guns!" cries Mac, regardless of the enemy's fire.

On the instant six terrific roars burst from the six field-pieces, each gun giving a frantic leap backward as the flame spouts from its throat.

Before the sound ceases the shells can be heard exploding in the opposite woods and the branches of trees be seen dropping to the ground, while the musketry stops utterly.

"Ha, ha! Johnny Reb! How does those pills suit your complaint?"

"But, Mac, it's only the musket that means business, you know."

"No—well—yes. But take a battery served like *that,* and—well, I'd full as lief have it on my side as against me." And Mac walks gayly back to his post on the left.

After a second round the battery ceases firing, the confederate musketry in the immediate front having suddenly stopped and the distant woods grown as silent as a forest primeval. No sign of life in sight, except two buzzards circling lazily about high in the air, floating with motionless wings—waiting, waiting. Their patience will be rewarded.

Meanwhile the distant battle rages to right and left, its horrid voice always advancing, and before long an aide is seen to gallop up from the rear, speak a few words to the battery officers and gallop back. Then the battery reopens, and Will says to himself:

"Thank God! I wonder why they stopped."

How do men fall in battle?

Forward, as fall other slaughtered animals. Homer says, not once, or twice, but often, "Death unstrung his limbs." Again: "Then the hero stayed fallen upon his knees, and with stout hand leant upon the earth, and the darkness of night veiled his eyes."

As they fall, so they lie, so they die and so they stiffen; and all the contortions seen by burial details and depicted by Verestschagin and other realistic painters are the natural result of the removal of bodies which have fallen with faces and limbs to the earth, and grown rigid without the rearrangement of "decent burial."

To learn all these things, one needs only to watch Company K through this day, Sunday, April 6, 1862. Then one must pause to remind himself that war did not invent death; nor does even blessed peace prevent it.

War is a game which, were their subjects wise,
Kings would not play at.—*Cowper*

Battle and Murder and Sudden Death

The battery was quickly enveloped in its own smoke, through which were dimly visible hurrying forms, wildly waving rammers and great spouts of flame at each discharge. Again the great roars burst out, and again, and again; and each explosion was sharp, ear-hurting, cruel. Not the grand, soul-stirring report and roll of a thunder-clap or a cannon afar off, but a *noise,* physically painful and abhorrent.

Will's mind sought relief from the dreadful tension of waiting for battle by straying off to untimely vagaries.

"That hideous sound is the sweetest music my ears ever listened to. No mother's lullaby to a frightened child was ever more comforting, consoling, soothing. How wretched must one be when *that* comforts him! Well, I am wretched! I am a miserable man—unhappy, low-spirited, *despairing*—in view of the things which this day has in store. This long, dreadful

day! How hellishly they are fighting over there toward our left! Musketry and artillery—it certainly seems further back than we are! But so long as our immediate neighbors are on our line, we must stand fast and support our battery, as Mac says.

"That's right, gunners! Fire fast—make a wall of iron against them! Don't let your music stop an instant—shut out that rattle from the left! A man must be falling there with every tick of the clock. Oh, when will our turn come? Load and fire, gunners, load and fire—and God bless you for it!"

Mac approached again.

"Those battery-men are doing wrong, and they know it! I'll bet my life that some fool brigadier-general is at the bottom of it—shooting away all their ammunition at nothing under God's Heaven but gopher-holes and birds' nests."

"Why, Mac, I was just wishing they would go on all day and prevent the rebels from coming across that open space at all."

"Oh, they can't do that. Amount of it will be that the rebs will bring up two or three batteries to silence them; then they can't help us when we need it. They ought to lie low now till the Johnnies show themselves again."

"Maybe they are told to keep firing for the sake of the moral effect on our men."

"Like enough. But I'd rather hold 'em for a physical effect on the other fellers."

They separated, much to Will's regret, for he loved to lean on Mac's cool strength and forgetfulness of danger. And then, too, the accurate instinct of the lieutenant made his captain now look with dread for an artillery attack directed against the laboring battery—and he did not have to look long before it came.

Several reports in rapid though irregular

succession sounded from the far front, and missiles came plunging over, all evidently meant for the battery, but some of them straying far enough to make the neighborhood very uncomfortable for the Sixth Illinois.

"How under Heaven can the battery-men stand that dreadful storm? Oh, don't! Oh, *don't! Look* what you are doing!" he added aloud, apostrophizing the enemy.

A moment after uttering this childish supplication, Will saw the full absurdity of it, and could have laughed out at himself if he could have laughed at anything.

The sound of galloping came from the rear. Will looked back and saw a riderless horse, with artillery harness on, coming toward him at full speed. He tried to stop the crazy brute, but it only swerved, and rushed on. As it passed he saw a rent in its side. A passed shell must have reached the place where the battery horses were held.

"Look out! Look out, men!" Too late. The beast dashed blindly through Company K. Three men went down; one got up and recovered his musket; one sat up and pressed his hand to his side; one lay still where he fell.

"Stand fast, men! *Stand* fast!" shouted Mac, restraining the overwhelming instinct of humanity to fly to the succor of a brother in distress.

"Sarg'nt Chipstone, take a file of men and bring those wounded here to me; then get back to your places." Then, turning to the rear, he called: "Litter-bearers, this way!"

One man, with ribs probably splintered, was helped back. But poor Harry Planter, just out of the hospital, was past help. His back was broken. Twice hit, both times from the rear, and his task was done.

The horse, on getting into the open place, stopped and looked about him, showing no consciousness of his wound except by ceaselessly brushing that side with his tail.

"Tolliver," said Mac, "see if you can fetch him." (Tolliver was a famous marksman.) While he was kneeling, waiting for the victim to present a favorable shot, the horse began to nibble at the herbage at his feet.

Will thought, "What a God's blessing it is to be without imagination!"

Tolliver's piece rang out.

"Missed him!"

"Missed him, did I?" cried Tolliver with sarcastic intonation while he reloaded his piece. At the same time the beast began to turn about as if on a pivot, and presently went down with a resounding thud. "Missed him right through the brain behind the eyes."

The battery, by irresistible impulse, had now turned its fire away from the point whence infantry was to be expected, and toward the artillery which was raining shell and schrapnel upon it. This left the opposite woods unmolested, and bullets began to come from there in deadly numbers. A good many of the Sixth's men had been carried back; and murmurs began to be heard.

"For God's sake, let us shoot, or lie down, or something!"

Lieut.-Colonel Isaacs, anxious for both the honor and safety of his regiment, came down to its left flank to hear what K's officers had to say. Mac spoke:

"Only one objection to lying down—that is that the men are almost sure to fire high. If you can stop that—"

"We'll do it. Lie down, boys, and mind what I'm going to tell you. Don't fire till I tell you, and then fire at the enemy's feet. Every man of you, try to put his bullet into the toe of a reb's boot! Tit for tat, and something to boot!"

Down went the company, officers and men, glad of the relief. Isaacs hurried along the line, repeating his orders, so that every man was sure to hear them. But the brave commander, now the most conspicuous mark, was soon laid low with a disabling wound; and then the group that gathered to help him off lost a man—killed stone dead. The major, stunned by the situation, seemed to have nothing to say, and the long line of gray coats now came into plain though distant view, advancing over the open space. Few of the men knew that the lieutenant-colonel was hurt, and all anxiously awaited his order to begin firing, as the regiments to right and left were doing.

At last Mac leaped to his feet and ran to where the major was squatting behind a slight rise of ground.

"Shall we open fire, sir?"

The major nodded dumbly, and Mac walked back along the line.

"Boys" (drawling), "if you're going to fire high, you can't fire at all; but if you'll aim low, why, then let 'em have it, and God have mercy on their damned souls."

The last words were inaudible in the volley that followed; probably one of the most destructive ever delivered by any six hundred men since the war began. The advancing enemy fairly withered away. Like ripe fruit when the gust first strikes the tree dropped the hurt, and like leaves before the wind fled the unhurt.

When the fugitives had melted into the woods again, the firing recommenced; evidently from a supporting line which would soon repeat the assault. Mac did not lie down again, but came to where Will crouched, saying:

"Major Colemason is rattled, and there is practically nobody in command. You must take it if nobody else does."

"Get down, Mac! Get down! You won't? Then I'll have to get up, though I hate to. There! Now, where's Chafferty? Where are all the other captains who rank me?"

"Blessed if I know. But somebody's got to take charge of this regiment. We may have to advance or retreat; and when we do it ought to be by orders, and not by accident. God knows what's become of brigade headquarters."

"Well, Mac, look out for the company, and I'll go and see what can be done. If I take charge nominally, you've got to have it really. Don't, I beg of you, *don't* expose yourself needlessly!"

Mac disdained to reply, but walked slowly up to take the captain's place on the right flank, and stood there erect, watching the point where the enemy must be forming, under cover of their own smoke, for a determined advance.

Fargeon found the ranking captain, and together they visited the group surrounding the stunned major, including the adjutant and two of the staff, crouching together.

"Major Colemason, the enemy is massing for another charge. Have you any orders to give?"

The poor fellow (who had always done well in all subordinate capacities) had nothing to say. He was too dazed either to command or to abdicate, and the two captains returned to their companies, through a scattering drive (not a storm) of bullets. Fargeon had well-nigh forgotten them; and again his mind wandered off on trivial things. He wondered what time it was; and found that he could not guess—could not remember whether it was morning or afternoon, and whether his last meal, which seemed a month ago, had been breakfast, dinner, or supper. There were the enemy, visible and advancing. There stood Mac like a statue; there lay the dead and wounded who had been dragged back, and there lay Company K awaiting orders to open fire.

Lacking the restraining force of their commander, the Sixth began firing earlier than before, and, of course, less effectively. The brave enemy continued to come on, firing as they came. But the charging rank, partly through wounds and partly through defections, grew thinner and thinner; and its proportionate losses grew larger as there were fewer left to fire at.

Human nature could not stand it, and the foe at last wavered, halted and turned back, leaving some of their fallen within what seemed only fifty paces of our front. Then, again, the absence of a restraining head worked ill for the Sixth. The men, unmindful of flank or rear, regardless of the absence of orders, jumped up with a hurrah and pursued the retreating line until it passed through and unmasked a solid brigade with loaded muskets, which met our force with a burst of fire that sent us reeling back in turn. We had a score or two of prisoners, wounded and unwounded; but almost a tenth of our brave fellows were laid low by that first volley or by the losses in the retreat. Most of our wounded—all who were not obviously past help—were lugged back by their comrades, some of whom were hit in the act of helping others. With difficulty were the flying men halted at their own color line; but Company K having set them the example (its officers calling "Halt, Company K! Steady, men! Steady!"), the others either stopped on the line or came back to it after drifting a few rods beyond.

As Fargeon recovered his breath and his pulse slowed down, thought resumed its mastery over feeling.

"Wholesale slaughter is less dreadful than retail killing. A dozen of my good friends—besides scores of men whom I know by sight—are dead or dying around me; and I am less affected than I should be by seeing any one of them lying there alone. Tolliver, the wit—he's gone. Those expressive brows will move nevermore while the world turns round. So is Aleck Thrush—that leaves the old mother with no son, those girls with no brother. Jeff Cobb is among the wounded. If Jeff goes under, what will the boys do for a laugh in their dreariest hours, without him to turn sufferings into drolleries? Oh, is there no God in Heaven?"

Now came cries from the right.

"Lie down, men! Lie flat down! The battery is going to fire over you!"

Down they went; lying closer from their friends' fire than they had from their enemies. Even the gravest situations have their ludicrous side, and here was wounded Jeff Cobb's chance. He called from his lying place among the wounded:

"Say, fellers, I'll bet you can find this spot a year from now by the line of holes your noses are rooting in the ground."

A smothered laugh greeted the suggestion, and each man with a prominent or peculiar organ was congratulated with the promise of being able to identify his spot.

In sober earnest, it was a most trying experience. The shriek of the missiles which were passing over from behind them was indescribably appalling, and there was constant apprehension that a shell with imperfect fuse might burst directly above our lines. Even short of this disaster there was the constant, vicious rain of fragments of the "sabots" or wooden sockets in which shells and schrapnel are encased; which give severe bruises, though not often dangerous wounds. All of the wounded whose hurts permitted it walked toward the rear; but the rest were left lying there, no stretchers having been available for a long, long time.

Company K, and indeed the whole left of the regiment, was comparatively out of the line of our artillery fire, which passed directly over the right flank; and McClintock continued to stand coolly erect. Presently he walked over to where Fargeon lay.

"The Johnnies are still coming, Captain."

"What!" cried Will, rising on his elbow. "Coming on through that hell-fire?"

"Ya-as. The shells are bursting mostly beyond them."

"Why don't we try grape and canister?"

"They aren't quite near enough for canister —couldn't fire it over our own men, anyhow —and we don't use grape-shot now except in the navy."

"Why, the newspapers always talk about 'grape and canister.' "

"That shows how much they know of what they're talking about."

Fargeon got upon his feet.

"Mac, suppose we let K open fire. We seem safe here from our artillery."

"Just what I'm thinking of. K and I, and maybe H, might do some good. If K sets the example it'll spread. We're bound to support our artillery, orders or no orders. And I'm afraid (with an anxious look toward our left) that the battery ought to be getting back *now,* by the way the firing seems to be drifting past us over there. But good Lord! if the old Fourth gets no order to go, they'll stay there till the last man falls."

As he walked back to his place he said, in his own bantering tone:

"Boys, what's the matter with your raising up jest enough to see the rebs, and send 'em your cards and then git down again to load? But fire slow and fire low. You hear me?"

Permission was all the boys wanted, and a rattling volley burst from their front. Whether it killed or not, it had one valuable effect—that of diverting part of the enemy's fire from the battery (which had been catching it all) to the direction of Company K. Several hundred confederate muskets responded to the sixty or seventy pieces which were all the effectives K now possessed (even including its impressed men), and the concentration, together with the battery fire, was very severe; more so than any previous experience that Will had met with. Two men in Company K, after a startled shock and a cry, clambered up and made their way rearward; one gave the cry—but lay still, half turned on his side, his knees drawn up. Fargeon, stooping, started over to get from dear, splendid, glorious Mac, either relief or strength to bear the strain.

"Mac must have dropped his pipe; he is looking down for something. There, he is stooping for it—he is on his knees feeling for it—he is on his face! Oh, my God! Oh, GOD in HEAVEN!"

No one but Will had seen Mac fall. No one else saw the rent in the back of his collar where the bullet had come out; no one helped turn him over; then a shriek from the grief-stricken captain brought others to his aid.

Fruitless the care that dragged the fallen hero a little aside. When they laid flat his broad shoulders his fine head fell back and showed the deadly wound—sheer through the neck, a little to the right of the windpipe. The brave eyes were already sightless, though the jaw had not yet dropped and the breath was still feebly passing.

Will fell upon his knees and bowed his breast on the shoulder of his friend. His lips sought the cruel laceration, whence red blood was slowly oozing, warm, saltish, and sickening. He leaped to his feet, and his voice called the name of the Deity—the name and some of the merciful attributes. Certain men of the awe-struck group thought he uttered a prayer; others—those nearest him—thought that his words were a blasphemous denial of his God and abjuration of his cherished faith.

He faced the bullets, coming thick and fast, and made as if he would rush at the enemy for revenge and death. But in his path were crouched, loading and firing, the soldiers of Company K—the great lieutenant's fellow-soldiers—now reduced almost to a single rank.

Mac's voice seemed to reach his ears; to whisper to him, drawling through the uproar:

"Duty first; then death. You hear me?"

A sudden calm fell upon him. Mac's spirit entered his breast. He walked slowly along the line, saying in almost Mac's tone:

"Fire slow and fire low, boys. Fire slow and fire low."

He came to where Morphy was crouching, and heard him ask:

"Is it true, Captain?"

"Yes, Barney. Go over and take his place."

Scarcely had the second lieutenant got to the flank when he shouted back:

"Captain! Captain! The other regiment is gone from our left."

Fargeon hurried back. Not a man was to be seen on that part of our line. He cried piteously, with tears in his tones:

"Oh, Mac! Mac! What shall I do?" But the beloved voice was silent.

A litter had come, and two litter-bearers, assisted by two of Company K's men, were placing Mac's body on it. When the litter started for the rear Will observed that his two soldiers were going with it.

"Come back! Come back here, you cowards! Take you places in the ranks."

One returned; the other, Dugong, pretended not to hear, but kept ahead of the litter, prepared to break into a run if followed.

"Dugong! Caleb Dugong!" He could have shot him through the heart without a pang.

"I will stop being myself. I will be Mac. Let me see—let me see—the last thing he said was 'we must support our battery.' No, after that he said 'the battery ought to be getting back.' That is my law."

He ran to the battery, now almost silenced by the deadly musketry, though one gun-squad seemed to be still working, sending its isolated missiles.

"Captain! Officer in command!"

"The captain and lieutenants are all killed or wounded. I am the sarg'nt in command. What do you want?"

"Get your battery back, for God's sake! We've got to go!"

"Very well, sir."

Then he saw the surviving artillery-men—splendid veteran soldiers—seize the prolonges and begin to pull the guns back by hand toward where the horses were held. He ran to where he had seen the major and adjutant, but failed to find them. He ran along the line of the Sixth, shouting:

"All our men are gone from the left of Company K. The battery is going. Let us get back in good order, boys, keeping between the enemy and the battery. It is all we can do." ["Was that like Mac? I hope so; I hope so."]

"Retreat! Retreat!"

The cry traveled along the regimental line faster than he did, and Company K had left its place before he got there. As he reached the line he observed that one man, Ed Ranney, lay still, as if he had not heard the order. He ran to him, touched him with his foot and screamed: "Retreat, Ed!"—to ears closed in death. Then he followed the rest, but not without a lingering look backward and a sob as he tore himself away from his dead friends.

"Steady, boys! Watch the colors and carry along our wounded, and don't go any faster than the flag goes." ["Was that like Mac?"]

"Load as you go, boys; and turn and fire when you can. Keep even with the colors." ["Was that like Mac?"]

They could easily get away from the enemies in their immediate front, but, alas! those on the left (now on their right hand) had passed them and were firing at them from that side. Friends fell faster and faster; it was in vain to try to care for them.

"Drop the wounded and close in toward the flag!" ["Was that like Mac? Oh, poor Jeff Cobb and the others! My God, my God!"]

As K crowded in toward the center, all order was soon lost, and the once glorious Sixth Illinois became a mere mob of running men and officers, protecting the flag more by the interposition of their bodies than by the use of their guns. Will was among the rearmost of the unwounded; while behind him came a pitiful, halting few of wounded, growing fewer as the strength gave out of one after another, though others were constantly dropping under the fire from front and flank.

The place of honor was with Will in the rear. Those who took no chances hurried forward, but the best and bravest would pause to fire back, while the rest outstripped and passed them. Will was gratified—and distressed—to observe that these were nearly all his blessed Company K men.

Suddenly the very nearest man to him dropped. It was George Friend. George climbed to his feet again—or, rather, to his foot—reversed his musket, gripped the butt, and began a frenzied effort to keep up by prodding the ground with the muzzle, and so helping himself along.

"Can you make it, George?"

"I could, Captain, if it wasn't for this cursed foot." Will looked down—the misshapen member was all awry and pointing inward. They were getting isolated—he must leave him.

"Oh, Cap! *Ca-an't* you take me alo-ong?"

Reverently be it said, there were tears furrowing the powder-grime on that brave face as Will saw it for the last time on earth.

Fargeon, running, gripped his own head with both hands, crying:

"Oh, God! I wish I were dead, dead, DEAD!"

The last word was a scream, but nobody heard it except himself.

Why can he no longer see plainly? What is this shadow they have run into?

Why—it is nightfall! He had forgotten there was any day or night—any flight of measured time. All seemed merged into an awful, hideous eternity.

The Private History of a Campaign that Failed

THE MILITARY CAREER OF MARK TWAIN (1835–1910) WAS SHORT AND AMBIGUOUS. AL-
though he spent two weeks as a second lieutenant in the Confederate Army, his wry account of
that period, "The Private History of a Campaign that Failed" (1892), is not autobiography. As
always, Twain changed experience into fiction, putting his brief knowledge of wartime service into
a tale that is both sardonic and tragic, funny and sad. It is an ironic story that shows how un-
glamorous war could be for a naïve volunteer.

Twain's story does stick fairly close to the facts. In 1861, when the Mississippi was blockaded,
the young pilot joined a loosely organized band of Confederate militia commanded by General
Thomas Harris. This force retreated steadily through Missouri along the Salt River until the group
reached a position near the village of Florida. When the men heard that Governor Jackson's army,
under General Sterling Price, had been routed at Boonville, there were wholesale defections among
the volunteers. Twain left to join his brother Orion who had become Territorial Secretary of
Nevada.

Some of Twain's severest critics felt that the author "deserted" the Southern cause, that he went
to Nevada to avoid conscription into the army. Twain, for his part, was never firmly committed to
the Confederacy; indeed, his whole family were staunch Unionists. Since he was too much of a
realist to fight for a cause in which he had no personal stake, by 1862 Twain was on the staff of the
Virginia City *Enterprise.* His history as a soldier was finished; his history as an author begun.

Twain consistently refused to accept either the romantic or the jingoistic views of war which
existed in the latter part of the century. In one of his most brutal passages, near the end of *A
Connecticut Yankee in King Arthur's Court,* he predicts the holocaust of modern mass warfare.
Dynamite, electrified barbed wire, torpedoes, and Gatling guns allow fifty-four boys to wipe out a
force of 30,000 armed men. Twain anticipates the impersonal cruelty of mechanized battle: "Of
course, we did not *count* the dead, because they did not exist as individuals, but merely as homo-
geneous protoplasm, with alloys of iron and buttons."

"The Private History of a Campaign that Failed" shows the same combination of satire (here, self-directed) and realism that leads to a rejection of the very idea of war. Rain, fatigue, foraging, inadequate leadership—these realities disenchant the narrator. The killing of the "enemy" only serves to put the final seal of disapproval on the occupation of war. The details, both grim and humorous, that Twain includes in the story undercut the view of war as a time of excitement and glory.

YOU HAVE HEARD FROM A GREAT MANY people who did something in the war; is it not fair and right that you listen a little moment to one who started out to do something in it, but didn't? Thousands entered the war, got just a taste of it, and then stepped out again permanently. These, by their very numbers, are respectable, and are therefore entitled to a sort of voice—not a loud one, but a modest one; not a boastful one, but an apologetic one. They ought not to be allowed much space among better people—people who did something. I grant that; but they ought at least to be allowed to state why they didn't do anything, and also to explain the process by which they didn't do anything. Surely this kind of light must have a sort of value.

Out West there was a good deal of confusion in men's minds during the first months of the great trouble—a good deal of unsettledness, of leaning first this way, then that, then the other way. It was hard for us to get our bearings. I call to mind an instance of this. I was piloting on the Mississippi when the news came that South Carolina had gone out of the Union on the 20th of December, 1860. My pilot mate was a New Yorker. He was strong for the Union; so was I. But he would not listen to me with any patience; my loyalty was smirched, to his eye, because my father had owned slaves. I said, in palliation of this dark fact, that I had heard my father say, some years before he died, that slavery was a great wrong, and that he would free the solitary Negro he

then owned if he could think it right to give away the property of the family when he was so straitened in means. My mate retorted that a mere impulse was nothing—anybody could pretend to a good impulse; and went on decrying my Unionism and libeling my ancestry. A month later the secession atmosphere had considerably thickened on the Lower Mississippi, and I became a rebel; so did he. We were together in New Orleans the 26th of January, when Louisiana went out of the Union. He did his full share of the rebel shouting, but was bitterly opposed to letting me do mine. He said that I came of bad stock—of a father who had been willing to set slaves free. In the following summer he was piloting a Federal gunboat and shouting for the Union again, and I was in the Confederate army. I held his note for some borrowed money. He was one of the most upright men I ever knew, but he repudiated that note without hesitation because I was a rebel and the son of a man who owned slaves.

In that summer—of 1861—the first wash of the wave of war broke upon the shores of Missouri. Our State was invaded by the Union forces. They took possession of St. Louis, Jefferson Barracks, and some other points. The Governor, Claib Jackson, issued his proclamation calling out fifty thousand militia to repel the invader.

I was visiting in the small town where my boyhood had been spent—Hannibal, Marion County. Several of us got together in a secret place by night and formed ourselves into a military company. One Tom Lyman, a young fellow of a good deal of spirit but of no military experience, was made captain; I was made second lieutenant. We had no first lieutenant; I do not know why; it was long ago. There were fifteen of us. By the advice of an innocent connected with the organization we called ourselves the Marion Rangers. I do not remember that anyone found fault with the name. I did not; I thought it sounded quite well. The young fellow who proposed this title was perhaps a fair sample of the kind of stuff we were made of. He was young, ignorant, good-natured, well-meaning, trivial, full of romance, and given to reading chivalric novels and singing forlorn love-ditties. He had some pathetic little nickel-plated aristocratic instincts, and detested his name, which was Dunlap; detested it, partly because it was nearly as common in that region as Smith, but mainly because it had a plebian sound to his ear. So he tried to ennoble it by writing it in this way: *d'Unlap.* That contented his eye, but left his ear unsatisfied, for people gave the new name the same old pronunciation—emphasis on the front end of it. He then did the bravest thing that can be imagined—a thing to make one shiver when one remembers how the world is given to resenting shams and affectations; he began to write his name so: *d'Un Lap.* And he waited patiently through the long storm of mud that was flung at this work of art, and he had his reward at last; for he lived to see that name accepted, and the emphasis put where he wanted it by people who had known him all his life, and to whom the tribe of Dunlaps had been as familiar as the rain and the sunshine for forty years. So sure of victory at last is the courage that can wait. He said he had found, by consulting some ancient French chronicles, that the name was rightly and originally written

d'Un Lap; and said that if it were translated into English it would mean Peterson: *Lap,* Latin or Greek, he said, for stone or rock, same as the French *pierre,* that is to say, Peter; *d',* of or from; *un,* a or one; hence, d'Un Lap, of or from a stone or a Peter; that is to say, one who is the son of a stone, the son of a Peter—Peterson. Our militia company were not learned, and the explanation confused them; so they called him Peterson Dunlap. He proved useful to us in his way; he named our camps for us, and he generally struck a name that was "no slouch," as the boys said.

That is one sample of us. Another was Ed Stevens, son of the town jeweler—trim-built, handsome, graceful, neat as a cat; bright, educated, but given over entirely to fun. There was nothing serious in life to him. As far as he was concerned, this military expedition of ours was simply a holiday. I should say that about half of us looked upon it in the same way; not consciously perhaps, but unconsciously. We did not think; we were not capable of it. As for myself, I was full of unreasoning joy to be done with turning out of bed at midnight and four in the morning for a while; grateful to have a change, new scenes, new occupations, a new interest. In my thoughts that was as far as I went; I did not go into the details; as a rule, one doesn't at twenty-four.

Another sample was Smith, the blacksmith's apprentice. This vast donkey had some pluck, of a slow and sluggish nature, but a soft heart; at one time he would knock a horse down for some impropriety, and at another he would get homesick and cry. However, he had one ultimate credit to his account which some of us hadn't: he stuck to the war, and was killed in battle at last.

Jo Bowers, another sample, was a huge, good-natured, flax-headed lubber; lazy, sentimental, full of harmless brag, a grumbler by nature; an experienced, industrious, ambitious, and often quite picturesque liar, and yet not a successful one, for he had had no intelligent training, but was allowed to come up just any way. This life was serious enough to him, and seldom satisfactory. But he was a good fellow anyway, and the boys all liked him. He was made orderly sergeant; Stevens was made corporal.

These samples will answer—and they are quite fair ones. Well, this herd of cattle started for the war. What could you expect of them? They did as well as they knew how; but really what was justly to be expected of them? Nothing, I should say. That is what they did.

We waited for a dark night, for caution and secrecy were necessary; then, toward midnight, we stole in couples and from various directions to the Griffith place, beyond the town; from that point we set out together on foot. Hannibal lies at the extreme southeastern corner of Marion County, on the Mississippi River; our objective point was the hamlet of New London, ten miles away, in Ralls County.

The first hour was all fun, all idle nonsense and laughter. But that could not be kept up. The steady trudging came to be like work; the play had somehow oozed out of it; the stillness of the woods and the somberness of the night began to throw a depressing influence over the spirits of the boys, and presently the talking died out and each person shut himself up in his own thoughts. During the last half of the second hour nobody said a word.

Now we approached a log farmhouse where, according to report, there was a guard of five Union soldiers. Lyman called a halt; and there, in the deep gloom of the overhanging branches, he began to whisper a plan of assault upon that house, which made the gloom more depressing than it was before. It was a crucial moment; we realized, with a cold suddenness, that here was no jest—we were standing face to face with actual war. We were equal to the occasion. In our response there was no hesitation, no indecision: we said that if Lyman wanted to meddle with those soldiers, he could go ahead and do it; but if he waited for us to follow him, he would wait a long time.

Lyman urged, pleaded, tried to shame us, but it had no effect. Our course was plain, our minds were made up: we would flank the farmhouse—go out around. And that was what we did.

We struck into the woods and entered upon a rough time, stumbling over roots, getting tangled in vines, and torn by briers. At last we reached an open place in a safe region, and sat down, blown and hot, to cool off and nurse our scratches and bruises. Lyman was annoyed, but the rest of us were cheerful; we had flanked the farmhouse, we had made our first military movement, and it was a success; we had nothing to fret about, we were feeling just the other way. Horse-play and laughing began again; the expedition was become a holiday frolic once more.

Then we had two more hours of dull trudging and ultimate silence and depression; then, about dawn, we straggled into New London, soiled, heel-blistered, fagged with our little march, and all of us except Stevens in a sour and raspy humor and privately down on the war. We stacked our shabby old shotguns in Colonel Ralls's barn, and then went in a body and breakfasted with that veteran of the Mexican War. Afterwards he took us to a distant meadow, and there in the shade of a tree we listened to an old-fashioned speech from him, full of gunpowder and glory, full of that adjective-piling, mixed metaphor, and windy declamation which were regarded as eloquence in that ancient time and that remote region; and then he swore us on the Bible to be faithful to the State of Missouri and drive all invaders from her soil, no matter whence they might come or under what flag they might march. This mixed us considerably, and we could not make out just what service we were embarked in; but Colonel Ralls, the practiced politician and phrase-juggler, was not similarly in doubt; he knew quite clearly that he had invested us in the cause of the Southern Confederacy. He closed the solemnities by belting around me the sword which his neighbor, Colonel Brown, had worn at Buena Vista and Molino del Rey; and he accompanied this act with another impressive blast.

Then we formed in line of battle and marched four miles to a shady and pleasant piece of woods on the border of the far-reaching expanses of a flowery prairie. It was an enchanting region for war—our kind of war.

We pierced the forest about half a mile, and took up a strong position, with some low, rocky, and wooded hills behind us, and a purling, limpid creek in front. Straightway half the command were in swimming and the other half fishing. The ass with the French name gave this position a romantic title, but it was too long, so the boys shortened and simplified it to Camp Ralls.

We occupied an old maple sugar camp, whose half-rotted troughs were still propped against the trees. A long corn-crib served for sleeping quarters for the battalion. On our left, half a mile away, were Mason's farm and house; and he was a friend to the cause. Shortly after noon the farmers began to arrive from several directions, with mules and horses for our use, and these they lent us for as long as

the war might last, which they judged would be about three months. The animals were of all sizes, all colors, and all breeds. They were mainly young and frisky, and nobody in the command could stay on them long at a time; for we were town boys, and ignorant of horsemanship. The creature that fell to my share was a very small mule, and yet so quick and active that it could throw me without difficulty; and it did this whenever I got on it. Then it would bray—stretching its neck out, laying its ears back, and spreading its jaws till you could see down to its works. It was a disagreeable animal in every way. If I took it by the bridle and tried to lead it off the grounds, it would sit down and brace back, and no one could budge it. However, I was not entirely destitute of military resources, and I did presently manage to spoil this game; for I had seen many a steamboat aground in my time, and knew a trick or two which even a grounded mule would be obliged to respect. There was a well by the corn-crib; so I substituted thirty fathom of rope for the bridle, and fetched him home with the windlass.

I will anticipate here sufficiently to say that we did learn to ride, after some days' practice, but never well. We could not learn to like our animals; they were not choice ones, and most of them had annoying peculiarities of one kind or another. Stevens's horse would carry him, when he was not noticing, under the huge excrescences which form on the trunks of oak trees, and wipe him out of the saddle; in this way Stevens got several bad hurts. Sergeant Bowers's horse was very large and tall, with slim, long legs, and looked like a railroad bridge. His size enabled him to reach all about, and as far as he wanted to, with his head; so he was always biting Bowers's legs. On the march, in the sun, Bowers slept a good deal; and as soon as the horse recognized that he was asleep he would reach around and bite him on the leg. His legs were black and blue with bites. This was the only thing that could ever make him swear, but this always did; whenever his horse bit him he always swore, and of course Stevens, who laughed at everything, laughed at this, and would even get into such convulsions over it as to lose his balance and fall off his horse; and then Bowers, already irritated by the pain of the horse-bite, would resent the laughter with hard language, and there would be a quarrel; so that horse made no end of trouble and bad blood in the command. ·

However I will get back to where I was— our first afternoon in the sugar-camp. The sugar-troughs came very handy as horse-troughs, and we had plenty of corn to fill them with. I ordered Sergeant Bowers to feed my mule; but he said that if I reckoned he went to war to be a dry-nurse to a mule, it wouldn't take me very long to find out my mistake. I believed that this was insubordination, but I was full of uncertainties about everything military, and so I let the thing pass, and went and ordered Smith, the blacksmith's apprentice, to feed the mule; but he merely gave me a large, cold, sarcastic grin, such as an ostensibly seven-year-old horse gives you when you lift his lip and find he is fourteen, and turned his back on me. I then went to the captain, and asked if it was not right and proper and military for me to have an orderly. He said it was, but as there was only one orderly in the corps, it was but right that he himself should have Bowers on his staff. Bowers said he wouldn't serve on anybody's staff; and if anybody thought he could make him, let him try it. So, of course, the thing had to be dropped; there was no other way.

Next, nobody would cook; it was considered a degradation; so we had no dinner. We lazied the rest of the pleasant afternoon away, some dozing under the trees, some smoking cob-pipes and talking sweethearts and war, some playing games. By late supper-time all hands were famished; and to meet the difficulty all hands turned to, on an equal footing, and gathered wood, built fires, and cooked the meal. Afterwards everything was smooth for a while; then trouble broke out between the corporal and the sergeant, each claiming to rank the other. Nobody knew which was the higher office; so Lyman had to settle the matter by making the rank of both officers equal. The commander of an ignorant crew like that has many troubles and vexations which probably do not occur in the regular army at all. However, with the song-singing and yarn-spinning around the camp-fire, everything presently became serene again; and by and by we raked the corn down level in one end of the crib, and all went to bed on it, tying a horse to the door, so that he would neigh if anyone tried to get in.*

We had some horsemanship drill every forenoon; then, afternoons, we rode off here and there in squads a few miles, and visited the farmers' girls, and had a youthful good time, and got an honest good dinner or supper, and

* It was always my impression that that was what the horse was there for, and I know that it was also the impression of at least one other of the command, for we talked about it at the time, and admired the military ingenuity of the device; but when I was out West, three years ago, I was told by Mr. A. G. Fuqua, a member of our company, that the horse was his; that the leaving him tied at the door was a matter of mere forgetfulness, and that to attribute it to intelligent invention was to give him quite too much credit. In support of his position he called my attention to the suggestive fact that the artifice was not employed again. I had not thought of that before.

then home again to camp, happy and content.

For a time life was idly delicious, it was perfect; there was nothing to mar it. Then came some farmers with an alarm one day. They said it was rumored that the enemy were advancing in our direction from over Hyde's prairie. The result was a sharp stir among us, and general consternation. It was a rude awakening from our pleasant trance. The rumor was but a rumor—nothing definite about it; so, in the confusion, we did not know which way to retreat. Lyman was for not retreating at all in these uncertain circumstances; but he found that if he tried to maintain that attitude he would fare badly, for the command were in no humor to put up with insubordination. So he yielded the point and called a council of war—to consist of himself and the three other officers; but the privates made such a fuss about being left out that we had to allow them to remain, for they were already present, and doing the most of the talking too. The question was, which way to retreat; but all were so flurried that nobody seemed to have even a guess to offer. Except Lyman. He explained in a few calm words that, inasmuch as the enemy were approaching from over Hyde's prairie, our course was simple: all we had to do was not to retreat *toward* him; any other direction would answer our needs perfectly. Everybody saw in a moment how true this was, and how wise; so Lyman got a great many compliments. It was now decided that we should fall back on Mason's farm.

It was after dark by this time, and as we could not know how soon the enemy might arrive, it did not seem best to try to take the horses and things with us; so we only took the guns and ammunition, and started at once. The route was very rough and hilly and rocky, and presently the night grew very black and rain began to fall; so we had a troublesome time of it, struggling and stumbling along in the dark; and soon some person slipped and fell, and then the next person behind stumbled over him and fell, and so did the rest, one after the other; and then Bowers came with the keg of powder in his arms, while the command were all mixed together, arms and legs, on the muddy slope; and so he fell, of course, with the keg, and this started the whole detachment down the hill in a body, and they landed in the brook at the bottom in a pile, and each that was undermost pulling the hair and scratching and biting those that were on top of him; and those that were being scratched and bitten scratching and biting the rest in their turn, and all saying they would die before they would ever go to war again if they ever got out of this brook this time, and the invader might rot for all they cared, and the country along with him—and all such talk as that, which was dismal to hear and take part in, in such smothered, low voices, and such a grisly dark place and so wet, and the enemy, maybe, coming any moment.

The keg of powder was lost, and the guns, too; so the growling and complaining continued straight along while the brigade pawed around the pasty hillside and slopped around in the brook hunting for these things; consequently we lost considerable time at this; and then we heard a sound, and held our breath and listened, and it seemed to be the enemy coming, though it could have been a cow, for it had a cough like a cow; but we did not wait, but left a couple of guns behind and struck out for Mason's again as briskly as we could scramble along in the dark. But we got lost presently among the rugged little ravines, and wasted a deal of time finding the way again, so it was after nine when we reached Mason's stile at last; and then before we could open our mouths to give the countersign several dogs came bounding over the fence, with great riot and noise, and each of them took a soldier by the slack of his trousers and began to back away with him. We could not shoot the dogs without endangering the persons they were attached to; so we had to look on helpless, at what was perhaps the most mortifying spectacle of the Civil War. There was light enough, and to spare, for the Masons had now run out on the porch with candles in their hands. The old man and his son came and undid the dogs without difficulty, all but Bowers's; but they couldn't undo his dog, they didn't know his combination; he was of the bull kind, and seemed to be set with a Yale time-lock; but they got him loose at last with some scalding water, of which Bowers got his share and returned thanks. Peterson Dunlap afterwards made up a fine name for this engagement, and also for the night march which preceded it, but both have long ago faded out of my memory.

We now went into the house, and they began to ask us a world of questions, whereby it presently came out that we did not know anything concerning who or what we were running from; so the old gentleman made himself very frank, and said we were a curious breed of soldiers, and guessed we could be depended on to end up the war in time, because no government could stand the expense of the shoe-leather we should cost it trying to follow us around. "Marion *Rangers!* good name, b'-gosh!" said he. And wanted to know why we hadn't had a picket-guard at the place where the road entered the prairie, and why we hadn't sent out a scouting party to spy out the enemy and bring us an account of his strength, and so on, before jumping up and stampeding

out of a strong position upon a mere vague rumor—and so on, and so forth, till he made us all feel shabbier than the dogs had done, not half so enthusiastically welcome. So we went to bed shamed and low-spirited; except Stevens. Soon Stevens began to devise a garment for Bowers which could be made to automatically display his battle-scars to the grateful, or conceal them from the envious, according to his occasions; but Bowers was in no humor for this, so there was a fight, and when it was over Stevens had some battle-scars of his own to think about.

Then we got a little sleep. But after all we had gone through, our activities were not over for the night; for about two o'clock in the morning we heard a shout of warning from down the lane, accompanied by a chorus from all the dogs, and in a moment everybody was up and flying around to find out what the alarm was about. The alarmist was a horseman who gave notice that a detachment of Union soldiers was on its way from Hannibal with orders to capture and hang any bands like ours which it could find, and said we had no time to lose. Farmer Mason was in a flurry this time himself. He hurried us out of the house with all haste, and sent one of his Negroes with us to show us where to hide ourselves and our telltale guns among the ravines half a mile away. It was raining heavily.

We struck down the lane, then across some rocky pasture-land which offered good advantages for stumbling; consequently we were down in the mud most of the time, and every time a man went down he blackguarded the war, and the people that started it, and everybody connected with it, and gave himself the master dose of all for being so foolish as to go into it. At last we reached the wooded mouth of a ravine, and there we huddled ourselves under the streaming trees, and sent the Negro back home. It was a dismal and heart-breaking time. We were like to be drowned with the rain, deafened with the howling wind and the booming thunder, and blinded by the lightning. It was, indeed, a wild night. The drenching we were getting was misery enough, but a deeper misery still was the reflection that the halter might end us before we were a day older. A death of this shameful sort had not occurred to us as being among the possibilities of war. It took the romance all out of the campaign, and turned our dreams of glory into a repulsive nightmare. As for doubting that so barbarous an order had been given, not one of us did that.

The long night wore itself out at last, and then the Negro came to us with the news that the alarm had manifestly been a false one, and that breakfast would soon be ready. Straightway we were light-hearted again, and the world was bright, and life as full of hope and promise as ever—for we were young then. How long ago that was! Twenty-four years.

The mongrel child of philology named the night's refuge Camp Devastation, and no soul objected. The Masons gave us a Missouri country breakfast, in Missourian abundance, and we needed it: hot biscuits; hot "wheat bread," prettily criss-crossed in a lattice pattern on top; hot corn pone; fried chicken; bacon, coffee, eggs, milk, buttermilk, etc.; and the world may be confidently challenged to furnish the equal of such a breakfast, as it is cooked in the South.

We stayed several days at Mason's; and after all these years the memory of the dullness, and stillness, and lifelessness of that slumberous farmhouse still oppresses my spirit as with a sense of the presence of death and mourning. There was nothing to do, nothing to think about; there was no interest in life. The male part of the household were away in the fields all day, the women were busy and out of our sight; there was no sound but the plaintive wailing of a spinning-wheel, forever moaning out from some distant room—the most lonesome sound in nature, a sound steeped and sodden with homesickness and the emptiness of life. The family went to bed about dark every night, and as we were not invited to intrude any new customs we naturally followed theirs. Those nights were a hundred years long to youths accustomed to being up till twelve. We lay awake and miserable till that hour every time, and grew old and decrepit waiting through the still eternities for the clock-strikes. This was no place for town boys. So at last it was with something very like joy that we received news that the enemy were on our track again. With a new birth of the old warrior spirit we sprang to our places in line of battle and fell back on Camp Ralls.

Captain Lyman had taken a hint from Mason's talk, and he now gave orders that our camp should be guarded against surprise by the posting of pickets. I was ordered to place a picket at the forks of the road in Hyde's prairie. Night shut down black and threatening. I told Sergeant Bowers to go out to that place and stay till midnight; and, just as I was expecting, he said he wouldn't do it. I tried to get others to go, but all refused. Some excused themselves on account of the weather; but the rest were frank enough to say they wouldn't go in any kind of weather. This kind of thing sounds odd now, and impossible, but there was no surprise in it at the time. On the contrary, it seemed a perfectly natural thing to do. There were scores of little camps scattered over Missouri where the same thing was happening. These camps were composed of young men who had been born and reared to a sturdy independence, and who did not know what it meant to be ordered around by Tom, Dick, and Harry, whom they had known familiarly all their lives, in the village or on the farm. It is quite within the probabilities that this same thing was happening all over the South. James Redpath recognized the justice of this assumption, and furnished the following instance in support of it. During a short stay in East Tennessee he was in a citizen colonel's tent one day talking, when a big private appeared at the door, and, without salute or other circumlocution, said to the colonel:

"Say, Jim, I'm a-goin' home for a few days."

"What for?"

"Well, I hain't b'en there for a right smart while, and I'd like to see how things is comin' on."

"How long are you going to be gone?"

" 'Bout two weeks."

"Well, don't be gone longer than that; and get back sooner if you can."

That was all, and the citizen officer resumed his conversation where the private had broken it off. This was in the first months of the war, of course. The camps in our part of Missouri were under Brigadier-General Thomas H. Harris. He was a townsman of ours, a first-rate fellow, and well liked; but we had all familiarly known him as the sole and modest-salaried operator in our telegraph office, where he had to send about one dispatch a week in ordinary times, and two when there was a rush of business; consequently, when he appeared in our midst one day, on the wing, and delivered a military command of some sort, in a large military fashion, nobody was surprised at the response which he got from the assembled soldiery:

"Oh, now, what'll you take to *don't,* Tom Harris?"

It was quite the natural thing. One might justly imagine that we were hopeless material for war. And so we seemed, in our ignorant state; but there were those among us who afterwards learned the grim trade; learned to obey like machines; became valuable soldiers; fought all through the war, and came out at the end with excellent records. One of the very boys who refused to go out on picket duty that night, and called me an ass for thinking he would expose himself to danger in such a foolhardy way, had become distinguished for intrepidity before he was a year older.

I did secure my picket that night—not by authority, but by diplomacy. I got Bowers to go by agreeing to exchange ranks with him for the time being, and go along and stand the watch with him as his subordinate. We stayed out there a couple of dreary hours in the pitchy darkness and the rain, with nothing to modify the dreariness but Bowers's monotonous growlings at the war and the weather; then we began to nod, and presently found it next to impossible to stay in the saddle; so we gave up the tedious job, and went back to the camp without waiting for the relief guard. We rode into camp without interruption or objection from anybody, and the enemy could have done the same, for there were no sentries. Everybody was asleep; at midnight there was nobody to send out another picket, so none was sent. We never tried to establish a watch at night again, as far as I remember, but we generally kept a picket out in the daytime.

In that camp the whole command slept on the corn in the big corn-crib; and there was usually a general row before morning, for the place was full of rats, and they would scramble over the boys' bodies and faces, annoying and irritating everybody; and now and then they would bite someone's toe, and the person who owned the toe would start up and magnify his English and begin to throw corn in the dark. The ears were half as heavy as bricks, and when they struck they hurt. The persons struck would respond, and inside of five minutes every man would be locked in a death-grip with his neighbor. There was a grievous deal of blood shed in the corn-crib, but this was all that was spilled while I was in the war. No, that is not quite true. But for one circumstance it would have been all. I will come to that now.

Our scares were frequent. Every few days rumors would come that the enemy were approaching. In these cases we always fell back on some other camp of ours; we never stayed where we were. But the rumors always turned out to be false; so at last even we began to grow indifferent to them. One night a Negro was sent to our corn-crib with the same old warning: the enemy was hovering in our neighborhood. We all said let him hover. We resolved to stay still and be comfortable. It was a fine warlike resolution, and no doubt we all felt the stir of it in our veins—for a moment. We had been having a very jolly time, that was full of horse-play and school-boy hilarity; but that cooled down now, and presently the fast-waning fire of forced jokes and forced laughs died out altogether, and the company became silent. Silent and nervous. And soon uneasy—worried—apprehensive. We had said we would stay, and we were committed. We could have been persuaded to go, but there was nobody brave enough to suggest it. An almost noiseless movement presently began in the dark by a general but unvoiced impulse. When the movement was completed each man knew that he was not the only person who had crept to the front wall and had his eye at a crack between the logs. No, we were all there; all there with our hearts in our throats, and staring out toward the sugar-troughs where the forest footpath came through. It was late, and there was a deep woodsy stillness everywhere. There was a veiled moonlight, which was only just strong enough to enable us to mark the general shape of objects. Presently a muffled sound caught our ears, and we recognized it as the hoof-beats of a horse or horses. And right away a figure appeared in the forest path; it could have been made of smoke, its mass had so little sharpness of outline. It was a man on horseback, and it seemed to me that there were others behind him. I got hold of a gun in the dark, and pushed it through a crack between the logs, hardly knowing what I was doing, I was so dazed with fright. Somebody said, "Fire!" I pulled the trigger. I seemed to see a hundred flashes and hear a hundred reports; then I saw the man fall down out of the saddle. My first feeling was of surprised gratification; my first impulse was an apprentice-sportsman's impulse to run and pick up his game. Somebody said, hardly audibly, "Good—we've got him!—wait for the rest." But the rest did not come. We waited—listened—still no more came. There was not a sound, not the whisper of a leaf; just perfect stillness; an uncanny kind of stillness, which was all the more uncanny on account of the damp, earthy, late-night smells now rising and pervading it. Then, wondering, we crept stealthily out, and approached the man. When we got to him the moon revealed him distinctly. He was lying on his back, with his arms abroad; his mouth was open and his chest heaving with long gasps, and his white shirt-front was all splashed with blood. The thought shot through me that I was a murderer; that

I had killed a man—a man who had never done me any harm. That was the coldest sensation that ever went through my marrow. I was down by him in a moment, helplessly stroking his forehead; and I would have given anything then—my own life freely—to make him again what he had been five minutes before. And all the boys seemed to be feeling in the same way; they hung over him, full of pitying interest, and tried all they could to help him, and said all sorts of regretful things. They had forgotten all about the enemy; they thought only of this one forlorn unit of the foe. Once my imagination persuaded me that the dying man gave me a reproachful look out of his shadowy eyes, and it seemed to me that I could rather he had stabbed me than done that. He muttered and mumbled like a dreamer in his sleep about his wife and his child; and I thought with a new despair, "This thing that I have done does not end with him; it falls upon *them* too, and they never did me any harm, any more than he."

In a little while the man was dead. He was killed in war; killed in fair and legitimate war; killed in battle, as you may say; and yet he was as sincerely mourned by the opposing force as if he had been their brother. The boys stood there a half-hour sorrowing over him, and recalling the details of the tragedy, and wondering who he might be, and if he were a spy, and saying that if it were to do over again they would not hurt him unless he attacked them first. It soon came out that mine was not the only shot fired; there were five others—a division of the guilt which was a great relief to me, since it in some degree lightened and diminished the burden I was carrying. There were six shots fired at once; but I was not in my right mind at the time, and my heated imagination had magnified my one shot into a volley.

The man was not in uniform, and was not armed. He was a stranger in the country; that was all we ever found out about him. The thought of him got to preying upon me every night; I could not get rid of it. I could not drive it away, the taking of that unoffending life seemed such a wanton thing. And it seemed an epitome of war; that all war must be just that—the killing of strangers against whom you feel no personal animosity; strangers whom, in other circumstances, you would help if you found them in trouble, and who would help you if you needed it. My campaign was spoiled. It seemed to me that I was not rightly equipped for this awful business; that war was intended for men, and I for a child's nurse. I resolved to retire from this avocation of sham soldiership while I could save some remnant of my self-respect. These morbid thoughts clung to me against reason; for at bottom I did not believe I had touched that man. The law of probabilities decreed me guiltless of his blood; for in all my small experience with guns I had never hit anything I had tried to hit, and I knew I had done my best to hit him. Yet there was no solace in the thought. Against a diseased imagination demonstration goes for nothing.

The rest of my war experience was of a piece with what I have already told of it. We kept monotonously falling back upon one camp or another, and eating up the country. I marvel now at the patience of the farmers and their families. They ought to have shot us; on the contrary, they were as hospitably kind and courteous to us as if we had deserved it. In one of these camps we found Ab Grimes, an Upper Mississippi pilot, who afterwards became famous as a dare-devil rebel spy, whose career bristled with desperate adventures. The look and style of his comrades suggested that they had not come into the war to play, and their deeds made good the conjecture later. They were fine horsemen and good revolver shots; but their favorite arm was the lasso. Each had one at his pommel, and could snatch a man out of the saddle with it every time, on a full gallop, at any reasonable distance.

In another camp the chief was a fierce and profane old blacksmith of sixty, and he had furnished his twenty recruits with gigantic home-made bowie-knives, to be swung with two hands, like the *machetes* of the Isthmus. It was a grisly spectacle to see that earnest band practicing their murderous cuts and slashes under the eye of that remorseless old fanatic.

The last camp which we fell back upon was in a hollow near the village of Florida, where I was born—in Monroe County. Here we were warned one day that a Union colonel was sweeping down on us with a whole regiment at his heel. This looked decidedly serious. Our boys went apart and consulted; then we went back and told the other companies present that the war was a disappointment to us, and we were going to disband. They were getting ready themselves to fall back on some place or other, and were only waiting for General Tom Harris, who was expected to arrive at any moment; so they tried to persuade us to wait a little while, but the majority of us said no, we were accustomed to falling back, and didn't need any of Tom Harris's help; we could get along perfectly well without him—and save time, too. So about half of our fifteen, including myself, mounted and left on the instant; the others yielded to persuasion and stayed—stayed through the war.

An hour later we met General Harris on the road, with two or three people in his company —his staff, probably, but we could not tell; none of them were in uniform; uniforms had not come into vogue among us yet. Harris ordered us back; but we told him there was a Union colonel coming with a whole regiment in his wake, and it looked as if there was going to be a disturbance; so we had concluded to go home. He raged a little, but it was of no use; our minds were made up. We had done our share; had killed one man, exterminated one army, such as it was; let him go and kill the rest, and that would end the war. I did not see that brisk young general again until last year; then he was wearing white hair and whiskers.

In time I came to know that Union colonel whose coming frightened me out of the war and crippled the Southern cause to that extent—General Grant. I came within a few hours of seeing him when he was as unknown as I was myself; at a time when anybody could have said, "Grant?—Ulysses S. Grant? I do not remember hearing the name before." It seems difficult to realize that there was once a time when such a remark could be rationally made; but there *was,* and I was within a few miles of the place and the occasion, too, though proceeding in the other direction.

The thoughtful will not throw this war paper of mine lightly aside as being valueless. It has this value: it is a not unfair picture of what went on in many and many a militia camp in the first months of the rebellion, when the green recruits were without discipline, without the steadying and heartening influence of trained leaders; when all their circumstances were new and strange, and charged with exaggerated terrors, and before the invaluable experience of actual collision in the field had turned them from rabbits into soldiers. If this side of the picture of that early day has not before been put into history, then history has been to that degree incomplete, for it had and has its rightful place there. There was more Bull Run material scattered through the early camps of this country than exhibited itself at Bull Run. And yet it learned its trade presently, and helped to fight the great battles later. I could have become a soldier myself if I had waited. I had got part of it learned; I knew more about retreating than the man that invented retreating.

The Brigade Commander

"UNDERNEATH WERE GREAT POOLS OF CLOTTED BLOOD, AMIDST WHICH LAY AMPUTATED fingers, hands, arms, feet, and legs, only a little more ghastly in color than the faces of those who waited their turn on the tables." Émile Zola did not write this description of operating tables in a field hospital. The passage comes from a novel with a most unlikely title for an exceedingly truthful and uncompromising treatment of the Civil War—*Miss Ravenel's Conversion from Secession to Loyalty* (1867) by John William De Forest (1826–1906).

In some ways this novel ranks as the best piece of fiction written about the war. According to William Dean Howells, De Forest was the "first to treat the war really and artistically. . . . His soldiers are the soldiers we actually know . . ." De Forest outlines an army in action. He catches the boredom of an interminable siege, the spang of the cannon, the red tape and graft, the ugliness of wounds, the depressing filth of mud. He clearly narrates two full-scale engagements, the siege of Port Hudson and the battle at Cane River. Still, the novel as a whole has great weaknesses: an affected romantic plot and a failure on the part of the author to *involve* his characters (or his readers) in the war experience. Unlike Tolstoy or Bierce or Crane, De Forest treats cowardice, for example, in an abstract manner. Although he shows the frightened reactions of a few hastily sketched figures, he refuses to touch upon their fears or motivations. After reading *War and Peace,* De Forest wrote Howells, "I actually did not dare state the extreme horror of battle, and the anguish with which the bravest soldiers struggle through it."

De Forest himself had a certain advantage for his times, one that did not become common in literary history until the first World War. Like Cooke, De Forest was a professional writer before he went into the army, having a history, two travel books, and two novels to his credit. He hurried back from Europe when the war broke out to become Captain of Company I, Twelfth Connecticut Volunteers. He took part in the battle of Georgia Landing, the assault on Port Hudson, and three other engagements before becoming Inspector General of the First Division of the XIX Corps. While on active duty, he wrote many factual accounts of camp life and combat, jotted down in the field and printed later as articles in *Harper's New Monthly Magazine.* He drew the combat passages of his novel from these notebooks (published in 1946 as *A Volunteer's Adventures*). After the war, De Forest continued to publish novels, *Kate Beaumont* and *Honest John Vane* being his most successful.

De Forest's "unknown" short story, "The Brigade Commander," first appeared in The New York *Times* in 1874. The tale shows De Forest's weaknesses and strengths. Although the plot holds few surprises, the battle description is brilliant in its clarity and scope.

THE COLONEL WAS THE IDOL OF HIS BRAG-
ging old regiment and of the bragging brigade which for the last six months he had commanded.

He was the idol, not because he was good and gracious, not because he spared his soldiers or treated them as fellow-citizens, but because he had led them to victory and made them famous. If a man will win battles and give his brigade a right to brag loudly of its doings, he may have its admiration and even its enthusiastic devotion, though he be as pitiless and as wicked as Lucifer.

"It's nothin' to me what the Currnell is in prrivit, so long as he shows us how to whack the rrebs," said Major Gahogan, commandant of the "Old Tenth." "Moses saw God in the burrnin' bussh, an' bowed down to it, an' worrshipt it. It wasn't the bussh he worrshipt; it was his God that was in it. An' I worrship this villin of a Currnell (if he is a villin) because he's almighty and gives us the vict'ry. He's nothin' but a human burrnin' bussh, perhaps, but he's got the god of war in um. Adjetant Wallis, it's a —— long time between dhrinks, as I think ye was sayin', an' with rayson. See if ye can't confiscate a canteen of whiskee somewhere in the camp. Bedad, if I can't buy it I'll stale it. We're goin' to fight tomorry, an' it may be it's the last chance we'll have for a dhrink, unless there's more lik'r now in the other worrld than Dives got."

The brigade was bivouacked in some invisi-ble region, amid the damp, misty darkness of a September night. The men lay in their ranks, each with his feet to the front and his head rearward, each covered by his overcoat and pillowed upon his haversack, each with his loaded rifle nestled close beside him. Asleep as they were, or dropping placidly into slumber, they were ready to start in order to their feet and pour out the red light and harsh roar of combat. There were two lines of battle, each of three regiments of infantry, the first some two hundred yards in advance of the second. In the space between them lay two four-gun batteries, one of them brass twelve-pounder "Napoleons," and the other rifled Parrotts. To the rear of the infantry were the recumbent troopers and picketed horses of a regiment of cavalry. All around, in the far, black distance, invisible and inaudible, paced or watched stealthily the sentinels of the grand guards.

There was not a fire, nor a torch, nor a star-beam in the whole bivouac to guide the feet of Adjutant Wallis in his pilgrimage after whisky. The orders from brigade headquarters had been strict against illuminations, for the Confederates were near at hand in force, and a surprise was purposed as well as feared. A tired and sleepy youngster, almost dropping with the heavy somnolence of wearied adolescence, he stumbled on through the trials of an undiscernible and unfamiliar footing, lifting his heavy riding-boots sluggishly over imaginary obstacles, and fearing the while lest his toil were labor misspent. It was a dry camp, he felt dolefully certain, or there would have been more noise in it. He fell over a sleeping Sergeant, and said to him hastily, "Steady, man—a friend!" as the half-roused soldier clutched his rifle. Then he found a Lieutenant, and shook him in vain; further on a Captain, and exchanged saddening murmurs with him; further still a camp-follower of African extraction, and blasphemed him.

"It's a God-forsaken camp, and there isn't a horn in it," said Adjutant Wallis to himself as he pursued his groping journey. "Bet you I don't find the first drop," he continued, for he was a betting boy, and frequently argued by wagers, even with himself. "Bet you two to one I don't. Bet you three to one—ten to one."

Then he saw, an indefinite distance beyond him, burning like red-hot iron through the darkness, a little scarlet or crimson gleam, as of a lighted cigar.

"That's Old Grumps, of the Bloody Fourteenth," he thought. "I've raided into his happy sleeping-grounds. I'll draw on him."

But Old Grumps, otherwise Colonel Lafayette Gildersleeve, had no rations—that is, no whisky.

"How do you suppose an officer is to have a drink, Lieutenant?" he grumbled.

"Don't you know that our would-be Brigadier sent all the commissary to the rear day before yesterday? A canteenful can't last two days. Mine went empty about five minutes ago."

"Oh, thunder!" groaned Wallis, saddened by that saddest of all thoughts, "Too late!" "Well, least said soonest mended. I must wobble back to my Major."

"He'll send you off to some other camp as dry as this one. Wait ten minutes, and he'll be asleep. Lie down on my blanket and light your pipe. I want to talk to you about official business—about our would-be Brigadier."

"Oh, *your* turn will come some day," mumbled Wallis, remembering Gildersleeve's jealousy of the brigade commander—a jealousy which only gave tongue when aroused by "commissary." "If you do as well as usual tomorrow you can have your own brigade."

"I suppose you think we are all going to do well to-morrow," scoffed Old Grumps, whose utterance by this time stumbled. "I suppose you expect to whip and to have a good time. I suppose you brag on fighting and enjoy it."

"I like it well enough when it goes right; and it generally does go right with this brigade. I should like it better if the rebs would fire higher and break quicker."

"That depends on the way those are commanded whose business it is to break them," growled Old Grumps. "I don't say but what we are rightly commanded," he added, remembering his duty to superiors. "I concede and acknowledge that our would-be Brigadier knows his military business. But the blessing of God, Wallis! I believe in Waldron as a soldier. But as a man and a Christian, faugh!"

Gildersleeve had clearly emptied his canteen unassisted; he never talked about Christianity when perfectly sober.

"What was your last remark?" inquired Wallis, taking his pipe from his mouth to grin. Even a superior officer might be chaffed a little in the darkness.

"I made no last remark," asserted the Colonel with dignity. "I'm not a-dying yet. If I said anything last it was a mere exclamation of disgust—the disgust of an officer and gentleman. I suppose you know something about our would-be Brigadier. I suppose you think you know something about him."

"Bet you I know *all* about him," affirmed

Wallis. "He enlisted in the old Tenth as a common soldier. Before he had been a week in camp they found that he knew his biz, and they made him a Sergeant. Before we started for the field the Governor got his eye on him and shoved him into a Lieutenancy. The first battle h'isted him to a Captain. And the second— bang! whiz! he shot up to Colonel, right over the heads of everybody, line and field. Nobody in the old Tenth grumbled. They saw that he knew his biz. I know *all* about him. What'll you bet?"

"I'm not a betting man, Lieutenant, except in a friendly game of poker," sighed Old Grumps. "You don't know anything about your Brigadier," he added in a sepulchral murmur, the echo of an empty canteen. "I have only been in this brigade a month, and I know more than you do, far, very far more, sorry to say it. He's a reformed clergyman. He's an apostatized minister." The Colonel's voice as he said this was solemn and sad enough to do credit to an undertaker. "It's a bad sort, Wallis," he continued, after another deep sigh, a very highly perfumed one, the sigh of a barkeeper. "When a clergyman falls, he falls for life and eternity, like a woman or an angel. I never knew a backslidden shepherd to come to good. Sooner or later he always goes to the devil, and takes down whomsoever hangs to him."

"He'll take down the old Tenth, then," asserted Wallis. "It hangs to him. Bet you two to one he takes it along."

"You're right, Adjutant; spoken like a soldier," swore Gildersleeve. "And the Bloody Fourteenth, too! It will march into the burning pit as far as any regiment; and the whole brigade, yes sir! But a backslidden shepherd, my God! Have we come to that? I often say to myself, in the solemn hours of the night, as I remember my Sabbath-school days, 'Great Scott, have we come to that?' A reformed clergyman! An apostatized minister! Think of it, Wallis, think of it! Why, sir, his very wife ran away from him. They had but just buried their first boy," pursued Old Grumps, his hoarse voice sinking to a whimper. "They drove home from the burial-place, where lay the new-made grave. Arrived at their door, *he* got out and extended his hand to help *her* out. Instead of accepting, instead of throwing herself into his arms and weeping there, she turned to the coachman and said, 'Driver, drive me to my father's house.' That was the end of their wedded life, Wallis."

The Colonel actually wept at this point, and the maudlin tears were not altogether insincere. His own wife and children he heartily loved, and remembered them now with honest tenderness. At home he was not a drinker and a rough; only amid the hardships and perils of the field.

"That was the end of it, Wallis," he repeated. "And what was it while it lasted? What does a woman leave her husband for? Why does she separate from him over the grave of her innocent first-born? There are twenty reasons, but they must all of them be good ones. I am sorry to give it as my decided opinion, Wallis, in perfect confidence, that they must all be whopping good ones. Well, that was the beginning; only the beginning. After that he held on for a while, breaking the bread of life to a skedaddling flock, and then he bolted. The next known of him, three years later, he enlisted in your regiment, a smart but seedy recruit, smelling strongly of whisky."

"I wish I smelt half as strong of it myself," grumbled Wallis. "It might keep out the swamp fever."

"That's the true story of Col. John James

Waldron," continued Old Grumps, with a groan which was very somnolent, as if it were a twin to a snore. "That's the true story."

"I don't believe the first word of it—that is to say, Colonel, I think you have been misinformed—and I'll bet you two to one on it. If he was nothing more than a minister, how did he know drill and tactics?"

"Oh, I forgot to say, he went through West Point—that is, nearly through. They graduated him in his third year by the back door, Wallis."

"Oh, that was it, was it? He was a West Pointer, was he? Well, then, the backsliding was natural, and oughtn't to count against him. A member of Benny Havens' church has a right to backslide anywhere, especially as the Colonel doesn't seem to be any worse than some of the rest of us, who haven't fallen from grace the least particle, but took our stand at the start just where we are now. A fellow that begins with a handful of trumps has a right to play a risky game."

"I know what euchered him, Wallis. It was the old Little Joker; and there's another of the same on hand now."

"On hand where? What are you driving at, Colonel?"

"He looks like a boy. I mean she looks like a boy. You know what I mean, Wallis; I mean the boy that makes believe wait on him. And her brother is in camp, got here to-night. There'll be an explanation to-morrow, and there'll be bloodshed."

"Good-night, Colonel, and sleep it off," said Wallis, rising from the side of a man whom he believed to be sillily drunk and altogether untrustworthy. "You know we get after the rebs at dawn."

"I know it—goo-night, Adjutant—gawblessyou," mumbled Old Grumps. "We'll lick those rebs, won't we?" he chuckled. "Goonight, ole fellow, an' gawblessyou."

Whereupon Old Grumps fell asleep, very absurdly overcome by liquor, we extremely regret to concede, but nobly sure to do his soldierly duty as soon as he should awake.

Stumbling wearily blanketward, Wallis found his Major and regimental commander, the genial and gallant Gahogan, slumbering in a peace like that of the just. He stretched himself a-near, put out his hand to touch his sabre and revolver, drew his caped great-coat over him, moved once to free his back of a root or pebble, glanced languidly at a single struggling star, thought for an instant of his far-away mother, turned his head with a sigh, and slept. In the morning he was to fight, and perhaps to die; but the boyish veteran was too seasoned, and also too tired, to mind that; he could mind but one thing—nature's pleading for rest.

In the iron-gray dawn, while the troops were falling dimly and spectrally into line, and he was mounting his horse to be ready for orders, he remembered Gildersleeve's drunken tale concerning the commandant, and laughed aloud. But turning his face toward brigade headquarters (a sylvan region marked out by the branches of a great oak), he was surprised to see a strange officer, a fair young man in Captain's uniform, riding slowly toward it.

"Is that the Boy's brother?" he said to himself; and in the next instant he had forgotten the whole subject; it was time to form and present the regiment.

Quietly and without tap of drum the small, battleworn battalions filed out of their bivouacs into the highway, ordered arms and waited for the word to march. With a dull rumble the field-pieces trundled slowly after, and halted in rear of the infantry. The cavalry trotted off circuitously through the fields, emerged upon the road in advance and likewise halted, all but a single company, which pushed on for half a mile, spreading out as it went into a thin line of skirmishers.

Meanwhile a strange interview took place near the great oak which had sheltered brigade headquarters. As the unknown officer, whom Wallis had noted, approached it, Col. Waldron was standing by his horse ready to mount. The commandant was a man of medium size, fairly handsome in person and features, and apparently about twenty-eight years of age. Perhaps it was the singular breadth of his forehead which made the lower part of his face look so unusually slight and feminine. His eyes were dark hazel, as clear, brilliant, and tender as a girl's, and brimming full of a pensiveness which seemed both loving and melancholy. Few persons, at all events few women, who looked upon him ever looked beyond his eyes. They were very fascinating, and in a man's countenance very strange. They were the kind of eyes which reveal passionate romances, and which make them.

By his side stood a boy, a singularly interesting and beautiful boy, fair-haired and blue-eyed, and delicate in color. When this boy saw the stranger approach he turned as pale as marble, slid away from the brigade commander's side, and disappeared behind a group of staff officers and orderlies. The new-comer also became deathly white as he glanced after the retreating youth. Then he dismounted, touched his cap slightly and, as if mechanically, advanced a few steps, and said hoarsely, "I believe this is Colonel Waldron. I am Captain Fitz Hugh, of the —th Delaware."

Waldron put his hand to his revolver, withdrew it instantaneously, and stood motionless.

"I am on leave of absence from my regi-

ment, Colonel," continued Fitz Hugh, speaking now with an elaborate ceremoniousness of utterance significant of a struggle to suppress violent emotion. "I suppose you can understand why I made use of it in seeking you."

Waldron hesitated; he stood gazing at the earth with the air of one who represses deep pain; at last, after a profound sigh, he raised his eyes and answered.

"Captain, we are on the eve of a battle. I must attend to my public duties first. After the battle we will settle our private affair."

"There is but one way to settle it, Colonel."

"You shall have your way if you will. You shall do what you will. I only ask what good will it do to *her?*"

"It will do good to *me,* Colonel," whispered Fitz Hugh, suddenly turning crimson. "You forget *me.*"

Waldron's face also flushed, and an angry sparkle shot from under his lashes in reply to this utterance of hate, but it died out in an instant.

"I have done a wrong, and I will accept the consequences," he said. "I pledge you my word that I will be at your disposal if I survive the battle. Where do you propose to remain meanwhile?"

"I will take the same chance, Sir. I propose to do my share in the fighting if you will use me."

"I am short of staff officers. Will you act as my aid?"

"I will, Colonel," bowed Fitz Hugh, with a glance which expressed surprise, and perhaps admiration, at this confidence.

Waldron turned, beckoned his staff officers to approach, and said, "Gentlemen, this is Captain Fitz Hugh of the —th Delaware. He has volunteered to join us for the day, and will act as my aid. And now, Captain, will you ride to the head of the column and order it forward? There will be no drum beat and no noise. When you have given your order and seen it executed, you will wait for me."

Fitz Hugh saluted, sprang into his saddle and galloped away. A few minutes later the whole column was plodding on silently toward its bloody goal. To a civilian, unaccustomed to scenes of war, the tranquillity of these men would have seemed very wonderful. Many of the soldiers were still munching the hard bread and raw pork of their meagre breakfasts, or drinking the cold coffee with which they had filled their canteens the day previous. Many more were chatting in an undertone, grumbling over their sore feet and other discomfits, chaffing each other, and laughing. The general bearing, however, was grave, patient, quietly enduring, and one might almost say stolid. You would have said, to judge by their expressions, that these sunburnt fellows were merely doing hard work, and thoroughly commonplace work, without a prospect of adventure, and much less of danger. The explanation of this calmness, so brutal perhaps to the eye of a sensitive soul, lies mainly in the fact that they were all veterans, the survivors of marches, privations, maladies, sieges, and battles. Not a regiment present numbered four hundred men, and the average was not above three hundred. The whole force, including artillery and cavalry, might have been about twenty-five hundred sabres and bayonets.

At the beginning of the march Waldron fell into the rear of his staff and mounted orderlies. Then the Boy who had fled from Fitz Hugh dropped out of the tramping escort, and rode up to his side.

"Well, Charlie," said Waldron, casting a pitying glance at the yet pallid face and anxious eyes of the youth, "you have had a sad fright. I make you very miserable."

"He has found us at last," murmured Charlie in a tremulous soprano voice. "What did he say?"

"We are to talk to-morrow. He acts as my aide-de-camp to-day. I ought to tell you frankly that he is not friendly."

"Of course, I knew it," sighed Charlie, while the tears fell.

"It is only one more trouble—one more danger, and perhaps it may pass. So many *have* passed."

"Did you tell him anything to quiet him? Did you tell him that we were married?"

"But we are not married yet, Charlie. We shall be, I hope."

"But you ought to have told him that we were. It might stop him from doing something—mad. Why didn't you tell him so? Why didn't you think of it?"

"My dear little child, we are about to have a battle. I should like to carry some honor and truth into it."

"Where is he?" continued Charlie, unconvinced and unappeased. "I want to see him. Is he at the head of the column? I want to speak to him, just one word. He won't hurt me."

She suddenly spurred her horse, wheeled into the fields, and dashed onward. Fitz Hugh was lounging in his saddle, and sombrely surveying the passing column, when she galloped up to him.

"Carrol!" she said, in a choked voice, reining in by his side, and leaning forward to touch his sleeve.

He threw one glance at her—a glance of aversion, if not of downright hatred, and turned his back in silence.

"He is my husband, Carrol," she went on rapidly. "I knew you didn't understand it. I ought to have written you about it. I thought I would come and tell you before you did anything absurd. We were married as soon as he heard that his wife was dead."

"What is the use of this?" he muttered hoarsely. "She is not dead. I heard from her a week ago. She was living a week ago."

"Oh, Carrol!" stammered Charlie. "It was some mistake then. Is it possible! And he was so sure! But he can get a divorce, you know. She abandoned him. Or *she* can get one. No, *he* can get it—of course, when she abandoned him. But, Carrol, she *must* be dead—he was *so* sure."

"She is *not* dead, I tell you. And there can be no divorce. Insanity bars all claim to a divorce. She is in an asylum. She had to leave him, and then she went mad."

"Oh, no, Carrol, it is all a mistake; it is not so, Carrol," she murmured in a voice so faint that he could not help glancing at her, half in fury and half in pity. She was slowly falling from her horse. He sprang from his saddle, caught her in his arms, and laid her on the turf, wishing the while that it covered her grave. Just then one of Waldron's orderlies rode up and exclaimed: "What is the matter with the —the Boy? Hullo, Charlie."

Fitz Hugh stared at the man in silence, tempted to tear him from his horse. "The boy is ill," he answered when he recovered his self-command. "Take charge of him yourself." He remounted, rode onward out of sight beyond a thicket, and there waited for the brigade commander, now and then fingering his revolver. As Charlie was being placed in an ambulance by the orderly and a sergeant's wife, Waldron came up, reined in his horse violently, and asked in a furious voice, "Is that boy hurt?"

"Ah—fainted," he added immediately. "Thank you, Mrs. Gunner. Take good care of

him—the best of care, my dear woman, and don't let him leave you all day."

Further on, when Fitz Hugh silently fell into his escort, he merely glanced at him in a furtive way, and then cantered on rapidly to the head of the cavalry. There he beckoned to the tall, grave, iron-gray Chaplain of the Tenth, and rode with him for nearly an hour, apart, engaged in low and seemingly impassioned discourse. From this interview Mr. Colquhoun returned to the escort with a strangely solemnized, tender countenance, while the commandant, with a more cheerful air than he had yet worn that day, gave himself to his martial duties, inspecting the landscape incessantly with his glass, and sending frequently for news to the advance scouts. It may properly be stated here that the Chaplain never divulged to any one the nature of the conversation which he had held with his Colonel.

Nothing further of note occurred until the little army, after two hours of plodding march, wound through a sinuous, wooded ravine, entered a broad, bare, slightly undulating valley, and for the second time halted. Waldron galloped to the summit of a knoll, pointed to a long eminence which faced him some two miles distant, and said tranquilly, "There is our battle-ground."

"Is that the enemy's position?" returned Captain Ives, his Adjutant-General. "We shall have a tough job if we go at it from here."

Waldron remained in deep thought for some minutes, meanwhile scanning the ridge and all its surroundings.

"What I want to know," he observed, at last, "is whether they have occupied the wooded knolls in front of their right and around their right flank."

Shortly afterward the commander of the

scouting squadron came riding back at a furious pace.

"They are on the hill, Colonel," he shouted.

"Yes, of course," nodded Waldron; "but have they occupied the woods which veil their right front and flank?"

"Not a bit of it; my fellows have cantered all through, and up to the base of the hill."

"Ah!" exclaimed the brigade commander, with a rush of elation. "Then it will be easy work. Go back, Captain, and scatter your men through the wood, and hold it, if possible. Adjutant, call up the regimental commanders at once. I want them to understand my plan fully."

In a few minutes Gahogan, of the Tenth; Gildersleeve, of the Fourteenth; Peck, of the First; Thomas, of the Seventh; Taylor, of the Eighth, and Colburn, of the Fifth, were gathered around their commander. There, too, was Bradley, the boyish, red-cheeked chief of the artillery; and Stilton, the rough, old, bearded regular, who headed the cavalry. The staff was at hand, also, including Fitz Hugh, who sat his horse a little apart, downcast and sombre and silent, but nevertheless keenly interested. It is worthy of remark, by the way, that Waldron took no special note of him, and did not seem conscious of any disturbing presence. Evil as the man may have been, he was a thoroughly good soldier, and just now he thought but of his duties.

"Gentlemen," he said, "I want you to see your field of battle. The enemy occupy that long ridge. How shall we reach it?"

"I think, if we go at it straight from here, we shan't miss it," promptly judged Old Grumps, his red-oak countenance admirably cheerful and hopeful, and his jealousy all dissolved in the interest of approaching combat.

"Nor they won't miss us nuther," laughed Major Gahogan. "Betther slide our infantree into thim wuds, push up our skirmishers, play away wid our guns for an hour, an' thin rowl in a couple o' col'ms."

There was a general murmur of approval. The limits of volunteer invention in tactics had been reached by Gahogan. The other regimental commanders looked upon him as their superior in the art of war.

"That would be well, Major, if we could do nothing better," said Waldron. "But I do not feel obliged to attack the front seriously at all. The rebels have been thoughtless enough to leave that long semicircle of wooded knolls unoccupied, even by scouts. It stretches from the front of their centre clear around their right flank. I shall use it as a veil to cover us while we get into position. I shall throw out a regiment, a battery, and five companies of cavalry, to make a feint against their centre and left. With the remainder of the brigade I shall skirt the woods, double around the right of the position, and close in upon it front and rear."

"Loike scissors blades upon a snip o' paper," snorted Gahogan, in delight. Then he turned to Fitz Hugh, who happened to be nearest him, and added, "I tell ye he's got the God o' War in um. He's the burrnin' bussh of humanity, wid a God o' Battles inside on't."

"But how if they come down on our thin right wing?" asked a cautious officer, Taylor, of the Eighth. "They might smash it and seize our line of retreat."

"Men who have taken up a strong position, a position obviously chosen for defense, rarely quit it promptly for an attack," replied Waldron. "There is not one chance in ten that these gentlemen will make a considerable forward movement early in the fight. Only the greatest geniuses jump from the defensive to the offensive. Besides, we must hold the wood. So long as we hold the wood in front of their centre we save the road."

Then came personal and detailed instructions. Each regimental commander was told whither he should march, the point where he should halt to form line, and the direction by which he should attack. The mass of the command was to advance in marching column toward a knoll where the highway entered and traversed the wood. Some time before reaching it Taylor was to deploy the Eighth to the right, throw out a strong skirmish line and open fire on the enemy's centre and left, supported by the battery of Parrotts, and, if pushed, by five companies of cavalry. The remaining troops would reach the knoll, file to the left under cover of the forest, skirt it for a mile as rapidly as possible, enfold the right of the Confederate position, and then move upon it concentrically. Counting from the left, the Tenth, the Seventh, and the Fourteenth were to constitute the first line of battle, while five companies of cavalry, then the First, and then the Fifth formed the second line. Not until Gahogan might have time to wind into the enemy's right rear should Gildersleeve move out of the wood and commence the real attack.

"You will go straight at the front of their right," said Waldron, with a gay smile, to this latter Colonel. "Send up two companies as skirmishers. The moment they are clearly checked, lead up the other eight in line. It will be rough work. But keep pushing. You won't have fifteen minutes of it before Thomas, on your left, will be climbing the end of the ridge to take the rebels in flank. In fifteen minutes more Gahogan will be running in on their backs. Of course they will try to change front and meet us. But they have extended their line a long way in order to cover the whole ridge. They will not be quick enough. We shall get

hold of their right, and we shall roll them up. Then, Colonel Stilton, I shall expect to see the troopers jumping into the gaps and making prisoners."

"All right, Colonel," answered Stilton in that hoarse growl which is apt to mark the old cavalry officer. "Where shall we find you if we want a fresh order?"

"I shall be with Colburn, in rear of Gildersleeve. That is our centre. But never mind me; you know what the battle is to be, and you know how to fight it. The whole point with the infantry is to fold around the enemy's right, go in upon it concentrically, smash it, and roll up their line. The cavalry will watch against the infantry being flanked, and when the latter have seized the hill, will charge for prisoners. The artillery will reply to the enemy's guns with shell, and fire grape at any offensive demonstration. You all know your duties, now, gentlemen. Go to your commands, and march!"

The Colonels saluted and started off at a gallop. In a few minutes twenty-five hundred men were in simultaneous movement. Five companies of cavalry wheeled into column of companies, and advanced at a trot through the fields, seeking to gain the shelter of the forest. The six infantry regiments slid up alongside of each other, and pushed on in six parallel columns of march, two on the right of the road and four on the left. The artillery, which alone left the highway, followed at a distance of two or three hundred yards. The remaining cavalry made a wide detour to the right, as if to flank the enemy's left.

It was a mile and a quarter—it was a march of fully twenty minutes—to the edge of the woodland, the proposed cover of the column. Ten minutes before this point was reached a tiny puff of smoke showed on the brow of the hostile ridge; then, at an interval of several seconds, followed the sound of a distant explosion; then, almost immediately, came the screech of a rifled shell. Every man who heard it swiftly asked himself, "Will it strike *me?*" But even as the words were thought out it had passed, high in air, clean to the rear, and burst harmlessly. A few faces turned upward and a few eyes glanced backward, as if to see the invisible enemy. But there was no pause in the column; it flowed onward quietly, eagerly, and with business-like precision; it gave forth no sound but the trampling of feet and the muttering of the officers, "Steady, men! Forward, men."

The Confederates, however, had got their range. A half minute later four puffs of smoke dotted the ridge, and a flight of hoarse humming shrieks tore the air. A little aureole cracked and splintered over the First, followed by loud cries of anguish and a brief, slight confusion. The voice of an officer rose sharply out of the flurry, "Close up, Company A! Forward, men!" The battalion column resumed its even formation in an instant, and tramped unitedly onward, leaving behind it two quivering corpses and a wounded man who tottered rearward.

Then came more screeches, and a shell exploded over the high road, knocking a gunner lifeless from his carriage. The brigade commander glanced anxiously along his batteries, and addressed a few words to his chief of artillery. Presently the four Napoleons set forward at a gallop for the wood, while the four Parrotts wheeled to the right, deployed, and advanced across the fields, inclining toward the left of the enemy. Next, Taylor's regiment (the Eighth) halted, fronted, faced to the right, and filed off in column of march at a double-quick until it had gained the rear of the

Parrotts, when it fronted again, and pushed on in support. A quarter of a mile further on these guns went into battery behind the brow of a little knoll, and opened fire. Four companies of the English spread out to the right as skirmishers, and commenced stealing toward the ridge, from time to time measuring the distance with rifle-balls. The remainder of the regiment lay down in line between the Parrotts and the forest. Far away to the right, five companies of cavalry showed themselves, maneuvering as if they proposed to turn the left flank of the Southerners. The attack on this side was in form and in operation.

Meantime the Confederate fire had divided. Two guns pounded away at Taylor's feint, while two shelled the main column. The latter was struck repeatedly; more than twenty men dropped silent or groaning out of the hurrying files; but the survivors pushed on without faltering, and without even caring for the wounded. At last a broad belt of green branches rose between the regiments and the ridge; and the rebel gunners, unable to see their foe, dropped suddenly into silence.

Here it appeared that the road divided. The highway traversed the forest, mounted the slope beyond and dissected the enemy's position, while a branch road turned to the left and skirted the exterior of the long curve of wooded hillocks. At the fork the battery of Napoleons had halted, and there it was ordered to remain for the present in quiet. There, too, the Fourteenth filed in among the dense greenery, threw out two companies of skirmishers toward the ridge, and pushed slowly after them into the shadows.

"Get sight of the enemy at once!" was Waldron's last word to Gildersleeve. "If they move down the slope, drive them back. But don't commence your attack under half an hour."

Next he filed the Fifth into the thickets, saying to Colburn, "I want you to halt a hundred yards to the left and rear of Gildersleeve. Cover his flank if he is attacked; but otherwise lie quiet. As soon as he charges, move forward to the edge of the wood, and be ready to support him. But make no assault yourself until further orders."

The two next regiments—the Seventh and First—he placed in *échelon,* in like manner, a quarter of a mile further along. Then he galloped forward to the cavalry, and had a last word with Stilton. "You and Gahogan must take care of yourselves. Push on four or five hundred yards, and then face to the right. Whatever Gahogan finds let him go at it. If he can't shake it, help him. You two *must* reach the top of the ridge. Only, look out for your left flank. Keep a squadron or two in reserve on that side."

"Currnel, if we don't raich the top of the hill, it'll be because it hasn't got wan," answered Gahogan. Stilton only laughed and rode forward.

Waldron now returned toward the fork of the road. On the way he sent a staff officer to the Seventh with renewed orders to attack as soon as possible after Gildersleeve. Then another staff officer was hurried forward to Taylor with directions to push his feint strongly, and drive his skirmishers as far up the slope as they could get. A third staff officer set the Parrotts in rear of Taylor to firing with all their might. By the time that the commandant had returned to Colburn's ambushed ranks, no one was with him but his enemy, Fitz Hugh.

"You don't seem to trust me with duty, Colonel," said the young man.

"I shall use you only in case of extremity, Captain," replied Waldron. "We have business to settle to-morrow."

"I ask no favors on that account. I hope you will offer me none."

"In case of need I shall spare no one," declared Waldron.

Then he took out his watch, looked at it impatiently, put it to his ear, restored it to his pocket, and fell into an attitude of deep attention. Evidently his whole mind was on his battle, and he was waiting, watching, yearning for its outburst.

"If he wins this fight," thought Fitz Hugh, "how can I do him a harm? And yet," he added, "how can I help it?"

Minutes passed. Fitz Hugh tried to think of his injury, and to steel himself against his chief. But the roar of battle on the right, and the suspense and imminence of battle on the left, absorbed the attention of even this wounded and angry spirit, as, indeed, they might have absorbed that of any being not more or less than human. A private wrong, insupportable though it might be, seemed so small amid that deadly clamor and awful expectation! Moreover, the intellect which worked so calmly and vigorously by his side, and which alone of all things near appeared able to rule the coming crisis, began to dominate him, in spite of his sense of injury. A thought crossed him to the effect that the great among men are too valuable to be punished for their evil deeds. He turned to the absorbed brigade commander, now not only his ruler but even his protector, with a feeling that he must accord him a word of peace, a proffer in some form of possible forgiveness and friendship. But the man's face was clouded and stern with responsibility and authority. He seemed at that moment too lofty to be approached with a message of pardon. Fitz Hugh gazed at him with a mixture of profound respect and smothered hate. He gazed, turned away, and remained silent.

Minutes more passed. Then a mounted orderly dashed up at full speed, with the words, "Colonel, Major Gahogan has fronted."

"Has he?" answered Waldron, with a smile which thanked the trooper and made him happy. "Ride on through the thicket here, my man, and tell Colonel Gildersleeve to push up his skirmishers."

With a thud of hoofs and a rustling of parting foliage the cavalryman disappeared amid the underwood. A minute or two later a thin, dropping rattle of musketry, five hundred yards or so to the front, announced that the sharpshooters of the Fourteenth were at work. Almost immediately there was an angry response, full of the threatenings and execution of death. Through the lofty leafage tore the screech of a shell, bursting with a sharp crash as it passed overhead, and scattering in humming slivers. Then came another, and another, and many more, chasing each other with hoarse hissings through the trembling air, a succession of flying serpents. The enemy doubtless believed that nearly the whole attacking force was massed in the wood around the road, and they had brought at least four guns to bear upon that point, and were working them with the utmost possible rapidity. Presently a large chestnut, not fifty yards from Fitz Hugh, was struck by a shot. The solid trunk, nearly three feet in diameter, parted asunder as if it were the brittlest of vegetable matter. The upper portion started aside with a monstrous groan, dropped in a standing posture to the earth, and then toppled slowly, sublimely prostrate, its branches crashing and all its leaves wailing. Ere long, a little further to the front, another Anak of the forest went down; and, mingled with the noise of its sylvan agony, there arose sharp cries of human suffering. Then Colonel Colburn, a broad-

chested and ruddy man of thirty-five, with a look of indignant anxiety in his iron-gray eyes, rode up to the brigade commander.

"This is very annoying, Colonel," he said. "I am losing my men without using them. That last tree fell into my command."

"Are they firing toward our left?" asked Waldron.

"Not a shot."

"Very good," said the chief, with a sigh of contentment. "If we can only keep them occupied in this direction! By the way, let your men lie down under the fallen tree, as far as it will go. It will protect them from others."

Colburn rode back to his regiment. Waldron looked impatiently at his watch. At that moment a fierce burst of line firing arose in front, followed and almost overborne by a long-drawn yell, the scream of charging men. Waldron put up his watch, glanced excitedly at Fitz Hugh, and smiled.

"I must forgive or forget," the latter could not help saying to himself. "All the rest of life is nothing compared with this."

"Captain," said Waldron, "ride off to the left at full speed. As soon as you hear firing at the shoulder of the ridge, return instantly and let me know."

Fitz Hugh dashed away. Three minutes carried him into perfect peace, beyond the whistling of ball or the screeching of shell. On the right was a tranquil, wide waving of foliage, and on the left a serene landscape of cultivated fields, with here and there an embowered farm-house. Only for the clamor of artillery and musketry far behind him, he could not have believed in the near presence of battle, of blood and suffering and triumphant death. But suddenly he heard to his right, assaulting and slaughtering the tranquility of nature, a tumultuous outbreak of file-firing, mingled with savage yells. He wheeled, drove spurs into his horse, and flew back to Waldron. As he re-entered the wood he met wounded men streaming through it, a few marching alertly upright, many more crouching and groaning, some clinging to their less injured comrades, but all haggard in face and ghastly.

"Are we winning?" he hastily asked of one man who held up a hand with three fingers gone and the bones projecting in sharp spikes through mangled flesh.

"All right, Sir; sailing in," was the answer.

"Is the brigade commander all right?" he inquired of another who was winding a bloody handkerchief around his arm.

"Straight ahead, Sir; hurrah for Waldron!" responded the soldier, and almost in the same instant fell lifeless with a fresh ball through his head.

"Hurrah for him!" Fitz Hugh answered frantically, plunging on through the underwood. He found Waldron with Colburn, the two conversing tranquilly in their saddles amid hissing bullets and dropping branches.

"Move your regiment forward now," the brigade commander was saying; "but halt it in the edge of the wood."

"Shan't I relieve Gildersleeve if he gets beaten?" asked the subordinate officer eagerly.

"No. The regiments on the left will help him out. I want your men and Peck's for the fight on top of the hill. Of course the rebels will try to retake it; then I shall call for you."

Fitz Hugh now approached and said, "Colonel, the Seventh has attacked in force."

"Good!" answered Waldron, with that sweet smile of his which thanked people who brought him pleasant news. "I thought I heard his fire. Gahogan will be on their right rear in ten minutes. Then we shall get the

ridge. Ride back now to Major Bradley, and tell him to bring his Napoleons through the wood, and set two of them to shelling the enemy's centre. Tell him my idea is to amuse them, and keep them from changing front."

Again Fitz Hugh galloped off as before on a comfortably safe errand, safer at all events than many errands of that day. "This man is sparing my life," he said to himself. "Would to God I knew how to spare his!"

He found Bradley lunching on a gun caisson, and delivered his orders. "Something to do at last, eh?" laughed the rosy-cheeked youngster. "The smallest favors thankfully received. Won't you take a bite of rebel chicken, Captain? This rebellion must be put down. No? Well, tell the Colonel I am moving on, and John Brown's soul not far ahead."

When Fitz Hugh returned to Waldron he found him outside of the wood, at the base of the long incline which rose into the rebel position. About the slope were scattered prostrate forms, most numerous near the bottom, some crawling slowly rearward, some quiescent. Under the brow of the ridge, decimated and broken into a mere skirmish line sheltered in knots and singly, behind rocks and knolls and bushes, lay the Fourteenth Regiment, keeping up a steady, slow fire. From the edge above, smokily dim against a pure, blue heaven, answered another rattle of musketry, incessant, obstinate, and spiteful. The combatants on both sides were lying down; otherwise neither party could have lasted ten minutes. From Fitz Hugh's point of view not a Confederate uniform could be seen. But the smoke of their rifles made a long gray line, which was disagreeably visible and permanent; and the sharp *whit! whit!* of their bullets continually passed him, and cheeped away in the leafage behind.

"Our men can't get on another inch," he ventured to say to his commander. "Wouldn't it be well for me to ride up and say a cheering word?"

"Every battle consists largely in waiting," replied Waldron thoughtfully. "They have undoubtedly brought up a reserve to face Thomas. But when Gahogan strikes the flank of the reserve, we shall win."

"I wish you would take shelter," begged Fitz Hugh. "Everything depends on your life."

"My life has been both a help and a hurt to my fellow-creatures," sighed the brigade commander. "Let come what will to it."

He glanced upward with an expression of profound emotion; he was evidently fighting two battles, an outward and an inward one.

Presently he added, "I think the musketry is increasing on the left. Does it strike you so?"

He was all eagerness again, leaning forward with an air of earnest listening, his face deeply flushed and his eye brilliant. Of a sudden the combat above rose and swelled into higher violence. There was a clamor far away —it seemed nearly a mile away—over the hill. Then the nearer musketry, first Thomas' on the shoulder of the ridge, next Gildersleeve's in front, caught fire and raged with new fury.

Waldron laughed outright. "Gahogan has reached them," he said to one of his staff who had just rejoined him. "We shall all be up there in five minutes. Tell Colburn to bring on his regiment slowly."

Then, turning to Fitz Hugh, he added, "Captain, we will ride forward."

They set off at a walk, now watching the smoking brow of the eminence, now picking their way among dead and wounded. Suddenly there was a shout above them and a sud-

den diminution of the firing; and looking upward, they saw the men of the Fourteenth running confusedly toward the summit. Without a word the brigade commander struck spurs into his horse and dashed up the long slope at a run, closely followed by his enemy and aid. What they saw when they overtook the straggling, running, panting, screaming pell-mell of the Fourteenth was victory!

The entire right wing of the Confederates, attacked on three sides at once, placed at enormous disadvantage, completely outgeneraled, had given way in confusion, was retreating, breaking, and flying. There were lines yet of dirty gray or butternut; but they were few, meagre, fluctuating, and recoiling, and there were scattered and scurrying men in hundreds. Three veteran and gallant regiments had gone all to wreck under the shock of three similar regiments far more intelligently directed. A strong position had been lost because the heroes who held it could not perform the impossible feat of forming successively two fresh fronts under a concentric fire of musketry. The inferior brain power had confessed the superiority of the stronger one.

On the victorious side there was wild, clamorous, fierce exultation. The hurrying, shouting, firing soldiers, who noted their commander riding among them, swung their rifles or their tattered hats at him, and screamed "Hurrah!" No one thought of the Confederate dead under foot, nor of the Union dead who dotted the slope behind. "What are you here for, Colonel?" shouted rough old Gildersleeve, one leg of his trousers dripping blood. "We can do it alone."

"It is a battle won," laughed Fitz Hugh, almost worshipping the man whom he had come to slay.

"It is a battle won, but not used," answered Waldron. "We haven't a gun yet, nor a flag. Where is the cavalry? Why isn't Stilton here? He must have got afoul of the enemy's horse, and been obliged to beat it off. Can anybody hear anything of Stilton?"

"Let him go," roared Old Grumps. "The infantry don't want any help."

"Your regiment has suffered, Colonel," answered Waldron, glancing at the scattered files of the Fourteenth. "Halt it and reorganize it, and let it fall in with the right of the First when Peck comes up. I shall replace you with the Fifth. Send your Adjutant back to Colburn and tell him to hurry along. Those fellows are making a new front over there," he added, pointing to the centre of the hill. "I want the Fifth, Seventh, and Tenth in *échelon* as quickly as possible. And I want that cavalry. Lieutenant," turning to one of his staff, "ride off to the left and find Colonel Stilton. Tell him that I need a charge in ten minutes."

Presently cannon opened from that part of the ridge still held by the Confederates, the shells tearing through or over the dissolving groups of their right wing, and cracking viciously above the heads of the victorious Unionists. The explosions followed each other with stunning rapidity, and the shrill whirring of the splinters was ominous. Men began to fall again in the ranks or to drop out of them wounded. Of all this Waldron took no further note than to ride hastily to the brow of the ridge and look for his own artillery.

"See how he attinds to iverything himself," said Major Gahogan, who had cantered up to the side of Fitz Hugh. "It's just a matther of plain business, an' he looks after it loike a business man. Did ye see us, though, Captin, whin we come in on their right flank? By George, we murthered um. There's more'n a hundred lyin' in hapes back there. As for old Stilton, I just caught sight of um behind that wood to our left, an' he's makin' for the enemy's right rair. He'll have lots o' prisoners in half an hour."

When Waldron returned to the group he was told of his cavalry's whereabouts, and responded to the information with a smile of satisfaction.

"Bradley is hurrying up," he said, "and Taylor is pushing their left smartly. They will make one more tussle to recover their line of retreat; but we shall smash them from end to end and take every gun."

He galloped now to his infantry, and gave the word "Forward!" The three regiments which composed the *échelon* were the Fifth on the right, the Seventh fifty yards to the rear and left of the Fifth, the Tenth to the rear and left of the Seventh. It was behind the Fifth, that is the foremost battalion, that the brigade commander posted himself.

"Do *you* mean to stay here, Colonel?" asked Fitz Hugh, in surprise and anxiety.

"It is a certain victory now," answered Waldron, with a singular glance upward. "My life is no longer important. I prefer to do my duty to the utmost in the sight of all men."

"I shall follow you and do mine, Sir," said the Captain, much moved, he could scarcely say by what emotions, they were so many and conflicting.

"I want you other wheres. Ride to Colonel Taylor at once, and hurry him up the hill. Tell him the enemy have greatly weakened their left. Tell him to push up everything, infantry, and cavalry, and artillery, and to do it in haste."

"Colonel, this is saving my life against my will," remonstrated Fitz Hugh.

"Go!" ordered Waldron, imperiously. "Time is precious."

Fitz Hugh dashed down the slope to the right at a gallop. The brigade commander turned tranquilly, and followed the march of his *échelon*. The second and decisive crisis of the little battle was approaching, and to understand it we must glance at the ground on which it was to be fought. Two hostile lines were marching toward each other along the broad, gently rounded crest of the hill and at right angles to its general course. Between these lines, but much the nearest to the Union troops, a spacious road came up out of the forest in front, crossed the ridge, swept down the smooth decline in rear, and led to a single wooden bridge over a narrow but deep rivulet. On either hand the road was hedged in by a close board fence, four feet or so in height. It was for the possession of this highway that the approaching lines were about to shed their blood. If the Confederates failed to win it, all their artillery would be lost, and their army captured or dispersed.

The two parties came on without firing. The soldiers on both sides were veterans, cool, obedient to orders, intelligent through long service, and able to reserve all their resources for a short-range and final struggle. Moreover, the fences as yet partially hid them from each other, and would have rendered all aim for the present vague and uncertain.

"Forward, Fifth!" shouted Waldron. "Steady. Reserve your fire." Then, as the regiment came up to the fence, he added, "Halt; right dress. Steady, men."

Meantime he watched the advancing array with an eager gaze. It was a noble sight, full of moral sublimity, and worthy of all admiration. The long, lean, sunburned, weather-beaten soldiers in ragged gray stepped forward, superbly, their ranks loose, but swift and firm, the men leaning forward in their haste, their tattered slouch hats pushed backward, their whole aspect business-like and virile. Their line was three battalions strong, far outflanking the Fifth, and at least equal to the entire *échelon*. When within thirty or forty yards of the further fence they increased their pace to nearly a double-quick, many of them stooping low in hunter fashion, and a few firing. Then Waldron rose in his stirrups and yelled, "Battalion! ready—aim—aim low. Fire!"

There was a stunning roar of three hundred and fifty rifles, and a deadly screech of bullets. But the smoke rolled out, the haste to reload was intense, and none could mark what execution was done. Whatever the Confederates may have suffered, they bore up under the volley, and they came on. In another minute each of those fences, not more than twenty-five yards apart, was lined by the shattered fragment of a regiment, each firing as fast as possible into the face of the other. The Fifth bled fearfully: it had five of its ten company commanders shot dead in three minutes; and its loss in other officers and in men fell scarcely short of this terrible ratio. On its left the Seventh and the Tenth were up, pouring in musketry, and receiving it in a fashion hardly less sanguinary. No one present had ever seen, or ever afterward saw, such another close and deadly contest.

But the strangest thing in this whole wonderful fight was the conduct of the brigade commander. Up and down the rear of the lacerated Fifth Waldron rode thrice, spurring his plunging and wounded horse close to the yelling and fighting file-closers, and shouting in a piercing voice encouragement to his men. Stranger still, considering the character which he had borne in the army, and considering the evil deed for which he was to account on the morrow, were the words which he was distinctly and repeatedly heard to utter. "Stand steady, men—God is with us!" was the extraordinary battle-cry of this backslidden clergyman, this sinner above many.

And it was a prophecy of victory. Bradley ran up his Napoleons on the right in the nick of time, and, although only one of them could be brought to bear, it was enough; the grape raked the Confederate left, broke it, and the battle was over. In five minutes more their whole array was scattered, and the entire position open to galloping cavalry, seizing guns, standards, and prisoners.

It was in the very moment of triumph, just as the stubborn Southern line reeled back from the fence in isolated clusters, that the miraculous impunity of Waldron terminated, and he received his death wound. A quarter of an hour later Fitz Hugh found a sorrowful group of officers gazing from a little distance upon their dying commander.

"Is the Colonel hit?" he asked, shocked and grieved, incredible as the emotion may seem.

"Don't go near him," called Gildersleeve, who, it will be remembered, knew or guessed his errand in camp. "The Chaplain and surgeon are there. Let him alone."

"He's going to render his account," added Gahogan. "An' whatever he's done wrong, he's made it square to-day. Let um lave it to his brigade."

Adjutant Wallis, who had been blubbering aloud, who had cursed the rebels and the luck energetically, and who had also been trying to pray inwardly, groaned out, "This is our

last victory. You see if it ain't. Bet you two to one."

"Hush, man!" replied Gahogan. "We'll win our share of um, though we'll have to work harder for it. We'll have to do more ourselves, an' get less done for us in the way of tactics."

"That so, Major," whimpered a drummer, looking up from his duty of attending to a wounded comrade. "He knowed how to put his men in the right place, and his men knowed when they was in the right place. But it's goin' to be uphill through the steepest part of hell the rest of the way."

Soldiers, some of them weeping, some of them bleeding, arrived constantly to inquire after their commander, only to be sent quietly back to their ranks or to the rear. Around lay other men—dead men, and senseless, groaning men—all for the present unnoticed. Everything, except the distant pursuit of the cavalry, waited for Waldron to die. Fitz Hugh looked on silently, with the tears of mingled emotions in his eyes, and with hopes and hatreds expiring in his heart. The surgeon supported the expiring victor's head, while Chaplain Colquhoun knelt beside him, holding his hand and praying audibly. Of a sudden the petition ceased, both bent hastily toward the wounded man, and after what seemed a long time exchanged whispers. Then the Chaplain rose, came slowly toward the now advancing group of officers, his hands outspread toward heaven in an attitude of benediction, and tears running down his haggard white face.

"I trust, dear friends," he said, in a tremulous voice, "that all is well with our brother and commander. His last words were, 'God is with us.'"

"Oh! but, man, *that* isn't well," broke out Gahogan, in a groan. "What did ye pray for his sowl for? Why didn't ye pray for his loife?"

Fitz Hugh turned his horse and rode silently away. The next day he was seen journeying rearward by the side of an ambulance, within which lay what seemed a strangely delicate boy, insensible, and, one would say, mortally ill.

from Tales of Soldiers

EASILY THE FINEST STORIES OF THE CIVIL WAR ARE THE FIFTEEN EXTREMELY SHORT *Tales of Soldiers* (1891) by Ambrose Bierce (1842–1914?). "Bitter Bierce," wit, cynic, savage columnist and editor, author of the mordant *Devil's Dictionary,* the terrifying *Fantastic Fables,* the misanthropic *Can Such Things Be?,* anticipated the disillusionment that was to mark the post World War I fiction. Like Remarque and Barbusse, Hemingway and Aldington, Bierce made the ironies of war part of his education.

Only nineteen at the Civil War's outbreak, he joined the Ninth Indiana Infantry and fought through the entire war with the western armies. He was severely wounded at Kenesaw Mountain, and served also at Shiloh, Stone River, Murfreesboro, Chickamauga, and Franklin, among other battles. He rose through the ranks to become a sergeant, then a first lieutenant. Finally, as a topographical engineer, he became an officer on the staff of General W. B. Hazen. In his autobiographical writings Bierce sums up his military experiences with an old soldier's quiet understatement: ". . . although hardly more than a boy in years, I had served at the front from the beginning of the trouble, and had seen enough of war to give me a fair understanding of it." In his fiction Bierce displays the awful misery, the macabre ugliness, the shocking brutality of war.

Bierce became a leading journalist in London and San Francisco after the war. In the '80's he was the literary dictator of the Pacific Coast, a feared and satiric commentator on the foibles of his times. Throughout his life he continued to write stories that were at once horrifying, suggestive, and unpopular. The death of Ambrose Bierce is still shrouded in mystery. He disappeared into a revolution-torn Mexico in 1913, and the rest is silence.

Tales of Soldiers are vignettes of cosmic irony. Man in all his insignificance learns the futility of "normal" actions and aspirations in the face of the all-encompassing universe of war. The keynote of these tales is frustration. The individual cannot see any reason; yet he must obey. The outcome of his most valiant efforts is usually failure. Bierce's brief, rapid anecdotes silhouette the blackest side of war.

The stories strike a mean between violently contrived naturalism, full of filth and coincidence, and the accumulation of exact, realistic details of combat life. The nature of war itself aids Bierce's controlled method. War has its own framework of irony, its own foreshortening of time, its own rapid transitions and swift confrontations. The Civil War provided the perfect vehicle for Bierce's sardonic excursions into fiction.

Like the tales of Eggleston, Bierce's stories are selective, fixing on the decisive, revealing moment. In each story, even in an allegory like "A Son of the Gods," Bierce evokes the sense of fact and place that makes war not an abstract moral condition but a concrete physical actuality. Bierce supplies "the very taste of battle." He draws on events from his wide Civil War experience, not concentrating on any particular battle. These stories have the universality of great fiction.

Chickamauga

ONE SUNNY AUTUMN AFTERNOON A CHILD strayed away from its rude home in a small field and entered a forest unobserved. It was happy in a new sense of freedom from control, happy in the opportunity of exploration and adventure; for this child's spirit, in bodies of its ancestors, had for thousands of years been trained to memorable feats of discovery and conquest—victories in battles whose critical moments were centuries, whose victors' camps were cities of hewn stone. From the cradle of its race it had conquered its way through two continents and passing a great sea had penetrated a third, there to be born to war and dominion as a heritage.

The child was a boy aged about six years, the son of a poor planter. In his younger manhood the father had been a soldier, had fought against naked savages and followed the flag of his country into the capital of a civilized race to the far South. In the peaceful life of a planter the warrior-fire survived; once kindled, it is never extinguished. The man loved military books and pictures and the boy had understood enough to make himself a wooden sword, though even the eye of his father would hardly have known it for what it was. This weapon he now bore bravely, as

became the son of an heroic race, and pausing now and again in the sunny space of the forest assumed, with some exaggeration, the postures of aggression and defense that he had been taught by the engraver's art. Made reckless by the ease with which he overcame invisible foes attempting to stay his advance, he committed the common enough military error of pushing the pursuit to a dangerous extreme, until he found himself upon the margin of a wide but shallow brook, whose rapid waters barred his direct advance against the flying foe that had crossed with illogical ease. But the intrepid victor was not to be baffled; the spirit of the race which had passed the great sea burned unconquerable in that small breast and would not be denied. Finding a place where some bowlders in the bed of the stream lay but a step or a leap apart, he made his way across and fell again upon the rear-guard of his imaginary foe, putting all to the sword.

Now that the battle had been won, prudence required that he withdraw to his base of operations. Alas; like many a mightier conqueror, and like one, the mightiest, he could not

curb the lust for war,
Nor learn that tempted Fate will leave the loftiest
    star.

Advancing from the bank of the creek he suddenly found himself confronted with a new and more formidable enemy: in the path that he was following, sat, bolt upright, with ears erect and paws suspended before it, a rabbit! With a startled cry the child turned and fled, he knew not in what direction, calling with inarticulate cries for his mother, weeping, stumbling, his tender skin cruelly torn by brambles, his little heart beating hard with terror—breathless, blind with tears— lost in the forest! Then, for more than an hour, he wandered with erring feet through the tangled undergrowth, till at last, overcome by fatigue, he lay down in a narrow space between two rocks, within a few yards of the stream and still grasping his toy sword, no longer a weapon but a companion, sobbed himself to sleep. The wood birds sang merrily above his head; the squirrels, whisking their bravery of tail, ran barking from tree to tree, unconscious of the pity of it, and somewhere far away was a strange, muffled thunder, as if the partridges were drumming in celebration of nature's victory over the son of her immemorial enslavers. And back at the little plantation, where white men and black were hastily searching the fields and hedges in alarm, a mother's heart was breaking for her missing child.

Hours passed, and then the little sleeper rose to his feet. The chill of the evening was in his limbs, the fear of the gloom in his heart. But he had rested, and he no longer wept. With some blind instinct which impelled to action he struggled through the undergrowth about him and came to a more open ground—on his right the brook, to the left a gentle acclivity studded with infrequent trees; over all, the gathering gloom of twilight. A thin, ghostly mist rose along the water. It frightened and repelled him; instead of recrossing, in the direction whence he had come, he turned his back upon it, and went forward toward the dark inclosing wood. Suddenly he saw before him a strange moving object which he took to be some large animal—a dog, a pig—he could not name it; perhaps it was a bear. He had seen pictures of bears, but knew of nothing to their discredit and had vaguely wished to meet one. But something in form or movement of this object—something in the awkwardness of its approach— told him that it was not a bear, and curiosity was stayed by fear. He stood still and as it came slowly on gained courage every moment, for he saw that at least it had not the long, menacing ears of the rabbit. Possibly his impressionable mind was half conscious of something familiar in its shambling, awkward gait. Before it had approached near enough to resolve his doubts he saw that it was followed by another and another. To right and to left were many more; the whole open space about him was alive with them—all moving toward the brook.

They were men. They crept upon their hands and knees. They used their hands only, dragging their legs. They used their knees only, their arms hanging idle at their sides. They strove to rise to their feet, but fell prone in the attempt. They did nothing naturally, and nothing alike, save only to advance foot by foot in the same direction. Singly, in pairs and in little groups, they came on through the gloom, some halting now and again while others crept slowly past them, then resuming their movement. They came by dozens and by hundreds; as far on either hand as one could see in the deepening gloom they extended and the black wood behind them appeared to be inexhaustible. The very ground seemed in motion toward the creek. Occasionally one who had paused did not again go on, but lay motionless. He was dead. Some, pausing, made strange gestures with their hands, erected their arms and lowered them again, clasped their heads; spread their palms upward, as men are sometimes seen to do in public prayer.

Not all of this did the child note; it is what would have been noted by an elder observer; he saw little but that these were men, yet crept like babes. Being men, they were not terrible, though unfamiliarly clad. He moved among them freely, going from one to another and peering into their faces with childish curiosity. All their faces were singularly white and many were streaked and gouted with red. Something in this—something too, perhaps, in their grotesque attitudes and movements —reminded him of the painted clown whom he had seen last summer in the circus, and he laughed as he watched them. But on and ever on they crept, these maimed and bleeding men, as heedless as he of the dramatic contrast between his laughter and their own ghastly gravity. To him it was a merry spectacle. He had seen his father's Negroes creep upon their hands and knees for his amusement—had ridden them so, "making believe" they were his horses. He now approached one of these crawling figures from behind and with an agile movement mounted it astride. The man sank upon his breast, recovered, flung the small boy fiercely to the ground as an un-broken colt might have done, then turned upon him a face that lacked a lower jaw— from the upper teeth to the throat was a great red gap fringed with hanging shreds of flesh and splinters of bone. The unnatural promi-nence of nose, the absence of chin, the fierce eyes, gave this man the appearance of a great bird of prey crimsoned in throat and breast by the blood of its quarry. The man rose to his knees, the child to his feet. The man shook his fist at the child; the child, terrified at last, ran to a tree near by, got upon the farther side of it and took a more serious view of the situation. And so the clumsy multitude dragged itself slowly and painfully along in hideous panto-mime—moved forward down the slope like a swarm of great black beetles, with never a sound of going—in silence profound, abso-lute.

Instead of darkening, the haunted land-scape began to brighten. Through the belt of trees beyond the brook shone a strange red light, the trunks and branches of the trees making a black lacework against it. It struck the creeping figures and gave them monstrous shadows, which caricatured their movements on the lit grass. It fell upon their faces, touch-ing their whiteness with a ruddy tinge, ac-centuating the stains with which so many of them were freaked and maculated. It sparkled on buttons and bits of metal in their clothing. Instinctively the child turned toward the growing splendor and moved down the slope with his horrible companions; in a few moments had passed the foremost of the throng—not much of a feat, considering his advantages. He placed himself in the lead, his wooden sword still in hand, and solemnly di-rected the march, conforming his pace to theirs and occasionally turning as if to see that his forces did not straggle. Surely such a leader never before had such a following.

Scattered about upon the ground now slowly narrowing by the encroachment of this awful march to water, were certain articles to which, in the leader's mind, were coupled no significant associations: an occasional blanket, tightly rolled lengthwise, doubled and the ends bound together with a string; a heavy knapsack here, and there a broken rifle—such things, in short, as are found in the rear of retreating troops, the "spoor" of men flying from their hunters. Everywhere near the creek, which here had a margin of lowland, the earth was trodden into mud by the feet of men and horses. An observer of better experience in the use of his eyes would have noticed that these footprints pointed in both directions; the ground had been twice passed over—in advance and in retreat. A few hours before, these desperate, stricken men, with their more fortunate and now distant comrades, had penetrated the forest in thousands. Their successive battalions, breaking into swarms and reforming in lines, had passed the child on every side —had almost trodden on him as he slept. The rustle and murmur of their march had not awakened him. Almost within a stone's throw of where he lay they had fought a battle; but all unheard by him were the roar of the musketry, the shock of the cannon, "the thunder of the captains and the shouting." He had slept through it all, grasping his little wooden sword with perhaps a tighter clutch in unconsciousness sympathy with his martial environment, but as heedless of the grandeur of the struggle as the dead who had died to make the glory.

The fire beyond the belt of woods on the farther side of the creek, reflected to earth from the canopy of its own smoke, was now suffusing the whole landscape. It transformed the sinuous line of mist to the vapor of gold. The water gleamed with dashes of red, and red, too, were many of the stones protruding above the surface. But that was blood; the less desperately wounded had stained them in crossing. On them, too, the child now crossed with eager steps; he was going to the fire. As he stood upon the farther bank he turned

about to look at the companions of his march. The advance was arriving at the creek. The stronger had already drawn themselves to the brink and plunged their faces into the flood. Three or four who lay without motion appeared to have no heads. At this the child's eyes expanded with wonder; even his hospitable understanding could not accept a phenomenon implying such vitality as that. After slaking their thirst these men had not had the strength to back away from the water, nor to keep their heads above it. They were drowned. In rear of these, the open spaces of the forest showed the leader as many formless figures of his grim command as at first; but not nearly so many were in motion. He waved his cap for their encouragement and smilingly pointed with his weapon in the direction of the guiding light—a pillar of fire to this strange exodus.

Confident of the fidelity of his forces, he now entered the belt of woods, passed through it easily in the red illumination, climbed a fence, ran across a field, turning now and again to coquet with his responsive shadow, and so approached the blazing ruin of a dwelling. Desolation everywhere! In all the wide glare not a living thing was visible. He cared nothing for that; the spectacle pleased, and he danced with glee in imitation of the wavering flames. He ran about, collecting fuel, but every object that he found was too heavy for him to cast in from the distance to which the heat limited his approach. In despair he flung in his sword—a surrender to the superior forces of nature. His military career was at an end.

Shifting his position, his eyes fell upon some outbuildings which had an oddly familiar appearance, as if he had dreamed of them. He stood considering them with wonder, when suddenly the entire plantation, with its inclosing forest, seemed to turn as if upon a pivot. His little world swung half around; the points of the compass were reversed. He recognized the blazing building as his own home!

For a moment he stood stupefied by the power of the revelation, then ran with stumbling feet, making a half-circuit of the ruin. There, conspicuous in the light of the conflagration, lay the dead body of a woman— the white face turned upward, the hands thrown out and clutched full of grass, the clothing deranged, the long dark hair in tangles and full of clotted blood. The greater part of the forehead was torn away, and from the jagged hole the brain protruded, overflowing the temple, a frothy mass of gray, crowned with clusters of crimson bubbles—the work of a shell.

The child moved his little hands, making wild, uncertain gestures. He uttered a series of inarticulate and indescribable cries—something between the chattering of an ape and the gobbling of a turkey—a startling, soulless, unholy sound, the language of a devil. The child was a deaf mute.

Then he stood motionless, with quivering lips, looking down upon the wreck.

A Son of the Gods
A Study in the Present Tense

A breezy day and a sunny landscape. An open country to right and left and forward; behind, a wood. In the edge of this wood, facing the open but not venturing into it, long lines of troops, halted. The wood is alive with them, and full of confused noises—the occasional rattle of wheels as a battery of artillery goes into position to cover the advance; the hum and murmur of the soldiers talking; a sound of innumerable feet in the dry leaves that strew the interspaces among the trees; hoarse commands of officers. Detached groups of horsemen are well in front—not altogether exposed—many of them intently regarding the crest of a hill a mile away in the direction of the interrupted advance. For this powerful army, moving in battle order through a forest, has met with a formidable obstacle—the open country. The crest of that gentle hill a mile away has a sinister look; it says, Beware! Along it runs a stone wall extending to left and right a great distance. Behind the wall is a hedge; behind the hedge are seen the tops of trees in rather straggling order. Among the trees—what? It is necessary to know.

Yesterday, and for many days and nights previously, we were fighting somewhere; always there was cannonading, with occasional keen rattlings of musketry, mingled with cheers, our own or the enemy's, we seldom knew, attesting some temporary advantage. This morning at daybreak the enemy was gone. We have moved forward across his earthworks, across which we have so often vainly attempted to move before, through the débris of his abandoned camps, among the graves of his fallen, into the woods beyond.

How curiously we had regarded everything! how odd it all had seemed! Nothing had appeared quite familiar; the most commonplace objects—an old saddle, a splintered wheel, a forgotten canteen—everything had related something of the mysterious personality of those strange men who had been killing us. The soldier never becomes wholly familiar with the conception of his foes as men like himself; he cannot divest himself of the feeling that they are another order of beings, differently conditioned, in an environment not altogether of the earth. The smallest vestiges of them rivet his attention and engage his interest. He thinks of them as inaccessible; and, catching an unexpected glimpse of them, they appear farther away, and therefore larger, than they really are—like objects in a fog. He is somewhat in awe of them.

From the edge of the wood leading up the acclivity are the tracks of horses and wheels—the wheels of cannon. The yellow grass is beaten down by the feet of infantry. Clearly they have passed this way in thousands; they have not withdrawn by the country roads. This is significant—it is the difference between retiring and retreating.

That group of horsemen is our commander, his staff and escort. He is facing the distant crest, holding his field-glass against his eyes with both hands, his elbows needlessly elevated. It is a fashion; it seems to dignify the act; we are all addicted to it. Suddenly he lowers the glass and says a few words to those about him. Two or three aides detach themselves from the group and canter away into the woods, along the lines in each direction. We did not hear his words, but we know them: "Tell General X. to send forward the skirmish line." Those of us who have been out of place resume our positions; the men resting at ease straighten themselves and the ranks are reformed without a command. Some of us staff officers dismount and look at our saddle girths; those already on the ground remount.

Galloping rapidly along in the edge of the open ground comes a young officer on a snow-white horse. His saddle blanket is scarlet. What a fool! No one who has ever been in action but remembers how naturally every rifle turns toward the man on a white horse; no one but has observed how a bit of red en-rages the bull of battle. That such colors are fashionable in military life must be accepted as the most astonishing of all the phenomena of human vanity. They would seem to have been devised to increase the death-rate.

This young officer is in full uniform, as if on parade. He is all agleam with bullion—a blue-and-gold edition of the Poetry of War. A wave of derisive laughter runs abreast of him all along the line. But how handsome he is!—with what careless grace he sits his horse!

He reins up within a respectful distance of the corps commander and salutes. The old soldier nods familiarly; he evidently knows him. A brief colloquy between them is going on; the young man seems to be preferring some request which the elder one is indisposed to grant. Let us ride a little nearer. Ah! too late—it is ended. The young officer salutes again, wheels his horse, and rides straight toward the crest of the hill!

A thin line of skirmishers, the men deployed at six paces or so apart, now pushes from the wood into the open. The commander speaks to his bugler, who claps his instrument to his lips. *Tra-la-la! Tra-la-la!* The skirmishers halt in their tracks.

Meantime the young horseman has advanced a hundred yards. He is riding at a walk, straight up the long slope, with never a turn of the head. How glorious! Gods! what would we not give to be in his place—with his soul! He does not draw his sabre; his right hand hangs easily at his side. The breeze catches the plume in his hat and flutters it smartly. The sunshine rests upon his shoulder-straps, lovingly, like a visible benediction. Straight on he rides. Ten thousand pairs of eyes are fixed upon him with an intensity that he can hardly fail to feel; ten thousand hearts keep quick time to the inaudible hoof-beats of his snowy steed. He is not alone—he draws all souls after him. But we remember that we laughed! On and on, straight for the hedge-lined wall, he rides. Not a look backward. O, if he would but turn—if he could but see the love, the adoration, the atonement!

Not a word is spoken; the populous depths of the forest still murmur with their unseen and unseeing swarm, but all along the fringe is silence. The burly commander is an equestrian statue of himself. The mounted staff officers, their field-glasses up, are motionless all. The line of battle in the edge of the wood stands at a new kind of "attention," each man in the attitude in which he was caught by the consciousness of what is going on. All these hardened and impenitent man-killers, to whom death in its awfulest forms is a fact familiar to their every-day observation; who sleep on hills trembling with the thunder of great guns, dine in the midst of streaming missiles, and play at cards among the dead faces of their dearest friends—all are watching with suspended breadth and beating hearts the outcome of an act involving the life of one man. Such is the magnetism of courage and devotion.

If now you should turn your head you would see a simultaneous movement among the spectators—a start, as if they had received an electric shock—and looking forward again to the now distant horseman you would see that he has in that instant altered his direction and is riding at an angle to his former course. The spectators suppose the sudden deflection to be caused by a shot, perhaps a wound; but take this field-glass and you will observe that he is riding toward a break in the wall and hedge. He means, if not killed, to ride through and overlook the country beyond.

You are not to forget the nature of this man's act; it is not permitted to you to think of it as an instance of bravado, nor, on the other hand, a needless sacrifice of self. If the enemy has not retreated he is in force on that ridge. The investigator will encounter nothing less than a line-of-battle; there is no need of pickets, videttes, skirmishers, to give warning of our approach; our attacking lines will be visible, conspicuous, exposed to an artillery fire that will shave the ground the moment they break from cover, and for half the distance to a sheet of rifle bullets in which nothing can live. In short, if the enemy is there, it would be madness to attack him in front; he must be manœuvred out by the immemorial plan of threatening his line of communication, as necessary to his existence as to the diver at the bottom of the sea his air tube. But how ascertain if the enemy is there? There is but one way,—somebody must go and see. The natural and customary thing to do is to send forward a line of skirmishers. But in this case they will answer in the affirmative with all their lives; the enemy, crouching in double ranks behind the stone wall and in cover of the hedge, will wait until it is possible to count each assailant's teeth. At the first volley a half of the questioning line will fall, the other half before it can accomplish the predestined retreat. What a price to pay for gratified curiosity! At what a dear rate an army must sometimes purchase knowledge! "Let me pay all," says this gallant man—this military Christ!

There is no hope except the hope against hope that the crest is clear. True, he might prefer capture to death. So long as he advances, the line will not fire—why should it? He can safely ride into the hostile ranks and become a prisoner of war. But this would defeat his object. It would not answer our question; it is necessary either that he return unharmed or be shot to death before our eyes. Only so shall we know how to act. If captured—why, that might have been done by a half-dozen stragglers.

Now begins an extraordinary contest of intellect between a man and an army. Our horseman, now within a quarter of a mile of the crest, suddenly wheels to the left and gallops in a direction parallel to it. He has caught sight of his antagonist; he knows all. Some slight advantage of ground has enabled him to overlook a part of the line. If he were here he could tell us in words. But that is now hopeless; he must make the best use of the few minutes of life remaining to him, by compelling the enemy himself to tell us as much and as plainly as possible—which, naturally, that discreet power is reluctant to do. Not a rifleman in those crouching ranks, not a cannoneer at those masked and shotted guns, but knows the needs of the situation, the imperative duty of forbearance. Besides, there has been time enough to forbid them all to fire. True, a single rifle-shot might drop him and be no great disclosure. But firing is infectious—and see how rapidly he moves, with never a pause except as he whirls his horse about to take a new direction, never directly backward toward us, never directly forward toward his executioners. All this is visible through the glass; it seems occurring within pistol-shot; we see all but the enemy, whose presence, whose thoughts, whose motives we infer. To the unaided eye there is nothing but a black figure on a white horse, tracing slow zigzags against the slope of a distant hill—so slowly they seem almost to creep.

Now—the glass again—he has tired of his failure, or sees his error, or has gone mad; he is dashing directly forward at the wall, as if to take it at a leap, hedge and all! One moment only and he wheels right about and is speeding like the wind straight down the slope—toward his friends, toward his death! Instantly the wall is topped with a fierce roll of smoke for a distance of hundreds of yards to right and left. This is as instantly dissipated by the wind, and before the rattle of the rifle reaches us he is down. No, he recovers his seat; he has but pulled his horse upon its haunches. They are up and away! A tremendous cheer bursts from our ranks, relieving the insupportable tension of our feelings. And the horse and its rider? Yes, they are up and away. Away, indeed—they are making directly to our left, parallel to the now steadily blazing and smoking wall. The rattle of the musketry is continuous, and every bullet's target is that courageous heart.

Suddenly a great bank of white smoke pushes upward from behind the wall. Another and another—a dozen roll up before the thunder of the explosions and the humming of the missiles reach our ears and the missiles themselves come bounding through clouds of dust into our covert, knocking over here and there a man and causing a temporary distraction, a passing thought of self.

The dust drifts away. Incredible!—that enchanted horse and rider have passed a ravine and are climbing another slope to unveil another conspiracy of silence, to thwart the will of another armed host. Another moment and that crest too is in eruption. The horse rears and strikes the air with its forefeet. They are down at last. But look again—the man has detached himself from the dead animal. He stands erect, motionless, holding his sabre in his right hand straight above his head. His face is toward us. Now he lowers his hand to a level with his face and moves it outward, the blade of the sabre describing a downward curve. It is a sign to us, to the world, to posterity. It is a hero's salute to death and history.

Again the spell is broken; our men attempt to cheer; they are choking with emotions; they utter hoarse, discordant cries; they clutch their weapons and press tumultuously forward into the open. The skirmishers, without orders, against orders, are going forward at a keen run, like hounds unleashed. Our cannon speak and the enemy's now open in full chorus; to right and left as far as we can see, the distant crest, seeming now so near, erects its towers of cloud and the great shot pitch roaring down among our moving masses. Flag after flag of ours emerges from the wood, line after line sweeps forth, catching the sunlight on its burnished arms. The rear battalions alone are in obedience; they preserve their proper distance from the insurgent front.

The commander has not moved. He now removes his field-glass from his eyes and glances to the right and left. He sees the human current flowing on either side of him and his huddled escort, like tide waves parted by a rock. Not a sign of feeling in his face; he is thinking. Again he directs his eyes forward; they slowly traverse that malign and awful crest. He addresses a calm word to his bugler. *Tra-la-la! Tra-la-la!* The injunction has an imperiousness which enforces it. It is repeated by all the bugles of all the subordinate commanders; the sharp metallic notes assert themselves above the hum of the advance and penetrate the sound of the cannon. To halt is to withdraw. The colors move slowly back; the lines face about and sullenly follow, bearing their wounded; the skirmishers return, gathering up the dead.

Ah, those many, many needless dead! That great soul whose beautiful body is lying over yonder, so conspicuous against the sere hillside—could it not have been spared the bitter

consciousness of a vain devotion? Would one exception have marred too much the pitiless perfection of the divine, eternal plan?

One of the Missing

Jerome Searing, a private soldier of General Sherman's army, then confronting the enemy at and about Kennesaw Mountain, Georgia, turned his back upon a small group of officers with whom he had been talking in low tones, stepped across a light line of earthworks, and disappeared in a forest. None of the men in line behind the works had said a word to him, nor had he so much as nodded to them in passing, but all who saw understood that this brave man had been intrusted with some perilous duty. Jerome Searing, though a private, did not serve in the ranks; he was detailed for service at division headquarters, being borne upon the rolls as an orderly. "Orderly" is a word covering a multitude of duties. An orderly may be a messenger, a clerk, an officer's servant—anything. He may perform services for which no provision is made in orders and army regulations. Their nature may depend upon his aptitude, upon favor, upon accident. Private Searing, an incomparable marksman, young, hardy, intelligent and insensible to fear, was a scout. The general commanding his division was not content to obey orders blindly without knowing what was in his front, even when his command was not on detached service, but formed a fraction of the line of the army; nor was he satisfied to receive his knowledge of his *vis-à-vis* through the customary channels; he wanted to know more than he was apprised of by the corps commander and the collisions of pickets and skirmishers. Hence Jerome Searing, with his extraordinary daring, his woodcraft, his sharp eyes, and truthful tongue. On this occasion his instructions were simple: to get as near the enemy's lines as possible and learn all that he could.

In a few moments he had arrived at the picket-line, the men on duty there lying in groups of two and four behind little banks of earth scooped out of the slight depression in which they lay, their rifles protruding from the green boughs with which they had masked their small defenses. The forest extended without a break toward the front, so solemn and silent that only by an effort of the imagination could it be conceived as populous with armed men, alert and vigilant—a forest formidable with possibilities of battle. Pausing a moment in one of these rifle-pits to apprise the men of his intention Searing crept stealthily forward on his hands and knees and was soon lost to view in a dense thicket of underbrush.

"That is the last of him," said one of the men; "I wish I had his rifle; those fellows will hurt some of us with it."

Searing crept on, taking advantage of every accident of ground and growth to give himself better cover. His eyes penetrated everywhere, his ears took note of every sound. He stilled his breathing, and at the cracking of a twig beneath his knee stopped his progress and hugged the earth. It was slow work, but not tedious; the danger made it exciting, but by no physical signs was the excitement manifest. His pulse was as regular, his nerves were as steady as if he were trying to trap a sparrow.

"It seems a long time," he thought, "but I cannot have come very far; I am still alive."

He smiled at his own method of estimating distance, and crept forward. A moment later he suddenly flattened himself upon the earth and lay motionless, minute after minute.

Through a narrow opening in the bushes he had caught sight of a small mound of yellow clay—one of the enemy's rifle-pits. After some little time he cautiously raised his head, inch by inch, then his body upon his hands, spread out on each side of him, all the while intently regarding the hillock of clay. In another moment he was upon his feet, rifle in hand, striding rapidly forward with little attempt at concealment. He had rightly interpreted the signs, whatever they were; the enemy was gone.

To assure himself beyond a doubt before going back to report upon so important a matter, Searing pushed forward across the line of abandoned pits, running from cover to cover in the more open forest, his eyes vigilant to discover possible stragglers. He came to the edge of a plantation—one of those forlorn, deserted homesteads of the last years of the war, upgrown with brambles, ugly with broken fences and desolate with vacant buildings having blank apertures in place of doors and windows. After a keen reconnaissance from the safe seclusion of a clump of young pines Searing ran lightly across a field and through an orchard to a small structure which stood apart from the other farm buildings, on a slight elevation. This he thought would enable him to overlook a large scope of country in the direction that he supposed the enemy to have taken in withdrawing. This building, which had originally consisted of a single room elevated upon four posts about ten feet high, was now little more than a roof; the floor had fallen away, the joists and planks loosely piled on the ground below or resting on end at various angles, not wholly torn from their fastenings above. The supporting posts were themselves no longer vertical. It looked as if the whole edifice would go down at the touch of a finger.

Concealing himself in the débris of joists

and flooring Searing looked across the open ground between his point of view and a spur of Kennesaw Mountain, a half-mile away. A road leading up and across this spur was crowded with troops—the rear-guard of the retiring enemy, their gun-barrels gleaming in the morning sunlight.

Searing had now learned all that he could hope to know. It was his duty to return to his own command with all possible speed and report his discovery. But the gray column of Confederates toiling up the mountain road was singularly tempting. His rifle—an ordinary "Springfield," but fitted with a globe sight and hair-trigger—would easily send its ounce and a quarter of lead hissing into their midst. That would probably not affect the duration and result of the war, but it is the business of a soldier to kill. It is also his habit if he is a good soldier. Searing cocked his rifle and "set" the trigger.

But it was decreed from the beginning of time that Private Searing was not to murder anybody that bright summer morning, nor was the Confederate retreat to be announced by him. For countless ages events had been so matching themselves together in that wondrous mosaic to some parts of which, dimly discernible, we give the name of history, that the acts which he had in will would have marred the harmony of the pattern. Some twenty-five years previously the Power charged with the execution of the work according to the design had provided against that mischance by causing the birth of a certain male child in a little village at the foot of the Carpathian Mountains, had carefully reared it, supervised its education, directed its desires into a military channel, and in due time made it an officer of artillery. By the concurrence of an infinite number of favoring influ-

ences and their preponderance over an infinite number of opposing ones, this officer of artillery had been made to commit a breach of discipline and flee from his native country to avoid punishment. He had been directed to New Orleans (instead of New York), where a recruiting officer awaited him on the wharf. He was enlisted and promoted, and things were so ordered that he now commanded a Confederate battery some two miles along the line from where Jerome Searing, the Federal scout, stood cocking his rifle. Nothing had been neglected—at every step in the progress of both these men's lives, and in the lives of their contemporaries and ancestors, and in the lives of the contemporaries of their ancestors, the right thing had been done to bring about the desired result. Had anything in all this vast concatenation been overlooked Private Searing might have fired on the retreating Confederates that morning, and would perhaps have missed. As it fell out, a Confederate captain of artillery, having nothing better to do while awaiting his turn to pull out and be off, amused himself by sighting a field-piece obliquely to his right at what he mistook for some Federal officers on the crest of a hill, and discharged it. The shot flew high of its mark.

As Jerome Searing drew back the hammer of his rifle and with his eyes upon the distant Confederates considered where he could plant his shot with the best hope of making a widow or an orphan or a childless mother,— perhaps all three, for Private Searing, although he had repeatedly refused promotion, was not without a certain kind of ambition,— he heard a rushing sound in the air, like that made by the wings of a great bird swooping down upon its prey. More quickly than he could apprehend the gradation, it increased to a hoarse and horrible roar, as the missile that made it sprang at him out of the sky, striking with a deafening impact one of the posts supporting the confusion of timbers above him, smashing it into matchwood, and bringing down the crazy edifice with a loud clatter, in clouds of blinding dust!

When Jerome Searing recovered consciousness he did not at once understand what had occurred. It was, indeed, some time before he opened his eyes. For a while he believed that he had died and been buried, and he tried to recall some portions of the burial service. He thought that his wife was kneeling upon his grave, adding her weight to that of the earth upon his breast. The two of them, widow and earth, had crushed his coffin. Unless the children should persuade her to go home he would not much longer be able to breathe. He felt a sense of wrong. "I cannot speak to her," he thought; "the dead have no voice; and if I open my eyes I shall get them full of earth."

He opened his eyes. A great expanse of blue sky, rising from a fringe of the tops of trees. In the foreground, shutting out some of the trees, a high, dun mound, angular in outline and crossed by an intricate, patternless system of straight lines; the whole an immeasurable distance away—a distance so inconceivably great that it fatigued him, and he closed his eyes. The moment that he did so he was conscious of an insufferable light. A sound was in his ears like the low, rhythmic thunder of a distant sea breaking in successive waves upon the beach, and out of this noise, seeming a part of it, or possibly coming from beyond it, and intermingled with its ceaseless undertone, came the articulate words: "Jerome Searing, you are caught like a rat in a trap—in a trap, trap, trap."

Suddenly there fell a great silence, a black darkness, an infinite tranquillity, and Jerome Searing, perfectly conscious of his rathood, and well assured of the trap that he was in, remembering all and nowise alarmed, again opened his eyes to reconnoitre, to note the strength of his enemy, to plan his defense.

He was caught in a reclining posture, his back firmly supported by a solid beam. Another lay across his breast, but he had been able to shrink a little away from it so that it no longer oppressed him, though it was immovable. A brace joining it at an angle had wedged him against a pile of boards on his left, fastening the arm on that side. His legs, slightly parted and straight along the ground, were covered upward to the knees with a mass of débris which towered above his narrow horizon. His head was as rigidly fixed as in a vise; he could move his eyes, his chin—no more. Only his right arm was partly free. "You must help us out of this," he said to it. But he could not get it from under the heavy timber athwart his chest, nor move it outward more than six inches at the elbow.

Searing was not seriously injured, nor did he suffer pain. A smart rap on the head from a flying fragment of the splintered post, incurred simultaneously with the frightfully sudden shock to the nervous system, had momentarily dazed him. His term of unconsciousness, including the period of recovery, during which he had had the strange fancies, had probably not exceeded a few seconds, for the dust of the wreck had not wholly cleared away as he began an intelligent survey of the situation.

With his partly free right hand he now tried to get hold of the beam that lay across, but not quite against, his breast. In no way could he do so. He was unable to depress the shoulder so as to push the elbow beyond that edge of the timber which was nearest his knees; failing in that, he could not raise the forearm and hand to grasp the beam. The brace that made an angle with it downward and backward prevented him from doing anything in that direction, and between it and his body the space was not half so wide as the length of his forearm. Obviously he could not get his hand under the beam nor over it; the hand could not, in fact, touch it at all. Having demonstrated his inability, he desisted, and began to think whether he could reach any of the débris piled upon his legs.

In surveying the mass with a view to determining that point, his attention was arrested by what seemed to be a ring of shining metal immediately in front of his eyes. It appeared to him at first to surround some perfectly black substance, and it was somewhat more than a half-inch in diameter. It suddenly occurred to his mind that the blackness was simply shadow and that the ring was in fact the muzzle of his rifle protruding from the pile of débris. He was not long in satisfying himself that this was so—if it was a satisfaction. By closing either eye he could look a little way along the barrel—to the point where it was hidden by the rubbish that held it. He could see the one side, with the corresponding eye, at apparently the same angle as the other side with the other eye. Looking with the right eye, the weapon seemed to be directed at a point to the left of his head, and *vice versa*. He was unable to see the upper surface of the barrel, but could see the under surface of the stock at a slight angle. The piece was, in fact, aimed at the exact centre of his forehead.

In the perception of this circumstance, in the recollection that just previously to the mischance of which this uncomfortable situation was the result he had cocked the rifle and set the trigger so that a touch would discharge it,

Private Searing was affected with a feeling of uneasiness. But that was as far as possible from fear; he was a brave man, somewhat familiar with the aspect of rifles from that point of view, and of cannon too. And now he recalled, with something like amusement, an incident of his experience at the storming of Missionary Ridge, where, walking up to one of the enemy's embrasures from which he had seen a heavy gun throw charge after charge of grape among the assailants he had thought for a moment that the piece had been withdrawn; he could see nothing in the opening but a brazen circle. What that was he had understood just in time to step aside as it pitched another peck of iron down that swarming slope. To face firearms is one of the commonest incidents in a soldier's life—firearms, too, with malevolent eyes blazing behind them. That is what a soldier is for. Still, Private Searing did not altogether relish the situation, and turned away his eyes.

After groping, aimless, with his right hand for a time he made an ineffectual attempt to release his left. Then he tried to disengage his head, the fixity of which was the more annoying from his ignorance of what held it. Next he tried to free his feet, but while exerting the powerful muscles of his legs for that purpose it occurred to him that a disturbance of the rubbish which held them might discharge the rifle; how it could have endured what had already befallen it he could not understand, although memory assisted him with several instances in point. One in particular he recalled, in which in a moment of mental abstraction he had clubbed his rifle and beaten out another gentleman's brains, observing afterward that the weapon which he had been diligently swinging by the muzzle was loaded, capped, and at full cock—knowledge of which circumstance would doubtless have cheered his antagonist to longer endurance. He had always smiled in recalling that blunder of his "green and salad days" as a soldier, but now he did not smile. He turned his eyes again to the muzzle of the rifle and for a moment fancied that it had moved; it seemed somewhat nearer.

Again he looked away. The tops of the distant trees beyond the bounds of the plantation interested him: he had not before observed how light and feathery they were, nor how darkly blue the sky was, even among their branches, where they somewhat paled it with their green; above him it appeared almost black. "It will be uncomfortably hot here," he thought, "as the day advances. I wonder which way I am looking."

Judging by such shadows as he could see, he decided that his face was due north; he would at least not have the sun in his eyes, and north—well, that was toward his wife and children.

"Bah!" he exclaimed aloud, "what have they to do with it?"

He closed his eyes. "As I can't get out I may as well go to sleep. The rebels are gone and some of our fellows are sure to stray out here foraging. They'll find me."

But he did not sleep. Gradually he became sensible of a pain in his forehead—a dull ache, hardly perceptible at first, but growing more and more uncomfortable. He opened his eyes and it was gone—closed them and it returned. "The devil!" he said, irrelevantly, and stared again at the sky. He heard the singing of birds, the strange metallic note of the meadow lark, suggesting the clash of vibrant blades. He fell into pleasant memories of his childhood, played again with his brother and sister, raced across the fields, shouting to alarm the sedentary larks, entered the sombre forest beyond and with timid steps followed the faint path to Ghost Rock, standing at last with audible heart-throbs before the Dead Man's Cave and seeking to penetrate its awful mystery. For the first time he observed that the opening of the haunted cavern was encircled by a ring of metal. Then all else vanished and left him gazing into the barrel of his rifle as before. But whereas before it had seemed nearer, it now seemed an inconceivable distance away, and all the more sinister for that. He cried out and, startled by something in his own voice—the note of fear—lied to himself in denial: "If I don't sing out I may stay here till I die."

He now made no further attempt to evade the menacing stare of the gun barrel. If he turned away his eyes an instant it was to look for assistance (although he could not see the ground on either side the ruin), and he permitted them to return, obedient to the imperative fascination. If he closed them it was from weariness, and instantly the poignant pain in his forehead—the prophecy and menace of the bullet—forced him to reopen them.

The tension of nerve and brain was too severe; nature came to his relief with intervals of unconsciousness. Reviving from one of these he became sensible of a sharp, smarting pain in his right hand, and when he worked his fingers together, or rubbed his palm with them, he could feel that they were wet and slippery. He could not see the hand, but he knew the sensation; it was running blood. In his delirium he had beaten it against the jagged fragments of the wreck, had clutched it full of splinters. He resolved that he would meet his fate more manly. He was a plain, common soldier, had no religion and not much philosophy; he could not die like a hero, with great and wise last words, even if there had been some one to hear them, but he could die "game," and he would. But if he could only know when to expect the shot!

Some rats which had probably inhabited the shed came sneaking and scampering about. One of them mounted the pile of débris that held the rifle; another followed and another. Searing regarded them at first with indifference, then with friendly interest; then, as the thought flashed into his bewildered mind that they might touch the trigger of his rifle, he cursed them and ordered them to go away. "It is no business of yours," he cried.

The creatures went away; they would return later, attack his face, gnaw away his nose, cut his throat—he knew that, but he hoped by that time to be dead.

Nothing could now unfix his gaze from the little ring of metal with its black interior. The pain in his forehead was fierce and incessant. He felt it gradually penetrating the brain more and more deeply, until at last its progress was arrested by the wood at the back of his head. It grew momentarily more insufferable: he began wantonly beating his lacerated hand against the splinters again to counteract that horrible ache. It seemed to throb with a slow, regular recurrence, each pulsation sharper than the preceding, and sometimes he cried out, thinking he felt the fatal bullet. No thoughts of home, of wife and children, of country, of glory. The whole record of memory was effaced. The world had passed away—not a vestige remained. Here in this confusion of timbers and boards is the sole universe. Here is immortality in time—each pain an everlasting life. The throbs tick off eternities.

Jerome Searing, the man of courage, the formidable enemy, the strong, resolute warrior, was as pale as a ghost. His jaw was fallen; his eyes protruded; he trembled in every fibre; a cold sweat bathed his entire body; he

screamed with fear. He was not insane—he was terrified.

In groping about with his torn and bleeding hand he seized at last a strip of board, and, pulling, felt it give way. It lay parallel with his body, and by bending his elbow as much as the contracted space would permit, he could draw it a few inches at a time. Finally it was altogether loosened from the wreckage covering his legs; he could lift it clear of the ground its whole length. A great hope came into his mind: perhaps he could work it upward, that is to say backward, far enough to lift the end and push aside the rifle; or, if that were too tightly wedged, so place the strip of board as to deflect the bullet. With this object he passed it backward inch by inch, hardly daring to breathe lest that act somehow defeat his intent, and more than ever unable to remove his eyes from the rifle, which might perhaps now hasten to improve its waning opportunity. Something at least had been gained: in the occupation of his mind in this attempt at self-defense he was less sensible of the pain in his head and had ceased to wince. But he was still dreadfully frightened and his teeth rattled like castanets.

The strip of board ceased to move to the suasion of his hand. He tugged at it with all his strength, changed the direction of its length all he could, but it had met some extended obstruction behind him and the end in front was still too far away to clear the pile of débris and reach the muzzle of the gun. It extended, indeed, nearly as far as the trigger guard, which, uncovered by the rubbish, he could imperfectly see with his right eye. He tried to break the strip with his hand, but had no leverage. In his defeat, all his terror returned, augmented tenfold. The black aperture of the rifle appeared to threaten a sharper and more imminent death in punishment of his rebellion. The track of the bullet through his head ached with an intenser anguish. He began to tremble again.

Suddenly he became composed. His tremor subsided. He clenched his teeth and drew down his eyebrows. He had not exhausted his means of defense; a new design had shaped itself in his mind—another plan of battle. Raising the front end of the strip of board, he carefully pushed it forward through the wreckage at the side of the rifle until it pressed against the trigger guard. Then he moved the end slowly outward until he could feel that it had cleared it, then, closing his eyes, thrust it against the trigger with all his strength! There was no explosion; the rifle had been discharged as it dropped from his hand when the building fell. But it did its work.

Lieutenant Adrian Searing, in command of the picket-guard on that part of the line through which his brother Jerome had passed on his mission, sat with attentive ears in his breastwork behind the line. Not the faintest sound escaped him; the cry of a bird, the barking of a squirrel, the noise of the wind among the pines—all were anxiously noted by his overstrained sense. Suddenly, directly in front of his line, he heard a faint, confused rumble, like the clatter of a falling building translated by distance. The lieutenant mechanically looked at his watch. Six o'clock and eighteen minutes. At the same moment an officer approached him on foot from the rear and saluted.

"Lieutenant," said the officer, "the colonel directs you to move forward your line and feel the enemy if you find him. If not, continue the advance until directed to halt. There is reason to think that the enemy has retreated."

The lieutenant nodded and said nothing; the other officer retired. In a moment the men, apprised of their duty by the non-commissioned officers in low tones, had deployed from their rifle-pits and were moving forward in skirmishing order, with set teeth and beating hearts.

This line of skirmishers sweeps across the plantation toward the mountain. They pass on both sides of the wrecked building, observing nothing. At a short distance in their rear their commander comes. He casts his eyes curiously upon the ruin and sees a dead body half buried in boards and timbers. It is so covered with dust that its clothing is Confederate gray. Its face is yellowish white; the cheeks are fallen in, the temples sunken, too, with sharp ridges about them, making the forehead forbiddingly narrow; the upper lip, slightly lifted, shows the white teeth, rigidly clenched. The hair is heavy with moisture, the face as wet as the dewy grass all about. From his point of view the officer does not observe the rifle; the man was apparently killed by the fall of the building.

"Dead a week," said the officer curtly, moving on and absently pulling out his watch as if to verify his estimate of time. Six o'clock and forty minutes.

One Kind of Officer

I. Of the Uses of Civility

"Captain Ransome, it is not permitted to you to know *anything*. It is sufficient that you obey my order—which permit me to repeat. If you perceive any movement of troops in your front you are to open fire, and if attacked hold this position as long as you can. Do I make myself understood, sir?"

"Nothing could be plainer. Lieutenant Price,"—this to an officer of his own battery, who had ridden up in time to hear the order —"the general's meaning is clear, is it not?"

"Perfectly."

The lieutenant passed on to his post. For a moment General Cameron and the commander of the battery sat in their saddles, looking at each other in silence. There was no more to say; apparently too much had already been said. Then the superior officer nodded coldly and turned his horse to ride away. The artillerist saluted slowly, gravely, and with extreme formality. One acquainted with the niceties of military etiquette would have said that by his manner he attested a sense of the rebuke that he had incurred. It is one of the important uses of civility to signify resentment.

When the general had joined his staff and escort, awaiting him at a little distance, the whole cavalcade moved off toward the right of the guns and vanished in the fog. Captain Ransome was alone, silent, motionless as an equestrian statue. The gray fog, thickening every moment, closed in about him like a visible doom.

II. Under What Circumstances Men Do Not Wish to Be Shot

The fighting of the day before had been desultory and indecisive. At the points of collision the smoke of battle had hung in blue sheets among the branches of the trees till beaten into nothing by the falling rain. In the softened earth the wheels of cannon and ammunition wagons cut deep, ragged furrows, and movements of infantry seemed impeded by the mud that clung to the soldiers' feet as, with soaken garments and rifles imperfectly protected by capes of overcoats they went dragging in sinuous lines hither and thither through dripping forest and flooded field. Mounted officers, their heads protruding from rubber ponchos that glittered like black armor, picked their way, singly and in loose groups, among the men, coming and going with apparent aimlessness and commanding attention from nobody but one another. Here and there a dead man, his clothing defiled with earth, his face covered with a blanket or showing yellow and claylike in the rain, added his dispiriting influence to that of the other dismal features of the scene and augmented the general discomfort with a particular dejection. Very repulsive these wrecks looked—not at all heroic, and nobody was accessible to the infection of their patriotic example. Dead upon the field of honor, yes; but the field of honor was so very wet! It makes a difference.

The general engagement that all expected did not occur, none of the small advantages accruing, now to this side and now to that, in isolated and accidental collisions being followed up. Half-hearted attacks provoked a sullen resistance which was satisfied with mere repulse. Orders were obeyed with mechanical fidelity; no one did any more than his duty.

"The army is cowardly to-day," said General Cameron, the commander of a Federal brigade, to his adjutant-general.

"The army is cold," replied the officer addressed, "and—yes, it doesn't wish to be like that."

He pointed to one of the dead bodies, lying in a thin pool of yellow water, its face and clothing bespattered with mud from hoof and wheel.

The army's weapons seemed to share its military delinquency. The rattle of rifles sounded flat and contemptible. It had no meaning and scarcely roused to attention and expectancy the unengaged parts of the line-of-battle and the waiting reserves. Heard at a little distance, the reports of cannon were feeble in volume and *timbre:* they lacked sting and resonance. The guns seemed to be fired with light charges, unshotted. And so the futile day wore on to its dreary close, and then to a night of discomfort succeeded a day of apprehension.

An army has a personality. Beneath the individual thoughts and emotions of its component parts it thinks and feels as a unit. And in this large, inclusive sense of things lies a wiser wisdom than the mere sum of all that it knows. On that dismal morning this great brute force, groping at the bottom of a white ocean of fog among trees that seemed as sea weeds, had a dumb consciousness that all was not well; that a day's manœuvring had resulted in a faulty disposition of its parts, a blind diffusion of its strength. The men felt insecure and talked among themselves of such tactical errors as with their meager military vocabulary they were able to name. Field and line officers gathered in groups and spoke more learnedly of what they apprehended with no greater clearness. Commanders of brigades and divisions looked anxiously to their connections on the right and on the left, sent staff officers on errands of inquiry and pushed skirmish lines silently and cautiously forward into the dubious region between the known and the unknown. At some points on the line the troops, apparently of their own volition, constructed such defenses as they could without the silent spade and the noisy ax.

One of these points was held by Captain Ransome's battery of six guns. Provided always with intrenching tools, his men had labored with diligence during the night, and now his guns thrust their black muzzles through the embrasures of a really formidable earthwork. It crowned a slight acclivity devoid of undergrowth and providing an unobstructed fire that would sweep the ground for an unknown distance in front. The position could hardly have been better chosen. It had this peculiarity, which Captain Ransome, who was greatly addicted to the use of the compass, had not failed to observe: it faced northward, whereas he knew that the general line of the army must face eastward. In fact, that part of the line was "refused"—that is to say, bent backward, away from the enemy. This implied that Captain Ransome's battery was somewhere near the left flank of the army; for an army in line of battle retires its flanks if the nature of the ground will permit, they being its vulnerable points. Actually, Captain Ransome appeared to hold the extreme left of the line, no troops being visible in that direction beyond his own. Immediately in rear of his guns occurred that conversation between him and his brigade commander, the concluding and more picturesque part of which is reported above.

III. How to Play the Cannon Without Notes

Captain Ransome sat motionless and silent on horseback. A few yards away his men were standing at their guns. Somewhere—everywhere within a few miles—were a hundred thousand men, friends and enemies. Yet he was alone. The mist had isolated him as completely as if he had been in the heart of a desert. His world was a few square yards of wet and trampled earth about the feet of his horse. His comrades in that ghostly domain were invisible and inaudible. These were conditions favorable to thought, and he was thinking. Of the nature of his thoughts his clear-cut handsome features yielded no attesting sign. His face was as inscrutable as that of the sphinx. Why should it have made a record which there was none to observe? At the sound of a footstep he merely turned his eyes in the direction whence it came; one of his sergeants, looking a giant in stature in the false perspective of the fog, approached, and when clearly defined and reduced to his true dimensions by propinquity, saluted and stood at attention.

"Well, Morris," said the officer, returning his subordinate's salute.

"Lieutenant Price directed me to tell you, sir, that most of the infantry has been withdrawn. We have not sufficient support."

"Yes, I know."

"I am to say that some of our men have been out over the works a hundred yards and report that our front is not picketed."

"Yes."

"They were so far forward that they heard the enemy."

"Yes."

"They heard the rattle of the wheels of artillery and the commands of officers."

"Yes."

"The enemy is moving toward our works."

Captain Ransome, who had been facing to the rear of his line—toward the point where the brigade commander and his cavalcade had been swallowed up by the fog—reined his horse about and faced the other way. Then he sat motionless as before.

"Who are the men who made that statement?" he inquired, without looking at the sergeant; his eyes were directed straight into the fog over the head of his horse.

"Corporal Hassman and Gunner Manning."

Captain Ransome was a moment silent. A slight pallor came into his face, a slight compression affected the lines of his lips, but it would have required a closer observer than Sergeant Morris to note the change. There was none in the voice.

"Sergeant, present my compliments to Lieutenant Price and direct him to open fire with all the guns. Grape."

The sergeant saluted and vanished in the fog.

IV. To Introduce General Masterson

Searching for his division commander, General Cameron and his escort had followed the line of battle for nearly a mile to the right of Ransome's battery, and there learned that the division commander had gone in search of the corps commander. It seemed that everybody was looking for his immediate superior—an ominous circumstance. It meant that nobody was quite at ease. So General Cameron rode on for another half-mile, where by good luck he met General Masterson, the division commander, returning.

"Ah, Cameron," said the higher officer, reining up, and throwing his right leg across the pommel of his saddle in a most unmilitary way—"anything up? Found a good position for your battery, I hope—if one place is better than another in a fog."

"Yes, general," said the other, with the greater dignity appropriate to his less exalted rank, "my battery is very well placed. I wish I could say that it is as well commanded."

"Eh, what's that? Ransome? I think him a fine fellow. In the army we should be proud of him."

It was customary for officers of the regular army to speak of it as "the army." As the greatest cities are most provincial, so the self-complacency of aristocracies is most frankly plebeian.

"He is too fond of his opinion. By the way,

in order to occupy the hill that he holds I had to extend my line dangerously. The hill is on my left—that is to say the left flank of the army."

"Oh, no, Hart's brigade is beyond. It was ordered up from Drytown during the night and directed to hook on to you. Better go and—"

The sentence was unfinished: a lively cannonade had broken out on the left, and both officers, followed by their retinues of aides and orderlies making a great jingle and clank, rode rapidly toward the spot. But they were soon impeded, for they were compelled by the fog to keep within sight of the line-of-battle, behind which were swarms of men, all in motion across their way. Everywhere the line was assuming a sharper and harder definition, as the men sprang to arms and the officers, with drawn swords, "dressed" the ranks. Color-bearers unfurled the flags, buglers blew the "assembly," hospital attendants appeared with stretchers. Field officers mounted and sent their impedimenta to the rear in care of Negro servants. Back in the ghostly spaces of the forest could be heard the rustle and murmur of the reserves, pulling themselves together.

Nor was all this preparation vain, for scarcely five minutes had passed since Captain Ransome's guns had broken the truce of doubt before the whole region was aroar: the enemy had attacked nearly everywhere.

V. How Sounds Can Fight Shadows

Captain Ransome walked up and down behind his guns, which were firing rapidly but with steadiness. The gunners worked alertly, but without haste or apparent excitement. There was really no reason for excitement; it is not much to point a cannon into a fog and fire it. Anybody can do as much as that.

The men smiled at their noisy work, performing it with a lessening alacrity. They cast curious regards upon their captain, who had now mounted the banquette of the fortification and was looking across the parapet as if observing the effect of his fire. But the only visible effect was the substitution of wide, low-lying sheets of smoke for their bulk of fog. Suddenly out of the obscurity burst a great sound of cheering, which filled the intervals between the reports of the guns with startling distinctness! To the few with leisure and opportunity to observe, the sound was inexpressibly strange—so loud, so near, so menacing, yet nothing seen! The men who had smiled at their work smiled no more, but performed it with a serious and feverish activity.

From his station at the parapet Captain Ransome now saw a great multitude of dim gray figures taking shape in the mist below him and swarming up the slope. But the work of the guns was now fast and furious. They swept the populous declivity with gusts of grape and canister, the whirring of which could be heard through the thunder of the explosions. In this awful tempest of iron the assailants struggled forward foot by foot across their dead, firing into the embrasures, reloading, firing again, and at last falling in their turn, a little in advance of those who had fallen before. Soon the smoke was dense enough to cover all. It settled down upon the attack and, drifting back, involved the defense. The gunners could hardly see to serve their pieces, and when occasional figures of the enemy appeared upon the parapet—having had the good luck to get near enough to it, between two embrasures, to be protected from the guns—they looked so unsubstantial that it seemed hardly worth while for the few infantrymen to go to work upon them with the bayonet and tumble them back into the ditch.

As the commander of a battery in action can find something better to do than cracking individual skulls, Captain Ransome had retired from the parapet to his proper post in rear of his guns, where he stood with folded arms, his bugler beside him. Here, during the hottest of the fight, he was approached by Lieutenant Price, who had just sabred a daring assailant inside the work. A spirited colloquy ensued between the two officers—spirited, at least, on the part of the lieutenant, who gesticulated with energy and shouted again and again into his commander's ear in the attempt to make himself heard above the infernal din of the guns. His gestures, if coolly noted by an actor, would have been pronounced to be those of protestation: one would have said that he was opposed to the proceedings. Did he wish to surrender?

Captain Ransome listened without a change of countenance or attitude, and when the other man had finished his harangue, looked him coldly in the eyes and during a seasonable abatement of the uproar said:

"Lieutenant Price, it is not permitted to you to know *anything.* It is sufficient that you obey my orders."

The lieutenant went to his post, and the parapet being now apparently clear Captain Ransome returned to it to have a look over. As he mounted the banquette a man sprang upon the crest, waving a great brilliant flag. The captain drew a pistol from his belt and shot him dead. The body, pitching forward, hung over the inner edge of the embankment, the arms straight downward, both hands still grasping the flag. The man's few followers

turned and fled down the slope. Looking over the parapet, the captain saw no living thing. He observed that no bullets were coming into the work.

He made a sign to the bugler, who sounded the command to cease firing. At all other points the action had already ended with a repulse of the Confederate attack; with the cessation of this cannonade the silence was absolute.

VI. Why, Being Affronted by A, It Is Not Best to Affront B

General Masterson rode into the redoubt. The men, gathered in groups, were talking loudly and gesticulating. They pointed at the dead, running from one body to another. They neglected their foul and heated guns and forgot to resume their outer clothing. They ran to the parapet and looked over, some of them leaping down into the ditch. A score were gathered about a flag rigidly held by a dead man.

"Well, my men," said the general cheerily, "you have had a pretty fight of it."

They stared; nobody replied; the presence of the great man seemed to embarrass and alarm.

Getting no response to his pleasant condescension, the easy-mannered officer whistled a bar or two of a popular air, and riding forward to the parapet, looked over at the dead. In an instant he had whirled his horse about and was spurring along in rear of the guns, his eyes everywhere at once. An officer sat on the trail of one of the guns, smoking a cigar. As the general dashed up he rose and tranquilly saluted.

"Captain Ransome!"—the words fell sharp and harsh, like the clash of steel blades— "you have been fighting our own men—our own men, sir; do you hear? Hart's brigade!"

"General, I know that."

"You know it—you know that, and you sit here smoking? Oh, damn it, Hamilton, I'm losing my temper,"—this to his provost-marshal. "Sir—Captain Ransome, be good enough to say—to say why you fought our own men."

"That I am unable to say. In my orders that information was withheld."

Apparently the general did not comprehend.

"Who was the aggressor in this affair, you or General Hart?" he asked.

"I was."

"And could you not have known—could you not see, sir, that you were attacking our own men?"

The reply was astounding!

"I knew that, general. It appeared to be none of my business."

Then, breaking the dead silence that followed his answer, he said:

"I must refer you to General Cameron."

"General Cameron is dead, sir—as dead as he can be—as dead as any man in this army. He lies back yonder under a tree. Do you mean to say that he had anything to do with this horrible business?"

Captain Ransome did not reply. Observing the altercation his men had gathered about to watch the outcome. They were greatly excited. The fog, which had been partly dissipated by the firing, had again closed in so darkly about them that they drew more closely together till the judge on horseback and the accused standing calmly before him had but a narrow space free from intrusion. It was the most informal of courts-martial, but all felt that the formal one to follow would but affirm its judgment.

It had no jurisdiction, but it had the significance of prophecy.

"Captain Ransome," the general cried impetuously, but with something in his voice that was almost entreaty, "if you can say anything to put a better light upon your incomprehensible conduct I beg you will do so."

Having recovered his temper this generous soldier sought for something to justify his naturally sympathetic attitude toward a brave man in the imminence of a dishonorable death.

"Where is Lieutenant Price?" the captain said.

That officer stood forward, his dark saturnine face looking somewhat forbidding under a bloody handkerchief bound about his brow. He understood the summons and needed no invitation to speak. He did not look at the captain, but addressed the general:

"During the engagement I discovered the state of affairs, and apprised the commander of the battery. I ventured to urge that the firing cease. I was insulted and ordered to my post."

"Do you know anything of the orders under which I was acting?" asked the captain.

"Of any orders under which the commander of the battery was acting," the lieutenant continued, still addressing the general, "I know nothing."

Captain Ransome felt his world sink away from his feet. In those cruel words he heard the murmur of the centuries breaking upon the shore of eternity. He heard the voice of doom; it said, in cold, mechanical, and measured tones: "Ready, aim, fire!" and he felt the bullets tear his heart to shreds. He heard the sound of the earth upon his coffin and (if the good God was so merciful) the song of a bird above his forgotten grave. Quietly detaching his sabre from its supports, he handed it up to the provost-marshal.

One Officer, One Man

Captain Graffenreid stood at the head of his company. The regiment was not engaged. It formed a part of the front line-of-battle, which stretched away to the right with a visible length of nearly two miles through the open ground. The left flank was veiled by woods; to the right also the line was lost to sight, but it extended many miles. A hundred yards in rear was a second line; behind this, the reserve brigades and divisions in column. Batteries of artillery occupied the spaces between and crowned the low hills. Groups of horsemen—generals with their staffs and escorts, and field officers of regiments behind the colors—broke the regularity of the lines and columns. Numbers of these figures of interest had field-glasses at their eyes and sat motionless, stolidly scanning the country in front; others came and went at a slow canter, bearing orders. There were squads of stretcher-bearers, ambulances, wagon-trains with ammunition, and officers' servants in rear of all—of all that was visible—for still in rear of these, along the roads, extended for many miles all that vast multitude of non-combatants who with their various impedimenta are assigned to the inglorious but important duty of supplying the fighters' many needs.

An army in line-of-battle awaiting attack, or prepared to deliver it, presents strange contrasts. At the front are precision, formality, fixity, and silence. Toward the rear these characteristics are less and less conspicuous, and finally, in point of space, are lost altogether in confusion, motion and noise. The homogene-ous becomes heterogeneous. Definition is lacking; repose is replaced by an apparently purposeless activity; harmony vanishes in hubbub, form in disorder. Commotion everywhere and ceaseless unrest. The men who do not fight are never ready.

From his position at the right of his company in the front rank, Captain Graffenreid had an unobstructed outlook toward the enemy. A half-mile of open and nearly level ground lay before him, and beyond it an irregular wood, covering a slight acclivity; not a human being anywhere visible. He could imagine nothing more peaceful than the appearance of that pleasant landscape with its long stretches of brown fields over which the atmosphere was beginning to quiver in the heat of the morning sun. Not a sound came from forest or field—not even the barking of a dog or the crowing of a cock at the half-seen plantation house on the crest among the trees. Yet every man in those miles of men knew that he and death were face to face.

Captain Graffenreid had never in his life seen an armed enemy, and the war in which his regiment was one of the first to take the field was two years old. He had had the rare advantage of a military education, and when his comrades had marched to the front he had been detached for administrative service at the capital of his State, where it was thought that he could be most useful. Like a bad soldier he protested, and like a good one obeyed. In close official and personal relations with the governor of his State, and enjoying his confidence and favor, he had firmly refused promotion and seen his juniors elevated above him. Death had been busy in his distant regiment; vacancies among the field officers had occurred again and again; but from a chivalrous feeling that war's rewards belonged of right to those who bore the storm and stress of battle he had held his humble rank and generously advanced the fortunes of others. His silent devotion to principle had conquered at last: he had been relieved of his hateful duties and ordered to the front, and now, untried by fire, stood in the van of battle in command of a company of hardy veterans, to whom he had been only a name, and that name a byword. By none—not even by those of his brother officers in whose favor he had waived his rights—was his devotion to duty understood. They were too busy to be just; he was looked upon as one who had shirked his duty, until forced unwillingly into the field. Too proud to explain, yet not too insensible to feel, he could only endure and hope.

Of all the Federal Army on that summer morning none had accepted battle more joyously than Anderton Graffenreid. His spirit was buoyant, his faculties were riotous. He was in a state of mental exaltation and scarcely could endure the enemy's tardiness in advancing to the attack. To him this was opportunity —for the result he cared nothing. Victory or defeat, as God might will; in one or in the other he should prove himself a soldier and a hero; he should vindicate his right to the respect of his men and the companionship of his brother officers—to the consideration of his superiors. How his heart leaped in his breast as the bugle sounded the stirring notes of the "assembly"! With what a light tread, scarcely conscious of the earth beneath his feet, he strode forward at the head of his company, and how exultingly he noted the tactical dispositions which placed his regiment in the front line! And if perchance some memory came to him of a pair of dark eyes that might take on a tenderer light in reading the account of that day's doings, who shall blame him for the un-

martial thought or count it a debasement of soldierly ardor?

Suddenly, from the forest a half-mile in front—apparently from among the upper branches of the trees, but really from the ridge beyond—rose a tall column of white smoke. A moment later came a deep, jarring explosion, followed—almost attended—by a hideous rushing sound that seemed to leap forward across the intervening space with inconceivable rapidity, rising from whisper to roar with too quick a gradation for attention to note the successive stages of its horrible progression! A visible tremor ran along the lines of men; all were startled into motion. Captain Graffenreid dodged and threw up his hands to one side of his head, palms outward. As he did so he heard a keen, ringing report, and saw on a hillside behind the line a fierce roll of smoke and dust—the shell's explosion. It had passed a hundred feet to his left! He heard, or fancied he heard, a low, mocking laugh and turning in the direction whence it came saw the eyes of his first lieutenant fixed upon him with an unmistakable look of amusement. He looked along the line of faces in the front ranks. The men were laughing. At him? The thought restored the color to his bloodless face—restored too much of it. His cheeks burned with a fever of shame.

The enemy's shot was not answered: the officer in command at that exposed part of the line had evidently no desire to provoke a cannonade. For the forbearance Captain Graffenreid was conscious of a sense of gratitude. He had not known that the flight of a projectile was a phenomenon of so appalling character. His conception of war had already undergone a profound change, and he was conscious that his new feeling was manifesting itself in visible perturbation. His blood was boiling in his veins; he had a choking sensation and felt that if he had a command to give it would be inaudible, or at least unintelligible. The hand in which he held his sword trembled; the other moved automatically, clutching at various parts of his clothing. He found a difficulty in standing still and fancied that his men observed it. Was it fear? He feared it was.

From somewhere away to the right came, as the wind served, a low, intermittent murmur like that of ocean in a storm—like that of a distant railway train—like that of wind among the pines—three sounds so nearly alike that the ear, unaided by the judgment, cannot distinguish them one from another. The eyes of the troops were drawn in that direction; the mounted officers turned their field-glasses that way. Mingled with the sound was an irregular throbbing. He thought it, at first, the beating of his fevered blood in his ears; next, the distant tapping of a bass drum.

"The ball is opened on the right flank," said an officer.

Captain Graffenreid understood: the sounds were musketry and artillery. He nodded and tried to smile. There was apparently nothing infectious in the smile.

Presently a light line of blue smoke-puffs broke out along the edge of the wood in front, succeeded by a crackle of rifles. There were keen, sharp hissings in the air, terminating abruptly with a thump near by. The man at Captain Graffenreid's side dropped his rifle; his knees gave way and he pitched awkwardly forward, falling upon his face. Somebody shouted "Lie down!" and the dead man was hardly distinguishable from the living. It looked as if those few rifle-shots had slain ten thousand men. Only the field officers remained erect; their concession to the emergency consisted in dismounting and sending their horses

to the shelter of the low hills immediately in rear.

Captain Graffenreid lay alongside the dead man, from beneath whose breast flowed a little rill of blood. It had a faint, sweetish odor that sickened him. The face was crushed into the earth and flattened. It looked yellow already, and was repulsive. Nothing suggested the glory of a soldier's death nor mitigated the loathsomeness of the incident. He could not turn his back upon the body without facing away from his company.

He fixed his eyes upon the forest, where all again was silent. He tried to imagine what was going on there—the lines of troops forming to attack, the guns being pushed forward by hand to the edge of the open. He fancied he could see their black muzzles protruding from the undergrowth, ready to deliver their storm of missiles—such missiles as the one whose shriek had so unsettled his nerves. The distension of his eyes became painful; a mist seemed to gather before them; he could no longer see across the field, yet would not withdraw his gaze lest he see the dead man at his side.

The fire of battle was not now burning very brightly in this warrior's soul. From inaction had come introspection. He sought rather to analyze his feelings than distinguish himself by courage and devotion. The result was profoundly disappointing. He covered his face with his hands and groaned aloud.

The hoarse murmur of battle grew more and more distinct upon the right; the murmur had, indeed, become a roar, the throbbing, a thunder. The sounds had worked round obliquely to the front; evidently the enemy's left was being driven back, and the propitious moment to move against the salient angle of his line would soon arrive. The silence and mystery in front were ominous; all felt that they boded evil to the assailants.

Behind the prostrate lines sounded the hoof-beats of galloping horses; the men turned to look. A dozen staff officers were riding to the various brigade and regimental commanders, who had remounted. A moment more and there was a chorus of voices, all uttering out of time the same words—"Attention, battalion!" The men sprang to their feet and were aligned by the company commanders. They awaited the word "forward"—awaited, too, with beating hearts and set teeth the gusts of lead and iron that were to smite them at their first movement in obedience to that word. The word was not given; the tempest did not break out. The delay was hideous, maddening! It unnerved like a respite at the guillotine.

Captain Graffenreid stood at the head of his company, the dead man at his feet. He heard the battle on the right—rattle and crash of musketry, ceaseless thunder of cannon, desultory cheers of invisible combatants. He marked ascending clouds of smoke from distant forests. He noted the sinister silence of the forest in front. These contrasting extremes affected the whole range of his sensibilities. The strain upon his nervous organization was insupportable. He grew hot and cold by turns. He panted like a dog, and then forgot to breathe until reminded by vertigo.

Suddenly he grew calm. Glancing downward, his eyes had fallen upon his naked sword, as he held it, point to earth. Foreshortened to his view, it resembled somewhat, he thought, the short heavy blade of the ancient Roman. The fancy was full of suggestion, malign, fateful, heroic!

The sergeant in the rear rank, immediately behind Captain Graffenreid, now observed a strange sight. His attention drawn by an uncommon movement made by the captain—a sudden reaching forward of the hands and their energetic withdrawal, throwing the elbows out, as in pulling an oar—he saw spring from between the officer's shoulders a bright point of metal which prolonged itself outward, nearly a half-arm's length—a blade! It was faintly streaked with crimson, and its point approached so near to the sergeant's breast, and with so quick a movement, that he shrank backward in alarm. That moment Captain Graffenreid pitched heavily forward upon the dead man and died.

A week later the major-general commanding the left corps of the Federal Army submitted the following official report:

"SIR: I have the honor to report, with regard to the action of the 19th inst., that owing to the enemy's withdrawal from my front to reinforce his beaten left, my command was not seriously engaged. My loss was as follows: Killed, one officer, one man."

The Mocking-Bird

The time, a pleasant Sunday afternoon in the early autumn of 1861. The place, a forest's heart in the mountain region of southwestern Virginia. Private Grayrock of the Federal Army is discovered seated comfortably at the root of a great pine tree, against which he leans, his legs extended straight along the ground, his rifle lying across his thighs, his hands (clasped in order that they may not fall away to his sides) resting upon the barrel of the weapon. The contact of the back of his head with the tree has pushed his cap downward over his eyes, almost concealing them; one seeing him would say that he slept.

Private Grayrock did not sleep; to have done so would have imperiled the interests of the United States, for he was a long way outside the lines and subject to capture or death at the hands of the enemy. Moreover, he was in a frame of mind unfavorable to repose. The cause of his perturbation of spirit was this: during the previous night he had served on the picket-guard, and had been posted as a sentinel in this very forest. The night was clear, though moonless, but in the gloom of the wood the darkness was deep. Grayrock's post was at a considerable distance from those to right and left, for the pickets had been thrown out a needless distance from the camp, making the line too long for the force detailed to occupy it. The war was young, and military camps entertained the error that while sleeping they were better protected by thin lines a long way out toward the enemy than by thicker ones close in. And surely they needed as long notice as possible of an enemy's approach, for they were at that time addicted to the practice of undressing—than which nothing could be more unsoldierly. On the morning of the memorable 6th of April, at Shiloh, many of Grant's men when spitted on Confederate bayonets were as naked as civilians; but it should be allowed that this was not because of any defect in their picket line. Their error was of another sort: they had no pickets. This is perhaps a vain digression. I should not care to undertake to interest the reader in the fate of an army; what we have here to consider is that of Private Grayrock.

For two hours after he had been left at his lonely post that Saturday night he stood stock-still, leaning against the trunk of a large tree, staring into the darkness in his front and trying to recognize known objects; for he had been posted at the same spot during the day.

But all was now different; he saw nothing in detail, but only groups of things, whose shapes, not observed when there was something more of them to observe, were now unfamiliar. They seemed not to have been there before. A landscape that is all trees and undergrowth, moreover, lacks definition, is confused and without accentuated points upon which attention can gain a foothold. Add the gloom of a moonless night, and something more than great natural intelligence and a city education is required to preserve one's knowledge of direction. And that is how it occurred that Private Grayrock, after vigilantly watching the spaces in his front and then imprudently executing a circumspection of his whole dimly visible environment (silently walking around his tree to accomplish it) lost his bearings and seriously impaired his usefulness as a sentinel. Lost at his post—unable to say in which direction to look for an enemy's approach, and in which lay the sleeping camp for whose security he was accountable with his life—conscious, too, of many another awkward feature of the situation and of considerations affecting his own safety, Private Grayrock was profoundly disquieted. Nor was he given time to recover his tranquillity, for almost at the moment that he realized his awkward predicament he heard a stir of leaves and a snap of fallen twigs, and turning with a stilled heart in the direction whence it came, saw in the gloom the indistinct outlines of a human figure.

"Halt!" shouted Private Grayrock, peremptorily as in duty bound, backing up the command with the sharp metallic snap of his cocking rifle—"who goes there?"

There was no answer; at least there was an instant's hesitation, and the answer, if it came, was lost in the report of the sentinel's rifle. In the silence of the night and the forest the sound was deafening, and hardly had it died away when it was repeated by the pieces of the pickets to right and left, a sympathetic fusillade. For two hours every unconverted civilian of them had been evolving enemies from his imagination, and peopling the woods in his front with them, and Grayrock's shot had started the whole encroaching host into visible existence. Having fired, all retreated, breathless, to the reserves—all but Grayrock, who did not know in what direction to retreat. When, no enemy appearing, the roused camp two miles away had undressed and got itself into bed again, and the picket line was cautiously re-established, he was discovered bravely holding his ground, and was complimented by the officer of the guard as the one soldier of that devoted band who could rightly be considered the moral equivalent of that uncommon unit of value, "a whoop in hell."

In the mean time, however, Grayrock had made a close but unavailing search for the mortal part of the intruder at whom he had fired, and whom he had a marksman's intuitive sense of having hit; for he was one of those born experts who shoot without aim by an instinctive sense of direction, and are nearly as dangerous by night as by day. During a full half of his twenty-four years he had been a terror to the targets of all the shooting-galleries in three cities. Unable now to produce his dead game he had the discretion to hold his tongue, and was glad to observe in his officer and comrades the natural assumption that not having run away he had seen nothing hostile. His "honorable mention" had been earned by not running away anyhow.

Nevertheless, Private Grayrock was far from satisfied with the night's adventure, and

when the next day he made some fair enough pretext to apply for a pass to go outside the lines, and the general commanding promptly granted it in recognition of his bravery the night before, he passed out at the point where that had been displayed. Telling the sentinel then on duty there that he had lost something, —which was true enough—he renewed the search for the person whom he supposed himself to have shot, and whom if only wounded he hoped to trail by the blood. He was no more successful by daylight than he had been in the darkness, and after covering a wide area and boldly penetrating a long distance into "the Confederacy" he gave up the search, somewhat fatigued, seated himself at the root of the great pine tree, where we have seen him, and indulged his disappointment.

It is not to be inferred that Grayrock's was the chagrin of a cruel nature balked of its bloody deed. In the clear large eyes, finely wrought lips, and broad forehead of that young man one could read quite another story, and in point of fact his character was a singularly felicitous compound of boldness and sensibility, courage and conscience.

"I find myself disappointed," he said to himself, sitting there at the bottom of the golden haze submerging the forest like a subtler sea —"disappointed in failing to discover a fellow-man dead by my hand! Do I then really wish that I had taken life in the performance of a duty as well performed without? What more could I wish? If any danger threatened, my shot averted it; that is what I was there to do. No, I am glad indeed if no human life was needlessly extinguished by me. But I am in a false position. I have suffered myself to be complimented by my officers and envied by my comrades. The camp is ringing with praise of my courage. That is not just; I know myself courageous, but this praise is for specific acts which I did not perform, or performed—otherwise. It is believed that I remained at my post bravely, without firing, whereas it was I who began the fusillade, and I did not retreat in the general alarm because bewildered. What, then, shall I do? Explain that I saw an enemy and fired? They have all said that of themselves, yet none believes it. Shall I tell a truth which, discrediting my courage, will have the effect of a lie? Ugh! it is an ugly business altogether. I wish to God I could find my man!"

And so wishing, Private Grayrock, overcome at last by the languor of the afternoon and lulled by the stilly sounds of insects droning and prosing in certain fragrant shrubs, so far forgot the interests of the United States as to fall asleep and expose himself to capture. And sleeping he dreamed.

He thought himself a boy, living in a far, fair land by the border of a great river upon which the tall steamboats moved grandly up and down beneath their towering evolutions of black smoke, which announced them long before they had rounded the bends and marked their movements when miles out of sight. With him always, at his side as he watched them, was one to whom he gave his heart and soul in love—a twin brother. Together they strolled along the banks of the stream; together explored the fields lying farther away from it, and gathered pungent mints and sticks of fragrant sassafras in the hills overlooking all—beyond which lay the Realm of Conjecture, and from which, looking southward across the great river, they caught glimpses of the Enchanted Land. Hand in hand and heart in heart they two, the only children of a widowed mother, walked in paths of light through valleys of peace, seeing new things under a new sun. And through all the golden days floated one unceasing sound— the rich, thrilling melody of a mocking-bird in a cage by the cottage door. It pervaded and possessed all the spiritual intervals of the dream, like a musical benediction. The joyous bird was always in song; its infinitely various notes seemed to flow from its throat, effortless, in bubbles and rills at each heart-beat, like the waters of a pulsing spring. That fresh, clear melody seemed, indeed, the spirit of the scene, the meaning and interpretation to sense of the mysteries of life and love.

But there came a time when the days of the dream grew dark with sorrow in a rain of tears. The good mother was dead, the meadowside home by the great river was broken up, and the brothers were parted between two of their kinsmen. William (the dreamer) went to live in a populous city in the Realm of Conjecture, and John, crossing the river into the Enchanted Land, was taken to a distant region whose people in their lives and ways were said to be strange and wicked. To him, in the distribution of the dead mother's estate, had fallen all that they deemed of value—the mocking-bird. They could be divided, but it could not, so it was carried away into the strange country, and the world of William knew it no more forever. Yet still through the aftertime of his loneliness its song filled all the dream, and seemed always sounding in his ear and in his heart.

The kinsmen who had adopted the boys were enemies, holding no communication. For a time letters full of boyish bravado and boastful narratives of the new and larger experience —grotesque descriptions of their widening lives and the new worlds they had conquered —passed between them; but these gradually became less frequent, and with William's removal to another and greater city ceased altogether. But ever through it all ran the song of the mocking-bird, and when the dreamer opened his eyes and stared through the vistas of the pine forest the cessation of its music first apprised him that he was awake.

The sun was low and red in the west; the level rays projected from the trunk of each giant pine a wall of shadow traversing the golden haze to eastward until light and shade were blended in undistinguishable blue.

Private Grayrock rose to his feet, looked cautiously about him, shouldered his rifle and set off toward camp. He had gone perhaps a half-mile, and was passing a thicket of laurel, when a bird rose from the midst of it and perching on the branch of a tree above, poured from its joyous breast so inexhaustible floods of song as but one of all God's creatures can utter in His praise. There was little in that— it was only to open the bill and breathe; yet the man stopped as if struck—stopped and let fall his rifle, looked upward at the bird, covered his eyes with his hands and wept like a child! For the moment he was, indeed, a child, in spirit and in memory, dwelling again by the great river, over-against the Enchanted Land! Then with an effort of the will he pulled himself together, picked up his weapon and audibly damning himself for an idiot strode on. Passing an opening that reached into the heart of the little thicket he looked in, and there, supine upon the earth, its arms all abroad, its gray uniform stained with a single spot of blood upon the breast, its white face turned sharply upward and backward, lay the image of himself!—the body of John Grayrock, dead of a gunshot wound, and still warm! He had found his man.

As the unfortunate soldier knelt beside that masterwork of civil war the shrilling bird upon the bough overhead stilled her song and, flushed with sunset's crimson glory, glided silently away through the solemn spaces of the wood. At roll-call that evening in the Federal camp the name William Grayrock brought no response, nor ever again thereafter.

3

The Aftermath of War

The Pickets

ROBERT W. CHAMBERS (1865–1933), FOR OVER FORTY YEARS A BEST-SELLING NOVELIST, became an author by chance. He started as an artist and illustrator and later began to write fiction to accompany his own pictures. Chambers turned out seventy-two books—short stories, historical adventures, verse, plays, children's tales, detective stories. Perhaps his greatest success was the melodramatic *The King in Yellow.*

Despite his avowed preference for the sensational, Chambers wrote a few sociological novels of surprising depth and power. His early short story, "The Pickets," appearing in *McClure's Magazine* in 1896, shows Chambers at his best. He neatly grasps the fraternal inclinations of soldiers in the ranks. Chambers avoids the kind of sentimentality that characterizes much Civil War writing dealing with the topic of lonely death. (The song "All Quiet Along the Potomac" is a good example.) The story depicts the irrationality of war that forces hostility upon men whose basic impulses are generous. This tightly constructed tale shows by indirection the genuine depth of feeling that often underlay the tough language of veteran troops.

> "We be of one blood, you and I!"
> —Kipling.

"HI, YANK!"

"Shut up!" replied Alden, wriggling to the edge of the rifle-pit. Connor also crawled a little higher and squinted through the chinks of the pine logs.

"Hey, Johnny!" he called across the river, "are you that clay-eatin' Cracker with green lamps on your pilot?"

"O Yank! Are yew the U.S. mewl with a C.S.A. brand on yewr head-stall?"

"Shut up!" replied Connor, sullenly.

A jeering laugh answered him from across the river.

"He had you there, Connor," observed Alden, with faint interest.

Connor took off his blue cap and examined the bullet-hole in the crown.

"C.S.A. brand on my head-stall, eh!" he repeated, savagely, twirling the cap between his dirty fingers.

"You called him a clay-eating Cracker," observed Alden; "and you referred to his spectacles as green lanterns on his pilot."

"I'll show him whose head-stall is branded," muttered Connor, shoving his smoky rifle through the log-crack.

Alden slid down to the bottom of the shallow pit, and watched him apathetically. He gasped once or twice, threw open his jacket at the throat, and stuffed a filthy handkerchief into the crown of his cap, arranging the ends as a shelter for his neck.

Connor lay silent, his right eye fastened upon the rifle-sight, his dusty army shoes crossed behind him. One yellow sock had slipped down over the worn shoe-heel and laid bare a dust-begrimed ankle-bone.

Suddenly Connor's rifle cracked; the echoes rattled and clattered away through the woods; a thin cloud of pungent vapor slowly drifted straight upward, shredding into filmy streamers among the tangled branches overhead.

"Get him?" asked Alden, after a silence.

"Nope," replied Connor. Then he addressed himself to his late target across the river:

"Hello, Johnny!"

"Hi, Yank!"

"How close?"

"Hey?"

"How close?"

"What, sonny?"

"My shot, you fool!"

"Why, sonny!" called back the Confederate, in affected surprise, "was yew a-shootin' at me?"

Bang! went Connor's rifle again. A derisive catcall answered him, and he turned furiously to Alden.

"Oh, let up," said the young fellow; "it's too hot for that."

Connor was speechless with rage, and he hastily jammed another cartridge into his long hot rifle; but Alden roused himself, brushed away a persistent fly, and crept up to the edge of the pit again.

"Hello, Johnny!" he shouted.

"That you, sonny?" replied the Confederate.

"Yes; say, Johnny, shall we call it square until four o'clock?"

"What time is it?" replied the cautious Confederate; "all our expensive gold watches is bein' repaired at Chickamauga."

At this taunt Connor showed his teeth, but Alden laid one hand on his arm and sang out: "It's two o'clock, Richmond time; Sherman has just telegraphed us from your Statehouse."

"Wall, in that case this crool war is over," replied the Confederate sharp-shooter; "we'll be easy on old Sherman."

"See here!" cried Alden; "is it a truce until four o'clock?"

"All right! Your word, Yank!"

"You have it!"

"Done!" said the Confederate, coolly rising to his feet and strolling down to the river bank, both hands in his pockets.

Alden and Connor crawled out of their ill-smelling dust-wallow, leaving their rifles behind them.

"Whew! It's hot, Johnny," said Alden, pleasantly. He pulled out a stained pipe, blew into the stem, polished the bowl with his sleeve, and sucked wistfully at the end. Then he went and sat down beside Connor, who had improvised a fishing outfit from his ramrod, a bit of string, and a rusty hook.

The Confederate rifleman also sat down on his side of the stream, puffing luxuriously on a fragrant corncob pipe. Alden watched him askance, sucking the stem of his own empty pipe. After a minute or two, Connor dug up a worm from the roots of a beech tree with his bayonet, fixed it to the hook, flung the line into the muddy current, and squatted gravely on his haunches, chewing a leaf stem.

Presently the Confederate soldier raised his head and looked across at Alden.

"What's yewr name, sonny?" he asked.

"Alden," replied the young fellow, briefly.

"Mine's Craig," observed the Confederate; "what's yewr regiment?"

"Two Hundred and Sixtieth New York; what's yours, Mr. Craig?"

"Ninety-third Maryland, *Mister* Alden."

"Quit that throwin' sticks in the water!" growled Connor. "How do you s'pose I'm goin' to catch anythin'?"

Alden tossed his stick back into the brush-heap and laughed.

"How's your tobacco, Craig?" he called out.

"Bully! How's yewr coffee 'n' tack, Alden?"

"First rate!" replied the youth.

After a silence he said, "Is it a go?"

"You bet," said Craig, fumbling in his pockets. He produced a heavy twist of Virginia tobacco, laid it on a log, hacked off about three inches with his sheath-knife, and folded it up in a big green sycamore leaf. This again he rolled into a corn-husk, weighted it with a pebble; then, stepping back, he hurled it into the air, saying, "Deal square, Yank!"

The tobacco fell at Alden's feet. He picked it up, measured it carefully with his clasp-knife, and called out: "Two and three-quarters, Craig. What do you want, hard-tack or coffee?"

"Tack," replied Craig; "don't stint!"

Alden laid out two biscuits. As he was about to hack a quarter from the third, he happened

to glance over the creek at his enemy. There was no mistaking the expression in his face. Starvation was stamped on every feature.

When Craig caught Alden's eye, he spat with elaborate care, whistled a bar of the "Bonny Blue Flag," and pretended to yawn.

Alden hesitated, glanced at Connor, then placed three whole biscuit in the corn-husk, added a pinch of coffee, and tossed the parcel over to Craig.

That Craig longed to fling himself upon the food and devour it was plain to Alden, who was watching his face. But he didn't; he strolled leisurely down the bank, picked up the parcel, weighed it critically before opening it, and finally sat down to examine the contents. When he saw that the third cracker was whole and that a pinch of coffee had been added, he paused in his examination and remained motionless on the bank, head bent. Presently he looked up and asked Alden if he had made a mistake. The young fellow shook his head and drew a long puff of smoke from his pipe, watching it curl out of his nose with interest.

"Then I'm obliged to yew, Alden," said Craig; " 'low I'll eat a snack to see it ain't pizened."

He filled his lean jaws with the dry biscuit, then scooped up a tin cup full of water from the muddy river and set the rest of the cracker to soak.

"Good?" queried Alden.

"Fair," drawled Craig, bolting an unchewed segment and choking a little. "How's the twist?"

"Fine," said Alden; "tastes like stable-sweepings."

They smiled at each other across the stream.

"Sa-a-y," drawled Craig, with his mouth

full, "when yew're out of twist, jest yew sing out, sonny."

"All right," replied Alden. He stretched back in the shadow of a sycamore and watched Craig with pleasant eyes.

Presently Connor had a bite and jerked his line into the air.

"Look yere," said Craig, "that ain't no way for to ketch red-horse. Yew want a ca'tridge on foh a sinker, sonny."

"What's that?" inquired Connor, suspiciously.

"Put on a sinker."

"Go on, Connor," said Alden.

Connor saw him smoking, and sniffed anxiously. Alden tossed him the twist, telling him to fill his pipe.

Presently Connor found a small pebble and improvised a sinker. He swung his line again into the muddy current, with a mechanical sidelong glance to see what Craig was doing, and settled down again on his haunches, smoking and grunting.

"Enny news, Alden?" queried Craig after a silence.

"Nothing much; except that Richmond has fallen," grinned Alden.

"Quit foolin'," urged the Southerner; "ain't there no news?"

"No. Some of our men down at Mud Pond got sick eating catfish. They caught them in the pond. It appears you Johnnys used the pond as a cemetery, and our men got sick eating the fish."

"That so?" drawled Craig; "too bad. Lots of yewr men was in Long Pond too, I reckon."

In the silence that followed two rifleshots sounded faint and dull from the distant forest.

"'Nother great Union victory," drawled Craig. "Extry! Extry! Richmond is took!"

Alden laughed and puffed his pipe.

"We licked the boots off of the 30th Texas last Monday," he said.

"Sho!" drawled Craig; "what did you go a lickin' their boots for—blackin'?"

"Oh, shut up!" said Connor from the bank; "I can't ketch no fish if you two fools don't quit jawin'."

The sun was dipping below the pine-clad ridge, flooding river and wood with a fierce radiance. The spruce needles glittered, edged with gold; every broad, green leaf wore a heart of gilded splendor, and the muddy waters of the river rolled onward like a flood of precious metal, heavy, burnished, noiseless.

From a balsam bough a thrush uttered three timid notes; a great, gauzy-winged grasshopper drifted blindly into a clump of sun-scorched weeds, click! click! cr-r-r-r!

"Purty, ain't it," said Craig, looking at the thrush. Then he swallowed the last morsel of muddy hard-tack, wiped his beard on his cuff, hitched up his trousers, took off his green glasses, and rubbed his eyes.

"A he catbird sings purtier, though," he said, with a yawn.

Alden drew out his watch, puffed once or twice, and stood up, stretching his arms in the air.

"It's four o'clock," he began, but was cut short by a shout from Connor.

"Gee whiz!" he yelled, "what have I got on this here pole?"

The ramrod was bending, the line swaying heavily in the current.

"It's four o'clock, Connor," said Alden, keeping a wary eye on Craig.

"That's all right!" called Craig; "the time's extended till yewr friend lands that there fish."

"Pulls like a porpoise," grunted Connor. "I bet it busts my ramrod!"

"Does it pull?" grinned Craig.

"Yes, a dead weight!"

"Don't it jerk kinder this way an' that," asked Craig, much interested.

"Naw," said Connor; "the bloody thing jest pulls steady."

"Then it ain't no red-horse; it's a catfish!"

"Huh!" sneered Connor; "don't I know a catfish? This ain't no catfish, lemme tell yer!"

"Then it's a log," laughed Alden.

"By gum! here it comes," panted Connor; "here, Alden, jest you ketch it with my knife; hook the blade, blame ye!"

Alden cautiously descended the red bank of mud, holding on to roots and branches, and bent over the water. He hooked the big-bladed clasp-knife like a scythe, set the spring, and leaned out over the water.

"Now!" muttered Connor.

An oily circle appeared upon the surface of the turbid water,—another and another. A few bubbles rose and floated upon the tide.

Then something black appeared just beneath the bubbles, and Alden hooked it with his knife and dragged it shoreward. It was the sleeve of a man's coat.

Connor dropped his ramrod and gaped at the thing. Alden would have loosed it, but the knife-blade was tangled in the sleeve.

He turned a sick face up to Connor.

"Pull it in," said the older man. "Here, give it to me, lad—"

When at last the silent visitor lay upon the bank, they saw it was the body of a Union cavalryman. Alden stared at the dead face, fascinated; Connor mechanically counted the yellow chevrons upon the blue sleeve, now soaked black. The muddy water ran over the baked soil, spreading out in dust-covered pools; the spurred boots trickled slime. After a while both men turned their heads and looked at Craig. The Southerner stood silent and grave, his battered cap in his hand. They eyed each other quietly for a moment, then, with a vague gesture, the Southerner walked back into his pit and presently reappeared, trailing his rifle.

Connor had already begun to dig with his bayonet, but he glanced up sharply at the rifle in Craig's hand. Then he looked searchingly into the eyes of the Southerner. Presently he bent his head and quietly continued digging.

It was after sunset before he and Alden finished the shallow grave, Craig watching them in silence, his rifle between his knees. When they were ready they rolled the body into the hole and stood up.

Craig also rose, raising his rifle to a "present." He held it there while the two Union soldiers shovelled the earth into the grave. Then Alden went back and lifted the two rifles from the pit, handed Connor his, and waited.

"Ready!" growled Connor. "Aim!"

Alden's rifle came to his shoulder. Craig also raised his rifle.

"Fire!"

Three times the three shots rang out in the wilderness, over the unknown grave. After a moment or two Alden nodded goodnight to Craig across the river, and walked slowly toward his rifle-pit. Connor shambled after him. As he turned to lower himself into the pit he called across the river, "Good-night, Craig!"

"Good-night, Connor," said Craig.

At the Twelfth Hour

As a boy growing up in Kentucky, Joseph Altsheler (1862–1919) read carefully his Scott and Thackeray and devoured at first hand tales and legends of the Civil War told him by both Confederate and Union veterans. Altsheler was a professional newspaperman who eventually became editor of the New York *World*. In 1897 he wrote an adventure story to fill a space in his paper. The success of this serial led Altsheler to write over forty novels, mostly boy's books, on subjects ranging from the French and Indian Wars to the settling of the West.

Nothing Altsheler wrote equalled his performance in "At the Twelfth Hour," published in 1898 in the *Atlantic Monthly*. Simple in conception, the impressionistic view of battle's terrors—including a vivid picture of wounded trapped in woods set aflame by heavy rifle and cannon fire—stands as one of the finest pieces of Civil War fiction. The exposition is full of the overwhelming sounds and sights of combat's inferno.

There was no pause in the clamor outside, which rose sometimes to a higher key, and then sank back to its level, like the rush of a storm. Every log and plank in the little house would tremble as if it were so much human flesh and blood, when a crash louder than the rest betokened the sudden discharge of all the guns in some battery. The loose windows rattled in their wooden frames alike before the roar of the artillery and the shriller note of the rifles, which clattered and buzzed without ceasing, and seemed to boast a sting sharper and more deadly than that of their comrades the big guns. Whiffs of smoke, like the scud blown about by the winds at sea, would pass before the windows and float off into the forest. Sometimes a yellow light, that wavered like heat-lightning, would shine through the glass and quiver for a moment or two across the wooden floor. In the east there was a haze, a mottled blur of red and yellow and blue, and whether the crash of the artillery rose or sank, whether the clatter of the rifles was louder or weaker, there came always the unbroken din of two hundred thousand men foot to foot in battle,—a shuffling, moaning noise, a shriek, then a roar.

The widow moved the table and its dim candle nearer the window, not that she might see better outside, but there she could have a stronger light on her sewing, which was important and must be finished. The blaze of the battle flared in at the window more than once, and flickered across her face, revealing the strong, harsh features, and the hundreds of fine wrinkles that crossed one another in countless mazes, and clustered under her eyes and around the corners of her mouth. She was not a handsome woman, nor had ever been, even on her bridal morning, but she was still tall and muscular, her figure clothed in a poor print dress,—one who had endured much, and could endure more. As she bent over her humble sewing, the dim light of the candle was reflected in hopeless eyes.

The battle rolled a little nearer from the east, and the flashes of its light grew more frequent. The trembling of the house never ceased. On the hearth-stone some tiny half-dead embers danced about under the incessant rocking, like popping grains of corn, and the windows in their frames droned out their steady rattle.

But the widow paid no heed, going on with her sewing. The battle was nothing to her. She did not care who won; she would not go out of her house to see. If men were such barbarians and brutes as to murder one another for they knew not what, then let them. The more human flesh and blood the war devoured, the greater its appetite grew; for upon such food it fattened and prospered. Her three sons had gone to the man-eater, gulped down, one, two, three, in the order of their age: first the eldest, then the second, and then her youngest, her

best beloved. She had thought that he, at least, who would not be a man for years, might be left to her; but the news had come from Shiloh, in a meagre letter written by a comrade, that he had fallen there, mortally wounded, and the enemy who kept the field had buried him, perhaps.

She had the letter yet, but she never looked at it. There was no need, when she knew every line, every word, every letter, and just how they looked and stood on the page. The two older sons, like so many of the men of those wild hill regions, had been worthless,—drinkers of whiskey, tellers of lies, squalid loafers blinking at the sun; but the third, the boy, had been different, and she had expected him to become a man such as a woman could admire, a man upon whom a woman could depend,—that is, one stronger than herself, and as good. He had been both son and daughter to her, for in that way a mother looks upon the youngest or only son when he has no sister; but fair hair and blue eyes and a girl face had not prevented him from following the others, and now she knew not even where his bones lay, save that the mould of a wide and desolate battle-field inclosed them, and, in some place, hid them.

This woman did not cry; no tears came from her eyes when the news of the boy's death was brought to her, and none came now, when she still saw him, fair-haired and white-faced, lying out there under the sky. She had merely become harsher and harder, and, never much given to speech, she spoke less than before.

The battle rolled yet a little nearer from the east, and the complaining windows rattled more loudly. Above the thud of the cannon and the unbroken crash of the rifles she could hear now the shouting of many men, a guttural tumult which brought to mind the roar and shriek of wild animals in combat. The coming of the twilight did not seem to diminish their ferocity, and, repeating her old formula, she said, "Let them fight on through the night, if it please them."

The earth rumbled and rocked beneath a mighty discharge of artillery, the old house shook, and the heap of coals rolled down and scattered over the hearth. She walked from the window and put them carefully in place with an iron shovel. Thrown back together they sent up little spears of flame, which cast a flickering light over the desolate room,—the bare wooden floor, the rough log walls spotted with a few old newspaper prints, the two pine tables, the cane-bottomed chairs, the homemade wooden stool, the iron kettle in one corner and the tin pans beside it, the low bed covered with a brown counterpane in another corner,—a room that suited the mind and the temper of the woman who owned it and lived in it.

The battle crept still closer; the departed sun, the twilight deepening into night, had no effect on the fury of the combatants. Gun answered gun, and the rifles hurled opposing showers of lead. The difference in the two notes of the battle, the sullen, bass thunder of the cannon with its curious trembling cadence, and the sharper, shriller crash of the small arms, like the wrath of little people, became clearer, more distinct. Over both, in irregular waves, swelled the shouting; the wild and piercing "rebel yell" and the hoarse Yankee cheer contending and mingling and rolling back and forth in a manner that would tell nothing to a listener save that men were in mortal combat.

She heard a shrieking noise, like the scream of a man, but far louder; a long trail of light appeared in the sky, curving and arching like a rainbow until it touched the earth, when it disappeared in one grand explosion, throwing red, blue, green, and yellow lights into the air, as if a little volcano had burst. She almost fancied she could hear pieces of the shell whizzing through the air, though it was only fancy; but she knew that the earth where it struck had been torn up, and the dead were scattered about like its own pieces. Up went another, and another, and the air was filled with them, shining and shrieking as if in delight because they gave the finish and crowning touch to the battle. She watched them with a certain pleasure as they curved so beautifully, and gave herself praise when she timed to the second the moment of striking the earth. Soon the air was filled with a shower of the curving lights, and then they ceased for a while.

Still the dim battle raged in the darkness. But presently a light flared up again and did not disappear. It burned with a steady red and blue flame that indicated something more than the flashing of cannon and rifles, and, looking through a window-pane, the widow saw the cause. The forest was on fire, the exploding gunpowder having served as a torch; the blaze ran high above the trees, adding a new rush and roar to the thunder and sweep of the battle. But she was calm; for the forest did not come near enough to place her house in danger of the fire, and there was no reason why she need disturb herself. She blew out the candle, carefully put away in the cupboard the piece remaining,—economy being both a virtue and a necessity with her,—and returned to her seat by the window, now lighted only by the blaze of the battle and the burning trees. The light from the flaming forest grew stronger, and flared through the window all the way across the room. When the flash of the guns joined it, the glare was so vivid that the widow was compelled to shield her eyes with her hand; she would have closed the shutter of the window and relighted the candle, had there been a shutter to close. Clouds of smoke—some light, white, and innocent-looking, others heavy and black—floated past the window. Such clouds were needed, she thought, to veil the horrors of the slaughter-yard outside. She looked at the little tin clock on the mantel, ticking placidly away, and saw that it was a quarter to ten. She would have gone to bed, but one could not sleep with all that noise outside and so near. She thought it wise to take her old seat by the window and watch the flames from the forest, because sparks driven by the wind might fall on her house and set it on fire. There were two buckets filled with water in the little lean-to that served as a kitchen, and she set them in a place that would be handy in case the dangerous sparks came.

But she did not think the water would be needed, since the wind, though light, was blowing the fire from her. This was indicated clearly by the streams of flame, red in the centre, blue and white at the edges, which leaned eastward. The fire had gathered full volume now, and gave her a gorgeous spectacle, the flames leaping far above the trees, where they united into cones and pyramids, flashing with many colors and sending forth millions of sparks, which curved up, and then fell like showers of fireflies. Under this flaming cloud, the cannon spouted and the rifles flashed with as much steadiness and vigor as ever. It seemed to be a vast panoramic effect in fire planned for her alone, after the fashion of the Roman emperors, of whom she had never heard.

By the light of the fire and the battle she saw, for the first time, some figures struggling in the chaos of flame and smoke. Human beings she knew them to be, though they looked but little like it, being mere writhing black lines in a whirl of red fire and blue smoke. It was a living picture, to her, of the infernal regions, in which she was a firm believer; those ghastly shapes straining and fighting among the eternal flames. She felt a little sympathy for the many—mostly boys like her own boy who had fallen at Shiloh—who were about to pass through the flames of this world into the flames of the next; for she had been taught that only one out of a hundred could be saved, and she never doubted it. If she felt doubt at all, it was about the deserts of the hundredth man.

The thunder of the cannon sank presently to a mutter and a growl, the rifles ceased entirely, and the sudden drop in the noise of the battle caused the fire's roar to be heard above it like a tempest. She could still see the black figures, so many jumping-jacks, through the veil of flame and smoke; but they were not now a confused and struggling heap, without plan or order; they had drawn apart in two lines, and for two or three minutes remained motionless, save for a few figures which strutted up and down and waved what looked through the fiery mist like little sticks, but which she knew to be long swords. She knew enough more to guess that one line was about to charge the other, or more likely, both would charge at the same time, and the sinking of the battle was but a pause to gather strength for a supreme effort.

She was interested, and her interest increased when she saw the opposing lines swing forward a little, as if making ready for the shock. The sudden ebb of the firing had made all other noises curiously distinct.

The ticking of the little clock on the mantel became a steady drumbeat. She even fancied that she could hear the commands given to the two lines of puny black figures, but she knew it was only fancy.

This silence, so heavy that it oppressed her, after all she had heard, was broken by the discharge of hidden batteries, so many great guns at once that the widow sprang up from her chair; she thought at first that the house was falling about her, and she clapped her hands to her ears to shut out the penetrating crash, which was succeeded by the fierce, unbroken shrieking of the small arms. The cloud of smoke at once thickened and darkened, but she could see through it the two lines, now dim gray images of men, rushing upon each other. She watched with eager, intent eyes. The whirling smoke would hide parts of one line for a moment, leaving it a series of disconnected fragments; then would drift away, revealing the unbroken ranks again. She could hear the ticking of the clock no longer, for the pounding of the guns was so terrific now that continuous thunder roared in her ears, inside her head, and seemed not to come from anything without. A window-pane broke under the impact of so much sound, and the fragments of glass rattled on the floor, but she did not take her eyes from the battle.

Over the heads of the rushing lines the smoke formed in a cloud so thick, so black, so threatening, and so low that it inclosed them, like a roof. The old likeness came back to the widow. It is the roof of hell, she said to herself; these walls and pillars of flame are its sides, and the men who fight in there, hemmed in by fire, are the damned, condemned to fight so forever.

On they rushed, some of the dim gray figures seeming to dance above the earth in the flames, like the imps they were, and the two lines met midway. She thought she could hear the smash of wave on wave above the red roar of the guns, and figures shot into the air as if hurled up by the meeting of tremendous and equal forces. A long cry, a yell, a shriek, and a wail, which could come only from human throats, thousands of them together, swelled again above everything else,—above the roar of the fire, above the crash of the rifles, above the thunder of the cannon.

In spite of her stoicism the watcher quivered a little and turned her eyes away from the window, but she turned them back again. The cry sank to a quaver, then rose again to a scream; and thus it sank and rose, as the battle surged from side to side in the flaming pit. She thought she could hear the clash of arms, bayonet on bayonet, sword on sword, and all the sounds of war became confused and mingled, like the two lines of men which had rushed so fiercely together. There were no longer two lines,—not even one line,—but a medley; struggling heaps, red whirlpools which threw out their dead and whirled on, grinding up the living like grain in a hopper. The soldiers fought in the very centre of the pit, and the shifting red curtain of flame between gave them strange shapes, enlarging some, belittling others, and then blending all into a blurred mass, a huddle of men without form or number.

Fantastic and horrible, the scene appealed strongly to the widow's hard religious sense. She could no longer doubt that the red chaos upon which she was looking was a picture of life from the regions of eternal torture, reserved for the damned, reproduced on earth for the benefit of men. It was, then, with a feeling of increased interest that she watched the battle as it blazed and shrieked to and fro.

The thunder of the cannon and the crash of the rifles were still as steady as the rush of a tempest, and the wild shouting of the men now rose above the din, then was crushed out by it, only to be heard again, fiercer and shriller than before.

The great clouds which lowered over the pit grew blacker and bigger, and rolled away in sombre waves on every side. Their vanguard reached even to her house and passed over it. The loathsome smell of burnt gunpowder and raw and roasted human flesh came in at the broken window. She stuffed a quilt into the open space, until neither smoke nor smell could enter; but some of the droppings of the black cloud, little balls and curls of smoke, came down the chimney and floated about the room, to remind the woman that the whirlwind of the battle whirled widely enough to draw her in, too. Her throat felt hot and scaly, and she took a gourd of water from one of the buckets and drank it. It was cool to the throat, and as smooth as oil. How some of those men lying out there, helpless on the ground, longed for water, cold water! How her own boy, doubtless, had longed for it, as he lay on the field of Shiloh waiting for the death that came! A feeling of pity, a strong feeling, swelled up in her soul. She walked again across the room and looked at the little tin clock on the mantel. Ten forty-five! It was time for the battle to close; it had been time long ago.

Then she went back as usual to the window, and she noticed at once that the roar and blaze of the battle were sinking. The thunder of the guns was not continuous, and the intervals increased in number and became longer. The fire of the rifles was broken into crackling showers, and spots of gray or white, where the air was breaking through, appeared in the wall of flame. The black roof of smoke lifted a little, and seemed to be losing length and breadth as the wind swept off cloudy patches and carried them away. The fire in the forest was dying, and she ceased to hear the rush of the flames from tree to tree. Once the human shout or shriek—she could not tell which—came to her ear, but she heard it no more just then. The men, more distinct now as the veil of flame thinned away or rose in vapor, still struggled, but with less ferocity. The groups were breaking up, and the two lines shrank apart, each seeming to abandon the ground for which it had fought.

It was nearly eleven o'clock, and the moon, able for the first time to send its beams through the battle-smoke, was beginning to cast a silvery radiance over the field. The flames sank fast. The fire in the forest burnt out. The great cloud of smoke broke up into many little clouds which drifted away westward before the wind. The showers of sparks ceased, and the bits of charred wood no longer fell. A fine cloud of ashes blown through the air began to form a film over the window-panes.

The battle died like the eruption of a volcano, which shoots up with all its strength, and then sinks from exhaustion. The human figures melted away, and the last was gone, though the widow knew that many must be lying in the ravines and on the hillsides beyond her view. There were four cannon-shots at irregular intervals, the fourth a long time after the third, a volley or two from the rifles, a pop-pop or two, and the firing was over. Some feeble flames from grass or bush still spurted up, but they fought in a lost cause, for the silver radiance of the moon grew, and they paled and sank before it.

The ticking of the clock made the cessation

of noise outside more noticeable. She opened the window, and the air that came in was strong with a fleshy smell. But so much smoke had come down the chimney, and the room was so close, that she kept the window open and let the air seek every corner. Outside, the unburnt trees were swaying in the west wind, but there was no other noise. The battlefield, unlighted by the fire of cannon and rifles, had become invisible; but she knew that many men were lying there, and the wind sobbing through the burnt and unburnt forest was their dead march.

Fine ashes, borne by the wind from the burnt forest, still fell; some came in at the open window, and fell in a faint whitish powder on the floor. The widow took her wisp broom and brushed the ashes carefully into the fire; but she did not close the window, for the fresh air which blew in had a tonic strength, though there was still about it some of that strange odor, the breath of slaughter.

She resolved to watch the field a little longer, and then she would go to bed; she had wasted enough time watching the struggles of lost souls. The light of the moon was beginning to wane, and the trees and hills were growing more shadowy; their silver gray was changing to black, the sombre hue borrowed from the skies above them. Flecks of fire like smouldering coals gleamed through the darkness, showing where a tree-trunk or a bush still burned in the wake of the battle or the fire. The wind rose again, and these tiny patches of flame blazed before it more brightly for a time, and then went out. But the wind moaned more loudly as it blew among the burned tree-trunks and the dead branches. Some trees, eaten through by the fire, fell, and the night, so still otherwise, echoed with the sound.

All the lights from the fire went out, but others took their place. She could see them far apart, but twinkling like little stars fallen to earth; probably the lanterns, she thought, of surgeons and soldiers come to look for those whose wounds were not mortal. Why not let them lie there and pay the price of their own folly? They had gone into the battle knowing its risks, and they should not seek to shun them. She would go to bed, and she put up her hand to pull down the window. She heard a prolonged cry, a wail and a sob; distant, perhaps, and feeble, but telling of pain and fear.

It came direct from the battlefield. She would have dismissed the sound, as she had dismissed all other signs of the battle, but it came again and was more penetrating. She thought that she had no fancy, no imagination, and that the battle had passed leaving her mind untouched, but the cry lingered. It rose for the third time, louder, fuller, more piercing than before, and the air ached with it. She was sure now that it was many voices in one, all groaning in their agony, and their groans uniting in a single lament, which rose above that of the wind and filled all the air with its wailing. She tried again to crush down her thoughts, and to hide the scenes that she saw with her mind, and not with her eyes; but her will refused to obey her, and yielded readily to imagination, which, held back so long, took possession of its kingdom with despotic power. Her face and hands became cold and wet at the sights and scenes that her fancy made her hear and see. It was easy to turn this field into the field of Shiloh, and her ready imagination, laughing at her will, did it for her. In that other battle her boy was lying at the foot of a hillock, his white face growing whiter, turned up to the stars; the dead lay around him, and there was no sound but his groans.

She closed the window with a sudden and violent gesture, as if she would shut out the sight, and would shut out too those cries which had stirred her imagination into such life. She walked angrily to the hearth and banked the coals for the last time, firmly resolved to go to bed and sleep. The clock ticked away loudly and clearly, as if to show its triumph over the battle, which was now gone, while it ticked on.

But the cry of anguish from the field reached her there; fainter, more muffled, but not to be mistaken. Whether it came through the glass or how else, she knew not, but she heard it,—a cry to her, a cry that would reach her even in bed and would not let her sleep. It was as if her own son had been crying to her for help, for water. She threw up the window again, and looked toward the battlefield. The air was filled with the cries of the wounded like the chorus of the lost, but of the field itself she could see nothing. The night had darkened fast, and the ground on which the men had fought was clothed in a ghostly vapor. The burnt trees were but a faint tracery of black, and the wind had ceased, leaving the night, hot, close, and breathless. The fine ashes from the fire no longer fell, and the air was free from them, but it was thick and heavy, and the repellent smell of human flesh lingered. It was a terrible night for the wounded. They would lie on the ground in the close heat and gasp for air, which would be like fire to their lungs.

The little clock struck midnight with a loud, emphatic tang, each stroke echoing and reminding her that it was time to go.

The two buckets filled with water, which she had brought to save her house from fire, still stood by the window. She put the drinking-gourd into one of them, lifted both, and passed out of the house. She was a strong woman, and she did not stagger beneath the weight of the water. This, she knew, was what they would want most; for in all that she had ever heard of battlefields the cry for water was loudest. Yet all her pity in that moment was for one,—not one of those who lay there, but her own boy on that other battlefield. She saw only him, only his face; like a girl's it had always looked to her, with its youthful flush and the fair hair around it. It was he, not the others, who was taking her out on the field, and she walked on with straight, strong steps, because he led her.

The mists and vapors seemed to drift away as she approached the battlefield, and the trees, holding out their burnt arms, rose distinct and clear from the darkness. The cries of the wounded increased, and were no longer a steady volume like the moaning of the wind; but she could distinguish in the tumult articulate sounds, even words, and they were always the same,—the cry for water rising above all others, just as she had been told. She reached the ground over which the fire had swept. Some clusters of sparks, invisible from the window, lingered yet in the clefts of roots and rocks, and glimmered like marsh lights.

The strange repellent odor that reminded her of the drippings of a slaughter-house attacked her with renewed strength. She turned a little sick, but she conquered her faintness and went on. Wisps of smoke were still drifting about, and she stumbled on something and nearly fell; but she saved the precious water, and saw that her foot had struck against a cannon-ball, which lay there, half buried in the earth, spent, after its mission. To her eyes the earth upon it was the color of blood, and giving it a look of repulsion she passed on. She saw two or three rifles upon the ground, abandoned by their owners; and here was a broken sword, and there a knapsack, still full, which some soldier had thrown away. Under the half-burned trunk of a tree was something dark and shapeless, and charred like the tree; but she knew what it was, and after the first glance kept her head turned away. She passed more like it, but all were motionless, for the fire had spared nothing over which it had gone.

The smell of roasted flesh was strong here, but the silence appalled her. All the cries came from the further part of the field, and around her no voice was raised. The figures, half hidden in the dark, did not stir. The trees waved their burnt arms, and gave forth a dry, parched sound when a whiff of wind struck them, like the rustle of a field of dead broom sedge.

She crossed the strip over which the fire had swept and burned out everything living, and entered the red battlefield beyond. It was lighter here, for there were fewer trees and the moon had cleared somewhat. She saw many figures of men: some motionless as they had been in the burnt woods; others twisting and distorting themselves like spiders on a pin; and still others half sitting or leaning against a stone or a stump, and trying to bind up their own wounds. The cries were a medley, chiefly groans and shrieks, but sometimes laughter, and twice a song. She had never seen ground so torn, for here the battle had trod to and fro in all its strength and ferocity. Three or four trees, cut down by cannon-balls, had fallen together, their boughs interlaced, and a hole in the earth showed where a huge shell had burst. Some sharp pieces of the exploding iron had been driven into a neighboring tree,

and a little further on a patch of bushes had been mowed down like grass in a hayfield.

A man, shot in the legs, who had propped himself against a rock, saw the water that she carried, and cried to her to come to him with it. He damned her from a full vocabulary because she did not make enough haste, and when she came tried to snatch the gourd from her hand. But with her stronger hand she pushed his away, and made him drink while she held the gourd. He was young, but it did not seem strange to her to hear such volleys of profanity from one who had the splendor of youth, for her older sons had been of his kind. She left him cursing her because she did not give him more water, and went on; for the face of her boy was still leading her, and the one she left was not like his.

The field extended further than she could see, but all around her was the lament of after-the-battle. Lights trembled or glimmered over the field; the surgeons and soldiers holding them were seeking the wounded, and she saw that some wore the blue and others the gray. Such a shambles as this was the only place in which they could meet like brethren, and here they passed each other without comment; nor did they notice her, save one, an old man with the shining tools of a surgeon in his hand, who gave her an approving nod.

She heard a moan which seemed to come from a little clump of bushes spared by the cannon-balls. A man,—a boy, rather,—with the animal instinct, had crawled in there that he might die unseen. He was in delirium with fever, and cried for his mother. The widow's heart was touched more deeply than before, for it was to such as he that her boy's face was leading her. She took him from out the bushes, stanched his wounds, and gave him of the cold water to drink. The fever abated, and his delirious talk sank to a mere mutter, while she stood and watched until one of the wagons gathering up the wounded came by; then she helped put him in, and passed on with the water to the others. She was eager to help; it was true pity, not a mere sense of duty, for she was now among the boys, the slender lads of eighteen and seventeen and sixteen; and very many of them there were, too, and she knew that her own boy had called her to help these. They lay thick upon the ground,—children they seemed to her; yet this war had such in scores of thousands, who went from the country schoolhouses to the battlefield.

Most of them were dead: sometimes they lay in long rows, as if they had been made ready for the grave; sometimes they lay in a heap, their bodies crossing; and here and there lay one who had found death alone. But amid the dead were a few living, and the widow's hands grew tenderer and more gentle as she raised their heads and let them drink. The water in her buckets was three fourths gone, and she was very careful of it now, for a little might mean a life.

The vapors still hung over the field, and the thick, clammy air was often death to the wounded who could not breathe it. The widow wished more than once for a little of the water, herself, but there were others who needed it far more, and she went on with her work among the boys. She thought often, as she looked at the white young faces around her, of that slaughter of the innocents of which the Bible told, and it seemed to her that this was as wicked and fruitless as that.

The lights were growing fewer, and the carts with the wounded rumbled past her less often; the cries, a volume of sound before, became solitary moans. The darkness, cut here and there by the vapors, hid most of the field, and she was forced to search closely to tell the living from the dead. She was tired, weary in bone and sinew, but the face of her boy led her on, and, while any of the living remained there, she would seek. She stumbled once, in the darkness, on a dead body, and, springing back with a shudder when she felt the yielding flesh under her feet, walked on into a little hollow.

She heard a boy groan,—very feebly, but still she could not mistake the sound for any of the fancied noises of the battlefield; and then the same faint voice calling his mother. She had heard other boys, on that night, calling for their mothers, but there was a new tone in this cry. She trembled and stood quite still, listening for the groan, which came again, feebler than before. It was so faint that she could not tell from what point it came, and all the shadows seemed to have gathered in the hollow. If she had only a light! She saw one of the lanterns glimmering far off in the field, but even if she obtained it she might not be able to find the place again. She advanced into the hollow, bending down low and searching the thick weeds and tangled bushes with her eyes. One of the buckets she had left behind; the other yet contained a gourdful of water, and she preserved it as if it were so much gold, now more jealously than ever.

She saw nothing. The place was larger than she had thought, and was thick with vines and weeds and heaped-up stones. She stumbled twice and fell upon her knees, but each time she held the water so well that not a drop was spilled. She stood erect again, listening, but hearing nothing. She called aloud, saying that help was there, but no answer came. Her heart was beating violently, but she neither wept nor cried aloud, for she was a woman of strength, and had always been of few words and less show.

Where she stood was the lowest point of the battlefield, and was on its outer edge. It was likewise the darkest spot, and the remainder of it seemed to curve before and above her in a great dusky amphitheatre, broken faintly by a few points of light where the lantern burned. She saw the formless bulk of a single cart moving slowly. In a little while the field would be abandoned to her and the dead.

She turned and continued the search, feeling her way through the mass of vegetation, and listening for the guiding groan. Again she stopped, and her heart was in the grip of fear lest she should not find him. She bent her ear close to the ground, and then she heard a cry so faint that it was but a sigh. She pushed her way through some bushes, and there he lay, his back against a rock, his white girlish face with its circle of fair hair turned up to the sky. The eyes were closed, and the chest seemed not to move. A great clot of blood hung upon his left shoulder and made a red gleam against the cloth of his coat.

Let it be said again that she was not a woman who showed her emotions, though at that first glance her face perhaps turned as white as his. She set the bucket down, knelt at his side, and, putting her face close to his, found that he was not dead, for she felt his breath upon her lips. She raised the head a little, and a sigh of pain, scarcely to be heard, escaped him. She poured some of the water, every drop more precious now than ever, into the gourd, and moistened his lips, which burned with the fever. Then she raised his head higher and dropped a little into his mouth. He sighed again, and his eyelids quivered and were lifted until a faint trace of the blue beneath appeared; then they closed. But she poured water into his mouth and down his throat a second time, and she could feel that pulse and breathing were stronger.

The blood was clotted and caked over his wound, but with wisdom she let it alone, knowing that there was no better bandage to stop the flow. She wet his hands and his face with water and gave him more to drink, and saw a trace of color appear in his cheeks. His eyes opened partly two or three times, and he talked, but not of anything she knew, speaking in confused words of other battlefields and long marches; and before a sentence or its sense was finished another would be begun. She wanted no help; she looked around in jealousy lest another should come, and saw how small was the chance of it. The last cart had disappeared from the field, so far as she could see; she could count but four lights, and they were far off. In that part of the field, she, the living, was alone with the dead and the boy who hung between life and death.

Never had she felt herself more strong of body and mind, more full of resource; never had she felt herself more ready of head and hand. She gave him the last of the water, and saw the spot of color in his cheek, which was not of fever, grow. Then she lifted him in her arms, and began to walk with her burden across the battlefield. She looked at the wound, and seeing no fresh blood knew that she had not strained it open in lifting. With that she was satisfied, and she went on with careful step.

She felt her way through the roughness of the hollow, where the bushes and the weeds clung to her dress and her feet and tried to trip her; but she thrust them all aside and went on toward the house. She passed out of the hollow, and into the space which had received the full sweep of the cannon-balls and bullets.

The field was clothed in vapors which floated around her like little clouds. The white faces of the dead looked up at her, and she seemed to be going between rows of them on either side.

She walked on with sure and steady step, not feeling the weight in her arms and against her shoulder, unmoved by the ghastly heaps and the dead faces. She reached the burnt ground, where the little patches of fire that she had seen as she passed the other way had ceased to burn, but the smoke was still rising and the ground was yet warm. She feared that the smoke would get into his throat and choke down the little life that was left. So she ran, and the burnt arms of the trees seemed to wave at her and to jeer her, as if they knew she would be too late. She stumbled a little, but recovered herself. The boy stirred and groaned. She was in dread lest the rough jolt had started his wound, but her hand could not feel the warmth of fresh blood, and, re-assured, she hastened through the burnt strip and toward home.

The house was silent and dark; apparently, no one had noticed the log cabin, its secluded position and the clump of woods perhaps hiding it from men whose attention had been devoted solely to the battle. She pushed open the door, and entered with her helpless burden. Some coals still glowed on the hearth, and threw out a warm light which bade her welcome. She put the boy on the bed, and covered the coals with ashes, for it was hot and close in the house. Then she lighted the piece of candle, and setting it where it could serve her with its light, and yet not shine into his eyes, she proceeded with her work.

Women who live such lives as hers must learn a little of all things, and she knew the duties of a surgeon. Twice she had bound up the wounds of her husband, received in some mountain fray. She undressed the young soldier, and as she did so she noticed the scar of a year-old wound under the shoulder,—a wound that might well have been mortal. The bullet of to-night had gone almost through, and she could feel it against the skin on the other side. She cut it out easily with the blade of a pocketknife, and put it in the cupboard. Then she bound up the wound the late bullet had made when it entered, leaving the congealed blood upon it as help against a fresh flow, and sat down to wait.

He was still talking, saying words that had no meaning, and threw his arms about a little; but he was stronger, and she hoped, though she knew, too, that he trembled on the edge.

She sat for a long time watching every movement, even the slightest. The little clock ticked so loudly that she thought once of stopping it; but the sound was so steady and regular that it lulled them, the boy as well as herself, and she let it alone.

He became quieter and grew stronger, too, as she could tell by his breathing, and slept. She spread a sheet over him, and opened the window that a little air might enter the close, warm room. She stood there for a while and looked toward the battlefield, but she could see nothing now to tell her of the combat. The vapors that floated over it hid it and all its ruin.

The wind rose, stirring the hot, close air and cooling the night. It whistled softly through the trees and among the hills, but it did not bring the smell of battle. That had vanished with the combat that had been so unreal itself, as she looked at it from her window. Now she could not see a human figure nor any sign of war. The cabin was just the same lone cabin among the hills that it had always been. She went outside and made the circuit of the house, but there was nothing for eye or ear to note. The night was darkening again, the wind had blown up clouds which hid the face of the moon, and but a few stars twinkled in the sky. The air felt damp, and scattered drops of rain whirled before the wind which was whistling, far off, as it drove away through the hills.

She went back into the house,—for she could not leave the boy more than a minute or two,—and found that he was sleeping well. She prepared some stimulants, and put them where they would be ready to her hand. Then she made over all her arrangements for the morrow, for two instead of one, and placed everything about the house in order, that it might put on its best look in the daylight. She finished her task, and sat down by the bed. Presently the sufferer began to talk of battle and strive to move, thinking he was in action on the field again. When she felt of his wrist and forehead, she saw that the fever was rising, and she thought he was going to die. She did all that her experience told her, and waited. Her bitterness came back, and she called them fools and barbarians once more; she was a fool herself to have had pity upon them.

The boy's wild talk was all of war. She followed him through march and camp, skirmish and battle, charge and retreat, and saw how they had taken their hold upon him, and what courage and energy he had put into his part. In half an hour he became quieter, and the fever sank. A cannon-shot boomed among the hills,—so far away that the sound was softened by the distance. But it echoed long; hill and valley took it up and passed it on to farther hill and valley; and she heard it again and again, until it died away in the farthest hills like the last throb of a distant drumbeat. It was as if it had been a minute gun for the dead, and she went in terror to the bed; but the boy was not dead. He had passed again from delirium to sleep, and, fearing everything now, she went outside to see if the cannon-shot, by any chance, foretold a renewal of the battle; but it must have been a stray shot, for, as before, nowhere could she see a light, nowhere a living figure, nor could she hear any sound of human beings. The air was cooler, and, shivering, she went back into the house.

Presently the drops changed to steady rain, which beat upon the windows; but it was peaceful and sheltered in the little house, and as she looked out at the rain, dashed past by the wind, there was a softness in her heart. The rain ceased after a while, and the trees and bushes dripped silver drops. The boy stirred; but it was some thought in his sleep that made him stir, not fever. She looked at him closely. His breathing was regular and easy, and she knew that he would live.

Going once more to the window, and with eyes to the skies, she gave her wordless thanks to God.

A broad bar of light appeared in the east. The day was coming.

The Burial of the Guns

ALTHOUGH THOMAS NELSON PAGE (1853–1922) WAS TOO YOUNG TO TAKE AN ACTIVE PART in the Civil War, he spent his youth in Virginia in the midst of the struggle. Throughout his life as lawyer, diplomat, and popular novelist, Page never forgot the Old South that died a bloody death during his adolescence.

Page's fiction deals with life in the South just before or immediately after the war. Novels and stories such as *In Ole Virginia* and *Red Rock* reflect his desire to preserve a sentimental past— sentimental in its emphasis on the good, golden days when men were gracious and dashing cavaliers, women proud and blushing beauties.

Page saw the war as the line of demarcation between the sweet past and the relatively harsh present. Thus in "The Burial of the Guns" (1894) his description of the last hours of the war for a group of artillerymen mixes bittersweet memories of glory with inflexible realities of defeat. The dream of victory died poignantly; the story evokes the sadness of the moment when no hope could remain. The war was over, and the South had lost.

LEE SURRENDERED THE REMNANT OF HIS army at Appomattox, April 9, 1865, and yet a couple days later the old Colonel's battery lay intrenched right in the mountain-pass where it had halted three days before. Two weeks previously it had been detailed with a light division sent to meet and repel a force which it was understood was coming in by way of the southwest valley to strike Lee in the rear of his long line from Richmond to Petersburg. It had done its work. The moun- tain-pass had been seized and held, and the Federal force had not gotten by that road within the blue rampart which guarded on that side the heart of Virginia. This pass, which was the key to the main line of passage over the mountains, had been assigned by the commander of the division to the old Colonel and his old battery, and they had held it. The position taken by the battery had been chosen with a soldier's eye. A better place could not have been selected to hold the pass. It was its highest point, just where the road crawled over the shoulder of the mountain along the limestone cliff, a hundred feet sheer above the deep river, where its waters had cut their way in ages past, and now lay deep and silent, as if resting after their arduous toil before they began to boil over the great bowlders which filled the bed a hundred or more yards below.

The little plateau at the top guarded the descending road on either side for nearly a mile, and the mountain on the other side of the river was the centre of a clump of rocky, heavily timbered spurs, so inaccessible that no feet but those of wild animals or of the hardiest hunter had ever climbed it. On the side of the river on which the road lay, the only path out over the mountain except the road itself was a charcoal-burner's track, dwindling at times to a footway known only to the mountain-folk, which a picket at the top could hold against an army. The position, well defended, was impregnable, and it was well defended. This the general of the division knew when he detailed the old Colonel and gave him his order to hold the pass until relieved, and not let his guns fall into the hands of the enemy. He knew both the Colonel and his battery. The battery was one of the oldest in the army. It had been in the service since April, 1861, and its commander had come to be known as "The Wheel Horse of his division." He was, perhaps, the oldest officer of his rank in his branch of the service. Although he had bitterly opposed secession, and was many years past the age of service when the war came on, yet as soon as the President called on the State for her quota of troops to coerce South Carolina, he had raised and uniformed an artillery company, and offered it, not to the President of the United States, but to the Governor of Virginia.

It is just at this point that he suddenly looms up to me as a soldier; the relation he never wholly lost to me afterward, though I knew him for many, many years of peace. His gray coat with the red facing and the bars on the collar; his military cap; his gray flannel shirt —it was the first time I ever saw him wear anything but immaculate linen—his high boots; his horse caparisoned with a black, high-peaked saddle, with crupper and breast-girth, instead of the light English hunting-saddle to which I had been accustomed, all come before me now as if it were but the other day. I remember but little beyond it, yet I remember, as if it were yesterday, his leaving home, and the scenes which immediately preceded it; the excitement created by the news of the President's call for troops; the unanimous judgment that it meant war; the immediate determination of the old Colonel, who had hitherto opposed secession, that it must be met; the suppressed agitation on the plantation, attendant upon the tender of his services and the Governor's acceptance of them. The prompt and continuous work incident to the enlistment of the men, the bustle of preparation, and all the scenes of that time, come before me now. It turned the calm current of the life of an old and placid country neighborhood, far from any city or centre, and stirred it into a boiling torrent, strong enough, or fierce enough to cut its way and join the general torrent which was bearing down and sweeping everything before it. It seemed but a minute before the quiet old plantation, in which the harvest, the corn-shucking, and the Christmas holidays alone marked the passage of the quiet seasons, and where a strange carriage or a single horseman coming down the big road was an event in life, was turned into a depot of war-supplies, and the neighborhood became a parade-ground. The old Colonel, not a colonel yet, nor even a captain, except by brevet, was on his horse by daybreak and off on his rounds through the plantations and the pines enlisting his company. The office in the yard, heretofore one in name only, became one now in reality, and a table was set out piled with papers, pens, ink, books of tactics and regulation, at which men were accepted and enrolled. Soldiers seemed to spring from the ground, as they did from the sowing of the dragon's teeth in the days of Cadmus. Men came up the high road or down the paths across the fields, sometimes singly, but oftener in little parties of two or three, and, asking for the Captain, entered the office as private citizens and came out soldiers enlisted for the war. There was nothing heard of on the plantation except fighting; white and black, all were at work, and all were eager; the servants contended for the honor of going with their master; the women flocked to the house to assist in the work of preparation, cutting out and making under-clothes, knitting socks, picking lint, preparing bandages, and sewing on uniforms; for many of the men who had enlisted were of the poorest class, far too poor to furnish anything themselves, and their equipment had to be contributed mainly by wealthier neighbors. The work was carried on at night as well as by day, for the occasion was urgent. Meantime the men were being drilled by the Captain and his lieutenants, who had been militia officers of old. We were carried to see the drill at the cross-roads, and a brave sight it seemed to us: the lines marching and countermarching in the field, with the horses galloping as they wheeled amid clouds of dust, at the hoarse commands of the excited officers, and the roadside lined with spectators of every age and condition. I recall the arrival of the messenger one night, with the tele-graphic order to the Captain to report with his company at "Camp Lee" immediately; the hush in the parlor that attended its reading; then the forced beginning of the conversation afterwards in a somewhat strained and unnatural key, and the Captain's quick and decisive outlining of his plans.

Within the hour a dozen messengers were on their way in various directions to notify the members of the command of the summons, and to deliver the order for their attendance at a given point next day. It seemed that a sudden and great change had come. It was the actual appearance of what had hitherto only been theoretical—war. The next morning the Captain, in full uniform, took leave of the assembled plantation, with a few solemn words commending all he left behind to God, and galloped away up the big road to join and lead his battery to the war, and to be gone just four years.

Within a month he was on "the Peninsula" with Magruder, guarding Virginia on the east against the first attack. His camp was first at Yorktown and then on Jamestown Island, the honor having been assigned his battery of guarding the oldest cradle of the race on this continent. It was at "Little Bethel" that his guns were first trained on the enemy, and that the battery first saw what they had to do, and from this time until the middle of April, 1865, they were in service, and no battery saw more service or suffered more in it. Its story was a part of the story of the Southern Army in Virginia. The Captain was a rigid disciplinarian, and his company had more work to do than most new companies. A pious churchman, of the old puritanical type not uncommon to Virginia, he looked after the spiritual as well as the physical welfare of his men, and his chaplain or he read prayers at the head of his company every morning during the war. At first he was not popular with the men, he made the duties of camp life so onerous to them, it was "nothing but drilling and praying all the time," they said. But he had not commanded very long before they came to know the stuff that was in him. He had not been in service a year before he had had four horses shot under him, and when later on he was offered the command of a battalion, the old company petitioned to be one of his batteries, and still remained under his command. Before the first year was out the battery had, through its own elements, and the discipline of the Captain, become a cohesive force, and a distinct integer in the Army of Northern Virginia. Young farmer recruits knew of its prestige and expressed preference for it of many batteries of rapidly growing or grown reputation. Owing to its high stand, the old and clumsy guns with which it had started out were taken from it, and in their place was presented a battery of four fine, brass, twelve-pound Napoleons of the newest and most approved kind, and two three-inch Parrotts, all captured. The men were as pleased with them as children with new toys. The care and attention needed to keep them in prime order broke the monotony of camp life. They soon had abundant opportunities to test their power. They worked admirably, carried far, and were extraordinarily accurate in their aim. The men from admiration of their guns grew to have first a pride in, and then an affection for them, and gave them nicknames as they did their comrades; the four Napoleons being dubbed, "The Evangelists," and the two rifles being "The Eagle," because of its scream and force, and "The Cat," because when it became hot from rapid firing "It jumped," they said, "like a cat." From many

a hill-top in Virginia, Maryland, and Pennsylvania "The Evangelists" spoke their hoarse message of battle and death, "The Eagle" screamed her terrible note, and "The Cat" jumped as she spat her deadly shot from her hot throat. In the Valley of Virginia; on the levels of Henrico and Hanover; on the slopes of Manassas; in the woods of Chancellorsville; on the heights of Fredericksburg; at Antietam and Gettysburg; in the Spottsylvania wilderness, and again on the Hanover levels and on the lines before Petersburg, the old guns through nearly four years roared from fiery throats their deadly messages. The history of the battery was bound up with the history of Lee's army. A rivalry sprang up among the detachments of the different guns, and their several records were jealously kept. The number of duels each gun was in was carefully counted, every scar got in battle was treasured, and the men around their camp-fires, at their scanty messes, or on the march, bragged of them among themselves and avouched them as witnesses. New recruits coming in to fill the gaps made by the killed and disabled, readily fell in with the common mood and caught the spirit like a contagion. It was not an uncommon thing for a wheel to be smashed in by a shell, but if it happened to one gun oftener than to another there was envy. Two of the Evangelists seemed to be especially favored in this line, while the Cat was so exempt as to become the subject of some derision. The men stood by the guns till they were knocked to pieces, and when the fortune of the day went against them, had with their own hands oftener than once saved them after most of their horses were killed.

This had happened in turn to every gun, the men at times working like beavers in mud up to their thighs and under a murderous fire to get their guns out. Many a man had been killed tugging at trail or wheel when the day was against them; but not a gun had ever been lost. At last the evil day arrived. At Winchester a sudden and impetuous charge for a while swept everything before it, and carried the knoll where the old battery was posted; but all the guns were got out by the toiling and rapidly dropping men, except the Cat, which was captured with its entire detachment working at it until they were surrounded and knocked from the piece by cavalrymen. Most of the men who were not killed were retaken before the day was over, with many guns; but the Cat was lost. She remained in the enemy's hands and probably was being turned against her old comrades and lovers. The company was inconsolable. The death of comrades was too natural and common a thing to depress the men beyond what such occurrences necessarily did; but to lose a gun! It was like losing the old Colonel; it was worse: a gun was ranked as a brigadier; and the Cat was equal to a major-general. The other guns seemed lost without her; the Eagle especially, which generally went next to her, appeared to the men to have a lonely and subdued air. The battery was no longer the same: it seemed broken and depleted, shrunken to a mere section. It was worse than Cold Harbor, where over half the men were killed or wounded. The old Captain, now Colonel of the battalion, appreciated the loss and apprehended its effect on the men as much as they themselves did, and application was made for a gun to take the place of the lost piece; but there was none to be had, as the men said they had known all along. It was added— perhaps by a department clerk—that if they wanted a gun to take the place of the one they had lost, they had better capture it. "By——,

we will," they said—adding epithets, intended for the department clerk in his "bomb-proof," not to be printed in this record—and they did. For some time afterwards in every engagement into which they got there used to be speculation among them as to whether the Cat were not there on the other side; some of the men swearing they could tell her report, and even going to the rash length of offering bets on her presence.

By one of those curious coincidences, as strange as anything in fiction, a new general had, in 1864, come down across the Rapidan to take Richmond, and the old battery had found a hill-top in the line in which Lee's army lay stretched across "the Wilderness" country to stop him. The day, though early in May, was a hot one, and the old battery, like most others, had suffered fearfully. Two of the guns had had wheels cut down by shells and the men had been badly cut up; but the fortune of the day had been with Lee, and a little before nightfall, after a terrible fight, there was a rapid advance, Lee's infantry sweeping everything before it, and the artillery, after opening the way for the charge, pushing along with it; now unlimbering as some vantage-ground was gained, and using canister with deadly effect; now driving ahead again so rapidly that it was mixed up with the muskets when the long line of breastworks was carried with a rush, and a line of guns were caught still hot from their rapid work. As the old battery, with lathered horses and smoke-grimed men, swung up the crest and unlimbered on the captured breastwork, a cheer went up which was heard even above the long general yell of the advancing line, and for a moment half the men in the battery crowded together around some object on the edge of the redoubt, yelling like madmen. The next instant they divided, and there was the Cat, smoke-grimed and blood-stained and still sweating hot from her last fire, being dragged from her muddy ditch by as many men as could get hold of trail-rope or wheel, and rushed into her old place beside the Eagle, in time to be double-shotted with canister to the muzzle, and to pour it from among her old comrades into her now retiring former masters. Still, she had a new carriage, and her record was lost, while those of the other guns had been faithfully kept by the men. This made a difference in her position for which even the bullets in her wheels did not wholly atone; even Harris, the sergeant of her detachment, felt that.

It was only a few days later, however, that abundant atonement was made. The new general did not retire across the Rapidan after his first defeat, and a new battle had to be fought: a battle, if anything, more furious, more terrible than the first, when the dead filled the trenches and covered the fields. He simply marched by the left flank, and Lee marching by the right flank to head him, flung himself upon him again at Spottsylvania Court-House. That day the Cat, standing in her place behind the new and temporary breastwork thrown up when the battery was posted, had the felloes of her wheels, which showed above the top of the bank, entirely cut away by Minie-bullets, so that when she jumped in the recoil her wheels smashed and let her down. This covered all old scores. The other guns had been cut down by shells or solid shot; but never before had one been gnawed down by musket-balls. From this time all through the campaign the Cat held her own beside her brazen and bloody sisters, and in the cold trenches before Petersburg that winter, when the new general—Starvation—had joined the

one already there, she made her bloody mark as often as any gun on the long lines.

Thus the old battery had come to be known, as its old commander, now colonel of a battalion, had come to be known by those in yet higher command. And when in the opening spring of 1865 it became apparent to the leaders of both armies that the long line could not longer be held if a force should enter behind it, and, sweeping the one partially unswept portion of Virginia, cut the railways in the southwest, and a man was wanted to command the artillery in the expedition sent to meet this force, it was not remarkable that the old Colonel and his battalion should be selected for the work. The force sent out was but small; for the long line was worn to a thin one in those days, and great changes were taking place, the consequences of which were known only to the commanders. In a few days the commander of the expedition found that he must divide his small force for a time, at least, to accomplish his purpose, and sending the old Colonel with one battery of artillery to guard one pass, must push on over the mountain by another way to meet the expected force, if possible, and repel it before it crossed the farther range. Thus the old battery, on an April evening of 1865, found itself toiling alone up the steep mountain road which leads above the river to the gap, which formed the chief pass in that part of the Blue Ridge. Both men and horses looked, in the dim and waning light of the gray April day, rather like shadows of the beings they represented than the actual beings themselves. And anyone seeing them as they toiled painfully up, the thin horses floundering in the mud, and the men, often up to their knees, tugging at the sinking wheels, now stopping to rest, and always moving so slowly that they seemed scarcely to advance at all, might have thought them the ghosts of some old battery lost from some long gone and forgotten war on that deep and desolate mountain road. Often, when they stopped, the blowing of the horses and the murmuring of the river in its bed below were the only sounds heard, and the tired voices of the men when they spoke among themselves seemed hardly more articulate sounds than they. Then the voice of the mounted figure on the roan horse half hidden in the mist would cut in, clear and inspiring, in a tone of encouragement more than of command, and everything would wake up: the drivers would shout and crack their whips; the horses would bend themselves on the collars and flounder in the mud; the men would spring once more to the mud-clogged wheels, and the slow ascent would begin again.

The orders of the Colonel, as has been said, were brief: To hold the pass until he received further instructions, and not to lose his guns. To be ordered, with him, was to obey. The last streak of twilight brought them to the top of the pass; his soldier's instinct and a brief reconnoissance made earlier in the day told him that this was his place, and before daybreak next morning the point was as well fortified as a night's work by weary and supperless men could make it. A prettier spot could not have been found for the purpose; a small plateau, something over an acre in extent, where a charcoal-burner's hut had once stood, lay right at the top of the pass. It was a little higher on either side than in the middle, where a small brook, along which the charcoal-burner's track was yet visible, came down from the wooded mountain above, thus giving a natural crest to aid the fortification on either side, with open space for the guns, while the edge of

the wood coming down from the mountain afforded shelter for the camp.

As the battery was unsupported it had to rely on itself for everything, a condition which most soldiers by this time were accustomed to. A dozen or so of rifles were in the camp, and with these pickets were armed and posted. The pass had been seized none too soon; a scout brought in the information before nightfall that the invading force had crossed the farther range before that sent to meet it could get there, and taking the nearest road had avoided the main body opposing it, and been met only by a rapidly moving detachment, nothing more than a scouting party, and now were advancing rapidly on the road on which they were posted, evidently meaning to seize the pass and cross the mountain at this point. The day was Sunday; a beautiful Spring Sunday; but it was no Sabbath for the old battery. All day the men worked, making and strengthening their redoubt to guard the pass, and by the next morning, with the old battery at the top, it was impregnable. They were just in time. Before noon their vedettes brought in word that the enemy were ascending the mountain, and the sun had hardly turned when the advance guard rode up, came within range of the picket, and were fired on.

It was apparent that they supposed the force there only a small one, for they retired and soon came up again reinforced in some numbers, and a sharp little skirmish ensued, hot enough to make them more prudent afterwards, though the picket retired up the mountain. This gave them encouragement and probably misled them, for they now advanced boldly. They saw the redoubt on the crest as they came on, and unlimbering a section or two, flung a few shells up at it, which either fell short or passed over without doing material damage. None of the guns was allowed to respond, as the distance was too great with the ammunition the battery had, and, indifferent as it was, it was too precious to be wasted in a duel at an ineffectual range. Doubtless deceived by this, the enemy came on in force, being obliged by the character of the ground to keep almost entirely to the road, which really made them advance in column. The battery waited. Under orders of the Colonel the guns standing in line were double-shotted with canister, and, loaded to the muzzle, were trained down to sweep the road at from four to five hundred yards' distance. And when the column reached this point the six guns, aimed by old and skilful gunners, at a given word swept road and mountain-side with a storm of leaden hail. It was a fire no mortal man could stand up against, and the practiced gunners rammed their pieces full again, and before the smoke had cleared or the reverberation had died away among the mountains, had fired the guns again and yet again. The road was cleared of living things when the draught setting down the river drew the smoke away; but it was no discredit to the other force; for no army that was ever uniformed could stand against that battery in that pass. Again and again the attempt was made to get a body of men up under cover of the woods and rocks on the mountain-side, while the guns below utilized their better ammunition from longer range; but it was useless. Although one of the lieutenants and several men were killed in the skirmish, and a number more were wounded, though not severely, the old battery commanded the mountain-side, and its skilful gunners swept it at every point the foot of man could scale. The sun went down flinging his last flame on a victorious battery still crowning the mountain pass. The dead were

buried by night in a corner of the little plateau, borne to their last bivouac on the old gun-carriages which they had stood by so often—which the men said would "sort of ease their minds."

The next day the fight was renewed, and with the same result. The old battery in its position was unconquerable. Only one fear now faced them; their ammunition was getting as low as their rations; another such day or half-day would exhaust it. A sergeant was sent back down the mountain to try to get more, or, if not, to get tidings. The next day it was supposed the fight would be renewed; and the men waited, alert, eager, vigilant, their spirits high, their appetite for victory whetted by success. The men were at their breakfast, or what went for breakfast, scanty at all times, now doubly so, hardly deserving the title of a meal, so poor and small were the portions of cornmeal, cooked in their frying-pans, which went for their rations, when the sound of artillery below broke on the quiet air. They were on their feet in an instant and at the guns, crowding upon the breastwork to look or to listen; for the road, as far as could be seen down the mountain, was empty except for their own picket, and lay as quiet as if sleeping in the balmy air. And yet volley after volley of artillery came rolling up the mountain. What could it mean? That the rest of their force had come up and was engaged with that at the foot of the mountain? The Colonel decided to be ready to go and help them; to fall on the enemy in the rear; perhaps they might capture the entire force. It seemed the natural thing to do, and the guns were limbered up in an incredibly short time, and a roadway made through the intrenchment, the men working like beavers under the excitement. Before they had left the redoubt, however, the vedettes sent out returned and reported that there was no engagement going on, and the firing below seemed to be only practising. There was quite a stir in the camp below; but they had not even broken camp. This was mysterious. Perhaps it meant that they had received reinforcements, but it was a queer way of showing it. The old Colonel sighed as he thought of the good ammunition they could throw away down there, and of his empty limber-chests. It was necessary to be on the alert, however; the guns were run back into their old places, and the horses picketed once more back among the trees. Meantime he sent another messenger back, this time a courier, for he had but one commissioned officer left, and the picket below was strengthened.

The morning passed and no one came; the day wore on and still no advance was made by the force below. It was suggested that the enemy had left; he had, at least, gotten enough of that battery. A reconnoissance, however, showed that he was still encamped at the foot of the mountain. It was conjectured that he was trying to find a way around to take them in the rear, or to cross the ridge by the footpath. Preparation was made to guard more closely the mountain-path across the spur, and a detachment was sent up to strengthen the picket there. The waiting told on the men and they grew bored and restless. They gathered about the guns in groups and talked; talked of each piece some, but not with the old spirit and vim; the loneliness of the mountain seemed to oppress them; the mountains stretching up so brown and gray on one side of them, and so brown and gray on the other, with their bare, dark forests soughing from time to time as the wind swept up the pass. The minds of the men seemed to go back to the time when they were not so alone, but

were part of a great and busy army, and some of them fell to talking of the past, and the battles they had figured in, and of the comrades they had lost. They told them off in a slow and colorless way, as if it were all part of the past as much as the dead they named. One hundred and nineteen times they had been in action. Only seventeen men were left of the eighty odd who had first enlisted in the battery, and of these four were at home crippled for life. Two of the oldest men had been among the half-dozen who had fallen in the skirmish just the day before. It looked tolerably hard to be killed that way after passing for four years through such battles as they had been in; and both had wives and children at home, too, and not a cent to leave them to their names. They agreed calmly that they'd have to "sort of look after them a little" if they ever got home. These were some of the things they talked about as they pulled their old worn coats about them, stuffed their thin, weather-stained hands in their ragged pockets to warm them, and squatted down under the breastwork to keep a little out of the wind. One thing they talked about a good deal was something to eat. They described meals they had had at one time or another as personal adventures, and discussed the chances of securing others in the future as if they were prizes of fortune. One listening and seeing their thin, worn faces and their wasted frames might have supposed they were starving, and they were, but they did not say so.

Towards the middle of the afternoon there was a sudden excitement in the camp. A dozen men saw them at the same time: a squad of three men down the road at the farthest turn, past their picket, but an advancing column could not have created as much excitement, for the middle man carried a white flag. In a minute every man in the battery was on the breastwork. What could it mean! It was a long way off, nearly half a mile, and the flag was small: possibly only a pocket-handkerchief or a napkin; but it was held aloft as a flag unmistakably. A hundred conjectures were indulged in. Was it a summons to surrender? A request for an armistice for some purpose? Or was it a trick to ascertain their number and position? Some held one view, some another. Some extreme ones thought a shot ought to be fired over them to warn them not to come on; no flags of truce were wanted. The old Colonel, who had walked to the edge of the plateau outside the redoubt and taken his position where he could study the advancing figures with his field-glass, had not spoken. The lieutenant who was next in command to him had walked out after him, and stood near him, from time to time dropping a word or two of conjecture in a half-audible tone; but the Colonel had not answered a word; perhaps none was expected. Suddenly he took his glass down, and gave an order to the lieutenant: "Take two men and meet them at the turn yonder; learn their business; and act as your best judgment advises. If necessary to bring the messenger farther, bring only the officer who has the flag, and halt him at that rock yonder, where I will join him." The tone was as placid as if such an occurrence came every day. Two minutes later the lieutenant was on his way down the mountain and the Colonel had the men in ranks. His face was as grave and his manner as quiet as usual, neither more nor less so. The men were in a state of suppressed excitement. Having put them in charge of the second sergeant the Colonel returned to the breastwork. The two officers were slowly ascending the hill, side by side, the bearer of the flag, now easily distinguish-

able in his jaunty uniform as a captain of cavalry, talking, and the lieutenant in faded gray, faced with yet more faded red, walking beside him with a face white even at that distance, and lips shut as though they would never open again. They halted at the big bowlder which the Colonel had indicated, and the lieutenant, having saluted ceremoniously, turned to come up to the camp; the Colonel, however, went down to meet him. The two men met, but there was no spoken question; if the Colonel inquired it was only with the eyes. The lieutenant spoke, however. "He says," he began and stopped, then began again —"he says, General Lee—"again he choked, then blurted out, "I believe it is all a lie—a damned lie."

"Not dead? Not killed?" said the Colonel, quickly.

"No, not so bad as that; surrendered: surrendered his entire army at Appomattox day before yesterday. I believe it is all a damned lie," he broke out again, as if the hot denial relieved him. The Colonel simply turned away his face and stepped a pace or two off, and the two men stood motionless back to back for more than a minute. Then the Colonel stirred.

"Shall I go back with you?" the lieutenant asked, huskily.

The Colonel did not answer immediately. Then he said: "No, go back to camp and await my return." He said nothing about not speaking of the report. He knew it was not needed. Then he went down the hill slowly alone, while the lieutenant went up to the camp.

The interview between the two officers beside the bowlder was not a long one. It consisted of a brief statement by the Federal envoy of the fact of Lee's surrender two days before near Appomattox Court-House, with the sources of his information, coupled with a formal demand on the Colonel for his surrender. To this the Colonel replied that he had been detached and put under command of another officer for a specific purpose, and that his orders were to hold that pass, which he should do until he was instructed otherwise by his superior in command. With that they parted, ceremoniously, the Federal captain returning to where he had left his horse in charge of his companions a little below, and the old Colonel coming slowly up the hill to camp. The men were at once set to work to meet any attack which might be made. They knew that the message was of grave import, but not of how grave. They thought it meant that another attack would be made immediately, and they sprang to their work with renewed vigor, and a zeal as fresh as if it were but the beginning and not the end.

The time wore on, however, and there was no demonstration below, though hour after hour it was expected and even hoped for. Just as the sun sank into a bed of blue cloud a horseman was seen coming up the darkened mountain from the eastward side, and in a little while practised eyes reported him one of their own men—the sergeant who had been sent back the day before for ammunition. He was alone, and had something white before him on his horse—it could not be the ammunition; but perhaps that might be coming on behind. Every step of his jaded horse was anxiously watched. As he drew near, the lieutenant, after a word with the Colonel, walked down to meet him, and there was a short colloquy in the muddy road; then they came back together and slowly entered the camp, the sergeant handing down a bag of corn which he had got somewhere below, with the grim remark to his comrades, "There's your rations," and going at once to the Colonel's

camp-fire, a little to one side among the trees, where the Colonel awaited him. A long conference was held, and then the sergeant left to take his luck with his mess, who were already parching the corn he had brought for their supper, while the lieutenant made the round of the camp; leaving the Colonel seated alone on a log by his camp-fire. He sat without moving, hardly stirring until the lieutenant returned from his round. A minute later the men were called from the guns and made to fall into line. They were silent, tremulous with suppressed excitement; the most sun-burned and weather-stained of them a little pale; the meanest, raggedest, and most insignificant not unimpressive in the deep and solemn silence with which they stood, their eyes fastened on the Colonel, waiting for him to speak. He stepped out in front of them, slowly ran his eye along the irregular line, up and down, taking in every man in his glance, resting on some longer than on others, the older men, then dropped them to the ground, and then suddenly, as if with an effort, began to speak. His voice had a somewhat metallic sound, as if it were restrained; but it was otherwise the ordinary tone of command. It was not much that he said; simply that it had become his duty to acquaint them with the information which he had received: that General Lee had surrendered two days before at Appomattox Court-House, yielding to overwhelming numbers; that this afternoon when he had first heard the report he had questioned its truth, but that it had been confirmed by one of their own men, and no longer admitted of doubt; that the rest of their own force, it was learned, had been captured, or had disbanded, and the enemy was now on both sides of the mountain; that a demand had been made on him that morning to surrender too; but that he had orders which he felt held good until they were countermanded, and he had declined. Later intelligence satisfied him that to attempt to hold out further would be useless, and would involve needless waste of life; he had determined, therefore, not to attempt to hold their position longer; but to lead them out, if possible, so as to avoid being made prisoners and enable them to reach home sooner and aid their families. His orders were not to let his guns fall into the enemy's hands, and he should take the only step possible to prevent it. In fifty minutes he should call the battery into line once more, and roll the guns over the cliff into the river, and immediately afterwards, leaving the wagons there, he would try to lead them across the mountain, and as far as they could go in a body without being liable to capture, and then he should disband them, and his responsibility for them would end. As it was necessary to make some preparations he would now dismiss them to prepare any rations they might have and get ready to march.

All this was in the formal manner of a common order of the day; and the old Colonel had spoken in measured sentences, with little feeling in his voice. Not a man in the line had uttered a word after the first sound, half exclamation, half groan, which had burst from them at the announcement of Lee's surrender. After that they had stood in their tracks like rooted trees, as motionless as those on the mountain behind them, their eyes fixed on their commander, and only the quick heaving up and down the dark line, as of horses overlaboring, told of the emotion which was shaking them. The Colonel, as he ended, half-turned to his subordinate officer at the end of the dim line, as though he were about to turn the company over to him to be dismissed; then

faced the line again, and taking a step nearer, with a sudden movement of his hands towards the men as though he would have stretched them out to them, began again:

"Men," he said, and his voice changed at the word, and sounded like a father's or a brother's, "My men, I cannot let you go so. We were neighbors when the war began— many of us, and some not here to-night; we have been more since then—comrades, brothers in arms; we have all stood for one thing— for Virginia and the South; we have all done our duty—tried to do our duty; we have fought a good fight, and now it seems to be over, and we have been overwhelmed by numbers, not whipped—and we are going home. We have the future before us—we don't know just what it will bring, but we can stand a good deal. We have proved it. Upon us depends the South in the future as in the past. You have done your duty in the past, you will not fail in the future. Go home and be honest, brave, self-sacrificing, God-fearing citizens, as you have been soldiers, and you need not fear for Virginia and the South. The war may be over; but you will ever be ready to serve your country. The end may not be as we wanted it, prayed for it, fought for it; but we can trust God; the end in the end will be the best that could be; even if the South is not free she will be better and stronger that she fought as she did. Go home and bring up your children to love her, and though you may have nothing else to leave them, you can leave them the heritage that they are sons of men who were in Lee's army."

He stopped, looked up and down the ranks again, which had instinctively crowded together and drawn around him in a half-circle; made a sign to the lieutenant to take charge, and turned abruptly on his heel to walk away.

But as he did so, the long pent-up emotion burst forth. With a wild cheer the men seized him, crowding around and hugging him, as with protestations, prayers, sobs, oaths—broken, incoherent, inarticulate—they swore to be faithful, to live loyal forever to the South, to him, to Lee. Many of them cried like children; others offered to go down and have one more battle on the plain. The old Colonel soothed them, and quieted their excitement, and then gave a command about the preparations to be made. This called them to order at once; and in a few minutes the camp was as orderly and quiet as usual: the fires were replenished; the scanty stores were being overhauled; the place was selected, and being got ready to roll the guns over the cliff; the camp was being ransacked for such articles as could be carried, and all preparations were being hastily made for their march.

The old Colonel having completed his arrangements sat down by his camp-fire with paper and pencil, and began to write; and as the men finished their work they gathered about in groups, at first around their camp-fires, but shortly strolled over to where the guns still stood at the breastwork, black and vague in the darkness. Soon they were all assembled about the guns. One after another they visited, closing around it and handling it from muzzle to trail as a man might a horse to try its sinew and bone, or a child to feel its fineness and warmth. They were for the most part silent, and when any sound came through the dusk from them to the officers at their fire, it was murmurous and fitful as of men speaking low and brokenly. There was no sound of the noisy controversy which was generally heard, the give-and-take of the camp-fire, the firing backwards and forwards that went on on the march; if a compliment was

paid a gun by one of its special detachment, it was accepted by the others; in fact, those who had generally run it down now seemed most anxious to accord the piece praise. Presently a small number of the men returned to a camp-fire, and, building it up, seated themselves about it, gathering closer and closer together until they were in a little knot. One of them appeared to be writing, while two or three took up flaming chunks from the fire and held them as torches for him to see by. In time the entire company assembled about them, standing in respectful silence, broken only occasionally by a reply from one or another to some question from the scribe. After a little there was a sound of a roll-call, and reading and a short colloquy followed, and then two men, one with a paper in his hand, approached the fire beside which the officers sat still engaged.

"What is it, Harris?" said the Colonel to the man with the paper, who bore remnants of the chevrons of a sergeant on his stained and faded jacket.

"If you please, sir," he said, with a salute, "we have been talking it over, and we'd like this paper to go in along with that you're writing." He held it out to the lieutenant, who was the nearer and had reached forward to take it. "We s'pose you're agoin' to bury it with the guns," he said, hesitatingly, as he handed it over.

"What is it?" asked the Colonel, shading his eyes with his hands.

"It's just a little list we made out in and among us," he said, "with a few things we'd like to put in, so's if anyone ever hauls 'em out they'll find it there to tell what the old battery was, and if they don't, it'll be in one of 'em down thar 'til judgment, an' it'll sort of ease our minds a bit." He stopped and waited as a man who had delivered his message. The old Colonel had risen and taken the paper, and now held it with a firm grasp, as if it might blow away with the rising wind. He did not say a word, but his hand shook a little as he proceeded to fold it carefully, and there was a burning gleam in his deep-set eyes, back under his bushy, gray brows.

"Will you sort of look over it, sir, if you think it's worth while? We was in a sort of hurry and we had to put it down just as we come to it; we didn't have time to pick our ammunition; and it ain't written the best in the world, nohow." He waited again, and the Colonel opened the paper and glanced down at it mechanically. It contained first a roster, headed by the list of six guns, named by name: "Matthew," "Mark," "Luke," and "John," "The Eagle," and "The Cat"; then of the men, beginning with the heading:

"Those killed."

Then had followed "Those wounded," but this was marked out. Then came a roster of the company when it first entered service; then of those who had joined afterward; then of those who were present now. At the end of all there was this statement, not very well written, nor wholly accurately spelt:

"To Whom it may Concern: We, the above members of the old battery known, etc., of six guns, named, etc., commanded by the said Col. etc., left on the 11th day of April, 1865, have made out this roll of the battery, them as is gone and them as is left, to bury with the guns which the same we bury this night. We're all volunteers, every man; we joined the army at the beginning of the war, and we've stuck through to the end; sometimes we aint had much to eat, and sometimes we aint had nothin', but we've fought the best we could 119 battles and skirmishes as near as we can make out in four years, and never lost a gun. Now we're agoin' home. We aint surrendered; just disbanded, and we pledges ourselves to teach our children to love the South and General Lee; and to come when we're called anywheres an' anytime, so help us God."

There was a dead silence whilst the Colonel read.

" 'Taint entirely accurite, sir, in one particular," said the sergeant, apologetically; "but we thought it would be playin' it sort o' low down on the Cat if we was to say we lost her unless we could tell about gittin' of her back, and the way she done since, and we didn't have time to do all that." He looked around as if to receive the corroboration of the other men, which they signified by nods and shuffling.

The Colonel said it was all right, and the paper should go into the guns.

"If you please, sir, the guns are all loaded," said the sergeant; "in and about our last charge, too; and we'd like to fire 'em off once more, jist for old times' sake to remember 'em by, if you don't think no harm could come of it?"

The Colonel reflected a moment and said it might be done; they might fire each gun separately as they rolled it over, or might get all ready and fire together, and then roll them over, whichever they wished. This was satisfactory.

The men were then ordered to prepare to march immediately, and withdrew for the purpose. The pickets were called in. In a short time they were ready, horses and all, just as they would have been to march ordinarily, except that the wagons and caissons were packed over in one corner by the camp with the harness hung on poles beside them, and the guns stood in their old places at the breastwork ready to defend the pass. The embers of the sinking campfires threw a faint light on them standing so still and silent. The old Colonel took his place, and at a command from him in a somewhat low voice, the men, except a detail left to hold the horses, moved into company-front facing the guns. Not a word was spoken, except the words of command. At the order each detachment went to its gun; the guns were run back and the men with their own hands ran them up on the edge of the perpendicular bluff above the river, where, sheer below, its waters washed its base, as if to face an enemy on the black mountain the other side. The pieces stood ranged in the order in which they had so often stood in battle, and the gray, thin fog rising slowly and silently from the river deep down between the cliffs, and wreathing the mountain-side above, might have been the smoke from some unearthly battle fought in the dim pass by ghostly guns, yet posted there in the darkness, manned by phantom gunners, while phantom horses stood behind, lit vaguely up by phantom camp-fires. At the given word the laniards were pulled together, and together as one the six black guns, belching flame and lead, roared their last challenge on the misty night, sending a deadly hail of shot and shell, tearing the trees and splintering the rocks of the farther side, and sending the thunder reverberating through the pass and down the mountain, startling from its slumber the sleeping camp on the hills below, and driving the browsing deer and the prowling mountain-fox in terror up the mountain.

There was silence among the men about the guns for one brief instant and then such a cheer burst forth as had never broken from them even in battle: cheer on cheer, the long, wild, old familiar rebel yell for the guns they had fought with and loved.

The noise had not died away and the men behind were still trying to quiet the frightened horses when the sergeant, the same who had written, received from the hand of the Colonel a long package or roll which contained the records of the battery furnished by the men and by the Colonel himself, securely wrapped to make them water-tight, and it was rammed down the yet warm throat of the nearest gun: the Cat, and then the gun was tamped to the muzzle to make her water-tight, and, like her sisters, was spiked, and her vent tamped tight. All this took but a minute, and the next instant the guns were run up once more to the edge of the cliff; and the men stood by them with their hands still on them. A deadly silence fell on the men, and even the horses behind seemed to feel the spell. There was a long pause, in which not a breath was heard from any man, and the soughing of the tree-tops above and the rushing of the rapids below were the only sounds. They seemed to come from far, very far away. Then the Colonel said, quietly, "Let them go, and God be our helper, Amen." There was the noise in the darkness of trampling and scraping on the cliff-top for a second; the sound as of men straining hard together, and then with a pant it ceased all at once, and the men held their breath to hear. One second of utter silence; then one prolonged, deep, resounding splash sending up a great mass of white foam as the brass-pieces together plunged into the dark water below, and then the soughing of the trees and the murmur of the river came again with painful distinctness. It was full ten minutes before the Colonel spoke, though there were other sounds enough in the darkness, and some of the men, as the dark, outstretched bodies showed, were lying on the ground flat on their faces. Then the Colonel gave the command to fall in in the same quiet, grave tone he had used all night. The line fell in, the men getting to their horses and mounting in silence; the Colonel put himself at their head and gave the order of march, and the dark line turned in the darkness, crossed the little plateau between the smouldering camp-fires and the spectral caissons with the harness hanging beside them, and slowly entered the dim charcoal-burner's track. Not a word was spoken as they moved off. They might all have been phantoms. Only, the sergeant in the rear, as he crossed the little breastwork which ran along the upper side and marked the boundary of the little camp, half turned and glanced at the dying fires, the low, newly made mounds in the corner, the abandoned caissons, and the empty redoubt, and said, slowly, in a low voice to himself,

"Well, by God!"

---

from The Little Regiment

WILFRED OWEN ONCE WROTE A PREFACE TO A BOOK THAT HE DID NOT LIVE LONG ENOUGH to prepare for publication: "This book is not about heroes. . . . Nor is it about deeds, or lands, nor anything about glory, honour, might, majesty, dominion, or power, except war." So it is with *The Red Badge of Courage* (1895)—a book about war, the Civil War. The novel is purely dedicated to the artistic reproduction of war, of man in war, of the horror and the beauty, the sacrifice and the triumph, the supreme test of mind and spirit in combat. Crane shows an individual's growth to maturity in war, moving from isolation to comradeship along with the regiment which also becomes battle-hardened.

Unlike Tolstoy, his only rival as a war novelist, Crane did not attempt an epic. There is neither history nor a view of society in his novel—only war and its impact upon the sensitive hero. As in all truly great fiction, the subject, here the Civil War, becomes a metaphor for life. *The Red Badge of Courage* has been called realistic, naturalistic, impressionistic, mythic, controlled. It is all these and something more. It is alive because it deals with basic verities, with the pain and triumph of a youth trapped in a world he never made.

How did Stephen Crane (1871–1900), who was not even born until six years after the war ended, understand the details and emotions of battle? Critics have bandied this question about for years. They have suggested influences such as Tolstoy, Zola, Stendhal, De Forest, Bierce, Whitman, Brady's photographs, *Battles and Leaders of the Civil War*. Crane himself denied any source and told Hamlin Garland that he learned all about the Civil War on the football field. Whatever the truth, somehow war and its meaning were revealed to the twenty-four year old author.

Crane's later career indicates that he felt a certain sense of guilty responsibility for writing knowingly about the war he had never seen. The incredibly precocious journalist, novelist, and poet ruined his health following wars to Greece and Cuba to test whether his vision of the Civil War had been correct. The vision had been. Crane died at the age of twenty-nine, the friend and associate of Conrad, James, and Ford. Among his works he left one great novel, some superb poems, and some of the best of American short stories—most notably "The Open Boat" and "The Blue Hotel."

Of the stories taken from *The Little Regiment* (1896), two, "A Gray Sleeve" and the title story, show Crane's attempt at the traditional popular and sentimental manner. Even so, his realistic bias enables him to bring forth the feel of battle. "A Mystery of Heroism" is a great war story. Crane studies the enigmatic quality of courage in battle, the irony of the gratuitous act. This short piece includes most of the effects used in the novel—impressionism, detailed realism, the emotion of fear, and the bitter triumph of the lone hero over a mechanistic universe. "The Veteran" shows the hero of *The Red Badge of Courage* as an old man. The tale indicates the influence the Civil War could have on the lives of those who served in the army during their impressionable youths.

A Gray Sleeve

I

"IT LOOKS AS IF IT MIGHT RAIN THIS AFTER-noon," remarked the lieutenant of artillery.

"So it does," the infantry captain assented. He glanced casually at the sky. When his eyes had lowered to the green-shadowed landscape before him, he said fretfully: "I wish those fellows out yonder would quit pelting at us. They've been at it since noon."

At the edge of a grove of maples, across wide fields, there occasionally appeared little puffs of smoke of a dull hue in this gloom of sky which expressed an impending rain. The long wave of blue and steel in the field moved uneasily at the eternal barking of the far-away sharpshooters, and the men, leaning upon their rifles, stared at the grove of maples. Once a private turned to borrow some tobacco from a comrade in the rear rank, but, with his hand still stretched out, he continued to twist his head and glance at the distant trees. He was afraid the enemy would shoot him at a time when he was not looking.

Suddenly the artillery officer said, "See what's coming!"

Along the rear of the brigade of infantry a column of cavalry was sweeping at a hard gal-lop. A lieutenant, riding some yards to the right of the column, bawled furiously at the four troopers just at the rear of the colours. They had lost distance and made a little gap, but at the shouts of the lieutenant they urged their horses forward. The bugler, careering along behind the captain of the troop, fought and tugged like a wrestler to keep his frantic animal from bolting far ahead of the column.

On the springy turf the innumerable hoofs thundered in a swift storm of sound. In the brown faces of the troopers their eyes were set like bits of flashing steel.

The long line of the infantry regiments standing at ease underwent a sudden movement at the rush of the passing squadron. The foot soldiers turned their heads to gaze at the torrent of horses and men.

The yellow folds of the flag fluttered back in silken, shuddering waves as if it were a reluctant thing. Occasionally a giant spring of a charger would rear the firm and sturdy figure of a soldier suddenly head and shoulders above his comrades. Over the noise of the scudding hoofs could be heard the creaking of leather trappings, the jingle and clank of steel, and the tense, low-toned commands or appeals of the men to their horses. And the horses were mad with the headlong sweep of this movement. Powerful under jaws bent back and straightened so that the bits were clamped as rigidly as vices upon the teeth, and glistening necks arched in desperate resistance to the hands at the bridles. Swinging their heads in rage at the granite laws of their lives, which compelled even their angers and their ardours to chosen directions and chosen faces, their flight was as a flight of harnessed demons.

The captain's bay kept its pace at the head of the squadron with the lithe bounds of a thoroughbred, and this horse was proud as a chief at the roaring trample of his fellows behind him. The captain's glance was calmly upon the grove of maples whence the sharpshooters of the enemy had been picking at the blue line. He seemed to be reflecting. He stolidly rose and fell with the plunges of his horse in all the indifference of a deacon's figure seated plumply in church. And it occurred to many of the watching infantry to wonder why this officer could remain imperturbable and reflective when his squadron was thundering and swarming behind him like the rushing of a flood.

The column swung in a sabre-curve toward a break in the fence, and dashed into a roadway. Once a little plank bridge was encountered, and the sound of the hoofs upon it was like the long roll of many drums. An old captain in the infantry turned to his first lieutenant and made a remark which was a compound of bitter disparagement of cavalry in general and soldierly admiration of this particular troop.

Suddenly the bugle sounded, and the column halted with a jolting upheaval amid sharp, brief cries. A moment later the men had tumbled from their horses, and, carbines in hand, were running in a swarm toward the grove of maples. In the road one of every four

of the troopers was standing with braced legs, and pulling and hauling at the bridles of four frenzied horses.

The captain was running awkwardly in his boots. He held his sabre low so that the point often threatened to catch in the turf. His yellow hair ruffled out from under his faded cap. "Go in hard now!" he roared, in a voice of hoarse fury. His face was violently red.

The troopers threw themselves upon the grove like wolves upon a great animal. Along the whole front of woods there was the dry, crackling of musketry, with bitter, swift flashes and smoke that writhed like stung phantoms. The troopers yelled shrilly and spanged bullets low into the foliage.

For a moment, when near the woods, the line almost halted. The men struggled and fought for a time like swimmers encountering a powerful current. Then with a supreme effort they went on again. They dashed madly at the grove, whose foliage from the high light of the field was as inscrutable as a wall.

Then suddenly each detail of the calm trees became apparent, and with a few more frantic leaps the men were in the cool gloom of the woods. There was a heavy odour as from burned paper. Wisps of gray smoke wound upward. The men halted and, grimy, perspiring, and puffing, they searched the recesses of the woods with eager, fierce glances. Figures could be seen flitting afar off. A dozen carbines rattled at them in an angry volley.

During this pause the captain strode along the line, his face lit with a broad smile of contentment. "When he sends this crowd to do anything, I guess he'll find we do it pretty sharp," he said to the grinning lieutenant.

"Say, they didn't stand that rush a minute, did they?" said the subaltern. Both officers were profoundly dusty in their uniforms, and their faces were soiled like those of two urchins.

Out in the grass behind them were three tumbled and silent forms.

Presently the line moved forward again. The men went from tree to tree like hunters stalking game. Some at the left of the line fired occasionally, and those at the right gazed curiously in that direction. The men still breathed heavily from their scramble across the field.

Of a sudden a trooper halted and said: "Hello! there's a house!" Every one paused. The men turned to look at their leader.

The captain stretched his neck and swung his head from side to side. "By George, it is a house!" he said.

Through the wealth of leaves there vaguely loomed the form of a large, white house. These troopers, brown-faced from many days of campaigning, each feature of them telling of their placid confidence and courage, were stopped abruptly by the appearance of this house. There was some subtle suggestion— some tale of an unknown thing—which watched them from they knew not what part of it.

A rail fence girded a wide lawn of tangled grass. Seven pines stood along a driveway which led from two distant posts of a vanished gate. The blue-clothed troopers moved forward until they stood at the fence peering over it.

The captain put one hand on the top rail and seemed to be about to climb the fence, when suddenly he hesitated, and said in a low voice, "Watson, what do you think of it?"

The lieutenant stared at the house. "Derned if I know!" he replied.

The captain pondered. It happened that the whole company had turned a gaze of profound awe and doubt upon this edifice which confronted them. The men were very silent.

At last the captain swore and said: "We are certainly a pack of fools. Derned old deserted house halting a company of Union cavalry, and making us gape like babies!"

"Yes, but there's something—something —" insisted the subaltern in a half stammer.

"Well, if there's 'something—something' in there, I'll get it out," said the captain. "Send Sharpe clean around to the other side with about twelve men, so we will sure bag your 'something—something,' and I'll take a few of the boys and find out what's in the d——d old thing!"

He chose the nearest eight men for his "storming party," as the lieutenant called it. After he had waited some minutes for the others to get into position, he said "Come ahead" to his eight men, and climbed the fence.

The brighter light of the tangled lawn made him suddenly feel tremendously apparent, and he wondered if there could be some mystic thing in the house which was regarding this approach. His men trudged silently at his back. They stared at the windows and lost themselves in deep speculations as to the probability of there being, perhaps, eyes behind the blinds—malignant eyes, piercing eyes.

Suddenly a corporal in the party gave vent to a startled exclamation, and threw his carbine into position. The captain turned quickly, and the corporal said: "I saw an arm move the blinds. An arm with a gray sleeve!"

"Don't be a fool, Jones, now!" said the captain sharply.

"I swear t'——" began the corporal, but the captain silenced him.

When they arrived at the front of the house, the troopers paused, while the captain went softly up the front steps. He stood before the large front door and studied it. Some crickets chirped in the long grass, and the nearest pine could be heard in its endless sighs. One of the privates moved uneasily, and his foot crunched the gravel. Suddenly the captain swore angrily and kicked the door with a loud crash. It flew open.

II

The bright lights of the day flashed into the old house when the captain angrily kicked open the door. He was aware of a wide hallway carpeted with matting and extending deep into the dwelling. There was also an old walnut hatrack and a little marble-topped table with a vase and two books upon it. Farther back was a great, venerable fireplace containing dreary ashes.

But directly in front of the captain was a young girl. The flying open of the door had obviously been an utter astonishment to her, and she remained transfixed there in the middle of the floor, staring at the captain with wide eyes.

She was like a child caught at the time of a raid upon the cake. She wavered to and fro upon her feet, and held her hands behind her. There were two little points of terror in her eyes, as she gazed up at the young captain in dusty blue, with his reddish, bronze complexion, his yellow hair, his bright sabre held threateningly.

These two remained motionless and silent, simply staring at each other for some moments.

The captain felt his rage fade out of him and leave his mind limp. He had been violently angry, because this house had made him feel hesitant, wary. He did not like to be wary.

He liked to feel confident, sure. So he had kicked the door open, and had been prepared to march in like a soldier of wrath.

But now he began, for one thing, to wonder if his uniform was so dusty and old in appearance. Moreover, he had a feeling that his face was covered with a compound of dust, grime, and perspiration. He took a step forward and said, "I didn't mean to frighten you." But his voice was coarse from his battle-howling. It seemed to him to have hempen fibres in it.

The girl's breath came in little, quick gasps, and she looked at him as she would have looked at a serpent.

"I didn't mean to frighten you," he said again.

The girl, still with her hands behind her, began to back away.

"Is there anyone else in the house?" he went on, while slowly following her. "I don't wish to disturb you, but we had a fight with some rebel skirmishers in the woods, and I thought maybe some of them might have come in here. In fact, I was pretty sure of it. Are there any of them here?"

The girl looked at him and said, "No!" He wondered why extreme agitation made the eyes of some women so limpid and bright.

"Who is here besides yourself?"

By this time his pursuit had driven her to the end of the hall, and she remained there with her back to the wall and her hands still behind her. When she answered this question, she did not look at him but down at the floor. She cleared her voice and then said, "There is no one here."

"No one?"

She lifted her eyes to him in that appeal that the human being must make even to falling trees, crashing boulders, the sea in a storm, and said, "No, no, there is no one here." He could plainly see her tremble.

Of a sudden he bethought him that she continually kept her hands behind her. As he recalled her air when first discovered, he remembered she appeared precisely as a child detected at one of the crimes of childhood. Moreover, she had always backed away from him. He thought now that she was concealing something which was an evidence of the presence of the enemy in the house.

"What are you holding behind you?" he said suddenly.

She gave a quick little moan, as if some grim hand had throttled her.

"What are you holding behind you?"

"Oh, nothing—please. I am not holding anything behind me; indeed I'm not."

"Very well, hold your hands out in front of you, then."

"Oh, indeed, I'm not holding anything behind me. Indeed, I'm not."

"Well," he began. Then he paused, and remained for a moment dubious. Finally, he laughed. "Well, I shall have my men search the house, anyhow. I'm sorry to trouble you, but I feel sure that there is some one here whom we want." He turned to the corporal, who with the other men was gaping quietly in at the door, and said, "Jones, go through the house."

As for himself, he remained planted in front of the girl, for she evidently did not dare to move and allow him to see what she held so carefully behind her back. So she was his prisoner.

The men rummaged around in the ground floor of the house. Sometimes the captain called to them, "Try that closet," "Is there any cellar?" But they found no one, and at last

they went trooping toward the stairs which led to the second floor.

But at this movement on the part of the men the girl uttered a cry—a cry of such fright and appeal that the men paused. "Oh, don't go up there! Please don't go up there!—ple-ease! There is no one there! Indeed—indeed there is not! Oh, ple-ease!"

"Go on, Jones," said the captain calmly.

The obedient corporal made a preliminary step, and the girl bounded toward the stairs with another cry.

As she passed him, the captain caught sight of that which she had concealed behind her back, and which she had forgotten in this supreme moment. It was a pistol.

She ran to the first step, and standing there, faced the men, one hand extended with perpendicular palm, and the other holding the pistol at her side. "Oh, please, don't go up there! Nobody is there—indeed, there is not! P-l-e-a-s-e!" Then suddenly she sank swiftly down upon the step, and, huddling forlornly, began to weep in the agony and with the convulsive tremors of an infant. The pistol fell from her fingers and rattled down to the floor.

The astonished troopers looked at their astonished captain. There was a short silence.

Finally, the captain stooped and picked up the pistol. It was a heavy weapon of the army pattern. He ascertained that it was empty.

He leaned toward the shaking girl, and said gently, "Will you tell me what you were going to do with the pistol?"

He had to repeat the question a number of times, but at last a muffled voice said, "Nothing."

"Nothing!" He insisted quietly upon a further answer. At the tender tones of the captain's voice, the phlegmatic corporal turned and winked gravely at the man next to him.

"Won't you tell me?"

The girl shook her head.

"Please tell me!"

The silent privates were moving their feet uneasily and wondering how long they were to wait.

The captain said, "Please won't you tell me?"

Then this girl's voice began in stricken tones half coherent, and amid violent sobbing: "It was grandpa's. He—he—he said he was going to shoot anybody who came in here— he didn't care if there were thousands of 'em. And—and I know he would, and I was afraid they'd kill him. And so—and—so I stole away his pistol—and I was going to hide it when you—you—you kicked open the door."

The men straightened up and looked at each other. The girl began to weep again.

The captain mopped his brow. He peered down at the girl. He mopped his brow again. Suddenly he said, "Ah, don't cry like that."

He moved restlessly and looked down at his boots. He mopped his brow again.

Then he gripped the corporal by the arm and dragged him some yards back from the others. "Jones," he said, in an intensely earnest voice, "will you tell me what in the devil I am going to do?"

The corporal's countenance became illuminated with satisfaction at being thus requested to advise a superior officer. He adopted an air of great thought, and finally said: "Well, of course, the feller with the gray sleeve must be upstairs, and we must get past the girl and up there somehow. Suppose I take her by the arm and lead her—"

"What!" interrupted the captain from between his clenched teeth. As he turned away from the corporal, he said fiercely over his shoulder, "You touch that girl and I'll split your skull!"

III

The corporal looked after his captain with an expression of mingled amazement, grief, and philosophy. He seemed to be saying to himself that there unfortunately were times, after all, when one could not rely upon the most reliable of men. When he returned to the group he found the captain bending over the girl and saying, "Why is it that you don't want us to search upstairs?"

The girl's head was buried in her crossed arms. Locks of her hair had escaped from their fastenings and these fell upon her shoulders.

"Won't you tell me?"

The corporal here winked again at the man next to him.

"Because," the girl moaned—"because— there isn't anybody up there."

The captain at last said timidly, "Well, I'm afraid—I'm afraid we'll have to—"

The girl sprang to her feet again, and implored him with her hands. She looked deep into his eyes with her glance, which was at this time like that of the fawn when it says to the hunter, "Have mercy upon me!"

These two stood regarding each other. The captain's foot was on the bottom step, but he seemed to be shrinking. He wore an air of being deeply wretched and ashamed. There was a silence.

Suddenly the corporal said in a quick, low tone, "Look out, captain!"

All turned their eyes swiftly toward the head of the stairs. There had appeared there a youth in a gray uniform. He stood looking coolly down at them. No word was said by the troopers. The girl gave vent to a little wail of desolation, "O Harry!"

He began slowly to descend the stairs. His right arm was in a white sling, and there were some fresh blood stains upon the cloth. His face was rigid and deathly pale, but his eyes flashed like lights. The girl was again moaning in an utterly dreary fashion, as the youth came slowly down toward the silent men in blue.

Six steps from the bottom of the flight he halted and said, "I reckon it's me you're looking for."

The troopers had crowded forward a trifle and, posed in lithe, nervous attitudes, were watching him like cats. The captain remained unmoved. At the youth's question he merely nodded his head and said, "Yes."

The young man in gray looked down at the girl, and then, in the same even tone which now, however, seemed to vibrate with suppressed fury, he said, "And is that any reason why you should insult my sister?"

At this sentence, the girl intervened, desperately, between the young man in gray and the officer in blue. "Oh, don't, Harry, don't! He was good to me! He was good to me, Harry—indeed he was!"

The youth came on in his quiet, erect fashion until the girl could have touched either of the men with her hand, for the captain still remained with his foot upon the first step. She continually repeated: "O Harry! O Harry!"

The youth in gray manoeuvred to glare into the captain's face, first over one shoulder of the girl and then over the other. In a voice that rang like metal, he said: "You are armed and unwounded, while I have no weapons and am wounded; but—"

The captain had stepped back and sheathed his sabre. The eyes of these two men were gleaming fire, but otherwise the captain's countenance was imperturbable. He said: "You are mistaken. You have no reason to—"

"You lie!"

All save the captain and the youth in gray started in an electric movement. These two words crackled in the air like shattered glass. There was a breathless silence.

The captain cleared his throat. His look at the youth contained a quality of singular and terrible ferocity, but he said in his stolid tone, "I don't suppose you mean what you say now."

Upon his arm he had felt the pressure of some unconscious little fingers. The girl was leaning against the wall as if she no longer knew how to keep her balance, but those fingers—he held his arm very still. She murmured, "O Harry, don't! He was good to me—indeed he was!"

The corporal had come forward until he in a measure confronted the youth in gray, for he saw those fingers upon the captain's arm, and he knew that sometimes very strong men were not able to move hand nor foot under such conditions.

The youth had suddenly seemed to become weak. He breathed heavily and clung to the rail. He was glaring at the captain, and apparently summoning all his will power to combat his weakness. The corporal addressed him with profound straightforwardness, "Don't you be a derned fool!" The youth turned toward him so fiercely that the corporal threw up a knee and an elbow like a boy who expects to be cuffed.

The girl pleaded with the captain. "You won't hurt him, will you? He don't know what he's saying. He's wounded, you know. Please don't mind him!"

"I won't touch him," said the captain, with rather extraordinary earnestness; "don't you worry about him at all. I won't touch him!"

Then he looked at her, and the girl suddenly withdrew her fingers from his arm.

The corporal contemplated the top of the stairs, and remarked without surprise, "There's another of 'em coming!"

An old man was clambering down the stairs with much speed. He waved a cane wildly. "Get out of my house, you thieves! Get out! I won't have you cross my threshold! Get out!" He mumbled and wagged his head in an old man's fury. It was plainly his intention to assault them.

And so it occurred that a young girl became engaged in protecting a stalwart captain, fully armed, and with eight grim troopers at his back, from the attack of an old man with a walking-stick!

A blush passed over the temples and brow of the captain, and he looked particularly savage and weary. Despite the girl's efforts, he suddenly faced the old man.

"Look here," he said distinctly, "we came in because we had been fighting in the woods yonder, and we concluded that some of the enemy were in this house, especially when we saw a gray sleeve at the window. But this young man is wounded, and I have nothing to say to him. I will even take it for granted that there are no others like him upstairs. We will go away, leaving your d——d old house just as we found it! And we are no more thieves and rascals than you are!"

The old man simply roared: "I haven't got a cow nor a pig nor a chicken on the place! Your soldiers have stolen everything they could carry away. They have torn down half my fences for firewood. This afternoon some of your accursed bullets even broke my window panes!"

The girl had been faltering: "Grandpa! O Grandpa!"

The captain looked at the girl. She returned his glance from the shadow of the old man's shoulder. After studying her face a moment, he said, "Well, we will go now." He strode toward the door and his men clanked docilely after him.

At this time there was the sound of harsh cries and rushing footsteps from without. The door flew open, and a whirlwind composed of blue-coated troopers came in with a swoop. It was headed by the lieutenant. "Oh, here you are!" he cried, catching his breath. "We thought—Oh, look at the girl!"

The captain said intensely, "Shut up, you fool!"

The men settled to a halt with a clash and a bang. There could be heard the dulled sound of many hoofs outside the house.

"Did you order up the horses?" inquired the captain.

"Yes. We thought—"

"Well, then, let's get out of here," interrupted the captain morosely.

The men began to filter out into the open air. The youth in gray had been hanging dismally to the railing of the stairway. He now was climbing slowly up to the second floor. The old man was addressing himself directly to the serene corporal.

"Not a chicken on the place!" he cried.

"Well, I didn't take your chickens, did I?"

"No, maybe you didn't, but——"

The captain crossed the hall and stood before the girl in rather a culprit's fashion. "You are not angry at me, are you?" he asked timidly.

"No," she said. She hesitated a moment, and then suddenly held out her hand. "You were good to me—and I'm—much obliged."

The captain took her hand, and then he blushed, for he found himself unable to formulate a sentence that applied in any way to the situation.

She did not seem to heed that hand for a time.

He loosened his grasp presently, for he was ashamed to hold it so long without saying anything clever. At last, with an air of charging an entrenched brigade, he contrived to say, "I would rather do anything than frighten or trouble you."

His brow was warmly perspiring. He had a sense of being hideous in his dusty uniform and with his grimy face.

She said, "Oh, I'm so glad it was you instead of somebody who might have—might have hurt brother Harry and grandpa!"

He told her, "I wouldn't have hurt 'em for anything!"

There was a little silence.

"Well, good-bye!" he said at last.

"Good-bye!"

He walked toward the door past the old man, who was scolding at the vanishing figure of the corporal. The captain looked back. She had remained there watching him.

At the bugle's order, the troopers standing beside their horses swung briskly into the saddle. The lieutenant said to the first sergeant:

"Williams, did they ever meet before?"

"Hanged if I know!"

"Well, say—"

The captain saw a curtain move at one of the windows. He cantered from his position at the head of the column and steered his horse between two flower beds.

"Well, good-bye!"

The squadron trampled slowly past.

"Good-bye!"

They shook hands.

He evidently had something enormously important to say to her, but it seems that he could not manage it. He struggled heroically. The bay charger, with his great mystically solemn eyes, looked around the corner of his shoulder at the girl.

The captain studied a pine tree. The girl inspected the grass beneath the window. The captain said hoarsely, "I don't suppose—I don't suppose—I'll ever see you again!"

She looked at him affrightedly and shrank back from the window. He seemed to have woefully expected a reception of this kind for his question. He gave her instantly a glance of appeal.

She said, "Why, no, I don't suppose we will."

"Never?"

"Why, no, 'tain't possible. You—you are a —Yankee!"

"Oh, I know it, but—" Eventually he continued, "Well, some day, you know, when there's no more fighting, we might—" He observed that she had again withdrawn suddenly into the shadow, so he said, "Well, good-bye!"

When he held her fingers she bowed her head, and he saw a pink blush steal over the curves of her cheek and neck.

"Am I never going to see you again?"

She made no reply.

"Never?" he repeated.

After a long time, he bent over to hear a faint reply: "Sometimes—when there are no troops in the neighbourhood—grandpa don't mind if I—walk over as far as that old oak tree yonder—in the afternoons."

It appeared that the captain's grip was very strong, for she uttered an exclamation and looked at her fingers as if she expected to find them mere fragments. He rode away.

The bay horse leaped a flower bed. They were almost to the drive, when the girl uttered a panic-stricken cry.

The captain wheeled his horse violently and upon his return journey went straight through a flower bed.

The girl had clasped her hands. She beseeched him wildly with her eyes. "Oh, please, don't believe it! I never walk to the old oak tree. Indeed, I don't! I never—never—never walk there."

The bridle drooped on the bay charger's neck. The captain's figure seemed limp. With an expression of profound dejection and gloom he stared off at where the leaden sky met the dark green line of the woods. The long-impending rain began to fall with a mournful patter, drop and drop. There was a silence.

At last a low voice said, "Well—I might—sometimes I might—perhaps—but only once in a great while—I might walk to the old tree—in the afternoons."

The Little Regiment

I

The fog made the clothes of the men of the column in the roadway seem of a luminous quality. It imparted to the heavy infantry overcoats a new colour, a kind of blue which was so pale that a regiment might have been merely a long, low shadow in the mist. However, a muttering, one part grumble, three parts joke, hovered in the air above the thick ranks, and blended in an undertoned roar, which was the voice of the column.

The town on the southern shore of the little river loomed spectrally, a faint etching upon the gray cloud-masses which were shifting with oily languor. A long row of guns upon the northern bank had been pitiless in their hatred, but a little battered belfry could be dimly seen still pointing with invincible resolution toward the heavens.

The enclouded air vibrated with noises made by hidden colossal things. The infantry tramplings, the heavy rumbling of the artillery, made the earth speak of gigantic preparation. Guns on distant heights thundered from time to time with sudden, nervous roar, as if unable to endure in silence a knowledge of hostile troops massing, other guns going to position. These sounds, near and remote, defined an immense battleground, described the tremendous width of the stage of the prospective drama. The voices of the guns, slightly casual, unexcited in their challenges and warnings, could not destroy the unutterable eloquence of the word in the air, a meaning of impending struggle which made the breath halt at the lips.

The column in the roadway was ankle-deep in mud. The men swore piously at the rain which drizzled upon them, compelling them to stand always very erect in fear of the drops that would sweep in under their coat-collars. The fog was as cold as wet cloths. The men stuffed their hands deep in their pockets, and huddled their muskets in their arms. The machinery of orders had rooted these soldiers deeply into the mud precisely as almighty nature roots mullein stalks.

They listened and speculated when a tumult of fighting came from the dim town across the river. When the noise lulled for a time they resumed their descriptions of the mud and graphically exaggerated the number of hours they had been kept waiting. The general commanding their division rode along the ranks, and they cheered admiringly, affectionately, crying out to him gleeful prophecies of the coming battle. Each man scanned him with a peculiarly keen personal interest, and afterward spoke of him with unquestioning devotion and confidence, narrating anecdotes which were mainly untrue.

When the jokers lifted the shrill voices which invariably belonged to them, flinging witticisms at their comrades, a loud laugh would sweep from rank to rank, and soldiers who had not heard would lean forward and demand repetition. When were borne past them some wounded men with gray and blood-smeared faces, and eyes that rolled in that helpless beseeching for assistance from the sky which comes with supreme pain, the soldiers in the mud watched intently, and from time to time asked of the bearers an account of the affair. Frequently they bragged of their corps, their division, their brigade, their regiment. Anon they referred to the mud and the cold drizzle. Upon this threshold of a wild scene of death they, in short, defied the proportion of events with that splendour of heedlessness which belongs only to veterans.

"Like a lot of wooden soldiers," swore Billie Dempster, moving his feet in the thick mass, and casting a vindictive glance indefinitely; "standing in the mud for a hundred years."

"Oh, shut up!" murmured his brother Dan. The manner of his words implied that this fraternal voice near him was an indescribable bore.

"Why should I shut up?" demanded Billie.

"Because you're a fool," cried Dan, taking no time to debate it; "the biggest fool in the regiment."

There was but one man between them, and he was habituated. These insults from brother to brother had swept across his chest, flown past his face, many times during two long campaigns. Upon this occasion he simply grinned first at one, then at the other.

The way of these brothers was not an unknown topic in regimental gossip. They had enlisted simultaneously, with each sneering loudly at the other for doing it. They left their little town, and went forward with the flag, exchanging protestations of undying suspicion. In the camp life they so openly despised each other that, when entertaining quarrels were lacking, their companions often contrived situations calculated to bring forth display of this fraternal dislike.

Both were large-limbed, strong young men, and often fought with friends in camp unless one was near to interfere with the other. This latter happened rather frequently, because Dan, preposterously willing for any manner of combat, had a very great horror of seeing Billie in a fight; and Billie, almost odiously ready himself, simply refused to see Dan stripped to his shirt and with his fists aloft. This sat queerly upon them, and made them the objects of plots.

When Dan jumped through a ring of eager soldiers and dragged forth his raving brother by the arm, a thing often predicted would almost come to pass. When Billie performed the same office for Dan, the prediction would again miss fulfillment by an inch. But indeed they never fought together, although they were perpetually upon the verge.

They expressed longing for such conflict. As a matter of truth, they had at one time made full arrangement for it, but even with the encouragement and interest of half of the regiment they somehow failed to achieve collision.

If Dan became a victim of police duty, no jeering was so destructive to the feelings as Billie's comment. If Billie got a call to appear at the headquarters, none would so genially prophesy his complete undoing as Dan. Small misfortunes to one were, in truth, invariably greeted with hilarity by the other, who seemed to see in them great re-enforcement of his opinion.

As soldiers, they expressed each for each a scorn intense and blasting. After a certain battle, Billie was promoted to corporal. When Dan was told of it, he seemed smitten dumb with astonishment and patriotic indignation. He stared in silence, while the dark blood rushed to Billie's forehead, and he shifted his weight from foot to foot. Dan at last found his tongue, and said: "Well, I'm durned!" If he had heard that an army mule had been appointed to the post of corps commander, his tone could not have had more derision in it. Afterward, he adopted a fervid insubordination, an almost religious reluctance to obey the new corporal's orders, which came near to developing the desired strife.

It is here finally to be recorded also that Dan, most ferociously profane in speech, very rarely swore in the presence of his brother; and that Billie, whose oaths came from his lips with the grace of falling pebbles, was seldom known to express himself in this manner when near his brother Dan.

At last the afternoon contained a suggestion of evening. Metallic cries rang suddenly from end to end of the column. They inspired at once a quick, business-like adjustment. The long thing stirred in the mud. The men had hushed, and were looking across the river. A moment later the shadowy mass of pale blue figures was moving steadily toward the stream. There could be heard from the town a clash of swift fighting and cheering. The noise of the shooting coming through the heavy air had its sharpness taken from it, and sounded in thuds.

There was a halt upon the bank above the pontoons. When the column went winding down the incline, and streamed out upon the bridge, the fog had faded to a great degree, and in the clearer dusk the guns on a distant ridge were enabled to perceive the crossing. The long whirling outcries of the shells came into the air above the men. An occasional solid shot struck the surface of the river, and dashed into view a sudden vertical jet. The distance was subtly illuminated by the lightning from the deep-booming guns. One by one the batteries on the northern shore aroused, the innumerable guns bellowing in angry oration at the distant ridge. The rolling thunder crashed and reverberated as a wild surf sounds on a still night, and to this music the column marched across the pontoons.

The waters of the grim river curled away in a smile from the ends of the great boats, and slid swiftly beneath the planking. The dark, riddled walls of the town upreared before the troops, and from a region hidden by these hammered and tumbled houses came incessantly the yells and firings of a prolonged and close skirmish.

When Dan had called his brother a fool, his voice had been so decisive, so brightly assured, that many men had laughed, considering it to be great humor under the circumstances. The incident happened to rankle deep in Billie. It was not any strange thing that his brother had called him a fool. In fact, he often called him a fool with exactly the same amount of cheerful and prompt conviction, and before large audiences, too. Billie wondered in his own mind why he took such profound offence in this case; but, at any rate, as he slid down the bank and on to the bridge with his regiment, he was searching his knowledge for something that would pierce Dan's blithesome spirit. But he could contrive nothing at this time, and his impotency made the glance which he was once able to give his brother still more malignant.

The guns far and near were roaring a fearful and grand introduction for this column which was marching upon the stage of death. Billie felt it, but only in a numb way. His heart was cased in that curious dissonant metal which covers a man's emotions at such times. The terrible voices from the hills told him that in this wide conflict his life was an insignificant fact, and that his death would be an insignificant fact. They portended the whirlwind to which he would be as necessary as a butterfly's waved wing. The solemnity, the sadness of it came near enough to make him wonder why he was neither solemn nor sad. When his mind vaguely adjusted events according to their importance to him, it appeared that the uppermost thing was the fact that upon the eve of battle, and before many comrades, his brother had called him a fool.

Dan was in a particularly happy mood. "Hurray! Look at 'em shoot," he said, when the long witches' croon of the shells came into the air. It enraged Billie when he felt the little thorn in him, and saw at the same time that his brother had completely forgotten it.

The column went from the bridge into more mud. At this southern end there was a chaos of hoarse directions and commands. Darkness was coming upon the earth, and regiments were being hurried up the slippery bank. As Billie floundered in the black mud, amid the swearing, sliding crowd, he suddenly resolved that, in the absence of other means of hurting Dan, he would avoid looking at him, refrain from speaking to him, pay absolutely no heed to his existence; and this done skillfully would, he imagined, soon reduce his brother to a poignant sensitiveness.

At the top of the bank the column again halted and rearranged itself, as a man after a climb rearranges his clothing. Presently the great steel-backed brigade, an infinitely graceful thing in the rhythm and ease of its veteran movement, swung up a little narrow, slanting street.

Evening had come so swiftly that the fighting on the remote borders of the town was indicated by thin flashes of flame. Some building was on fire, and its reflection upon the clouds was an oval of delicate pink.

II

All demeanour of rural serenity had been wrenched violently from the little town by the guns and by the waves of men which had surged through it. The hand of war laid upon this village had in an instant changed it to a thing of remnants. It resembled the place of a monstrous shaking of the earth itself. The windows, now mere unsightly holes, made the tumbled and blackened dwellings seem skeletons. Doors lay splintered to fragments. Chimneys had flung their bricks everywhere. The artillery fire had not neglected the rows of gentle shade-trees which had lined the streets. Branches and heavy trunks cluttered the mud in driftwood tangles, while a few shattered forms had contrived to remain dejectedly, mournfully upright. They expressed an innocence, a helplessness, which perforce created a pity for their happening into this cauldron of battle. Furthermore, there was under foot a vast collection of odd things reminiscent of the charge, the fight, the retreat. There were boxes and barrels filled with earth, behind which riflemen had lain snugly, and in these little trenches were the dead in blue with the dead in gray, the poses eloquent of the struggles for possession of the town until the history of the whole conflict was written plainly in the streets.

And yet the spirit of this little city, its quaint individuality, poised in the air above the ruins, defying the guns, the sweeping volleys; holding in contempt those avaricious blazes which had attacked many dwellings. The hard earthen sidewalks proclaimed the games that had been played there during long lazy days, in the careful shadows of the trees. "General Merchandise," in faint letters upon a long board, had to be read with a slanted glance, for the sign dangled by one end; but the porch of the old store was a palpable legend of wide-hatted men, smoking.

This subtle essence, this soul of the life that had been, brushed like invisible wings the thoughts of the men in the swift columns that came up from the river.

In the darkness a loud and endless humming arose from the great blue crowds bivouacked in the streets. From time to time a sharp spatter of firing from far picket lines entered this bass chorus. The smell from the smouldering ruins floated on the cold night breeze.

Dan, seated ruefully upon the doorstep of a shot-pierced house, was proclaiming the campaign badly managed. Orders had been issued forbidding camp-fires.

Suddenly he ceased his oration, and scanning the group of his comrades, said: "Where's Billie? Do you know?"

"Gone on picket."

"Get out! Has he?" said Dan. "No business to go on picket. Why don't some of them other corporals take their turn?"

A bearded private was smoking his pipe of confiscated tobacco, seated comfortably upon a horse-hair trunk which he had dragged from the house. He observed: "*Was* his turn."

"No such thing," cried Dan. He and the man on the horse-hair trunk held discussion in which Dan stoutly maintained that if his brother had been sent on picket it was an injustice. He ceased his argument when another soldier, upon whose arms could faintly be seen the two stripes of a corporal, entered the circle. "Humph," said Dan, "where you been?"

The corporal made no answer. Presently Dan said: "Billie, where you been?"

His brother did not seem to hear these inquiries. He glanced at the house which towered above them and remarked casually to the man on the horse-hair trunk: "Funny, ain't it? After the pelting this town got, you'd think there wouldn't be one brick left on another."

"Oh," said Dan, glowering at his brother's back. "Getting mighty smart, ain't you?"

The absence of camp-fires allowed the evening to make apparent its quality of faint silver light in which the blue clothes of the throng became black, and the faces became white expanses, void of expression. There was considerable excitement a short distance from the group around the doorstep. A soldier had chanced upon a hoop-skirt, and arrayed in it he was performing a dance amid the applause of his companions. Billie and a greater part of the men immediately poured over there to witness the exhibition.

"What's the matter with Billie?" demanded Dan of the man upon the horse-hair trunk.

"How do I know?" rejoined the other in mild resentment. He arose and walked away. When he returned he said briefly, in a weather-wise tone, that it would rain during the night.

Dan took a seat upon one end of the horse-hair trunk. He was facing the crowd around the dancer, which in its hilarity swung this way and that way. At times he imagined that he could recognize his brother's face.

He and the man on the other end of the trunk thoughtfully talked of the army's position. To their minds, infantry and artillery were in a most precarious jumble in the streets of the town; but they did not grow nervous over it, for they were used to having the army appear in a precarious jumble to their minds. They had learned to accept such puzzling situations as a consequence of their position in the ranks, and were now usually in possession of a simple but perfectly immovable faith that somebody understood the jumble. Even if they had been convinced that the army was a headless monster, they would merely have nodded with the veteran's singular cynicism. It was none of their business as soldiers. Their duty was to grab sleep and food when occasion permitted, and cheerfully fight wherever their feet were planted until more orders came. This was a task sufficiently absorbing.

They spoke of other corps, and this talk being confidential, their voices dropped to tones of awe. "The Ninth"—"The First"—"The Fifth"—"The Sixth"—"The Third"—the simple numerals rang with eloquence, each having a meaning which was to float through many years as no intangible arithmetical mist, but as pregnant with individuality as the names of cities.

Of their own corps they spoke with a deep veneration, an idolatry, a supreme confidence which apparently would not blanch to see it match against everything.

It was as if their respect for other corps was due partly to a wonder that organizations not blessed with their own famous numeral could take such an interest in war. They could prove that their division was the best in the corps, and that their brigade was the best in the division. And their regiment—it was plain that no fortune of life was equal to the chance which caused a man to be born, so to speak, into this command, the keystone of the defending arch.

At times Dan covered with insults the character of a vague, unnamed general to whose petulance and busy-body spirit he ascribed the order which made hot coffee impossible.

Dan said that victory was certain in the coming battle. The other man seemed rather dubious. He remarked upon the fortified line of hills, which had impressed him even from the other side of the river. "Shucks," said Dan. "Why, we—" He pictured a splendid overflowing of these hills by the sea of men in blue. During the period of this conversation Dan's glance searched the merry throng about the dancer. Above the babble of voices in the street a far-away thunder could sometimes be heard—evidently from the very edge of the horizon—the boom-boom of restless guns.

III

Ultimately the night deepened to the tone of black velvet. The outlines of the fireless camp were like the faint drawings upon ancient tapestry. The glint of a rifle, the shine of a button, might have been threads of silver and gold sewn upon the fabric of night. There was little presented to the vision, but to a sense more subtle there was discernible in the atmosphere something like a pulse; a mystic beating which would have told a stranger of the presence of a giant thing—the slumbering mass of regiments and batteries.

With fires forbidden, the floor of a dry old

kitchen was thought to be a good exchange for the cold earth of December, even if a shell had exploded in it and knocked it so out of shape that when a man lay curled in his blanket his last waking thought was likely to be of the wall that bellied out above him as if strongly anxious to topple upon the score of soldiers.

Billie looked at the bricks ever about to descend in a shower upon his face, listened to the industrious pickets plying their rifles on the border of the town, imagined some measure of the din of the coming battle, thought of Dan and Dan's chagrin, and rolling over in his blanket went to sleep with satisfaction.

At an unknown hour he was aroused by the creaking of boards. Lifting himself upon his elbow, he saw a sergeant prowling among the sleeping forms. The sergeant carried a candle in an old brass candle-stick. He would have resembled some old farmer on an unusual midnight tour if it were not for the significance of his gleaming buttons and striped sleeves.

Billie blinked stupidly at the light until his mind returned from the journeys of slumber. The sergeant stooped among the unconscious soldiers, holding the candle close, and peering into each face.

"Hello, Haines," said Billie. "Relief?"

"Hello, Billie," said the sergeant. "Special duty."

"Dan got to go?"

"Jameson, Hunter, McCormack, D. Dempster. Yes. Where is he?"

"Over there by the winder," said Billie, gesturing. "What is it for, Haines?"

"You don't think I know, do you?" demanded the sergeant. He began to pipe sharply but cheerily at men upon the floor. "Come, Mac, get up here. Here's a special for you. Wake up, Jameson. Come along, Dannie, me boy."

Each man at once took this call to duty as a personal affront. They pulled themselves out of their blankets, rubbed their eyes, and swore at whoever was responsible. "Them's orders," cried the sergeant. "Come! Get out of here." An undetailed head with dishevelled hair thrust out from a blanket, and a sleepy voice said: "Shut up, Haines, and go home."

When the detail clanked out of the kitchen, all but one of the remaining men seemed to be again asleep. Billie, leaning on his elbow, was gazing into darkness. When the footsteps died to silence, he curled himself into his blanket.

At the first cool lavender lights of daybreak he aroused again, and scanned his recumbent companions. Seeing a wakeful one he asked: "Is Dan back yet?"

The man said: "Hain't seen 'im."

Billie put both hands behind his head, and scowled into the air. "Can't see the use of these cussed details in the night-time," he muttered in his most unreasonable tones. "Darn nuisances. Why can't they—" He grumbled at length and graphically.

When Dan entered with the squad, however, Billie was convincingly asleep.

IV

The regiment trotted in double time along the street, and the colonel seemed to quarrel over the right of way with many artillery officers. Batteries were waiting in the mud, and the men of them, exasperated by the bustle of this ambitious infantry, shook their fists from saddle and caisson, exchanging all manner of taunts and jests. The slanted guns continued to look reflectively at the ground.

On the outskirts of the crumbled town a fringe of blue figures were firing into the fog. The regiment swung out into skirmish lines, and the fringe of blue figures departed, turning their backs and going joyfully around the flank.

The bullets began a low moan off toward a ridge which loomed faintly in the heavy mist. When the swift crescendo had reached its climax, the missiles zipped just overhead, as if piercing an invisible curtain. A battery on the hill was crashing with such tumult that it was as if the guns had quarrelled and had fallen pell-mell and snarling upon each other. The shells howled on their journey toward the town. From short range distance there came a spatter of musketry, sweeping along an invisible line and making faint sheets of orange light.

Some in the new skirmish lines were beginning to fire at various shadows discerned in the vapour, forms of men suddenly revealed by some humour of the laggard masses of clouds. The crackle of musketry began to dominate the purring of the hostile bullets. Dan, in the front rank, held his rifle poised, and looked into the fog keenly, coldly, with the air of a sportsman. His nerves were so steady that it was as if they had been drawn from his body, leaving him merely a muscular machine; but his numb heart was somehow beating to the pealing march of the fight.

The waving skirmish line went backward and forward, ran this way and that way. Men got lost in the fog, and men were found again. Once they got too close to the formidable ridge, and the thing burst out as if repulsing a general attack. Once another blue regiment was apprehended on the very edge of firing into them. Once a friendly battery began an elaborate and scientific process of extermination. Always as busy as brokers, the men slid here and there over the plain, fighting their foes, escaping from their friends,

leaving a history of many movements in the wet yellow turf, cursing the atmosphere, blazing away every time they could identify the enemy.

In one mystic changing of the fog, as if the fingers of spirits were drawing aside these draperies, a small group of the gray skirmishers, silent, statuesque, were suddenly disclosed to Dan and those about him. So vivid and near were they that there was something uncanny in the revelation.

There might have been a second of mutual staring. Then each rifle in each group was at the shoulder. As Dan's glance flashed along the barrel of his weapon, the figure of a man suddenly loomed as if the musket had been a telescope. The short black beard, the slouch hat, the pose of the man as he sighted to shoot, made a quick picture in Dan's mind. The same moment, it would seem, he pulled his own trigger, and the man, smitten, lurched forward, while his exploding rifle made a slanting crimson streak in the air, and the slouch hat fell before the body. The billows of the fog, governed by singular impulses, rolled between.

"You got that feller sure enough," said a comrade to Dan. Dan looked at him absentmindedly.

V

When the next morning calmly displayed another fog, the men of the regiment exchanged eloquent comments; but they did not abuse it at length, because the streets of the town now contained enough galloping aides to make three troops of cavalry, and they knew that they had come to the verge of the great fight.

Dan conversed with the man who had once

possessed a horse-hair trunk; but they did not mention the line of hills which had furnished them in more careless moments with an agreeable topic. They avoided it now as condemned men do the subject of death, and yet the thought of it stayed in their eyes as they looked at each other and talked gravely of other things.

The expectant regiment heaved a long sigh of relief when the sharp call: "Fall in," repeated indefinitely, arose in the streets. It was inevitable that a bloody battle was to be fought, and they wanted to get it off their minds. They were, however, doomed again to spend a long period planted firmly in the mud. They craned their necks, and wondered where some of the other regiments were going.

At last the mists rolled carelessly away. Nature made at this time all provisions to enable foes to see each other, and immediately the roar of guns resounded from every hill. The endless cracking of the skirmishers swelled to rolling crashes of musketry. Shells screamed with panther-like noises at the houses. Dan looked at the man of the horse-hair trunk, and the man said: "Well, here she comes!"

The tenor voices of younger officers and the deep and hoarse voices of the older ones rang in the streets. These cries pricked like spurs. The masses of men vibrated from the suddenness with which they were plunged into the situation of troops about to fight. That the orders were long-expected did not concern the emotion.

Simultaneous movement was imparted to all these thick bodies of men and horses that lay in the town. Regiment after regiment swung rapidly into the streets that faced the sinister ridge.

This exodus was theatrical. The little sober-hued village had been like the cloak which disguises the king of drama. It was now put aside, and an army, splendid thing of steel and blue, stood forth in the sunlight.

Even the soldiers in the heavy columns drew deep breaths at the sight, more majestic than they had dreamed. The heights of the enemy's position were crowded with men who resembled people come to witness some mighty pageant. But as the column moved steadily to their positions, the guns, matter-of-fact warriors, doubled their number, and shells burst with red thrilling tumult on the crowded plain. One came into the ranks of the regiment, and after the smoke and the wrath of it had faded, leaving motionless figures, everyone stormed according to the limits of his vocabulary, for veterans detest being killed when they are not busy.

The regiment sometimes looked sideways at its brigade companions composed of men who had never been in battle; but no frozen blood could withstand the heat of the splendour of this army before the eyes on the plain, these lines so long that the flanks were little streaks, this mass of men of one intention. The recruits carried themselves heedlessly. At the rear was an idle battery, and three artillery men in a foolish row on a caisson nudged each other and grinned at the recruits. "You'll catch it pretty soon," they called out. They were impersonally gleeful, as if they themselves were not also likely to catch it pretty soon. But with this picture of an army in their hearts, the new men perhaps felt the devotion which the drops may feel for the wave; they were of its power and glory; they smiled jauntily at the foolish row of gunners, and told them to go to blazes.

The column trotted across some little bridges, and spread quickly into lines of battle. Before them was a bit of plain, and back of the plain was the ridge. There was no time left for considerations. The men were staring at the plain, mightily wondering how it would feel to be out there, when a brigade in advance yelled and charged. The hill was all gray smoke and fire-points.

That fierce elation in the terrors of war, catching a man's heart and making it burn with such ardour that he becomes capable of dying, flashed in the faces of the men like coloured lights, and made them resemble leashed animals, eager, ferocious, daunting at nothing. The line was really in its first leap before the wild, hoarse crying of the orders.

The greed for close quarters which is the emotion of a bayonet charge, came then into the minds of the men and developed until it was a madness. The field, with its faded grass of a Southern winter, seemed to this fury miles in width.

High, slow-moving masses of smoke, with an odour of burning cotton, engulfed the line until the men might have been swimmers. Before them the ridge, the shore of this gray sea, was outlined, crossed, and recrossed by sheets of flame. The howl of the battle rose to the noise of innumerable wind demons.

The line, galloping, scrambling, plunging like a herd of wounded horses, went over a field that was sown with corpses, the records of other charges.

Directly in front of the black-faced, whooping Dan, carousing in this onward sweep like a new kind of fiend, a wounded man appeared, raising his shattered body, and staring at this rush of men down upon him. It seemed to occur to him that he was to be trampled; he made a desperate, piteous effort to escape; then finally huddled in a waiting heap. Dan and the soldier near him widened the interval between them without looking down, without appearing to heed the wounded man. This little

clump of blue seemed to reel past them as boulders reel past a train.

Bursting through a smoke-wave, the scampering, unformed bunches came upon the wreck of the brigade that had preceded them, a floundering mass stopped afar from the hill by the swirling volleys.

It was as if a necromancer had suddenly shown them a picture of the fate which awaited them; but the line with muscular spasm hurled itself over this wreckage and onward, until men were stumbling amid the relics of other assaults, the point where the fire from the ridge consumed.

The men, panting, perspiring, with crazed faces, tried to push against it; but it was as if they had come to a wall. The wave halted, shuddered in an agony from the quick struggle of its two desires, then toppled, and broke into a fragmentary thing which has no name.

Veterans could now at last be distinguished from recruits. The new regiments were instantly gone, lost, scattered, as if they never had been. But the sweeping failure of the charge, the battle, could not make the veterans forget their business. With a last throe, the band of maniacs drew itself up and blazed a volley at the hill, insignificant to those iron intrenchments, but nevertheless expressing that singular final despair which enables men coolly to defy the walls of a city of death.

After this episode the men renamed their command. They called it the Little Regiment.

VI

"I seen Dan shoot a feller yesterday. Yes sir. I'm sure it was him that done it. And maybe he thinks about that feller now, and wonders if *he* tumbled down just about the same way. Them things come up in a man's mind."

Bivouac fires upon the sidewalks, in the streets, in the yards, threw high their wavering reflections, which examined, like slim, red fingers, the dingy, scarred walls and the piles of tumbled brick. The droning of voices again rose from great blue crowds.

The odour of frying bacon, the fragrance from countless little coffee-pails floated among the ruins. The rifles, stacked in the shadows, emitted flashes of steely light. Wherever a flag lay horizontally from one stack to another was the bed of an eagle which had led men into the mystic smoke.

The men about a particular fire were engaged in holding in check their jovial spirits. They moved whispering around the blaze, although they looked at it with a certain fine contentment, like labourers after a day's hard work.

There was one who sat apart. They did not address him save in tones suddenly changed. They did not regard him directly, but always in little sidelong glances.

At last a soldier from a distant fire came into this circle of light. He studied for a time the man who sat apart. Then he hesitatingly stepped closer, and said: "Got any news, Dan?"

"No," said Dan.

The new-comer shifted his feet. He looked at the fire, at the sky, at the other men, at Dan. His face expressed a curious despair; his tongue was plainly in rebellion. Finally, however, he contrived to say: "Well, there's some chance yet, Dan. Lots of the wounded are still lying out there, you know. There's some chance yet."

"Yes," said Dan.

The soldier shifted his feet again, and looked miserably into the air. After another struggle he said: "Well, there's some chance yet, Dan." He moved hastily away.

One of the men of the squad, perhaps encouraged by this example, now approached the still figure. "No news yet, hey?" he said, after coughing behind his hand.

"No," said Dan.

"Well," said the man, "I've been thinking of how he was fretting about you the night you went on special duty. You recollect? Well, sir, I was surprised. He couldn't say enough about it. I swan, I don't believe he slep' a wink after you left, but just lay awake cussing special duty and worrying. I was surprised. But there he lay cussing. He—"

Dan made a curious sound, as if a stone had wedged in his throat. He said: "Shut up, will you?"

Afterward the men would not allow this moody contemplation of the fire to be interrupted.

"Oh, let him alone, can't you?"

"Come away from there, Casey!"

"Say, can't you leave him be?"

They moved with reverence about the immovable figure, with its countenance of mask-like invulnerability.

VII

After the red round eye of the sun had stared long at the little plain and its burden, darkness, a sable mercy, came heavily upon it, and the wan hands of the dead were no longer seen in strange frozen gestures.

The heights in front of the plain shone with tiny camp-fires, and from the town in the rear, small shimmerings ascended from the blazes of the bivouac. The plain was a black expanse upon which, from time to time, dots of light, lanterns, floated slowly here and there. These fields were long steeped in grim mystery.

Suddenly, upon one dark spot, there was a resurrection. A strange thing had been groaning there, prostrate. Then it suddenly dragged itself to a sitting posture, and became a man.

The man stared stupidly for a moment at the lights on the hill, then turned and contemplated the faint colouring over the town. For some moments he remained thus, staring with dull eyes, his face unemotional, wooden.

Finally he looked around him at the corpses dimly to be seen. No change flashed into his face upon viewing these men. They seemed to suggest merely that his information concerning himself was not too complete. He ran his fingers over his arms and chest, bearing always the air of an idiot upon a bench at an almshouse door.

Finding no wound in his arms nor in his chest, he raised his hand to his head, and the fingers came away with some dark liquid upon them. Holding these fingers close to his eyes, he scanned them in the same stupid fashion, while his body gently swayed.

The soldier rolled his eyes again toward the town. When he arose, his clothing peeled from the frozen ground like wet paper. Hearing the sound of it, he seemed to see reason for deliberation. He paused and looked at the ground, then at his trousers, then at the ground.

Finally he went slowly off toward the faint reflection, holding his hands palm outward before him, and walking in the manner of a blind man.

VIII

The immovable Dan again sat unaddressed in the midst of comrades, who did not joke aloud. The dampness of the usual morning fog seemed to make the little camp-fires furious.

Suddenly a cry arose in the streets, a shout of amazement and delight. The men making breakfast at the fire looked up quickly. They broke forth in clamorous exclamation: "Well! Of all things! Dan! Dan! Look who's coming! Oh, Dan!"

Dan the silent raised his eyes and saw a man, with a bandage of the size of a helmet about his head, receiving a furious demonstration from the company. He was shaking hands, and explaining, and haranguing to a high degree.

Dan started. His face of bronze flushed to his temples. He seemed about to leap from the ground, but then suddenly he sank back, and resumed his impassive gazing.

The men were in a flurry. They looked from one to the other. "Dan! Look! See who's coming!" some cried again. "Dan! Look!"

He scowled at last, and moved his shoulders sullenly. "Well, don't I know it?"

But they could not be convinced that his eyes were in service. "Dan! Why can't you look? See who's coming!"

He made a gesture then of irritation and rage. "Curse it! Don't I know it?"

The man with a bandage the size of a helmet moved forward, always shaking hands and explaining. At times his glance wandered to Dan, who saw with his eyes riveted.

After a series of shiftings, it occurred naturally that the man with the bandage was very near to the man who saw the flames. He paused, and there was a little silence. Finally he said: "Hello, Dan."

"Hello, Billie."

A Mystery of Heroism

The dark uniforms of the men were so coated with dust from the incessant wrestling of the two armies that the regiment almost seemed a part of the clay bank which shielded them from the shells. On the top of the hill a battery was arguing in tremendous roars with some other guns, and to the eye of the infantry, the artillerymen, the guns, the caissons, the horses, were distinctly outlined upon the blue sky. When a piece was fired, a red streak as round as a log flashed low in the heavens, like a monstrous bolt of lightning. The men of the battery wore white duck trousers, which somehow emphasized their legs; and when they ran and crowded in little groups at the bidding of the shouting officers, it was more impressive than usual to the infantry.

Fred Collins, of A Company, was saying: "Thunder! I wisht I had a drink. Ain't there any water round here?" Then somebody yelled, "There goes th' bugler!"

As the eyes of half the regiment swept in one machinelike movement there was an instant's picture of a horse in a great convulsive leap of a death wound and a rider leaning back with a crooked arm and spread fingers before his face. On the ground was the crimson terror of an exploding shell, with fibres of flame that seemed like lances. A glittering bugle swung clear of the rider's back as fell headlong the horse and the man. In the air was an odour as from a conflagration.

Sometimes they of the infantry looked down at a fair little meadow which spread at their feet. Its long, green grass was rippling gently in a breeze. Beyond it was the gray form of a house half torn to pieces by shells and by the busy axes of soldiers who had pursued firewood. The line of an old fence was now dimly marked by long weeds and by an occasional post. A shell had blown the wellhouse to fragments. Little lines of gray smoke ribboning upward from some embers indicated the place where had stood the barn.

From beyond a curtain of green woods there came the sound of some stupendous scuffle, as if two animals of the size of islands were fighting. At a distance there were occasional appearances of swift-moving men, horses, batteries, flags, and, with the crashing of infantry volleys were heard, often, wild and frenzied cheers. In the midst of it all Smith and Ferguson, two privates of A Company, were engaged in a heated discussion, which involved the greatest questions of the national existence.

The battery on the hill presently engaged in a frightful duel. The white legs of the gunners scampered this way and that way, and the officers redoubled their shouts. The guns, with their demeanours of stolidity and courage, were typical of something infinitely self-possessed in this clamour of death that swirled around the hill.

One of a "swing" team was suddenly smitten quivering to the ground, and his maddened brethren dragged his torn body in their struggle to escape from this turmoil and danger. A young soldier astride one of the leaders swore and fumed in his saddle, and furiously jerked at the bridle. An officer screamed out an order so violently that his voice broke and ended the sentence in a falsetto shriek.

The leading company of the infantry regiment was somewhat exposed, and the colonel ordered it moved more fully under the shelter of the hill. There was the clank of steel against steel.

A lieutenant of the battery rode down and passed them, holding his right arm carefully in his left hand. And it was as if this arm was not at all a part of him, but belonged to another man. His sober and reflective charger went slowly. The officer's face was grimy and perspiring, and his uniform was tousled as if he had been in direct grapple with an enemy. He smiled grimly when the men stared at him. He turned his horse toward the meadow.

Collins, of A Company, said: "I wisht I had a drink. I bet there's water in that there ol' well yonder!"

"Yes; but how you goin' to git it?"

For the little meadow which intervened was now suffering a terrible onslaught of shells. Its green and beautiful calm had vanished utterly. Brown earth was being flung in monstrous handfuls. And there was a massacre of the young blades of grass. They were being torn, burned, obliterated. Some curious fortune of the battle had made this gentle little meadow the object of the red hate of the shells, and each one as it exploded seemed like an imprecation in the face of a maiden.

The wounded officer who was riding across this expanse said to himself, "Why, they couldn't shoot any harder if the whole army was massed here!"

A shell struck the gray ruins of the house, and as, after the roar, the shattered wall fell in fragments, there was a noise which resembled the flapping of shutters during a wild gale of winter. Indeed, the infantry paused in the shelter of the bank appeared as men standing upon a shore contemplating a madness of the sea. The angel of calamity had under its glance the battery upon the hill. Fewer white-legged men laboured about the guns. A shell had smitten one of the pieces, and after the flare, the smoke, the dust, the wrath of this blow were gone, it was possible to see white legs stretched horizontally upon the ground. And at that interval to the rear, where it is the business of battery horses to stand with their noses to the fight awaiting the command to drag their guns out of the destruction or into it or wheresoever these incomprehensible hu-

mans demanded with whip and spur—in this line of passive and dumb spectators, whose fluttering hearts yet would not let them forget the iron laws of man's control of them—in this rank of brute-soldiers there had been relentless and hideous carnage. From the ruck of bleeding and prostrate horses, the men of the infantry could see one animal raising its stricken body with its fore legs, and turning its nose with mystic and profound eloquence toward the sky.

Some comrades joked Collins about his thirst. "Well, if yeh want a drink so bad, why don't yeh go git it!"

"Well, I will in a minnet, if yeh don't shut up!"

A lieutenant of artillery floundered his horse straight down the hill with as great concern as if it were level ground. As he galloped past the colonel of the infantry, he threw up his hand in swift salute. "We've got to get out of that," he roared angrily. He was a black-bearded officer, and his eyes, which resembled beads, sparkled like those of an insane man. His jumping horse sped along the column of infantry.

The fat major, standing carelessly with his sword held horizontally behind him and with his legs far apart, looked after the receding horseman and laughed. "He wants to get back with orders pretty quick, or there'll be no batt'ry left," he observed.

The wise young captain of the second company hazarded to the lieutenant colonel that the enemy's infantry would probably soon attack the hill, and the lieutenant colonel snubbed him.

A private in one of the rear companies looked out over the meadow, and then turned to a companion and said, "Look there, Jim!" It was the wounded officer from the battery, who some time before had started to ride across the meadow, supporting his right arm carefully with his left hand. This man had encountered a shell apparently at a time when no one perceived him, and he could now be seen lying face downward with a stirruped foot stretched across the body of his dead horse. A leg of the charger extended slantingly upward precisely as stiff as a stake. Around this motionless pair the shells still howled.

There was a quarrel in A Company. Collins was shaking his fist in the faces of some laughing comrades. "Dern yeh! I ain't afraid t' go. If yeh say much, I will go!"

"Of course, yeh will! You'll run through that there medder, won't yeh?"

Collins said, in a terrible voice, "You see now!" At this ominous threat his comrades broke into renewed jeers.

Collins gave them a dark scowl and went to find his captain. The latter was conversing with the colonel of the regiment.

"Captain," said Collins, saluting and standing at attention—in those days all trousers bagged at the knees—"captain, I want t' get permission to go git some water from that there well over yonder!"

The colonel and the captain swung about simultaneously and stared across the meadow. The captain laughed. "You must be pretty thirsty, Collins?"

"Yes, sir, I am."

"Well—ah," said the captain. After a moment, he asked, "Can't you wait?"

"No, sir."

The colonel was watching Collins's face. "Look here, my lad," he said, in a pious sort of a voice—"look here, my lad"—Collins was not a lad—"don't you think that's taking pretty big risks for a little drink of water?"

"I dunno," said Collins uncomfortably. Some of the resentment toward his companions, which perhaps had forced him into this affair, was beginning to fade. "I dunno whether 'tis."

The colonel and the captain contemplated him for a time.

"Well," said the captain finally.

"Well," said the colonel, "if you want to go, why, go."

Collins saluted. "Much obliged t' yeh."

As he moved away the colonel called after him. "Take some of the other boys' canteens with you an' hurry back now."

"Yes, sir, I will."

The colonel and the captain looked at each other then, for it had suddenly occurred that they could not for the life of them tell whether Collins wanted to go or whether he did not.

They turned to regard Collins, and as they perceived him surrounded by gesticulating comrades, the colonel said: "Well, by thunder! I guess he's going."

Collins appeared as a man dreaming. In the midst of the questions, the advice, the warnings, all the excited talk of his company mates, he maintained a curious silence.

They were very busy in preparing him for his ordeal. When they inspected him carefully it was somewhat like the examination that grooms give a horse before a race; and they were amazed, staggered by the whole affair. Their astonishment found vent in strange repetitions.

"Are yeh sure a-goin'?" they demanded again and again.

"Certainly I am," cried Collins, at last furiously.

He strode sullenly away from them. He was swinging five or six canteens by their cords. It seemed that his cap would not remain firmly on his head, and often he reached and pulled it down over his brow.

There was a general movement in the compact column. The long animal-like thing moved slightly. Its four hundred eyes were turned upon the figure of Collins.

"Well, sir, if that ain't th' derndest thing! I never thought Fred Collins had the blood in him for that kind of business."

"What's he goin' to do, anyhow?"

"He's goin' to that well there after water."

"We ain't dyin' of thirst, are we? That's foolishness."

"Well, somebody put him up to it, an' he's doin' it."

"Say, he must be a desperate cuss."

When Collins faced the meadow and walked away from the regiment, he was vaguely conscious that a chasm, the deep valley of all prides, was suddenly between him and his comrades. It was provisional, but the provision was that he return as a victor. He had blindly been led by quaint emotions, and laid himself under an obligation to walk squarely up to the face of death.

But he was not sure that he wished to make a retraction, even if he could do so without shame. As a matter of truth, he was sure of very little. He was mainly surprised.

It seemed to him supernaturally strange that he had allowed his mind to manoeuvre his body into such a situation. He understood that it might be called dramatically great.

However, he had no full appreciation of anything, excepting that he was actually conscious of being dazed. He could feel his dulled mind groping after the form and colour of this incident. He wondered why he did not feel some keen agony of fear cutting his sense like a knife. He wondered at this, because human expression had said loudly for cen-

turies that men should feel afraid of certain things, and that all men who did not feel this fear were phenomena—heroes.

He was, then, a hero. He suffered that disappointment which we would all have if we discovered that we were ourselves capable of those deeds which we most admire in history and legend. This, then, was a hero. After all, heroes were not much.

No, it could not be true. He was not a hero. Heroes had no shames in their lives, and, as for him, he remembered borrowing fifteen dollars from a friend and promising to pay it back the next day, and then avoiding that friend for ten months. When at home his mother had aroused him for the early labour of his life on the farm, it had often been his fashion to be irritable, childish, diabolical; and his mother had died since he had come to the war.

He saw that, in this matter of the well, the canteens, the shells, he was an intruder in the land of fine deeds.

He was now about thirty paces from his comrades. The regiment had just turned its many faces toward him.

From the forest of terrific noises there suddenly emerged a little uneven line of men. They fired fiercely and rapidly at distant foliage on which appeared little puffs of white smoke. The spatter of skirmish firing was added to the thunder of the guns on the hill. The little line of men ran forward. A colour sergeant fell flat with his flag as if he had slipped on ice. There was hoarse cheering from this distant field.

Collins suddenly felt that two demon fingers were pressed into his ears. He could see nothing but flying arrows, flaming red. He lurched from the shock of this explosion, but he made a mad rush for the house, which he viewed as a man submerged to the neck in a boiling surf might view the shore. In the air, little pieces of shell howled and the earthquake explosions drove him insane with the menace of their roar. As he ran the canteens knocked together with a rhythmical tinkling.

As he neared the house, each detail of the scene became vivid to him. He was aware of some bricks of the vanished chimney lying on the sod. There was a door which hung by one hinge.

Rifle bullets called forth by the insistent skirmishers came from the far-off bank of foliage. They mingled with the shells and the pieces of shells until the air was torn in all directions by hootings, yells, howls. The sky was full of fiends who directed all their wild rage at his head.

When he came to the well, he flung himself face downward and peered into its darkness. There were furtive silver glintings some feet from the surface. He grabbed one of the canteens and, unfastening its cap, swung it down by the cord. The water flowed slowly in with an indolent gurgle.

And now as he lay with his face turned away he was suddenly smitten with the terror. It came upon his heart like the grasp of claws. All the power faded from his muscles. For an instant he was no more than a dead man.

The canteen filled with a maddening slowness, in the manner of all bottles. Presently he recovered his strength and addressed a screaming oath to it. He leaned over until it seemed as if he intended to try to push water into it with his hands. His eyes as he gazed down into the well shone like two pieces of metal and in their expression was a great appeal and a great curse. The stupid water derided him.

There was the blaring thunder of a shell.

Crimson light shone through the swift-boiling smoke and made a pink reflection on part of the wall of the well. Collins jerked out his arm and canteen with the same motion that a man would use in withdrawing his head from a furnace.

He scrambled erect and glared and hesitated. On the ground near him lay the old well bucket, with a length of rusty chain. He lowered it swiftly into the well. The bucket struck the water and then, turning lazily over, sank. When, with hand reaching tremblingly over hand, he hauled it out, it knocked often against the walls of the well and spilled some of its contents.

In running with a filled bucket, a man can adopt but one kind of gait. So through this terrible field over which screamed practical angels of death Collins ran in the manner of a farmer chased out of a dairy by a bull.

His face went staring white with anticipation—anticipation of a blow that would whirl him around and down. He would fall as he had seen other men fall, the life knocked out of them so suddenly that their knees were no more quick to touch the ground than their heads. He saw the long blue line of the regiment, but his comrades were standing looking at him from the edge of an impossible star. He was aware of some deep wheel ruts and hoofprints in the sod beneath his feet.

The artillery officer who had fallen in this meadow had been making groans in the teeth of the tempest of sound. These futile cries, wrenched from him by his agony, were heard only by shells, bullets. When wild-eyed Collins came running, this officer raised himself. His face contorted and blanched from pain, he was about to utter some great beseeching cry. But suddenly his face straightened and he called: "Say, young man, give me a drink of water, will you?"

Collins had no room amid his emotions for surprise. He was mad from the threats of destruction.

"I can't!" he screamed, and in his reply was a full description of his quaking apprehension. His cap was gone and his hair was riotous. His clothes made it appear that he had been dragged over the ground by the heels. He ran on.

The officer's head sank down and one elbow crooked. His foot in its brass-bound stirrup still stretched over the body of his horse and the other leg was under the steed.

But Collins turned. He came dashing back. His face had now turned gray and in his eyes was all terror. "Here it is! here it is!"

The officer was as a man gone in drink. His arm bent like a twig. His head drooped as if his neck were of willow. He was sinking to the ground, to lie face downward.

Collins grabbed him by the shoulder. "Here it is. Here's your drink. Turn over. Turn over, man, for God's sake!"

With Collins hauling at his shoulder, the officer twisted his body and fell with his face turned toward that region where lived the unspeakable noises of the swirling missiles. There was the faintest shadow of a smile on his lips as he looked at Collins. He gave a sigh, a little primitive breath like that from a child.

Collins tried to hold the bucket steadily, but his shaking hands caused the water to splash all over the face of the dying man. Then he jerked it away and ran on.

The regiment gave him a welcoming roar. The grimed faces were wrinkled in laughter.

His captain waved the bucket away. "Give it to the men!"

The two genial, skylarking young lieutenants were the first to gain possession of it. They played over it in their fashion.

When one tried to drink the other teasingly knocked his elbow. "Don't, Billie! You'll make me spill it," said the one. The other laughed.

Suddenly there was an oath, the thud of wood on the ground, and a swift murmur of astonishment among the ranks. The two lieutenants glared at each other. The bucket lay on the ground empty.

The Veteran

Out of the low window could be seen three hickory trees placed irregularly in a meadow that was resplendent in springtime green. Farther away, the old, dismal belfry of the village church loomed over the pines. A horse meditating in the shade of one of the hickories lazily swished his tail. The warm sunshine made an oblong of vivid yellow on the floor of the grocery.

"Could you see the whites of their eyes?" said the man who was seated on a soap box.

"Nothing of the kind," replied old Henry warmly. "Just a lot of flitting figures, and I let go at where they 'peared to be the thickest. Bang!"

"Mr. Fleming," said the grocer, his deferential voice expressed somehow the old man's exact social weight—"Mr. Fleming, you never was frightened much in them battles, was you?"

The veteran looked down and grinned. Observing his manner, the entire group tittered. "Well, I guess I was," he answered finally. "Pretty well scared, sometimes. Why, in my first battle I thought the sky was falling down.

I thought the world was coming to an end. You bet I was scared."

Every one laughed. Perhaps it seemed strange and rather wonderful to them that a man should admit the thing, and in the tone of their laughter there was probably more admiration than if old Fleming had declared he had always been a lion. Moreover, they knew that he had ranked as an orderly sergeant, and so their opinion of his heroism was fixed. None, to be sure, knew how an orderly sergeant ranked, but then it was understood to be somewhere just shy of a major general's stars. So, when old Henry admitted that he had been frightened, there was a laugh.

"The trouble was," said the old man, "I thought they were all shooting at me. Yes, sir, I thought every man in the other army was aiming at me in particular, and only me. And it seemed so darned unreasonable, you know. I wanted to explain to 'em what an almighty good fellow I was, because I thought then they might quit all trying to hit me. But I couldn't explain, and they kept on being unreasonable —blim!—blam!—bang! So I run!"

Two little triangles of wrinkles appeared at the corners of his eyes. Evidently he appreciated some comedy in this recital. Down near his feet, however, little Jim, his grandson, was visibly horror-stricken. His hands were clasped nervously, and his eyes were wide with astonishment at this terrible scandal, his most magnificent grandfather telling such a thing.

"That was at Chancellorsville. Of course, afterward I kind of got used to it. A man does. Lots of men, though, seem to feel all right from the start. I did, as soon as I 'got on to it,' as they say now; but at first I was pretty well flustered. Now, there was young Jim Conklin, old Si Conklin's son—that used to keep the tannery—you none of you recollect him—well, he went into it from the start just as if he was born to it. But with me it was different. I had to get used to it."

When little Jim walked with his grandfather he was in the habit of skipping along on the stone pavement in front of the three stores and the hotel of the town and betting that he could avoid the cracks. But upon this day he walked soberly, with his hand gripping two of his grandfather's fingers. Sometimes he kicked abstractedly at dandelions that curved over the walk. Any one could see that he was much troubled.

"There's Sickles's colt over in the medder, Jimmie," said the old man. "Don't you wish you owned one like him?"

"Um," said the boy, with a strange lack of interest. He continued his reflections. Then finally he ventured, "Grandpa—now—was that true what you was telling those men?"

"What?" asked the grandfather. "What was I telling them?"

"Oh, about your running."

"Why, yes, that was true enough, Jimmie. It was my first fight, and there was an awful lot of noise, you know."

Jimmie seemed dazed that this idol, of its own will, should so totter. His stout boyish idealism was injured.

Presently the grandfather said: "Sickles's colt is going for a drink. Don't you wish you owned Sickles's colt, Jimmie?"

The boy merely answered, "He ain't as nice as our'n." He lapsed into another moody silence.

* * *

One of the hired men, a Swede, desired to drive to the county seat for purposes of his own. The old man loaned a horse and an unwashed buggy. It appeared later that one of the purposes of the Swede was to get drunk.

After quelling some boisterous frolic of the farm hands and boys in the garret, the old man had that night gone peacefully to sleep, when he was aroused by clamouring at the kitchen door. He grabbed his trousers, and they waved out behind as he dashed forward. He could hear the voice of the Swede, screaming and blubbering. He pushed the wooden button, and, as the door flew open, the Swede, a maniac, stumbled inward, chattering, weeping, still screaming: "De barn fire! Fire! Fire! De barn fire! Fire! Fire! Fire!"

There was a swift and indescribable change in the old man. His face ceased instantly to be a face; it became a mask, a gray thing, with horror written about the mouth and eyes. He hoarsely shouted at the foot of the little rickety stairs, and immediately, it seemed, there came down an avalanche of men. No one knew that during this time the old lady had been standing in her night clothes at the bedroom door, yelling: "What's th' matter? What's th' matter? What's th' matter?"

When they dashed toward the barn it presented to their eyes its usual appearance, solemn, rather mystic in the black night. The Swede's lantern was overturned at a point some yards in front of the barn doors. It contained a wild little conflagration of its own, and even in their excitement some of those who ran felt a gentle secondary vibration of the thrifty part of their minds at sight of this overturned lantern. Under ordinary circumstances it would have been a calamity.

But the cattle in the barn were trampling, trampling, trampling, and above this noise could be heard a humming like the song of innumerable bees. The old man hurled aside the great doors, and a yellow flame leaped out at one corner and sped and wavered frantically up the old gray wall. It was glad, terrible, this single flame, like the wild banner of deadly and triumphant foes.

The motley crowd from the garret had come with all the pails of the farm. They flung themselves upon the well. It was a leisurely old machine, long dwelling in indolence. It was in the habit of giving out water with a sort of reluctance. The men stormed at it, cursed it; but it continued to allow the buckets to be filled only after the wheezy windlass had howled many protests at the mad-handed men.

With his opened knife in his hand old Fleming himself had gone headlong into the barn, where the stifling smoke swirled with the air currents, and where could be heard in its fulness the terrible chorus of the flames, laden with tones of hate and death, a hymn of wonderful ferocity.

He flung a blanket over an old mare's head, cut the halter close to the manger, led the mare to the door, and fairly kicked her out to safety. He returned with the same blanket, and rescued one of the work horses. He took five horses out, and then came out himself, with his clothes bravely on fire. He had no whiskers, and very little hair on his head. They soused five pailfuls of water on him. His eldest son made a clean miss with the sixth pailful, because the old man had turned and was running down the decline and around to the basement of the barn, where were the stanchions of the cows. Some one noticed at the time that he ran very lamely, as if one of the frenzied horses had smashed his hip.

The cows, with their heads held in the heavy stanchions, had thrown themselves, strangled themselves, tangled themselves; done everything which the ingenuity of their exuberant fear could suggest to them.

Here, as at the well, the same thing happened to every man save one. Their hands went mad. They became incapable of everything save the power to rush into dangerous situations.

The old man released the cow nearest the door, and she, blind drunk with terror, crashed into the Swede. The Swede had been running to and fro babbling. He carried an empty milk pail, to which he clung with an unconscious, fierce enthusiasm. He shrieked like one lost as he went under the cow's hoofs, and the milk pail, rolling across the floor, made a flash of silver in the gloom.

Old Fleming took a fork, beat off the cow, and dragged the paralyzed Swede to the open air. When they had rescued all the cows save one, which had so fastened herself that she could not be moved an inch, they returned to the front of the barn and stood sadly, breathing like men who had reached the final point of human effort.

Many people had come running. Some one had even gone to the church, and now, from the distance, rang the tocsin note of the old bell. There was a long flare of crimson on the sky, which made remote people speculate as to the whereabouts of the fire.

The long flames sang their drumming chorus in voices of the heaviest bass. The wind whirled clouds of smoke and cinders into the faces of the spectators. The form of the old barn was outlined in black amid these masses of orange-hued flames.

And then came this Swede again, crying as one who is the weapon of the sinister fates. "De colts! De colts! You have forgot de colts!"

Old Fleming staggered. It was true; they had forgotten the two colts in the box stalls at the back of the barn. "Boys," he said, "I must try to get 'em out." They clamoured about him then, afraid for him, afraid of what they should see. Then they talked wildly each to each. "Why, it's sure death!" "He would never get out!" "Why, it's suicide for a man to go in there!" Old Fleming stared absent-mindedly at the open doors. "The poor little things!" he said. He rushed into the barn.

When the roof fell in, a great funnel of smoke swarmed toward the sky, as if the old man's mighty spirit, released from its body— a little bottle—had swelled like the genie of fable. The smoke was tinted rose-hue from the flames, and perhaps the unutterable midnights of the universe will have no power to daunt the colour of this soul.

The Return of a Private

HAMLIN GARLAND (1860–1940) WAS A LEADER IN THE STRUGGLE FOR REALISM IN AMERICAN writing. Like Joseph Kirkland (whom Garland considered his literary mentor) a product of the midwest, Garland in his finest work deals with the farmer's lonely struggle for survival on the Middle Border. His best stories appeared in *Main-Travelled Roads* (1891); "The Return of a Private" comes from this collection. Garland went on to write a few propagandist novels designed to help the farmer's lot, many volumes of autobiography and biography—*A Son of the Middle Border* came out in 1917, and its sequel, *A Daughter of the Middle Border* won the Pulitzer Prize in 1922. In his old age he concentrated on psychic research.

Garland experienced the war only vicariously, through the remembrances of his father, a Union Army veteran. The author comprehended the realities of an ex-soldier's lot, the usual results of military triumph.

In part elegiac, in part naturalistic, "The Return of a Private" stresses the anti-romantic side of war—and peace. The blue-coated cogs in a vast destructive machine, the gaunt veterans gain no cheers from welcoming crowds; only a few loafers notice the soldiers' return from the wars, and only the soldiers themselves remember the dead. There are no heroes, no flashing swords and fluttering banners here. Garland's common soldier returns from the war with the South to take up his weapons in the war with nature and injustice.

I

THE NEARER THE TRAIN DREW TOWARD LA Crosse, the soberer the little group of "vets" became. On the long way from New Orleans they had beguiled tedium with jokes and friendly chaff; or with planning with elabo-rate detail what they were going to do now, after the war. A long journey, slowly, irregularly, yet persistently pushing northward. When they entered on Wisconsin territory they gave a cheer, and another when they reached Madison, but after that they sank into a dumb expectancy. Comrades dropped off at one or two points beyond, until there were only four or five left who were bound for La Crosse County.

Three of them were gaunt and brown, the fourth was gaunt and pale, with signs of fever and ague upon him. One had a great scar down his temple, one limped, and they all had unnaturally large, bright eyes, showing emaciation. There were no hands greeting them at the station, no banks of gayly dressed ladies waving handkerchiefs and shouting "Bravo!" as they came in on the caboose of a freight train into the towns that had cheered and blared at them on their way to war. As they looked out or stepped upon the platform for a moment, while the train stood at the station, the loafers looked at them indifferently. Their blue coats, dusty and grimy, were too familiar now to excite notice, much less a friendly word. They were the last of the army to return, and the loafers were surfeited with such sights.

The train jogged forward so slowly that it seemed likely to be midnight before they should reach La Crosse. The little squad grumbled and swore, but it was no use; the train would not hurry, and, as a matter of fact, it was nearly two o'clock when the engine whistled "down brakes."

All of the group were farmers, living in districts several miles out of the town, and all were poor.

"Now, boys," said Private Smith, he of the fever and ague, "we are landed in La Crosse in the night. We've got to stay somewhere till mornin'. Now I ain't got no two dollars to waste on a hotel. I've got a wife and children, so I'm goin' to roost on a bench and take the cost of a bed out of my hide."

"Same here," put in one of the other men. "Hide'll grow on again, dollars'll come hard.

It's going to be mighty hot skirmishin' to find a dollar these days."

"Don't think they'll be a deputation of citizens waitin' to 'scort us to a hotel, eh?" said another. His sarcasm was too obvious to require an answer.

Smith went on, "Then at daybreak we'll start for home—at least, I will."

"Well, I'll be dummed if I'll take two dollars out o' *my* hide," one of the younger men said. "I'm goin' to a hotel, ef I don't never lay up a cent."

"That'll do f'r you," said Smith; "but if you had a wife an' three young uns dependin' on yeh—"

"Which I ain't, thank the Lord! and don't intend havin' while the court knows itself."

The station was deserted, chill, and dark, as they came into it at exactly a quarter to two in the morning. Lit by the oil lamps that flared a dull red light over the dingy benches, the waiting room was not an inviting place. The younger man went off to look up a hotel, while the rest remained and prepared to camp down on the floor and benches. Smith was attended to tenderly by the other men, who spread their blankets on the bench for him, and, by robbing themselves, made quite a comfortable bed, though the narrowness of the bench made his sleeping precarious.

It was chill, though August, and the two men, sitting with bowed heads, grew stiff with cold and weariness, and were forced to rise now and again and walk about to warm their stiffened limbs. It did not occur to them, probably, to contrast their coming home with their going forth, or with the coming home of the generals, colonels, or even captains—but to Private Smith, at any rate, there came a sickness at heart almost deadly as he lay there on his hard bed and went over his situation.

In the deep of the night, lying on a board in the town where he had enlisted three years ago, all elation and enthusiasm gone out of him, he faced the fact that with the joy of home-coming was already mingled the bitter juice of care. He saw himself sick, worn out, taking up the work on his half-cleared farm, the inevitable mortgage standing ready with open jaw to swallow half his earnings. He had given three years of his life for a mere pittance of pay, and now!—

Morning dawned at last, slowly, with a pale yellow dome of light rising silently above the bluffs, which stand like some huge storm-devastated castle, just east of the city. Out to the left the great river swept on its massive yet silent way to the south. Bluejays called across the water from hillside to hillside through the clear, beautiful air, and hawks began to skim the tops of the hills. The older men were astir early, but Private Smith had fallen at last into a sleep, and they went out without waking him. He lay on his knapsack, his gaunt face turned toward the ceiling, his hands clasped on his breast, with a curious pathetic effect of weakness and appeal.

An engine switching near woke him at last, and he slowly sat up and stared about. He looked out of the window and saw that the sun was lightening the hills across the river. He rose and brushed his hair as well as he could, folded his blankets up, and went out to find his companions. They stood gazing silently at the river and at the hills.

"Looks natcher'l, don't it?" they said, as he came out.

"That's what it does," he replied. "An' it looks good. D' yeh see that peak?" He pointed at a beautiful symmetrical peak, rising like a slightly truncated cone, so high that it seemed the very highest of them all. It was touched by the morning sun and it glowed like a beacon, and a light scarf of gray morning fog was rolling up its shadowed side.

"My farm's just beyond that. Now, if I can only ketch a ride, we'll be home by dinnertime."

"I'm talkin' about breakfast," said one of the others.

"I guess it's one more meal o' hardtack f'r me," said Smith.

They foraged around, and finally found a restaurant with a sleepy old German behind the counter, and procured some coffee, which they drank to wash down their hardtack.

"Time'll come," said Smith, holding up a piece by the corner, "when this'll be a curiosity."

"I hope to God it will! I bet I've chawed hardtack enough to shingle every house in the coolly. I've chawed it when my lampers was down, and when they wasn't. I've took it dry, soaked, and mashed. I've had it wormy, musty, sour, and blue-mouldy. I've had it in little bits and big bits; 'fore coffee an' after coffee. I'm ready f'r a change. I'd like t' git holt jest about now o' some of the hot biscuits my wife c'n make when she lays herself out f'r company."

"Well, if you set there gabblin', you'll never *see* yer wife."

"Come on," said Private Smith. "Wait a moment, boys; less take suthin'. It's on me." He led them to the rusty tin dipper which hung on a nail beside the wooden water-pail, and they grinned and drank. Then shouldering their blankets and muskets, which they were "takin' home to the boys," they struck out on their last march.

"They called that coffee Jayvy," grumbled one of them, "but it never went by the road where government Jayvy resides. I reckon I know coffee from peas."

They kept together on the road along the turnpike, and up the winding road by the river, which they followed for some miles. The river was very lovely, curving down along its sandy beds, pausing now and then under broad basswood trees, or running in dark, swift, silent currents under tangles of wild grapevines, and drooping alders, and haw trees. At one of these lovely spots the three vets sat down on the thick green sward to rest, "on Smith's account." The leaves of the trees were as fresh and green as in June, the jays called cheery greetings to them, and kingfishers darted to and fro with swooping, noiseless flight.

"I tell yeh, boys, this knocks the swamps of Loueesiana into kingdom come."

"You bet. All they c'n raise down there is snakes, niggers, and p'rticler hell."

"An' fightin' men," put in the older man.

"An' fightin' men. If I had a good hook an' line I'd sneak a pick'rel out o' that pond. Say, remember that time I shot that alligator—"

"I guess we'd better be crawlin' along," interrupted Smith, rising and shouldering his knapsack, with considerable effort, which he tried to hide.

"Say, Smith, lemme give you a lift on that."

"I guess I c'n manage," said Smith grimly.

"Course. But, yo' see, I may not have a chance right off to pay you back for the times you've carried my gun and hull caboodle. Say, now, gimme that gun, anyway."

"All right, if yeh feel like it, Jim," Smith replied, and they trudged along doggedly in the sun, which was getting higher and hotter each half-mile.

"Ain't it queer there ain't no teams comin' along," said Smith, after a long silence.

"Well, no, seein's it's Sunday."

"By jinks, that's a fact. It *is* Sunday. I'll get home in time f'r dinner, sure!" he exulted.

"She don't hev dinner usually till about *one* on Sundays." And he fell into a muse, in which he smiled.

"Well, I'll git home jest about six o'clock, jest about when the boys are milkin' the cows," said old Jim Cranby. "I'll step into the barn, an' then I'll say: 'He*ah!* why ain't this milkin' done before this time o' day?' An' then won't they yell!" he added, slapping his thigh in great glee.

Smith went on. "I'll jest go up the path. Old Rover'll come down the road to meet me. He won't bark; he'll know me, an' he'll come down waggin' his tail an' showin' his teeth. That's his way of laughin'. An' so I'll walk up to the kitchen door, an' I'll say, '*Dinner* f'r a hungry man!' An' then she'll jump up, an'—"

He couldn't go on. His voice choked at the thought of it. Saunders, the third man, hardly uttered a word, but walked silently behind the others. He had lost his wife the first year he was in the army. She died of pneumonia, caught in the autumn rains while working in the fields in his place.

They plodded along till at last they came to a parting of the ways. To the right the road continued up the main valley; to the left it went over the big ridge.

"Well, boys," began Smith, as they grounded their muskets and looked away up the valley, "here's where we shake hands. We've marched together a good many miles, an' now I s'pose we're done."

"Yes, I don't think we'll do any more of it f'r a while. I don't want to, I know."

"I hope I'll see yeh once in a while, boys, to talk over old times."

"Of course," said Saunders, whose voice trembled a little, too. "It ain't *exactly* like dyin'." They all found it hard to look at each other.

"But we'd ought'r go home with you," said Cranby. "You'll never climb that ridge with all them things on yer back."

"Oh, I'm all right! Don't worry about me. Every step takes me nearer home, yeh see. Well, good-by, boys."

They shook hands. "Good-by. Good luck!"

"Same to you. Lemme know how you find things at home."

"Good-by."

"Good-by."

He turned once before they passed out of sight, and waved his cap, and they did the same, and all yelled. Then all marched away with their long, steady, loping, veteran step. The solitary climber in blue walked on for a time, with his mind filled with the kindness of of his comrades, and musing upon the many wonderful days they had had together in camp and field.

He thought of his chum, Billy Tripp. Poor Billy! A "minie" ball fell into his breast one day, fell wailing like a cat, and tore a great ragged hole in his heart. He looked forward to a sad scene with Billy's mother and sweetheart. They would want to know all about it. He tried to recall all that Billy had said, and the particulars of it, but there was little to remember, just that wild wailing sound high in the air, a dull slap, a short, quick, expulsive groan, and the boy lay with his face in the dirt in the ploughed field they were marching across.

That was all. But all the scenes he had since been through had not dimmed the horror, the terror of that moment, when his boy comrade fell, with only a breath between a laugh and a death-groan. Poor handsome Billy! Worth millions of dollars was his young life.

These sombre recollections gave way at length to more cheerful feelings as he began to approach his home coolly. The fields and houses grew familiar, and in one or two he was greeted by people seated in the doorways. But he was in no mood to talk, and pushed on steadily, though he stopped and accepted a drink of milk once at the well-side of a neighbor.

The sun was burning hot on that slope, and his step grew slower, in spite of his iron resolution. He sat down several times to rest. Slowly he crawled up the rough, reddish-brown road, which wound along the hillside, under great trees, through dense groves of jack oaks, with tree-tops far below him on his left hand, and the hills far above him on his right. He crawled along like some minute, wingless variety of fly.

He ate some hardtack, sauced with wild berries, when he reached the summit of the ridge, and sat there for some time, looking down into his home coolly.

Sombre, pathetic figure! His wide, round, gray eyes gazing down into the beautiful valley, seeing and not seeing, the splendid cloud-shadows sweeping over the western hills and across the green and yellow wheat far below. His head drooped forward on his palm, his shoulders took on a tired stoop, his cheek-bones showed painfully. An observer might have said, "He is looking down upon his own grave."

II

Sunday comes in a Western wheat harvest with such sweet and sudden relaxation to man and beast that it would be holy for that reason, if for no other, and Sundays are usually fair in harvest-time. As one goes out into the field in the hot morning sunshine, with no sound abroad save the crickets and the indescribably pleasant silken rustling of the ripened grain, the reaper and the very sheaves in the stubble seem to be resting, dreaming.

Around the house, in the shade of the trees, the men sit, smoking, dozing, or reading the papers, while the women, never resting, move about at the housework. The men eat on Sundays about the same as on other days, and breakfast is no sooner over and out of the way than dinner begins.

But at the Smith farm there were no men dozing or reading. Mrs. Smith was alone with her three children, Mary, nine, Tommy, six, and little Ted, just past four. Her farm, rented to a neighbor, lay at the head of a coolly or narrow gully, made at some far-off post-glacial period by the vast and angry floods of water which gullied these tremendous furrows in the level prairie—furrows so deep that undisturbed portions of the original level rose like hills on either side, rose to quite considerable mountains.

The chickens wakened her as usual that Sabbath morning from dreams of her absent husband, from whom she had not heard for weeks. The shadows drifted over the hills, down the slopes, across the wheat, and up the opposite wall in leisurely way, as if, being Sunday, they could take it easy also. The fowls clustered about the housewife as she went out into the yard. Fuzzy little chickens swarmed out from the coops, where their clucking and perpetually disgruntled mothers tramped about, petulantly thrusting their heads through the spaces between the slats.

A cow called in a deep, musical bass, and a calf answered from a little pen near by, and a pig scurried guiltily out of the cabbages. Seeing all this, seeing the pig in the cabbages, the tangle of grass in the garden, the broken fence which she had mended again and again—

the little woman, hardly more than a girl, sat down and cried. The bright Sabbath morning was only a mockery without him!

A few years ago they had bought this farm, paying part, mortgaging the rest in the usual way. Edward Smith was a man of terrible energy. He worked "nights and Sundays," as the saying goes, to clear the farm of its brush and of its insatiate mortgage! In the midst of his Herculean struggle came the call for volunteers, and with the grim and unselfish devotion to his country which made the Eagle Brigade able to "whip its weight in wild-cats," he threw down his scythe and grub-axe, turned his cattle loose, and became a blue-coated cog in a vast machine for killing men, and not thistles. While the millionaire sent his money to England for safe-keeping, this man, with his girl-wife and three babies, left them on a mortgaged farm, and went away to fight for an idea. It was foolish, but it was sublime for all that.

That was three years before, and the young wife, sitting on the well-curb on this bright Sabbath harvest morning, was righteously rebellious. It seemed to her that she had borne her share of the country's sorrow. Two brothers had been killed, the renter in whose hands her husband had left the farm had proved a villain; one year the farm had been without crops, and now the overripe grain was waiting the tardy hand of the neighbor who had rented it, and who was cutting his own grain first.

About six weeks before, she had received a letter saying, "We'll be discharged in a little while." But no other word had come from him. She had seen by the papers that his army was being discharged, and from day to day other soldiers slowly percolated in blue streams back into the State and county, but still *her* hero did not return.

Each week she had told the children that he was coming, and she had watched the road so long that it had become unconscious; and as she stood at the well, or by the kitchen door, her eyes were fixed unthinkingly on the road that wound down the coolly.

Nothing wears on the human soul like waiting. If the stranded mariner, searching the sun-bright seas, could once give up hope of a ship, that horrible grinding on his brain would cease. It was this waiting, hoping, on the edge of despair, that gave Emma Smith no rest.

Neighbors said, with kind intentions: "He's sick, maybe, an' can't start north just yet. He'll come along one o' these days."

"Why don't he write?" was her question, which silenced them all. This Sunday morning it seemed to her as if she could not stand it longer. The house seemed intolerably lonely. So she dressed the little ones in their best calico dresses and home-made jackets, and, closing up the house, set off down the coolly to old Mother Gray's.

"Old Widder Gray" lived at the "mouth of the coolly." She was a widow woman with a large family of stalwart boys and laughing girls. She was the visible incarnation of hospitality and optimistic poverty. With Western open-heartedness she fed every mouth that asked food of her, and worked herself to death as cheerfully as her girls danced in the neighborhood harvest dances.

She waddled down the path to meet Mrs. Smith with a broad smile on her face.

"Oh, you little dears! Come right to your granny. Gimme me a kiss! Come right in, Mis' Smith. How are yeh, anyway? Nice mornin', ain't it? Come in an' set down. Everything's in a clutter, but that won't scare you any."

She led the way into the best room, a sunny, square room, carpeted with a faded and patched rag carpet, and papered with white-and-green wall-paper, where a few faded effigies of dead members of the family hung in variously sized oval walnut frames. The house resounded with singing, laughter, whistling, tramping of heavy boots, and riotous scufflings. Half-grown boys came to the door and crooked their fingers at the children, who ran out, and were soon heard in the midst of the fun.

"Don't s'pose you've heard from Ed?" Mrs. Smith shook her head. "He'll turn up some day, when you ain't lookin' for 'm." The good old soul had said that so many times that poor Mrs. Smith derived no comfort from it any longer.

"Liz heard from Al the other day. He's comin' some day this week. Anyhow, they expect him."

"Did he say anything of——"

"No, he didn't," Mrs. Gray admitted. "But then it was only a short letter, anyhow. Al ain't much for writin', anyhow.—But come out and see my new cheese. I tell yeh, I don't believe I ever had better luck in my life. If Ed should come, I want you should take him up a piece of this cheese."

It was beyond human nature to resist the influence of that noisy, hearty, loving household, and in the midst of the singing and laughing the wife forgot her anxiety, for the time at least, and laughed and sang with the rest.

About eleven o'clock a wagon-load more drove up to the door, and Bill Gray, the widow's oldest son, and his whole family, from Sand Lake Coolly, piled out amid a good-natured uproar. Every one talked at once, except Bill, who sat in the wagon with his wrists on his knees, a straw in his mouth, and an amused twinkle in his blue eyes.

"Ain't heard nothin' o' Ed, I s'pose?" he asked in a kind of bellow. Mrs. Smith shook her head. Bill, with a delicacy very striking in such a great giant, rolled his quid in his mouth, and said:

"Didn't know but you had. I hear two or three of the Sand Lake boys are comin'. Left New Orleenes some time this week. Didn't write nothin' about Ed, but no news is good news in such cases, mother always says."

"Well, go put out yer team," said Mrs. Gray, "an' go'n bring me in some taters, an', Sim, you go see if you c'n find some corn. Sadie, you put on the water to bile. Come now, hustle yer boots, all o' yeh. If I feed this yer crowd, we've got to have some raw materials. If y' think I'm goin' to feed yeh on pie—you're just mightily mistaken."

The children went off into the field, the girls put dinner on to boil, and then went to change their dresses and fix their hair. "Somebody might come," they said.

"Land sakes, I hope not! I don't know where in time I'd set 'em, 'less they'd eat at the second table," Mrs. Gray laughed, in pretended dismay.

The two older boys, who had served their time in the army, lay out on the grass before the house, and whittled and talked desultorily about the war and the crops, and planned buying a threshing-machine. The older girls and Mrs. Smith helped enlarge the table and put on the dishes, talking all the time in that cheery, incoherent, and meaningful way a group of such women have,—a conversation to be taken for its spirit rather than for its letter, though Mrs. Gray at last got the ear of them all and dissertated at length on girls.

"Girls in love ain' no use in the whole

blessed week," she said. "Sundays they're a-lookin' down the road, expectin' he'll *come.* Sunday afternoons they can't think o' nothin' else, 'cause he's *here.* Monday mornin's they're sleepy and kind o' dreamy and slimpsy, and good f'r nothin' on Tuesday and Wednesday. Thursday they git absent-minded, an' begin to look off toward Sunday agin, an' mope aroun' and let the dishwater git cold, right under their noses. Friday they break dishes, an' go off in the best room an' snivel, an' look out o' the winder. Saturdays they have queer spurts o' workin' like all p'ssessed, an' spurts o' frizzin' their hair. An' Sunday they begin it all over agin."

The girls giggled and blushed, all through this tirade from their mother, their broad faces and powerful frames anything but suggestive of lackadaisical sentiment. But Mrs. Smith said:

"Now, Mrs. Gray, I hadn't ought to stay to dinner. You've got——"

"Now you set right down! If any of them girls' beaus comes, they'll have to take what's left, that's all. They ain't s'posed to have much appetite, nohow. No, you're goin' to stay if they starve, an' they ain't no danger o' that."

At one o'clock the long table was piled with boiled potatoes, cords of boiled corn on the cob, squash and pumpkin pies, hot biscuit, sweet pickles, bread and butter, and honey. Then one of the girls took down a conch-shell from a nail, and going to the door, blew a long, fine, free blast, that showed there was no weakness of lungs in her ample chest.

Then the children came out of the forest of corn, out of the creek, out of the loft of the barn, and out of the garden.

"They come to their feed f'r all the world jest like the pigs when y' holler 'poo-ee!' See 'em scoot!" laughed Mrs. Gray, every wrinkle on her face shining with delight.

The men shut up their jack-knives, and surrounded the horse-trough to souse their faces in the cold, hard water, and in a few moments the table was filled with a merry crowd, and a row of wistful-eyed youngsters circled the kitchen wall, where they stood first on one leg and then on the other, in impatient hunger.

"Now pitch in, Mrs. Smith," said Mrs. Gray, presiding over the table. "You know these men critters. They'll eat every grain of it, if yeh give 'em a chance. I swan, they're made o' India-rubber, their stomachs is, I know it."

"Haf to eat to work," said Bill, gnawing a cob with a swift, circular motion that rivalled a corn-sheller in results.

"More like workin' to eat," put in one of the girls, with a giggle. "More eat 'n work with you."

"*You* needn't say anything, Net. Any one that'll eat seven ears——"

"I didn't, no such thing. You piled your cobs on my plate."

"That'll do to tell Ed Varney. It won't go down here where we know yeh."

"Good land! Eat all yeh want! They's plenty more in the fiel's, but I can't afford to give you young uns tea. The tea is for us women-folks, and 'specially f'r Mis' Smith an' Bill's wife. We're a-goin' to tell fortunes by it."

One by one the men filled up and shoved back, and one by one the children slipped into their places, and by two o'clock the women alone remained around the débris-covered table, sipping their tea and telling fortunes.

As they got well down to the grounds in the cup, they shook them with a circular motion in the hand, and then turned them bottom-side-up quickly in the saucer, then twirled them

three or four times one way, and three or four times the other, during a breathless pause. Then Mrs. Gray lifted the cup, and, gazing into it with profound gravity, pronounced the impending fate.

It must be admitted that, to a critical observer, she had abundant preparation for hitting close to the mark, as when she told the girls that "somebody was comin'." "It's a man," she went on gravely. "He is cross-eyed ——"

"Oh, you hush!" cried Nettie.

"He has red hair, and is death on b'iled corn and hot biscuit."

The others shrieked with delight.

"But he's goin' to get the mitten, that red-headed feller is, for I see another feller comin' up behind him."

"Oh, lemme see, lemme see!" cried Nettie.

"Keep off," said the priestess, with a lofty gesture. "His hair is black. He don't eat so much, and he works more."

The girls exploded in a shriek of laughter, and pounded their sister on the back.

At last came Mrs. Smith's turn, and she was trembling with excitement as Mrs. Gray again composed her jolly face to what she considered a proper solemnity of expression.

"Somebody is comin' to *you*," she said, after a long pause. "He's got a musket on his back. He's a soldier. He's almost here. See?"

She pointed at two little tea-stems, which really formed a faint suggestion of a man with a musket on his back. He had climbed nearly to the edge of the cup. Mrs. Smith grew pale with excitement. She trembled so she could hardly hold the cup in her hand as she gazed into it.

"It's Ed," cried the old woman. "He's on the way home. Heavens an' earth! There he is now!" She turned and waved her hand out toward the road. They rushed to the door to look where she pointed.

A man in a blue coat, with a musket on his back, was toiling slowly up the hill on the sun-bright, dusty road, toiling slowly, with bent head half hidden by a heavy knapsack. So tired it seemed that walking was indeed a process of falling. So eager to get home he would not stop, would not look aside, but plodded on, amid the cries of the locusts, the welcome of the crickets, and the rustle of the yellow wheat. Getting back to God's country, and his wife and babies!

Laughing, crying, trying to call him and the children at the same time, the little wife, almost hysterical, snatched her hat and ran out into the yard. But the soldier had disappeared over the hill into the hollow beyond, and, by the time she had found the children, he was too far away for her voice to reach him. And, besides, she was not sure it was her husband, for he had not turned his head at their shouts. This seemed so strange. Why didn't he stop to rest at his old neighbor's house? Tortured by hope and doubt, she hurried up the coolly as fast as she could push the baby wagon, the blue-coated figure just ahead pushing steadily, silently forward up the coolly.

When the excited, panting little group came in sight of the gate they saw the blue-coated figure standing, leaning upon the rough rail fence, his chin on his palms, gazing at the empty house. His knapsack, canteen, blankets, and musket lay upon the dusty grass at his feet.

He was like a man lost in a dream. His wide, hungry eyes devoured the scene. The rough lawn, the little unpainted house, the field of clear yellow wheat behind it, down across which streamed the sun, now almost ready to touch the high hill to the west, the crickets crying merrily, a cat on the fence near

by, dreaming, unmindful of the stranger in blue——

How peaceful it all was. O God! How far removed from all camps, hospitals, battle lines. A little cabin in a Wisconsin coolly, but it was majestic in its peace. How did he ever leave it for those years of tramping, thirsting, killing?

Trembling, weak with emotion, her eyes on the silent figure, Mrs. Smith hurried up to the fence. Her feet made no noise in the dust and grass, and they were close upon him before he knew of them. The oldest boy ran a little ahead. He will never forget that figure, that face. It will always remain as something epic, that return of the private. He fixed his eyes on the pale face covered with a ragged beard.

"Who *are* you, sir?" asked the wife, or, rather, started to ask, for he turned, stood a moment, and then cried:

"Emma!"

"Edward!"

The children stood in a curious row to see their mother kiss this bearded, strange man, the elder girl sobbing sympathetically with her mother. Illness had left the soldier partly deaf, and this added to the strangeness of his manner.

But the youngest child stood away, even after the girl had recognized her father and kissed him. The man turned then to the baby, and said in a curiously unpaternal tone:

"Come here, my little man; don't you know me?" But the baby backed away under the fence and stood peering at him critically.

"My little man!" What meaning in those words! This baby seemed like some other woman's child, and not the infant he had left in his wife's arms. The war had come between him and his baby—he was only a strange man to him, with big eyes; a soldier, with mother hanging to his arm, and talking in a loud voice.

"And this is Tom," the private said, drawing the oldest boy to him. "*He'll* come and see me. *He* knows his poor old pap when he comes home from the war."

The mother heard the pain and reproach in his voice and hastened to apologize.

"You've changed so, Ed. He can't know yeh. This is papa, Teddy; come and kiss him —Tom and Mary do. Come, won't you?" But Teddy still peered through the fence with solemn eyes, well out of reach. He resembled a half-wild kitten that hesitates, studying the tones of one's voice.

"I'll fix him," said the soldier, and sat down to undo his knapsack, out of which he drew three enormous and very red apples. After giving one to each of the older children, he said:

"*Now* I guess he'll come. Eh, my little man? Now come see your pap."

Teddy crept slowly under the fence, assisted by the overzealous Tommy, and a moment later was kicking and squalling in his father's arms. Then they entered the house, into the sitting room, poor, bare, art-forsaken little room, too, with its rag carpet, its square clock, and its two or three chromos and pictures from *Harper's Weekly* pinned about.

"Emma, I'm all tired out," said Private Smith, as he flung himself down on the carpet as he used to do, while his wife brought a pillow to put under his head, and the children stood about munching their apples.

"Tommy, you run and get me a pan of chips, and Mary, you get the tea-kettle on, and I'll go and make some biscuit."

And the soldier talked. Question after question he poured forth about the crops, the cattle, the renter, the neighbors. He slipped his heavy government brogan shoes off his poor, tired, blistered feet, and lay out with

utter, sweet relaxation. He was a free man again, no longer a soldier under a command. At supper he stopped once, listened and smiled. "That's old Spot. I know her voice. I s'pose that's her calf out there in the pen. I can't milk her to-night, though. I'm too tired. But I tell you, I'd like a drink of her milk. What's become of old Rove?"

"He died last winter. Poisoned, I guess." There was a moment of sadness for them all. It was some time before the husband spoke again, in a voice that trembled a little.

"Poor old feller! He'd 'a' known me half a mile away. I expected him to come down the hill to meet me. It 'ud 'a' been more like comin' home if I could 'a' seen him comin' down the road an' waggin' his tail, an' laughin' that way he has. I tell yeh, it kind o' took hold o' me to see the blinds down an' the house shut up."

"But, yeh see, we—we expected you'd write again 'fore you started. And then we thought we'd see you if you *did* come," she hastened to explain.

"Well, I ain't worth a cent on writin'. Besides, it's just as well yeh didn't know when I was comin'. I tell you, it sounds good to hear them chickens out there, an' turkeys, an' the crickets. Do you know they don't have just the same kind o' crickets down South? Who's Sam hired t' help cut yer grain?"

"The Ramsey boys."

"Looks like a good crop; but I'm afraid I won't do much gettin' it cut. This cussed fever an' ague has got me down pretty low. I don't know when I'll get rid of it. I'll bet I've took twenty-five pounds of quinine if I've taken a bit. Gimme another biscuit. I tell yeh, they taste good, Emma. I ain't had anything like it —— Say, if you'd 'a' hear'd me braggin' to th' boys about your butter 'n' biscuits I'll bet your ears 'ud 'a' burnt."

The private's wife colored with pleasure. "Oh, you're always a-braggin' about your things. Everybody makes good butter."

"Yes; old lady Snyder, for instance."

"Oh, well, she ain't to be mentioned. She's Dutch."

"Or old Mis' Snively. One more cup o' tea, Mary. That's my girl! I'm feeling better already. I just b'lieve the matter with me is, I'm *starved*."

This was a delicious hour, one long to be remembered. They were like lovers again. But their tenderness, like that of a typical American family, found utterance in tones, rather than in words. He was praising her when praising her biscuit, and she knew it. They grew soberer when he showed where he had been struck, one ball burning the back of his hand, one cutting away a lock of hair from his temple, and one passing through the calf of his leg. The wife shuddered to think how near she had come to being a soldier's widow. Her waiting no longer seemed hard. This sweet, glorious hour effaced it all.

Then they rose, and all went out into the garden and down to the barn. He stood beside her while she milked old Spot. They began to plan fields and crops for next year.

His farm was weedy and encumbered, a rascally renter had run away with his machinery (departing between two days), his children needed clothing, the years were coming upon him, he was sick and emaciated, but his heoric soul did not quail. With the same courage with which he had faced his Southern march he entered upon a still more hazardous future.

Oh, that mystic hour! The pale man with big eyes standing there by the well, with his young wife by his side. The vast moon swinging above the eastern peaks, the cattle winding down the pasture slopes with jangling bells, the crickets singing, the stars blooming out sweet and far and serene; the katydids rhythmically calling, the little turkeys crying querulously, as they settled to roost in the poplar tree near the open gate. The voices at the well drop lower, the little ones nestle in their father's arms at last, and Teddy falls asleep there.

The common soldier of the American volunteer army had returned. His war with the South was over, and his fight, his daily running fight with nature and against the injustice of his fellow-men, was begun again.

The Disbandment
of the Army of Northern Virginia

A WARMLY SYMPATHETIC VIEW OF THE NOSTALGIA FOR DEPARTED GLORY FELT BY THE OLD soldiers who never die, "The Disbandment of the Army of Northern Virginia" came out in 1898 in *McClure's Magazine*. Marshall Putnam Thompson (1869–1929) was a Boston attorney who occasionally wrote fiction. His works include a novel of South American love and intrigue, *The Lieutenant, the Girl, and the Viceroy*.

This short story typifies the halo of sentiment that was beginning to hover over the memories of the Civil War by the end of the nineteenth century.

WE RODE PAST THE CURVE, AND SAW IN THE gathering twilight the yellow Virginia road winding ahead for miles, nothing else to break the monotony of the ranks of pines except a weather-beaten shanty that stood lonely among the trees. In front, a rude flag-pole sentineled the way; and at the peak fluttered in the evening breeze, thirty years after the war had ended, the tattered and faded, but still to be distinguished, red field, divided by the blue St. Andrew's Cross, of the last battle-flag of the Southern Confederacy.

As the sun slowly sank behind the pines, the notes of a bugle sounded among the trees. Then a rifle shot rang from the cabin, and an old man, erect as a soldier, walked, or rather marched, to the flag-pole, and gently lowered the flag. As it fluttered to the ground, I noticed that the Virginia colonel with whom I rode had uncovered and that a look of other days had come into his face.

"What does it mean?" I asked.

"It is the last headquarters of the Army of Northern Virginia," he laughed in reply.

Afterwards I heard the story, partly from the Colonel, partly from others.

When the War broke out and the strains of "Dixie," from the Gulf to Baltimore, were setting bright eyes and brave hearts a-dancing, Company F was being recruited in Albemarle County, Virginia. The privates were gentlemen's sons from neighboring plantations; the officers, wealthy land-owners of the vicinity; the equipment of the best, the uniforms being of fine gray cloth and made in London; and Company F was considered—at least in Albemarle County—"the finest company of the finest State in or out of the Union, sah."

In the community of Ivy Church there was only one man of military age not in Company F. He was an Irishman, Patrick Murphy, once a sergeant in the British army, now a "land-owner and a gintleman." He had an acre or two in the country. He raised vegetables, and sold them when he could, smoked his pipe, and was happy. Patrick had not been asked to join the company when it was organized, for the young cavaliers had no desire for the society of a man who worked with his hands and was, in their opinion, "little better than a nigger."

As the days of drilling wore away, all was not sunshine in Company F. The officers, with the best intentions in the world, knew absolutely nothing of drill and military discipline, and of course the men could not be blamed for ignorance when there was no adequate instruction. Meanwhile, Patrick Murphy stood an on-looker and watched with amused contempt the movements of "th' recruities."

When Captain De Courcy (ex-West-Pointer) took charge of the company, things rapidly changed for the better; but it took all the company's enthusiasm and all its respect for De Courcy to keep from open protest when the captain announced that Patrick Murphy must and should be enlisted.

"He is an ex-sergeant," said De Courcy; "has served in the British army; and we've got to have a good non-commissioned officer or we'll go all to pieces at the first fire; the men marched this afternoon like a lot of brats with broomsticks."

"But a common Irishman to be placed over gentlemen!"

"And mighty lucky for the gentlemen," said De Courcy. "You gentlemen must learn that there are just two classes in the army—officers and privates. Other things being equal, I should prefer to have gentlemen privates; but I have had Irishmen, Englishmen, Germans, and niggers, and they all come out about the same under a good sergeant."

"Not niggers!"

"Yes, niggers. They're all right when properly drilled, and you fellows will admit it too before this war is over," and with this heretical remark De Courcy went to his quarters.

So Patrick Murphy was enlisted. He knew something of the feeling in the company, and when he had signed the papers and taken the oath of allegiance to the sovereign State of Virginia, he turned to the on-lookers and said:

"I'm the lasht man of this coompany to enlisht; but tak' notice, I'll be th' lasht wan to dishband."

The influence of Murphy as drill-master was immediately apparent: the lines straightened out, the men became erect, the company wheeled like clockwork, and the manual of arms went with the click and precision of machinery. Then came the day when they marched off—

"Away down South in Dixie,
Look away, look away."

How well the old Virginians remember it! The line in front of the court-house steps; the girls in their big bonnets and voluminous skirts; the fathers and mothers and sweethearts; the cheer, the sob, and the laugh! The presentation of the flag—"the blue flag of

Virginia—blue as the sky, woven by the fair hands of the ladies of Albemarle County—given to the sons of heroic sires, the best blood of the Old Dominion—gentlemen." "May it wave in victory!" "May it never know defeat!" "Hurrah!—three cheers for the ladies of Albemarle County!" "Good-by! Good-by!"

> "Away down South in Dixie,
> Look away,—look—"

The line has passed down the street, out on the yellow road, and the pine trees hide it.

More than thirty years ago, ladies and gentlemen of Virginia; but the days of '61 still live in the hearts of your faded women and white-haired men who entertain us, the sons of the Northern invaders of other days, with your generous hospitality; still live in your hearts, with no thought of bitterness or disloyalty; but they were your boys, and they lie from Bull Run to Appomattox—but to you, still young, still confident, ever marching on in the spring sunshine, the bonny blue flag waving over them—

> "Away down South in Dixie,
> Look away, look away."

Patrick Murphy marched away with the company; in the first engagement saved the flag, and became color-sergeant; went to West Virginia and back to Manassas; fought at Fair Oaks and Seven Pines; tramped on the wonderful night march through the Shenandoah valley; kept time to the

> "Maryland, my Maryland"

of the bands, as regiment after regiment crossed the river in the shadow of the hills, and swung over the dusty road on the march to Frederick. After Antietam, was offered and refused a commission; stood in the line of flame and death at Fredericksburg and Chancellorsville; marched with the tattered and ragged, but till now victorious, Army of Northern Virginia on the second invasion of the North; retreated, as light-hearted in defeat as in victory, from Gettysburg, and after each reverse of the Wilderness laughed and said, "We'll lick 'em worse nixt toime."

The next times grew sad for the Army of Northern Virginia. Day by day came news of fresh losses, fresh defeats on the Gulf, in the West. Rumors of Sherman's march thickened, while in front their old enemy, the Army of the Potomac, ever persistent, with a commander at last who understood his trade, pressed relentlessly forward. At last came the feeling that the very stars in their courses fought for the Northern battalions—Petersburg, Cold Harbor—and the army, starving, ragged, but gallant still, was for the first time in its history in real retreat. Here and there a man slipped away in the night, sure that the war was practically over; now a company lost ten and a regiment a hundred; but the majority, ragged, shoeless, shirtless, munched their parched corn, marched on, fought on, to Appomattox; and with the majority marched and fought Patrick Murphy.

As General Lee, "flower of Southern chivalry" indeed, rode back from his interview with Grant, his escort, respecting his feelings, fell back, while the General with head bowed, let his horse choose his own way back to the defeated army. Suddenly his revery was disturbed; a thin, sun-burned sergeant, carrying a flag, stepped from the bushes, halted, and came to attention.

"Gineral Lee."

"Yes, my man."

"Me name is Patrick Murphy."

"Well?"

"Gineral Lee, the bys say that the Arrmy of Northern Virginia is surrindered and will dishband."

"Yes, my man. The army is to give its parole never to bear arms against the United States, turn in its arms and accoutrements, but keep its horses, and disband."

Patrick Murphy shifted uneasily from foot to foot, while the General watched him curiously, doubtless glad that the train of his gloomy thoughts should be broken by the interruption. Suddenly a twinkle came into Murphy's eyes.

"Gineral Lee, if wan division of th' Arrmy of Northern Virginia should refuse to dishband, that wad still be the Arrmy of Northern Virginia, wouldn't it, Gineral Lee?"

"Yes, my man."

"If two regiments or a brigade should refuse to dishband, that wad be the Arrmy, wouldn't it?"

"Yes, my man," replied the General, wondering what the whimsical Celtic brain was evolving.

"Gineral Lee, if all th' officers an' all th' soldiers of the Arrmy of Northern Virginia except wan coompany should dishband, that coompany wad be the Arrmy of Northern Virginia?"

"Yes, yes, my man." The General was getting impatient, and lifted his bridle rein.

"Wan minute more—if th' Gineral plaze, sor! If all that wan coompany should dishband except wan man, that man wad be the Arrmy, sor, wouldn't he, Gineral Lee?"

The General's eyes twinkled at the conceit, but answered gravely as before, "Yes, my man, I suppose he would."

Murphy stood even more erect than before.

"Gineral Lee, I refuse to dishband." Then turning half front, his voice ringing with the tone of command, "Arrmy of Northern Virginia, about face! Forward march! Report at Ivy Church, Virginia!" and off he marched whistling, not "Dixie," but the "Wearing of the Green."

When Colonel Marshall, who was on escort duty, rode up, he wondered as he heard for the first time in many weary months a hearty laugh ring from the General's lips.

General Lee forgot the matter entirely; but when the Army of Northern Virginia gave in its parole, one name was missing—that of Patrick Murphy—and one battle-flag was never accounted for; it was the one I had seen fluttering down from the staff among the pine trees thirty years after the war ended, where Patrick Murphy, in sunshine and shadow, held his cabin, the last stronghold of the dead Confederacy, against his one enemy—old age, and maintained under the branches of the pines the organization of the Army of Northern Virginia.

Here I suppose the story of the disbandment of the Army of Northern Virginia would end; but in May of this year I again rode down through the pines, and again the Colonel rode with me. This time he rode in a blue uniform, and the letters U.S.V. glittered on the collar. In front marched, as in '61, the young men of Ivy Church; but their uniforms were blue, and the national flag kissed the sunlight above the marching ranks. There had been the scenes of 1861 reënacted before the court-house steps, and a new picture of marching men and a proudly tossing flag had been painted, never to fade by the years, and again the old Confederate tune set the eyes and the hearts a-dancing:

> "Away down South in Dixie,
> Look away, look away."

Patrick Murphy came from his cabin, and saluted the Colonel. He was dressed in the tattered gray of Company F, in his hands the furled battle-flag.

"I want th' officer commanding this coompany."

"I am he," said the Colonel.

"Captain—for that's your rank now—the Arrmy of Northern Virginia"—a twinkle danced in the faded blue eyes—"the Arrmy of Northern Virginia wants to enlist as an organization, to fight"—his eyes lost their twinkle, and his face took on a new look of dignity—"for the United States."

The Colonel waited a moment. "You are too old," he said.

"Then it's toime to tak' th' oath of alle-giance and dishband," said Murphy. "There is wan flag for us now, and it's not this," and he held up the old flag.

Fresh and clear came the music of the band:

> "Away down South in Dixie,
> Look away, look away."

As the flag passed—his flag at last—the old man uncovered and stood at salute.

> "In Dixie's land I take my stand,
> To live and die for Dixie."

The Colonel was silent. Wilder and more rollicking came the music, the dust rolled up in a cloud, and still Patrick Murphy stood at attention.

"By Jove, the war is over!" exclaimed the Colonel. "Order them to play the 'Star Spangled Banner.'"

Decoration Day

SARAH ORNE JEWETT (1849–1909), WHO WAS PERHAPS THE MOST SKILLED OF AMERICAN regional writers, supplies a fitting story to close a book of Civil War fiction. "Decoration Day," which appeared in *Harper's New Monthly Magazine* in 1892, calls forth in Miss Jewett's precise style a final mood of commemoration for the war that was over and done.

In all her stories the author used her intimate knowledge of the people and environment of her native state of Maine to create delicate local color studies. Writing with clarity and poetic serenity, she established characterizations marked by intuitive sensitivity. Her quiet career started in 1869 when she published the first of a series of stories that were collected in *Deephaven* in 1887. Over a dozen other works of provincial realism followed. Her masterpiece, *The Country of the Pointed Firs*, shows the same quality that marks this short story—the ability to recall the strength and isolation of the New England natives.

"Decoration Day" is a peaceful hymn to those who survived as well as to those who gave their lives in the Civil War. The flavor of a small town Memorial Day furnishes an end to a collection of stories about a war whose passions once flamed brightly and whose banked fires still give off a glitter.

I

A WEEK BEFORE THE 30TH OF MAY, THREE friends—John Stover and Henry Merrill and Asa Brown—happened to meet on Saturday evening at Barton's store at the Plains. They were enjoying this idle hour after a busy week. After long easterly rains, the sun had at last come out bright and clear, and all the Barlow farmers had been planting. There was even a good deal of ploughing left to be done, the season was so backward.

The three middle-aged men were old friends. They had been school-fellows, and when they were hardly out of their boyhood the war came on, and they enlisted in the same company, on the same day, and happened to march away elbow to elbow. Then came the great experience of a great war, and the years that followed their return from the South had come to each almost alike. They might have been members of the same rustic household, they knew each other's history so well.

They were sitting on a low wooden bench at the left of the store door as you went in. People were coming and going on their Saturday night errands—the post-office was in Barton's store—but the friends talked on eagerly, without interrupting themselves, except by an occasional nod of recognition. They appeared to take no notice at all of the neighbors whom they saw oftenest. It was a most beautiful evening; the two great elms were almost half in leaf over the blacksmith shop which stood across the wide road. Farther along were two small old-fashioned houses and the old white church, with its pretty belfry of four arched sides and a tiny dome at the top. The large cockerel on the vane was pointing a little south of west, and there was still light enough to make it shine bravely against the deep blue eastern sky. On the western side of the road, near the store, were the parsonage and the storekeeper's modern house, which had a French roof and some attempt at decoration, which the long-established Barlow people called gingerbread-work, and regarded with mingled pride and disdain. These buildings made the tiny village called Barlow Plains. They stood in the middle of a long narrow strip of level ground. They were islanded by green fields and pastures. There were hills beyond; the mountains themselves seemed very near. Scattered about on the hill slopes were farm-houses, which stood so far apart, with their clusters of out-buildings, that each looked lonely, and the pine woods above seemed to beseige them all. It was lighter on the uplands than it was in the valley where the three men sat on their bench, with their backs to the store and the western sky.

"Well, here we be 'most into June, an' I ain't got a bush bean aboveground," lamented Henry Merrill.

"Your land's always late, ain't it? But you always catch up with the rest on us," Asa Brown consoled him. "I've often observed that your land, though early planted, is late to sprout. I view it there's a good week's difference betwixt me an' Stover an' your folks, but come 1st o' July we all even up."

" 'Tis just so," said John Stover, taking his pipe out of his mouth, as if he had a good deal more to say, and then replacing it, as if he had changed his mind.

"Made it extry hard having that long wet spell. Can't none on us take no day off this season," said Asa Brown; but nobody thought it worth his while to respond to such evident truth.

"Next Saturday'll be the 30th o' May— that's Decoration Day, ain't it?—come round again. Lord! how the years slip by after you git to be forty-five an' along there!" said Asa again. "I s'pose some o' our folks'll go over to Alton to see the procession, same's usual. I've got to git one o' them small flags to stick on our Joel's grave, an' Mis' Dexter always counts on havin' some for Harrison's lot. I calculate to get 'em somehow. I must make time to ride over, but I don't know where the time's comin' from out o' next week. I wish the women folks would tend to them things. There's the spot where Eb Munson an' John Tighe lays in the poor-farm lot, an' I did mean certain to buy flags for 'em last year an' year before, but I went an' forgot it. I'd like to have folks that rode by notice 'em for once, if they was town paupers. Eb Munson was as darin' a man as ever stepped out to tuck o' drum."

"So he was," said John Stover, taking out his pipe with decision and knocking out the ashes. "Drink was his ruin; but I wa'n't one that could be harsh with Eb, no matter what he done. He worked hard long's he could, too; but he wa'n't like a sound man, an' I think he took somethin' first not so much 'cause he loved it, but to kind of keep his strength up so's he could work, an' then, all of a sudden, rum clinched with him an' threw him. Eb was talkin' 'long o' me one day when he was about half full, an' says he, right out, 'I wouldn't have fell to this state,' says he, 'if I'd had me a home an' a little fam'ly; but it don't make no difference to nobody, and it's the best comfort I seem to have, an' I ain't goin' to do without it. I'm ailin' all the time,' says he, 'an' if I keep middlin' full, I make out to hold my own an' to keep along o' my work.' I pitied Eb. I says to him, 'You ain't goin' to bring no shame on us old army boys, be you, Eb?' An' he says no, he wa'n't. I think if he'd lived to get one o' them big fat pensions, he'd had it easier. Eight dollars a month paid his board, while he'd pick up what cheap work he could, an' then he got so that decent folks didn't seem to want the bother of him, an' so he come on the town."

"There was somethin' else to it," said Henry Merrill, soberly. "Drink come natural to him, 'twas born in him, I expect, an' there wa'n't nobody that could turn the divil out same's they did in Scriptur'. His father an' his gran'-father was drinkin' men; but they was kind-hearted an' good neighbors, an' never set out to wrong nobody. 'Twas the custom to drink in their day; folks was colder an' lived poorer in early times, an' that's how most of 'em kept a-goin'. But what stove Eb all up was his dis-

app'ntment with Marthy Peck—her forsakin' of him an' marryin' old John Down whilst Eb was off to war. I've always laid it up ag'inst her."

"So've I," said Asa Brown. "She didn't use the poor fellow right. I guess she was full as well off, but it's one thing to show judgment, an' another thing to have heart."

There was a long pause; the subject was too familiar to need further comment.

"There ain't no public sperit here in Barlow," announced Asa Brown, with decision. "I don't s'pose we could ever get up anything for Decoration Day. I've felt kind of 'shamed, but it always comes in a busy time; 'twa'n't no time to have it, anyway, right in late plantin'."

"'Tain't no use to look for public sperit 'less you've got some yourself," observed John Stover, soberly; but something had pleased him in the discouraged suggestion. "Perhaps we could mark the day this year. It comes on a Saturday; that ain't nigh so bad as bein' in the middle of the week."

Nobody made any answer, and presently he went on:

"There was a time along back when folks was too near the war-time to give much thought to the bigness of it. The best fellows was them that had staid to home an' worked their trades an' laid up money; but I don't know's it's so now."

"Yes, the fellows that staid at home got all the fat places, an' when we come back we felt dreadful behind the times," grumbled Asa Brown. "I remember how 'twas."

"They begun to call us hero an' old stick-in-the-mud just about the same time," resumed Stover, with a chuckle. "We wa'n't no hand for strippin' woodland nor tradin' hosses them first few years. I don' know why 'twas we were so beat out. The best most on us could do was to sag right on to the old folks. Father he never wanted me to go to the war—'twas partly his Quaker breed—an' he used to be dreadful mortified with the way I hung round down here to the store an' loafed round a-talkin' about when I was out South, an' arguin' with folks that didn't know nothin' about what the generals done. There! I see me now just as he see me then; but after I had my boy strut out, I took holt o' the old farm 'long o' father, an' I've made it bounce. Look at them old meadows an' see the herds' grass that come off of 'em last year! I ain't ashamed o' my place, if I did go to the war."

"It all looks a sight bigger to me now than it did then," said Henry Merrill. "Our goin' to the war I refer to. We didn't sense it no more than other folks did. I used to be sick o' hearin' their stuff about patriotism an' lovin' your country, an' them pieces o' poetry women-folks wrote for the papers on the old flag, an' our fallen heroes, an' them things; they didn't seem to strike me in the right place; but I tell ye it kind o' starts me now every time I come on the flag sudden—it does so. A spell ago—'long in the fall, I guess it was—I was over to Alton tradin', an' there was a fire company paradin'. They'd got a prize at a fair, an' had just come home on the cars, an' I heard the band; so I stepped to the front o' the store where me an' my woman was, an' the company felt well, an' was comin' along the street 'most as good as troops. I see the old flag a-comin', kind of blowin' back, an' it went all over me. Somethin' worked round in my throat; I vow I come near cryin'. I was glad nobody see me."

"I'd go to war again in a minute," declared Stover, after an expressive pause; "but I expect we should know better what we was about. I don' know but we've got too many

rooted opinions now to make us the best o' soldiers."

"Martin Tighe an' John Tighe was considerable older than the rest, and they done well," answered Henry Merrill, quickly. "We three was the youngest of any, but we did think at the time we knew the most."

"Well, whatever you may say, that war give the country a great start," said Asa Brown. "I tell ye we just begin to see the scope on't. There was my cousin, you know, Dan'l Evans, that stopped with us last winter; he was tellin' me that one o' his coastin' trips he was into the port o' Beaufort lo'din' with yaller-pine lumber, an' he was into an old buryin'-ground there is there, an' he see a stone that had on it some young Southern fellow's name that was killed in the war, an' under it, 'He died for his country.' Dan'l knowed how I used to feel about them South Car'lina goings on, an' I did feel kind o' red an' ugly for a minute, an' then somethin' come over me, an' I says, 'Well, I don' know but what the poor chap did, Dan Evans, when you come to view it all round.' "

The other men made no answer.

"Le's see what we can do this year. I don't care if we be a poor han'ful," urged Henry Merrill. "The young folks ought to have the good of it; I'd like to have my boys see somethin' different. Le's get together what men there is. How many's left, anyhow? I know there was thirty-seven went from old Barlow, three-month men an' all."

"There can't be over eight, countin' out Martin Tighe; he can't march," said Stover. "No, 'tain't worth while." But the others did not notice his disapproval.

"There's nine in all," announced Asa Brown, after pondering and counting two or three times on his fingers. "I can't make us no more. I never could carry figgers in my head."

"I make nine," said Merrill. "We'll have Martin ride, an' Jesse Dean too, if he will. He's awful lively on them canes o' his. An' there's Jo Wade with his crutch; he's amazin' spry for a short distance. But we can't let 'em go afoot; they're decripped men. We'll make 'em all put on what they've got left o' their uniforms, an' we'll scratch round an' have us a fife an' drum, an' make the best show we can."

"Why, Martin Tighe's boy, the next to the oldest, is an excellent hand to play the fife!" said John Stover, suddenly growing enthusiastic. "If you two are set on it, let's have a word with the minister to-morrow, an' see what he says. Perhaps he'll give out some kind of a notice. You have to have a good many bunches o' flowers. I guess we'd better call a meetin', some few on us, an' talk it over first o' the week. 'Twouldn't be no great of a range for us to take to march from the old buryin'-ground at the meetin'-house here up to the poor-farm an' round by Deacon Elwell's lane, so's to notice them two stones he set up for his boys that was sunk on the man-o'-war. I expect they notice stones same's if the folks laid there, don't they?"

He spoke wistfully. The others knew that Stover was thinking of the stone he had set up to the memory of his only brother, whose nameless grave had been made somewhere in the Wilderness.

"I don't know but what they'll be mad if we don't go by every house in town," he added, anxiously, as they rose to go home. "'Tis a terrible scattered population in Barlow to favor with a procession."

It was a mild starlit night. The three friends took their separate ways presently, leaving the Plains road and crossing the fields by footpaths toward their farms.

II

The week went by, and the next Saturday morning brought fair weather. It was a busy morning on the farms—like any other; but long before noon the teams of horses and oxen were seen going home from work in the fields, and everybody got ready in haste for the great event of the afternoon. It was so seldom that any occasion roused public interest in Barlow that there was an unexpected response, and the green before the old white meeting-house was covered with country wagons and groups of people, whole families together, who had come on foot. The old soldiers were to meet in the church; at half past one the procession was to start, and on its return the minister was to make an address in the old burying-ground. John Stover had been a lieutenant in the army, so he was made captain of the day. A man from the next town had offered to drum for them, and Martin Tighe's proud boy was present with his fife. He had a great longing—strange enough in that peaceful sheep-raising neighborhood—to go into the army; but he and his elder brother were the mainstay of their crippled father, and he could not be spared from the large household until a younger brother could take his place; so that all his fire and military zeal went for the present into martial tunes, and the fife was the safety-valve for his enthusiasm.

The army men were used to seeing each other; everybody knew everybody in the little country town of Barlow; but when one comrade after another appeared in what remained of his accoutrements, they felt the day to be greater than they had planned, and the simple ceremony proved more solemn than any one expected. They could make no use of their everyday jokes and friendly greetings. Their old blue coats and tarnished army caps looked faded and antiquated enough. One of the men had nothing left but his rusty canteen and rifle; but these he carried like sacred emblems. He had worn out all his army clothes long ago, because when he was discharged he was too poor to buy any others.

When the door of the church opened, the veterans were not abashed by the size and silence of the crowd. They came walking two by two down the steps, and took their places in line as if there were nobody looking on. Their brief evolutions were like a mystic rite. The two lame men refused to do anything but march, as best they could; but poor Martin Tighe, more disabled than they, was brought out and lifted into Henry Merrill's best wagon, where he sat up, straight and soldierly, with his boy for driver. There was a little flag in the whip socket before him, which flapped gayly in the breeze. It was such a long time since he had been seen out-of-doors that everybody found him a great object of interest, and paid him much attention. Even those who were tired of being asked to contribute to his support, who resented the fact of his having a helpless wife and great family; who always insisted that with his little pension and hopeless lameness, his fingerless left hand and failing sight, he could support himself and his household if he chose—even those persons came forward now to greet him handsomely and with large approval. To be sure, he enjoyed the conversation of idlers, and his wife had a complaining way that was the same as begging, especially since her boys began to grow up and be of some use; and there were one or two near neighbors who never let them

really want; so other people, who had cares enough of their own, could excuse themselves for forgetting him the year round, and even call him shiftless. But there were none to look askance at Martin Tighe on Decoration Day, as he sat in the wagon, with his bleached face like a captive's, and his thin, afflicted body. He stretched out his whole hand impartially to those who had remembered him and those who had forgotten both his courage at Fredericksburg and his sorry need in Barlow.

Henry Merrill had secured the engine company's large flag in Alton, and now carried it proudly. There were eight men in line, two by two, and marching a good bit apart, to make their line the longer. The fife and drum struck up gallantly together, and the little procession moved away slowly along the country road. It gave an unwonted touch of color to the landscape—the scarlet, the blue, between the new-ploughed fields and budding road-side thickets, between the wide dim ranges of the mountains, under the great white clouds of the spring sky. Such processions grow more pathetic year by year; it will not be so long now before wondering children will have seen the last. The aging faces of the men, the renewed comradeship, the quick beat of the hearts that remember, the tenderness of those who think upon old sorrows—all these make the day a lovelier and a sadder festival. So men's hearts were stirred, they knew not why, when they heard the shrill fife and the incessant drum along the quiet Barlow road, and saw the handful of old soldiers marching by. Nobody thought of them as familiar men and neighbors alone—they were a part of that army which saved its country. They had taken their lives in their hands and gone out to fight—plain John Stover and Jesse Dean and the rest. No matter if every other day in the year they counted for little or much, whether they were lame-footed and despised, whether their farms were of poor soil or rich.

The little troop went in slender line along the road; the crowded country wagons and all the people who went afoot followed Martin Tighe's wagon as if it were a great gathering at a country funeral. The route was short, and the long straggling line marched slowly; it could go no faster than the lame men could walk.

In one of the houses by the road-side an old woman sat by a window, in an old-fashioned black gown, and clean white cap with a prim border which bound her thin sharp features closely. She had been for a long time looking out eagerly over the snowberry and cinnamon-rose bushes; her face was pressed close to the pane, and presently she caught sight of the great flag.

"Let me see 'em! I've got to see 'em go by!" she pleaded, trying to rise from her chair alone when she heard the fife, and the women helped her to the door, and held her so that she could stand and wait. She had been an old woman when the war began; she had sent two sons and two grandsons to the field; they were all gone now. As the men came by, she straightened her bent figure with all the vigor of youth. The fife and drum stopped suddenly; the colors dipped. She did not heed that, but her old eyes flashed and then filled with tears to see the flag going to salute the soldiers' graves. "Thank ye, boys; thank ye!" she cried, in her quavering voice, and they all cheered her. The cheer went back along the straggling line for old Grandmother Dexter, standing there in her front door between the lilacs. It was one of the great moments of the day.

The few old people at the poorhouse, too, were waiting to see the show. The keeper's young son, knowing that it was a day of festivity, and not understanding exactly why, had put his toy flag out of the gable window, and there it showed against the gray clapboards like a gay flower. It was the only bit of decoration along the veterans' way, and they stopped and saluted it before they broke ranks and went out to the field corner beyond the poor-farm barn to the bit of ground that held the paupers' unmarked graves. There was a solemn silence while Asa Brown went to the back of Tighe's wagon, where such light freight was carried, and brought two flags, and he and John Stover planted them straight in the green sod. They knew well enough where the right graves were, for these had been made in a corner by themselves, with unwonted sentiment. And so Eben Munson and John Tighe were honored like the rest, both by their flags and by great and unexpected nosegays of spring flowers, daffies and flowering currant and red tulips, which lay on the graves already. John Stover and his comrade glanced at each other curiously while they stood singing, and then laid their own bunches of lilacs down and came away.

Then something happened that almost none of the people in the wagons understood. Martin Tighe's boy, who played the fife, had studied well his part, and on his poor short-winded instrument now sounded taps as well as he could. He had heard it done once in Alton at a soldier's funeral. The plaintive notes called sadly over the fields, and echoed back from the hills. The few veterans could not look at each other; their eyes brimmed up with tears; they could not have spoken. Nothing called back old army days like that. They had a sudden vision of the Virginian camp, the hillside dotted white with tents, the twinkling lights in other camps, and far away the glow of smouldering fires. They heard the bugle call from post to post; they remembered the chilly winter night, the wind in the pines, the laughter of the men. Lights out! Martin Tighe's boy sounded it again sharply. It seemed as if poor Eb Munson and John Tighe must hear it too in their narrow graves.

The procession went on, and stopped here and there at the little graveyards on the farms, leaving their bright flags to flutter through summer and winter rains and snows, and to bleach in the wind and sunshine. When they returned to the church, the minister made an address about the war, and every one listened with new ears. Most of what he said was familiar enough to his listeners; they were used to reading those phrases about the results of the war, the glorious future of the South, in their weekly newspapers; but there never had been such a spirit of patriotism and loyalty waked in Barlow as was waked that day by the poor parade of the remnant of the Barlow soldiers. They sent flags to all the distant graves, and proud were those households who claimed kinship with valor, and could drive or walk away with their flags held up so that others could see that they, too, were of the elect.

III

It is well that the days are long in the last of May, but John Stover had to hurry more than usual with his evening work, and then, having the longest distance to walk, he was much the latest comer to the Plains store, where his two triumphant friends were waiting for him impatiently on the bench. They also had made excuse of going to the post-office and doing an unnecessary errand for their wives, and were talking together so busily that they had gathered a group about them before the store. When they saw Stover coming, they rose hastily and crossed the road to meet him, as if they were a committee in special session. They leaned against the post-and-board fence, after they had shaken hands with each other solemnly.

"Well, we've had a great day, ain't we, John?" asked Henry Merrill. "You did lead off splendid. We've done a grand thing, now, I tell you. All the folks say we've got to keep it up every year. Everybody had to have a talk about it as I went home. They say they had no idea we should make such a show. Lord! I wish we'd begun while there was more of us!"

"That han'some flag was the great feature," said Asa Brown, generously. "I want to pay my part for hirin' it. An' then folks was glad to see poor old Martin made o' some consequence."

"There was half a dozen said to me that another year they're goin' to have flags out, and trim up their places somehow or 'nother. Folks has feelin' enough, but you've got to rouse it," said Merrill.

"I have thought o' joinin' the Grand Army over to Alton time an' again, but it's a good ways to go, an' then the expense has been o' some consideration," Asa continued. "I don't know but two or three over there. You know, most o' the Alton men nat'rally went out in the rigiments t'other side o' the line, an' they was in other battles, an' never camped no-wheres nigh us. Seems to me we ought to have home feelin' enough to do what we can right here."

"The minister says to me this afternoon that he was goin' to arrange an' have some talks in the meetin'-house next winter, an' have some of us tell where he was in the

South; an' one night 'twill be about camp life, an' one about the long marches, an' then about the battles—that would take some time—an' tell all we could about the boys that was killed, an' their record, so they wouldn't be forgot. He said some of the folks must have the letters we wrote home from the front, an' we could make out quite a history of us. I call Elder Dallas a very smart man; he'd planned it all out a'ready, for the benefit o' the young folks, he said," announced Henry Merrill, in a tone of approval.

"I s'pose there ain't none of us but could add a little somethin'," answered John Stover, modestly. "'Twould re'lly learn the young folks a good deal. I should be scared numb to try an' speak from the pulpit. That ain't what the elder means, is it? Now I had a good chance to see somethin' o' Washin'ton. I shook hands with President Lincoln, an' I always think I'm worth lookin' at for that, if I ain't for nothin' else. 'Twas that time I was just out o' hospit'l, an' able to crawl about some. Well, we'll see how 'tis when winter comes. I never thought I had no gift for public speakin', 'less 'twas for drivin' cattle or pollin' the house town-meetin' days. Here! I've got somethin' in mind. You needn't speak about it if I tell it to ye," he added, suddenly. "You know all them han'some flowers that was laid on to Eb Munson's grave an' Tighe's? I mistrusted you thought the same thing I did by the way you looked. They come from Marthy Down's front yard. My woman told me when we got home that she knew 'em in a minute; there wa'n't nobody in town had that kind o' red flowers but her. She must ha' kind o' harked back to the days when she was Marthy Peck. She must have come with 'em after dark, or else dreadful early in the mornin'.'"

Henry Merrill cleared his throat. "There ain't nothin' half-way 'bout Mis' Down," he said. "I wouldn't ha' spoken 'bout this 'less you had led right on to it; but I overtook her when I was gittin' towards home this afternoon, an' I see by her looks she was worked up a good deal; but we talked about how well things had gone off, an' she wanted to know what expenses we'd been put to, an' I told her; an' she said she'd give five dollars any day I'd stop in for it. An' then she spoke right out. 'I'm alone in the world,' says she, 'and somethin' to do with, an' I'd like to have a plain stone put up to Eb Munson's grave, with the number of his rigiment on it, an' I'll pay the bill. 'Tain't out o' Mr. Down's money,' she says; ' 'tis mine, an' I want you to see to it.' I said I would, but we'd made a plot to git some o' them soldiers' head-stones that's provided by the government. 'Twas a shame it had been overlooked so long. 'No,' says she; 'I'm goin' to pay for Eb's myself.' An' I told her there wouldn't be no objection. Don't ary one o' you speak about it. 'Twouldn't be fair. She was real well-appearin'. I never felt to respect Marthy so before."

"We was kind o' hard on her sometimes, but folks couldn't help it. I've seen her pass Eb right by in the road an' never look at him when he first come home," said John Stover.

"If she hadn't felt bad, she wouldn't have cared one way or t'other," insisted Henry Merrill. " 'Tain't for us to judge. Sometimes folks has to get along in years before they see things fair. Come; I must be goin'. I'm tired as an old dog."

"It seemed kind o' natural to be steppin' out together again. Strange we three got through with so little damage, an' so many dropped round us," said Asa Brown. "I've never been one mite sorry I went out in old A Company. I was thinkin' when I was marchin' to-day, though, that we should all have to take to the wagons before long an' do our marchin' on wheels, so many of us felt kind o' stiff. There's one thing—folks won't never say again that we don't show no public sperit here in old Barlow."